More Praise for *Who Lost Russia?*

'Clear, thought-provoking, disturbing. Anyone who wants to understand the rise of Vladimir Putin and the resurgence of Russian nationalism should read Peter Conradi's impeccably researched and impressive book.'

Victor Sebestyen, author of
1946: The Making of the Modern World

'How the world careened from one Cold War into another with a friendly but all too brief pit stop between them is the subject of this quite wonderful book. Bringing to bear his seven years as a Moscow correspondent, and a gift for clear, sparkling prose, Peter Conradi's spirited, well-informed narrative brings to life the ups and downs, colourful characters, and turning points that didn't turn along the way.'

William Taubman, Pulitzer Prize-winning author of
Khrushchev: The Man and his Era

'Peter Conradi takes a calm, considered look at developments in East–West relations that threaten to divide the world. In an era of inflamed partisan debate, he provides the historical context vital for a rational assessment of where we stand and where we are headed.'

Martin Sixsmith, author of
Russia: A 1,000-Year Chronicle of the Wild East

WHO LOST RUSSIA?

HOW THE WORLD ENTERED A NEW COLD WAR

PETER CONRADI

ONEWORLD

A Oneworld Book

First published by Oneworld Publications, 2017

ISBN 978-1-78607-041-8
EISBN 978-1-78607-042-5

Typeset by Palimpsest Book Production Ltd, Falkirk, Stirlingshire
Printed and bound in Great Britain by Clays Ltd, St Ives plc

Oneworld Publications Ltd
10 Bloomsbury Street
London WC1B 3SR
England

Contents

Map vii

Preface ix

Introduction xi

I. THE TIME OF TROUBLES

1 The ties that bind 3

2 The boys in pink trousers 20

3 In search of a new Marshall Plan 30

4 Stockholm Syndrome 40

5 Eastward bound 55

6 Bill and Ol' Boris 67

7 A fatal error? 76

8 Kosovo 92

II. REBIRTH

9 A new start 105

10 A sense of Putin's soul 128

11 From 9/11 to Iraq 138

12 Mission Accomplished 152

13   The Colour Revolutions 162

14   Munich 176

15   The trap 186

III.   THE HOT PEACE

16   Overload 207

17   Silicon Valley 220

18   The return of the chief 229

19   Ukraine 247

20   A piece of paradise 261

21   'You do it too' 278

22   Towards Eurasia 294

23   The Siberian Candidate 308

24   Three faces of Russia 324

Epilogue 333

Acknowledgements 343

Notes 345

Index 363

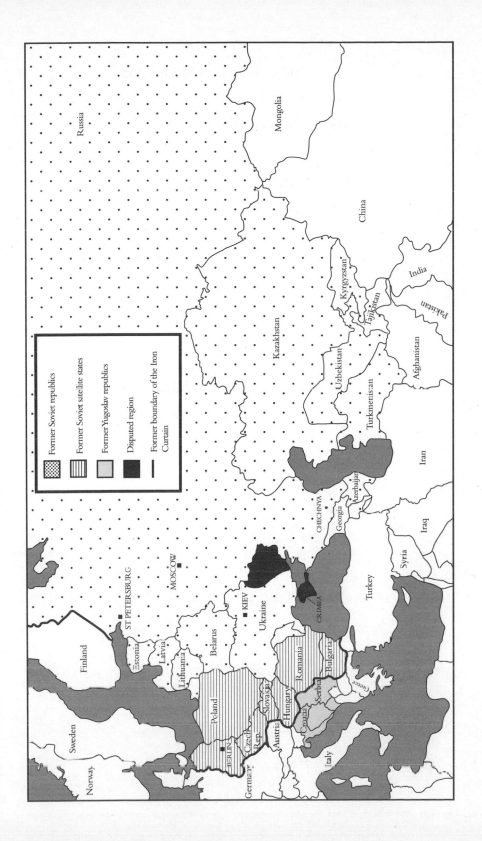

To Julia

Preface

I WENT TO WORK IN MOSCOW IN August 1988 as a young correspondent for the Reuters news agency. My wife, Roberta, and I
arrived in the city after a road trip across Europe and through Ukraine
that took us perilously close to the Chernobyl nuclear plant, which
had exploded two years earlier. Our shiny new Volvo estate car was
piled so high with supplies that when we opened the back doors they
began to cascade out. Stashed away beneath the jumble of clothes and
shoes and household appliances were more than a hundred bottles of
wine. I had been warned by my future colleagues that it was difficult
to find any wine – or anything much else for that matter – in Russian
shops. They were right.

Home was a gloomy little ground-floor flat in a complex for
foreigners near the Rizhsky Market in the north of the city. Just up the
road was the Exhibition of the Achievements of the National Economy
(VDNKh), which by then was turning into something of a joke. A
policeman in a cubicle at the gate of our compound checked the documents of everyone who came in and out. The Reuters office was in a
rather grander complex in Sadovaya Samotechnaya Street, known
among the expat community as Sad Sam. We wrote our stories on
primitive computer terminals that turned our words into holes on a
punched tape that we fed into a telex machine. A team of three interpreters, hired through the Directorate for Servicing the Diplomatic
Corps (UPDK), the all-powerful organisation that took care of
foreigners, watched over us in shifts. They all also worked for the KGB.
At night we went to parties with an extraordinary *fin de siècle* feel.

When we drove around Moscow in the Volvo, now bearing number plates that began K001 – 'K' for correspondent and '001' for Great Britain – we took it for granted that we were being watched. Returning home, we often found the drawer in which we kept our documents had been left open. Sometimes the phone would ring a few minutes later: there was never anyone there. Nina, who visited every morning to teach me Russian, structured her grammar questions in such a way as to extract details about my private life; she was especially interested in our Russian friends. When we wanted to travel outside Moscow we had to give our handlers twenty-four hours' notice – or forty-eight in the case of sensitive places – to allow them time to arrange surveillance teams.

The Soviet Union, even in its final days, was a curious place in which nothing worked quite in the same way as it did in the West. But, thanks to Mikhail Gorbachev, who had come to power in 1985, it was changing fast. In the years that followed, I had a privileged front-row seat as the political, economic and socialist system built up since the Bolsheviks seized power in 1917 unravelled before my eyes and something wild, new and untested emerged to take its place. There was a sense of freedom and exhilaration in the air, but also a sense of foreboding mingled with that perennial Russian fear of chaos. When I left for good in 1995 the country's future path seemed uncertain.

The Moscow to which I returned in 2016 to research this book was a very different city. People complained about the collapsing rouble and Western sanctions and how tough life had become. But I couldn't get over how affluent the place looked compared with my time there. In the intervening two decades Russians had come to take for granted the shops, bars, restaurants and other trappings of a modern developed economy that had seemed so exotic when the first McDonalds opened in Moscow in 1990. Yet the optimism and euphoria that had reigned in my early days in the city had long since been replaced by a sense of resignation, grievance and wounded national pride.

This book sets out to track how Russia has changed over the past quarter of a century through the prism of its relations with the West. It is a story of high hopes and goodwill but also of misunderstandings and missed opportunities.

Peter Conradi
London, December 2016

Introduction

O NE AFTER THE OTHER, the SS-N-30A Kalibr cruise missiles streaked into the air, the plumes of flame beneath them lighting up the early morning skies over the Caspian Sea. There were twenty-six in total, fired in rapid succession from four Russian warships. Turning to the West, they flew for more than 900 miles across Iran and Northern Iraq at speeds of up to 600mph before hitting eleven targets near the Syrian city of Aleppo. Each missile was packed with 990lb of explosives.

It was not the most efficient or cost-effective way to hit the rebels trying to topple President Bashar al-Assad. Pentagon sources claimed that at least four of the missiles, which are similar to US Tomahawks, crashed way short of their target in Iran – an assertion Moscow angrily denied. Yet it was the perfect way of showcasing Russia's growing military might. Within hours, footage of the missiles' launch, cut together with animated graphics of their path, appeared in a two-minute video posted on YouTube by the country's defence ministry. The release of the video coincided with President Vladimir Putin's sixty-third birthday. He made a televised appearance with Sergey Shoygu, the defence minister. 'The fact that we launched precision weapons from the Caspian Sea to the distance of about 1,500 kilometres and hit all the designated targets shows good work by military industrial plants and good personnel skills,' said Putin, in what sounded like a sales pitch for Russian military technology.

The cruise missile strikes took place a week after Russian warplanes had for the first time provided air cover for a ground offensive by Syrian government forces. In the days that followed, the Russian defence ministry's official Twitter account posted daily video clips taken by surveillance drones showing the deadly results of its air strikes on sites in Syria. The ministry's Facebook page was updated with details like the number of sorties flown and targets hit. It was as if the Kremlin had watched how the US government and media had presented Washington's wars in Afghanistan and Iraq and tried to follow suit.

Russian television viewers, who for the previous eighteen months had been bombarded with images of Moscow-backed separatists fighting in Ukraine, were now shown their armed forces' heroics in Syria. The pictures of the new intervention were accompanied by a different but equally powerful narrative. While the enemy in Ukraine had been portrayed as neo-Fascists nostalgic for the days of their Second World War collaboration with Nazi Germany, the battle in Syria was an equally black-and-white one, between the country's elected president and bloodthirsty Islamists.

Putin's intervention in Syria – which followed his defiant seizure of the Crimean peninsula from Ukraine in March 2014 – underlined just how much had changed in the quarter of a century since the newly independent Russian Federation emerged from the wreck of the Soviet Union on 31 December 1991. Putin's message to the world was clear: Russia was back.

When George H. W. Bush, starting the final year of his momentous single term as president, approached the lectern to deliver his State of the Union speech in January 1992, he could be excused a swagger in his step. The United States was now the sole superpower. 'In the past twelve months, the world has known changes of almost biblical proportions,' Bush told Congress. 'And even now . . . I'm not sure we've absorbed the full impact, the full import of what happened . . . But communism died this year . . . The biggest thing that has happened in the world in my life, in our lives, is this. By the grace of God, America won the Cold War.'

Bush's hyperbole was understandable. For the previous four decades the world had been divided into two rival camps, one centred in Washington, the other in Moscow. Capitalism and communism were locked in a global battle for influence. Events from Cuba to Angola to Vietnam were viewed through the prism of the Cold War. The massive nuclear arsenals accumulated on each side meant the threat of total annihilation was only ever minutes away.

But the communist bloc was no more. Mikhail Gorbachev, the last Soviet president, had tried to save his country by humanising it, but instead he unleashed forces that would destroy it. First its satellite states, then the Soviet Union itself began to splinter. When some of Gorbachev's closest allies staged a failed coup in August 1991 in a last attempt to save their country, they unwittingly dealt it a fatal blow. Just over four months later, the Soviet Union disappeared. An extraordinary experiment begun in 1917 to create a new kind of society like no other before it had ended not with a bang but a whimper. As Francis Fukuyama argued in his book *The End of History and the Last Man*, which was published a few days after Bush spoke, the fundamental values of liberal democracy and market capitalism on which America had been built now reigned unchallenged across the planet.

How was the West to deal with the fifteen new states that emerged from the wreckage of the Soviet Union – and especially with Russia, by far the largest and most challenging of them all? It may no longer have been an adversary, but was it already an ally? And what would replace the policy of containment that had guided the United States since the early days of the Cold War? This was the question that Zbigniew Brzezinski, a former National Security Adviser, posed in an article in the March/April 1994 edition of the influential journal *Foreign Affairs*, in which he despaired at America's failure to come up with a 'well-considered and historically relevant successor to the grand strategy of the Cold War years'.

Much has happened in the years since Brzezinski's article: the tentative cooperation of the 1990s and early 2000s has been replaced by confrontation; Russia has annexed the Crimea and fomented a war in eastern Ukraine that has killed more than six thousand people – among them the 298 people on board a Malaysian airliner flying from Amsterdam to Kuala Lumpur. Russia's muscle-flexing in Syria has added another source of friction. While commentators in America and Europe rail against Putin's aggression, opinion polls in Russia show that fascination with the West and all things Western has been replaced with a level of hostility not seen even at the height of Soviet rule. The world is in danger of sliding into a new Cold War.

Yet, remarkably, the West has still not put together the 'well-considered and historically relevant' policy that Brzezinski called for more than two decades ago. Sanctions imposed on Russia over Crimea have not prompted the Kremlin to climb down. Barack Obama, for all his attempts to bring a new, more cerebral approach to American foreign policy, proved no more adept at managing relations with Russia than the two Bushes and Bill Clinton before him. Devising an effective strategy to deal with the Kremlin is one of the major challenges that faces the new President Trump, following his victory over Hillary Clinton in the 2016 presidential election. Trump promised during his campaign to adopt a collaborative rather than confrontational approach towards the Kremlin. It remains to be seen whether his policy will succeed where his predecessors' failed.

Just as America was convulsed by the question of 'Who lost China?' in the aftermath of Chairman Mao's victory over the nationalists in 1949, so now we must ask: 'Who lost Russia?'

I.

THE TIME OF TROUBLES

1

THE TIES THAT BIND

THE FOUNDING OF THE SOVIET UNION was proclaimed from the stage of the Bolshoi Theatre in Moscow on 30 December 1922. Its death warrant was signed almost seven decades later in a forest in Belarus. On 8 December 1991, in a hunting lodge in the Belavezha national park, Boris Yeltsin, president of the Russian Federation, and his Ukrainian and Belorussian counterparts, signed a treaty that formally abolished the USSR and replaced it with a looser entity called the Commonwealth of Independent States.

'We, the Republic of Belarus, the Russian Federation (RSFSR), and Ukraine, as founder states of the USSR and signatories to the union treaty of 1922 . . . state that the USSR as a subject of international law and a geopolitical reality is terminating its existence,' the document began. Yeltsin toasted the agreement of each of the treaty's fourteen articles with Soviet champagne. A meeting with the press afterwards was brought to a close after only a few minutes when it became clear that the celebrations had left him barely coherent.

The treaty marked the final failure of attempts by Mikhail Gorbachev, the Soviet president, to prevent his country from being pulled apart by the separatist forces he unleashed after coming to power in 1985. Over the course of the previous few months, Gorbachev's power had been gradually usurped by the leaders of the fifteen Soviet republics, chief among them Yeltsin. A charismatic larger-than-life figure whose ruddy cheeks betrayed his weakness for alcohol, Yeltsin had once been

3

Gorbachev's protégé, brought from the provinces to head the Moscow city Communist Party, with a seat in the Politburo.* But the two men fell out over Yeltsin's impatience at the slow pace of reform, and after Gorbachev sacked him, Yeltsin became a bitter rival. Now he was getting his revenge: that June, taking advantage of the democratic reforms Gorbachev had introduced, Yeltsin had been elected as president of the largest republic, the Russian Federation, which was home to almost half of the Soviet Union's 293 million people and much of its economic might. It gave him the ideal power base from which to attack his erstwhile mentor.

Yeltsin had travelled to Belarus with the aim of finding a way of maintaining the union – although without a role for Gorbachev, who had not been invited to join their meeting, giving it a conspiratorial character. But Yeltsin's hopes foundered in the face of opposition from Leonid Kravchuk, president of Ukraine, whose people had just voted in a referendum in favour of independence by a margin of nine to one. For any reformed union to be viable, it had to include Ukraine, the second most powerful republic after Russia, and Kravchuk refused to sign up to anything that smacked of central control. Yeltsin changed tack and, desperate to salvage something from the meeting, agreed to the treaty hastily drafted by the Ukrainian leader as they sat there. Rather than save the Soviet Union, it buried it.

In the days that followed, as the other Soviet republics wavered and the West looked on with a mixture of fascination and horror, Gorbachev sought ways of undoing the deal done in Belavezha. Yet the tide of history was against him. On 21 December, in the Kazakh capital of Almaty, the new treaty was signed by the heads of the remaining Soviet republics (save Georgia, which sent an observer and was to join later, and the three Baltic states, which had definitively gone their own way that September). At the insistence of the Central Asian leaders, it was agreed that they would all be considered founding members.

In a televised speech on the evening of 25 December 1991, Gorbachev announced his resignation as Soviet president. At 7:32P.M., a few minutes after he left the Kremlin for the last time, the red Soviet hammer-and-sickle flag was lowered. At 7:45P.M., the tricolour of the Russian

---

* Yeltsin was actually a non-voting 'candidate' member of the Politburo rather than a full one.

Federation was raised in its place and the chimes of the Kremlin's Spassky Tower clock rang out for several minutes. The next day, the Council of Republics, the upper chamber of parliament, issued a declaration that the Soviet Union had ceased to exist as a functioning state.

THE SEEDS OF THE SOVIET UNION'S destruction were sown by its own creators. Russia under the Tsars was an empire rather than a nation state. Its people had been divided into Russians and *inorodtsy* ('aliens'), with no doubt over who was in control. Lenin famously described Russia as the *tyurma narodov* ('prison of peoples').

The Bolsheviks adopted a different policy after seizing power in 1917: they set out to undo centuries of Russification and, despite their dismissal of national culture as a bourgeois fiction, encouraged the development of the bewildering number of ethnic groups who lived on the territory of the Soviet Union – 176, according to the first population census conducted in 1926.

It was not just a matter of making amends for the 'great power chauvinism' of the Tsars. Lenin realised that force alone was not enough to consolidate Soviet power. He had to convince the tens of millions of non-Russians that the new state being created was theirs, too, and persuade them to be active participants in his great socialist experiment. Paradoxical as it seemed, he believed the best way to do this was to develop individual languages and cultures, to foster the creation of ethnic leaders who could mediate with their respective peoples, and to set up institutions that would encourage mass participation. Where a language did not exist, or had no written form, linguists were dispatched from Moscow or St Petersburg to formulate one.

This policy was reflected in the administrative structure of the new state. Although power in reality was concentrated in the Kremlin, in the Politburo of the ruling Communist Party, the Soviet Union was formally divided up in such a way that each of the ethnic minorities had its own national territory. The main building blocks were the union republics, of which there were eventually fifteen: created between 1917 and 1940, they enjoyed equal rights and equal powers under the constitution, despite vast differences in their sizes, populations and economic might.

Each had its own branch of the Communist Party, parliament and government and other attributes of nationhood such as a flag, coat of arms and anthem.* Their sense of cultural identity was reinforced by their respective writers' unions, theatres, opera companies and national academies that specialised in their history, language and literature. The Ukrainian and Belorussian republics even each had their own seat in the United Nations. The right of each member republic to 'freely withdraw from the union', granted in the 1924 constitution, was confirmed by those that replaced it in both 1936 and 1977. No details were given of how secession would work in practice, but there was no need: the right to secede was as much a fiction as many of the other rights outlined in the constitution.

The Russian Federation – or the Russian Soviet Federative Socialist Republic, to give it its full name – was divided during the early 1920s into some thirty autonomous republics and oblasts, which were themselves subdivided into a bewildering number of individual ethnic units, right down to district level. The same was true in several of the other union republics. The structure of the Soviet Union, according to one expert, was reminiscent of a 'puzzling and apparently limitless collection of ethnic nesting dolls'.[1]

The policy swung wildly over the years. In the late 1930s, under Stalin, the cultivation of individual national groups was largely abandoned and replaced by a glorification of Russian culture and history. The Russian people became the 'elder brother' of the 'socialist family of nations'. As war against Germany loomed, greater prominence was given to Soviet patriotism and a willingness to fight for the socialist motherland. At the same time, entire national groups were deported from one end of the country to the other in a process of ethnic cleansing that accelerated after the outbreak of the Second World War. Between 1941 and 1949 nearly 3.3 million people accused of collaboration with the Germans or of anti-Soviet activity were sent to Siberia and the Central Asian republics. Conditions were appalling: by some estimates more than four out of ten died of disease or starvation. In the years following Stalin's death these 'collaborators' were rehabilitated, but many were not allowed to return to their ancestral homelands until decades later.

Writing in 1924, I. Vareikis, secretary of the central committee of the Turkestani Communist Party, likened the USSR to a giant *kommunalka*, the communal apartments that many Soviet families were obliged

---

* With the exception of Russia.

to share. Every national grouping – or family, in his analogy – was entitled to a separate room of its own. 'Only through free national self-determination could we arrive in this apartment,' argued Vareikis, 'for only because of this self-determination can any formerly oppressed nation shed its legitimate mistrust of larger nations.'[2]

Yuri Slezkine, a Russian academic, took up the analogy in an article published eighty years later, after the end of the Soviet Union, in which he looked back on the communists' policy on nationality. Such a policy endured for decades, he wrote, even if by the late 1930s the Russians, who inhabited 'the enormous hall, corridor and the kitchen where all the major decisions were made', began to 'bully their neighbours and decorate their part of the communal apartment'. Yet even then, they 'did not claim that the whole apartment was theirs or that the other (large) families were not entitled to their own rooms. The tenants were increasingly unequal but reassuringly separate.'[3]

Despite the complicated system of national divisions that Lenin bequeathed to his successors, he had assumed that the crutch of national consciousness among the various Soviet peoples would ultimately fall away to be replaced by a shared class consciousness. Stalin and his immediate successors brutally repressed any manifestations of nationalism. But when Gorbachev began to relax control over the political system in the mid-1980s, this national consciousness began to reassert itself and was mixed with calls for political and economic reform. For many in the non-Russian republics, the demand for democracy was synonymous with the demand for autonomy or even independence.

The first open show of nationalism during the Gorbachev era erupted in December 1986 when Dinmukhamed Konayev, the veteran Kazakh Communist Party leader, was replaced by Gennady Kolbin, a Russian who had no connection with the republic. Gorbachev had been trying to fight corruption there. But the move was regarded by Kazakhs as a breach of the tradition under which the non-Russian republics were headed by one of their own. The security forces were called to put down protests, during which at least two people died and hundreds were injured. Two years later, a centuries-old dispute between Armenia and Azerbaijan over the disputed territory of Nagorno-Karabakh turned into open warfare that rumbles on today. There was also ethnic-based violence in Georgia and parts of Central Asia, where equally ancient grievances between different ethnic groups erupted into fighting.

This violence went hand in hand with the emergence of organised national movements, initially in the Baltic republics of Estonia, Latvia and Lithuania, then in the Caucasus, Moldova and beyond. Far from trying to crush the separatists, however, the republics' leaders began to co-opt them. The effect was most pronounced in the Baltic states, whose reform-minded Communist Party offices effectively merged with the newly formed Popular Fronts that were leading the drive for independence.

Ironically, by opting for the structure of a federation that divided the country along national lines, the Soviet Union's founding fathers had marked out the lines of any future split: those pushing for independence had formal structures within which to work and ready-made borders for their putative independent states. Thanks to the first steps towards democracy that began with the election of the first Congress of People's Deputies in March 1989, republican leaders started to derive their legitimacy from their own electorate rather than from Moscow. The individual republics' parliaments, for decades little more than rubber stamps, began to behave like proper legislatures themselves. The Estonians led the way: in November 1988, the republic's parliament adopted a declaration of sovereignty, announcing that only those Soviet laws it approved would come into force on its territory. In the months that followed, most of the other republics did the same.

The situation in Ukraine was of particular concern to the Kremlin. With a population of fifty-two million people, it was of considerable importance to both Soviet industry and agriculture. Its people had always been closely linked with the Russians: their languages are very similar and the families of many Russians and Ukrainians are intertwined, in much the same way as the Scots are with the English. Ukrainians' attitudes were dictated to a large degree by their country's history: separatist feeling was strongest in the west, which had been part of the Soviet Union only since the Second World War, when it was annexed by Stalin under the secret protocols of the 1939 Molotov-Ribbentrop Pact. Here intellectuals and former dissidents took the lead, with events following a similar path to those in the Baltic states, which had been seized at the same time. Sentiments were more mixed in the east, especially in industrial areas where ethnic Russians and 'Russified' Ukrainians predominated, and support for the Communist Party was stronger.

As the threats to Gorbachev's authority mounted, he set out to try to remake the Soviet Union in such a way as to satisfy some of the demands for autonomy while maintaining a 'centre' in Moscow – and a role for himself. After many months of negotiation, agreement was finally reached on 23 April 1991 to turn the Soviet Union into the Union of Soviet Sovereign Republics, a federation of independent republics with a common president, foreign policy and military. The new formulation had the added advantage of retaining the USSR acronym. Six of the republics – Georgia, Moldova, Armenia and the three Baltic states – refused to join, but its chances of success were buoyed by a referendum held the previous month in which it was backed by seventy-six per cent of voters in the remaining nine republics. The formal signing ceremony of the new Union Treaty was set for 20 August.

Gorbachev, who had spent the previous months flip-flopping between the reformists and the reactionaries, antagonising both sides in the process, could take satisfaction from the fact that he had salvaged something from the chaos. Yet the deal was already beginning to crumble: as 20 August approached, the Ukrainians began to waver and Gorbachev worried that Yeltsin, too, would refuse to sign. Unbeknown to Gorbachev, though, the real threat was from the hardliners he had himself appointed to key positions in the Soviet leadership.

IT WAS IN THE MIDST OF this turmoil that President George H. W. Bush arrived in Moscow on 29 July 1991 for a summit with Gorbachev. Since entering the White House at the beginning of the tumultuous year of 1989, Bush had welcomed the far-reaching changes in Soviet policy that had occurred under Gorbachev, who had allowed Germany to reunify and the former Soviet satellite states such as Poland and Hungary* to break free without a fight. The Soviet leader also backed the US-led coalition's freeing of Kuwait after Saddam Hussein's invasion, and proved a willing partner in negotiating away nuclear weapons. Although still an avowed communist, Gorbachev introduced elements of democracy through partially free elections, put an end to decades of repression and implemented market reforms that would open up

---

* The German Democratic Republic, Poland, Czechoslovakia, Hungary, Romania and Bulgaria had been part of a broader Soviet 'bloc' of countries with communist governments that were members of the Warsaw Pact and under the direct influence of the Soviet Union.

the Soviet economy to the world, providing new opportunities for Western companies. The Cold War appeared to be giving way to a new era of superpower cooperation.

Contrary to the impression that Bush gave in his State of the Union address the following January, America had not wanted the Soviet Union to dissolve. Bush feared that such a process could be violent and destabilising. He was also worried about the fate of the country's vast arsenal of nuclear weapons, which were divided between Russia, Ukraine, Belarus and Kazakhstan.* Even giving the impression that America was in favour of break-up risked undermining Gorbachev's standing with his hard-line communist critics. 'Whatever the course, however long the process took, and whatever its outcome, I wanted to see stable, and above all peaceful, change,' Bush wrote in his memoirs. 'I believed the key to this would be a politically strong Gorbachev and an effectively working central structure. The outcome depended on what Gorbachev was willing to do.'[4]

What was billed as the first post-Cold War summit was Bush's third meeting with Gorbachev, but the first on Soviet soil. The formal centrepiece of the summit was the signature of the Strategic Arms Reduction Treaty, known as START, which for the first time obliged the two countries to reduce their holdings of the weapons, rather than merely slow down the rate at which stocks were growing. The two sides pledged to cooperate on the Middle East, and Gorbachev agreed to cut economic support for Fidel Castro's regime in Cuba. The Soviet leader also lobbied for financial assistance and some form of membership in the International Monetary Fund.

Before the START signing ceremony at the Grand Kremlin Palace on the second day of the summit, Bush and Gorbachev spent several hours in the informal setting of Novo-Ogaryovo, a state dacha west of Moscow. Here, dressed casually and with no formal agenda, they were free to talk about how to move on from the mutual antagonism of the Cold War. Gorbachev, who was losing control at home and desperately in need of economic help from the West, was in a weak position. Yet as the two men sat for five hours on wicker chairs at a circular table,

---

* The only exception was the three Baltic states, which the United States, along with Britain and several other countries, had always considered to have been illegally occupied and whose independence was a long-standing American demand.

with the dacha on one side and the woods on the other, he set out an ambitious vision according to which the Soviet Union and the United States could work together to sort out the world's problems. As he saw it, the era of confrontation between the superpowers was to be replaced by one of cooperation.

Gorbachev was delighted at the hearing he received from Bush, describing their discussion as 'a moment of glory' for his new approach to foreign policy. Yet he was deluding himself if he thought America was ready to establish a new partnership of equals. The Soviet Union's days as a superpower were over. In his memoirs, Bush says of their discussion merely: 'Gorbachev began with a lengthy monologue, during which I barely managed to squeeze in a comment.'[5]

The summit had also brought to the fore the question of how to deal with the unravelling of the Soviet Union. Bush had displeased his host by making clear his intention to travel on after the summit to Kiev, the Ukrainian capital. It was only a five-hour stopover but it held enormous symbolic importance. As Serhii Plokhy pointed out in his authoritative account of the break-up of the Soviet Union,[6] the White House wanted to signal its realisation that it was no longer enough to talk to the central authorities in Moscow; it also had to take into account the views of the individual Soviet republics. Ukraine was chosen for good reason: not only because of its size but also because the nationalist movement there was popular and peaceful, and its leaders were pushing for more sovereignty rather than complete independence.

With only just over a week to go, the Kremlin had tried to persuade Bush to cancel the Ukraine leg of his trip, citing unspecified tensions in Kiev. The White House stood firm, however, and Bush denied any malign intentions. 'I want to assure you that during my trip to Kiev neither I nor any of those accompanying me will do anything that might complicate existing problems or interfere in the question of when Ukraine might sign the Union Treaty,' he insisted.[7]

Bush was as good as his word. In a speech to the Verkhovna Rada, the Ukrainian parliament, he praised Gorbachev for the reforms he had introduced and described as a 'false choice' the need to decide between him and pro-independence leaders. Though vowing to back those who strove for freedom, democracy and economic liberty, Bush added: 'Freedom is not the same as independence. Americans will not support those who seek independence in order to replace a far-off tyranny with a local despotism. They will not aid those who promote a suicidal nationalism based on ethnic hatred.'[8]

Bush's words reflected the balancing act that his administration was trying to perform: although sensitive to the aspirations of Ukraine and the other fourteen republics, he did not want to jeopardise his relationship with the Soviet leadership, especially over negotiations on nuclear arms – a point he made clear in talks with Kravchuk. 'There is a delicate balance here and I want to deal respectfully with the centre,' Bush told the Ukrainian leader, stressing his 'deep respect for President Gorbachev'.[9] Although Bush's speech was greeted with standing applause in the parliament, it was denounced by Rukh, the group leading the drive for Ukrainian independence. Ivan Drach, its chairman, told reporters that he thought Bush had been 'hypnotised by Gorbachev'. Another nationalist politician, Stepan Pavluk, complained the American leader did not appreciate that Ukrainians were fighting against a totalitarian state. Even the Georgian government, fighting its own battle for independence, weighed in, mocking Bush. 'Why didn't he call on Kuwait to sign the Union Treaty with Iraq?' it asked in a statement.[10]

Bush's desire to preserve the Soviet Union also went down badly with many people back home, not least with America's 750,000 Ukrainians, who usually voted Republican. William Safire, the conservative *New York Times* columnist, famously dubbed it the 'Chicken Kiev speech'. Bush, he claimed in an excoriating piece, had 'lectured Ukrainians against self-determination, foolishly placing Washington on the side of Moscow centralism and against the tide of history'.[11]

Yet events moved faster than Bush – or anyone else – could have predicted. On 18 August, just over two weeks after the American president left for Ukraine, eight high-ranking Soviet officials took control of the government of the USSR in the name of the self-proclaimed State Committee of the State of Emergency. Gorbachev, on holiday in Crimea, was placed under house arrest. But the plotters lacked the determination and ruthlessness to turn back the clock, their ineffectiveness epitomised by a press conference at which the vice president, Gennady Yanayev, was so nervous – and also perhaps drunk – that his hands were shaking as he announced that Gorbachev was 'resting' and that he was now in charge of the country.

But it was Yeltsin who saw them down. Drawing on his authority as president of Russia and his enormous popularity with Muscovites, he rushed to the White House, the Russian parliament building, where defiant crowds were gathering, despite the menacing presence of tanks on the streets. In what became one of the most enduring images of the coup, Yeltsin climbed onto one of the tanks and read an appeal to the people of Russia. Its crew did nothing to stop him. The plotters had failed to appreciate that a successful coup means having the army on your side. Less than seventy-two hours after the coup started it had collapsed in farce, but it would change the course of history in a way that no one – certainly not the plotters themselves – could have foreseen.

Gorbachev, who arrived back in Moscow in the early hours of 22 August, tried to reassert control. Recognising the complicity in the coup of leading members of the Communist Party, most of them his own appointees, he dissolved its central committee and resigned as its head. Yet the balance of power in the country had changed in the course of those three tumultuous days: Yeltsin's defiance of the plotters had boosted his standing and he moved quickly to strengthen the powers of the government of the Russian Federation, which he headed, at the expense of the Soviet authorities, who answered to Gorbachev.

Yet Yeltsin no more wanted the Soviet Union to break up than Gorbachev did. When Ukraine's parliament declared the republic's independence on 24 August, Yeltsin's press secretary warned that Russia might retaliate by laying claim to some of its territory – citing Crimea and the Donetsk region of eastern Ukraine, as well as Abkhazia in Georgia and a swathe of northern Kazakhstan.

The Ukrainians were furious. In an attempt to calm the situation, a delegation headed by Aleksandr Rutskoi, Yeltsin's vice president, was dispatched to Kiev. The gulf between the two countries came into focus when one member of the delegation, Anatoly Sobchak, the mayor of Leningrad and a leading reformist, left the talks to address a crowd gathered outside the Ukrainian parliament. 'What is important is for us to be together,' Sobchak declared – only to be met with boos and whistles. What Russians characterised as 'togetherness' was seen by many in Ukraine as the domination of a larger neighbour.

The talks ended with Russia recognising Ukraine's right to independence. The two sides also agreed to adhere to a treaty dating from 1990 confirming their respective borders. Nursultan Nazarbayev, the Kazakh leader, who was equally concerned about Russian territorial claims, demanded that Rutskoi's delegation fly on to his republic to provide similar guarantees. The Russians nevertheless continued to believe in a federation and considered the Ukrainians' independence declaration nothing more than a ploy to obtain better terms – an accusation angrily denied by officials in Kiev.

The other republics now had the bit between their teeth. The Baltic states took advantage of the coup to assert their independence, which was recognised by the United States on 2 September and by the Soviet Union four days later. One by one the other republics did the same – although similar recognition did not follow. Even in quasi-feudal Central Asia, where the demand for independence had been weaker and economic ties with Russia were seen as vital for survival, the republics' leaders embraced the opportunity to become presidents of sovereign states rather than the Kremlin's pawns.

The Soviet collapse came closer on 1 December when Ukrainians were asked whether they supported the declaration of independence that had been made by their parliament on 24 August. The 'yes' vote was an overwhelming 92.3%, and close to 100% in parts of the west, based on a turnout of more than 84%. Such was the degree of disenchantment with the Soviet Union that even in the Crimean peninsula, which was overwhelmingly populated by Russians, 54% voted to throw in their lot with an independent Ukraine. The union's fate was sealed.

At the end of the Belavezha meeting a week later, Yeltsin called Bush to tell him what had been decided, stressing that he and the pact's two other signatories had agreed to accept responsibility for Soviet debts and to keep the country's massive nuclear arsenal under a single command. Bush was satisfied on both counts, but was reluctant to give premature approval or disapproval of what was a momentous change, replying merely: 'I see.' It was only then that Yeltsin called Gorbachev. He was furious at the destruction of his country, his anger compounded by the fact that Bush had learnt about it before he had.

WHEN THE SOVIET UNION SPLIT AT the end of 1991, it was on the basis of article 72 of the 1977 version of the constitution, which gave each union republic the right to secede. The borders between the republics, hitherto administrative divisions, became the national borders between the newly proclaimed sovereign states. The Soviet Union had always been erroneously portrayed as a free association of nations. Now the nationalities policy pursued all those years had reached its logical conclusion.

The relative bloodlessness with which this happened was remarkable, especially compared with the series of wars that followed the break-up of Yugoslavia, which took place at around the same time. Both countries were home to a patchwork of different ethno-national groups with age-old grudges against one another and potential territorial disputes that had been suppressed during decades of authoritarian rule. Russia dominated the Soviet Union economically and politically to an even greater extent than Serbia had dominated Yugoslavia. A large number of Russians, like Serbs, lived outside the borders of their home republic. Slobodan Milošević, the Serbian (and later, Yugoslav) leader, exploited this situation with his drive to create a Greater Serbia, with disastrous consequences for his own country and its neighbours.

Yet while Yugoslavia's constituent republics became embroiled in a series of wars over territory that raged for much of the 1990s, the internal borders between the Soviet Union's fifteen republics were largely accepted, even though they were arbitrary – in some cases deliberately so – having been drawn in Soviet times not so much to unite ethnic groups as to divide them. Much of the credit for this peaceful transition was due to Yeltsin.

Unlike Milošević, he had no interest in stirring up national hatred. Far from it: Yeltsin appreciated that the only way to turn Russia into a democratic country was to allow the other republics their freedom. As reformers around him put it, the choice was between an authoritarian Soviet Union and a democratic Russia. For that reason Yeltsin did not try to use force to stop Ukraine's drive for independence. Nor, despite some initial sabre-rattling, did he attempt to challenge Ukraine's borders. Where interethnic violence did take place, although bloody it was largely between non-Russian nationalities in the Caucasus and Central Asia, though some saw Russia's hand in stirring up conflicts in Georgia and Moldova.

Yet the equanimity with which Russians appeared to accept the loss of lands they had ruled, in most cases for hundreds of years, was deceptive. For a people brought up to believe in a single, indissoluble Soviet nation, the loss of a large slice of their territory for the second time in a century was a massive blow to national pride. Since the sixteenth century, Russia had been expanding outwards, stopping only when it came up against strong powers: Germany (and Austria) to the west, China and Japan to the east and the British Empire to the south. Up until 1991 the area within those boundaries – about one-sixth of the world's land mass – was dominated by Russia, whether it was called the Russian Empire or the Soviet Union. The extent of this territory provided what has been called the 'strategic depth' that Russia needed to defend itself, and which it made use of to see off first Napoleon and then Hitler. Russia's desire to retain its influence over these lands – especially Ukraine – and to bind them together was reflected in its support for the attempt at Belavezha to set up the Commonwealth of Independent States.

In September 1990, as the Soviet Union began to crumble, the dissident writer Alexander Solzhenitsyn, living in exile in Vermont, had warned in an essay entitled *Rebuilding Russia* against attempts to destroy the country's Slavic core. It was no problem if the Baltic, Central Asian and Caucasian republics broke away – indeed they should be encouraged to do so, he argued – but the Slavs should remain together in one country. Despite being a fierce anti-communist, Solzhenitsyn was an old-style Russian nationalist. He was especially critical of those trying to 'hack off' Ukraine, which he considered inseparable from Russia, in particular Crimea and other parts of the south and east that had not been part of 'old Ukraine'.

'To separate off the Ukraine today would mean to cut across the lives of millions of individuals and families,' he wrote in his essay, which was also published in *Komsomolskaya Pravda*, the bestselling Russian newspaper.[12] 'The two populations are thoroughly intermingled; there are entire regions where Russians predominate; many individuals would be hard put to choose between the two nationalities; many others are of mixed origin, and there are plenty of mixed marriages (marriages which have indeed never been viewed as "mixed"). There is not even a hint of intolerance between Russians and Ukrainians on the level of the ordinary people.' More controversially, he, too, had suggested that the north of Kazakhstan should be part of this Slavic core.

The Russian's anguish over the break-up of the Soviet Union was compounded by concerns about the fate of their twenty-five million compatriots who, after December 1991, found themselves on the wrong side of the borders of the new independent Russia – just as German nationalists agitated in the 1920s and 1930s for the rights of the ten million *Volksdeutsche* living outside the borders of Weimar Germany. Through a process begun under the Tsars and continued in Soviet times, ethnic Russians had colonised the Baltic states, the Caucasus and Central Asia not just to provide skilled labour but also as a deliberate policy of Russification. Now, overnight, they were living in a foreign country.

The fate of the colonisers is one of the more fraught issues that accompanies the break-up of any empire: they can be transformed from members of a privileged elite into a hated minority. The problem becomes far greater in the case of contiguous empires such as the Soviet Union. Unlike the British in India or the French in Africa, few of the Russians who had settled in other republics saw themselves as representative of a colonial power. Raised on propaganda that extolled the fraternal nature of the Soviet peoples, they saw themselves as moving between regions of a single country in search of better opportunities, much as an American would travel from the Rust Belt to California to find work.

Their position became especially problematic in the Baltic states. While official Soviet history held that Estonia, Latvia and Lithuania had voluntarily become Soviet republics in 1940, those who championed the drive for their independence in the late 1980s maintained that these countries, which had achieved independence from Tsarist Russia after the First World War, had been illegally occupied – a position also adhered to by the United States and Britain, among others.

The leaders of the newly independent Baltic states considered Russians who had settled there as members of an illegal occupying force and were therefore not willing to grant them automatic citizenship. On independence, some thirty per cent of residents in Estonia were deemed stateless. The policy was logical in its own terms and not based on ethnicity as such; the small minority of Russians who had lived in the country since Tsarist times and were better integrated were all granted citizenship. Yet it inevitably prompted accusations of discrimination from Russia and raised eyebrows in Europe.

None of the other former republics claimed to have been occupied in such a way – and consequently none took such an uncompromising line against their Russian minorities. Yet all were aware of the impact of centuries of Russification. This was especially the case in Ukraine, although the ethnic dividing line was blurred by the large number of ethnic Ukrainians who chose to speak Russian rather than Ukrainian but were nevertheless loyal to Kiev rather than to Moscow.

Some in the Kremlin quickly appreciated that this new diaspora could be a potential asset. In a much-quoted article published in November 1992, Sergei Karaganov, deputy director of the Institute of Europe in the Russian Academy of Science, suggested that Russia was entitled to pose as a defender of the rights of the millions of its compatriots in the Baltic states, and elsewhere in the former Soviet Union. Far from mourning the loss of those left on the wrong side of the borders, Karaganov argued that the Kremlin should see them as an instrument to help them retain influence over its former republics, an idea that came to be known as the Karaganov Doctrine. Shortly after the article appeared in the *Diplomaticeskij Vestnik* ('Diplomatic Herald'), the Kremlin's foreign policy statements began to insist that the withdrawal of troops from Estonia was contingent on an end to the alleged 'systematic discrimination' against Russian speakers there.

In the years after 1991, the end of the Soviet Union was dismissed by communists and Russian nationalists – who formed a 'red-brown' front – as a few months of madness, in which peoples who had lived together for centuries had been ripped apart by the machinations of power-hungry politicians. Just as the civilian leaders of the Weimar Republic were accused by the far right of stabbing Germany in the back in the dying days of the First World War by doing a deal with the Allies, so the legend would grow of the 'traitors of Belavezha'.

This narrative was given an inadvertent boost by Bush, who, beginning with his January 1992 State of the Union address, attempted to portray himself as the man who had brought about the end of communism and of the Soviet Union and, in doing so, had 'won' the Cold War. Yet this was rewriting history. Far from pushing for the disintegration of the Soviet Union, Bush had made clear in his 'Chicken Kiev' speech – and in separate talks with Yeltsin and Kravchuk – that America wanted Ukraine and the other republics to enter the voluntary federation Gorbachev was proposing. An exception was made only for the three Baltic states. Nor could Bush claim credit for ending the Communist Party's monopoly on power: that was down to Gorbachev, even though he might not have done so if he had foreseen how voters would turn against it. As for the Cold War, it had already effectively ended two years earlier with the fall of the Berlin Wall, as Gorbachev and Bush made clear the following month at their Malta summit in December 1989 when the Soviet leader declared: 'We stated, both of us, that the world leaves one epoch of cold war and enters another epoch.'

'The fact is that the end of the Cold War, the end of communist rule in the Soviet Union and the end of the Soviet Union itself are three separate events, interconnected but not identical,' observed Jack Matlock, who was US ambassador to the Soviet Union until shortly before the August coup.[13] 'The U.S. attitude differed greatly in regard to those three events, and our contribution to them differed greatly.' Yet by 1992 Bush had an election to fight, and with the American economy tanking, he had pinned hopes of his return to the White House on a recognition by voters of his successful handling of the dramatic events the previous year in the Soviet Union and in Kuwait.

During the early 1990s, such arguments were of little interest to the majority of Russians, who were more preoccupied with providing for themselves and their families in the difficult economic times that followed the end of the Soviet Union. Over time, however, this was replaced by a Russian sense of victimhood and a feeling that they had been taken advantage of. As Matlock argued, such American triumphalism was also to have a damaging impact on US foreign policy in the years that followed, encouraging an excessive reliance on the use of military force. 'After all, the logic went, if military pressure brought down communism and started the successor states of the Soviet Union on the road to democracy and market economies, it must be a reliable instrument not only in responding to potential threats but also in implementing other aspects of foreign policy, including spreading democracy,' he wrote.[14]

2

THE BOYS IN PINK TROUSERS

IT WAS A TYPICAL RUSSIAN QUEUE. The women stood in front of the *gastronom* in Moscow's Tverskaya Street, their fur hats pulled down over their heads, and muttered quietly to themselves. But when they finally made it inside the dimly lit shop, there was nothing on the shelves but milk and bread, and both cost three times more than they had the day before. If this had been anywhere else, there might have been riots. But this was Russia. The women stood stoically in line. If bread and milk was all there was on offer, then that was what they would buy, regardless of how much they had to pay.

Similar scenes played out across the country on 2 January 1992. The first day of Russia's transition to a free market proved to be a life-defining moment. The previous six months had seen a series of political events, each more dramatic than the last, culminating in the dissolution of the Soviet Union. Yet none had such a direct and immediate impact as the Yeltsin government's decision to end the price controls that had been a feature of Soviet life since the 1920s. The Big Bang had come. It was not just milk and bread that soared in price. Sugar became four times more expensive than before; butter seven times. The cost of a bottle of vodka quintupled.

Over the previous few years, Western products had started to find their way into the shops, while foreign restaurants began to open for business. When the first branch of McDonald's opened its doors in Pushkin Square, in the heart of Moscow, on 31 January 1990, five thousand people were queuing; by the end of the day it had served a record thirty thousand customers. (A quarter of a century later, there are more than five hundred outlets across Russia.) Where Ronald McDonald led, others followed. *Importnyi* became synonymous with high quality. Who now wanted to eat *pelmeni* or borscht when they could enjoy pizza or sushi? Why wear Russian clothes when they could dress in Armani or Versace, or have a Lada or a Moskvitch when they could drive a Toyota or a BMW? Provided they had the money, that is.

Hand in hand with Western goods came Western ideas. American-style democracy was the ideal. A steady flow of US and European advisers arrived in Russia to spread democracy and economic liberalism. The country's new rulers were clear about what had to be done: the replacement of the old Soviet command economy with a market-based system. What was not so clear was how to get from one to the other.

Since the days of Peter the Great, Russia had been engaged in a struggle between the *Zapadniki* ('Westernisers'), who held that the country must follow a Western model of development, and the Slavophiles, who stressed the unique nature of Orthodox Russia. Now, thanks to the dramatic changes of the previous few months, the *Zapadniki* were firmly in control. The new Russia was to be remade in the image of America. This shift was all the more remarkable because, since its foundation almost seven decades earlier, the Soviet Union had developed into the heartland of an alternative worldview, in which almost every aspect of economic, social and political life worked according to its own specific rules.

The speed of the change represented by what happened on that January day in 1992 was breathtaking. The end of price controls was part of a broader process that challenged everything the Soviets had been brought up to believe in. Buying and selling for a profit had once been denounced as speculation and been punishable with jail. Now it was the foundation of the economy. Money-changing used to be conducted by shady characters on street corners; now it was carried out by financial experts sitting at rows of computer screens in swanky offices. Other exotic manifestations of the capitalist system such as loans, credit cards and mortgages were to follow. The greatest social, political and economic experiment of the twentieth century had ended in abject failure, and a new one was beginning. Russia was embarking on a revolution just as far-reaching as the one begun in 1917. No one paused to consider where it would end.

'BEFORE 1985 AND GORBACHEV, THE WEST was a different, inaccessible planet for us, just like Mars,' recalls Aleksandr Oslon, a veteran pollster who has been charting public opinion in Russia and the Soviet Union for more than two decades.[1] 'Spaceships used to be sent there for research and to write reports on what they found. We knew that there were many good things on that planet that were not available here. But at the same time there were a lot of bad things that we did not want to have.'

It is January 2016 and I am sitting with Oslon in the plush new offices of his organisation, the Public Opinion Fund, talking about relations between Russia and the West: how, a quarter of a century ago, these two worlds came together after decades apart and how, in the past few years, they have drifted away from each other. One of Russia's leading social scientists, Oslon has had a ringside seat, advising Yeltsin in his re-election campaign in 1996, which in retrospect set the tone for the development of modern Russia. He has also worked for Yeltsin's successor, Vladimir Putin.

During the Soviet years, perceptions of the outside world were shaped largely by the official media. Travel was a privilege extended only to the few, and the high-profile defections of sportspeople or members of the Bolshoi Ballet while on foreign tours an occasional embarrassment. The West was an alien place, even to the country's leaders: when Nikita Khrushchev went on a twelve-week tour of America in 1959, he appears to have been genuinely surprised by the enormity of the range of products available in a San Francisco supermarket and disappointed when his planned trip to Disneyland was cancelled.

The picture of the United States presented by Soviet media was unremittingly hostile, viewed through the narrow prism of Marxist-Leninist ideology. Americans were depicted as warmongers or fat businessmen in tailcoats and stovepipe hats. 'Every Marxist work on the economics of capitalist countries must be a bill of indictment,' declared *Pravda*, the Communist Party newspaper,[2] during the early years of the Cold War. America, according to the official line, was run by a small clique of Wall Street finance capital: everything from the political process, the press, social arrangements, culture and foreign policy was subordinated to those interests. 'America resembles more closely the horrid fantasy of Orwell's *Nineteen Eighty-Four* than the country we know,' wrote Frederick Barghoorn, a well-known scholar of the Soviet Union in 1950.[3] 'The America in Soviet propaganda is ruled by force and fraud. Its handful of rulers pull the strings to which their subjects dance like puppets. Its domestic policy is one of exploitation and oppression and its foreign policy is characterised by deception and aggression.'

Attitudes softened under Khrushchev, but respect for the efficiency of America's industry and agriculture was tempered by criticism of its enormous wealth disparity, economic deprivation and social injustice. Approved authors such as Steinbeck, Sinclair Lewis, Caldwell and Dreiser were read as though life in 1950s America was still as it had been portrayed in their books – a land of robber barons and bloated merchants, of exploited factory workers, impoverished sharecroppers and blacks under constant threat of lynching. There were also moments of extreme tension such as the Cuban Missile Crisis of October 1962 when the Cold War came close to escalating into a full-blown nuclear conflict. 'Capitalism is not simply an unjust economic system. It is a way of life that leads to a corruption of important values,' declared Khrushchev.[4] He believed that the Soviet Union would 'bury' or outlive capitalist America.

In the 1970s a desire on both sides to reduce the threat of nuclear war and boost trade brought detente, which was marked by a series of arms control treaties between America and the Soviet Union and some further softening of attitudes to the West. The joint Apollo-Soyuz mission of 1975, the first in which the two rivals cooperated in space, was a dramatic moment that symbolised a new era of peaceful coexistence. Russians smoked a new brand of Apollo-Soyuz cigarettes, produced in a joint venture between Philip Morris and the Soviet Yava tobacco factory, their packs decorated with an image of the two vessels coming together. Detente went only so far, however: the two countries may have started to talk to each other but they remained fierce geopolitical and ideological rivals. Soviet media continued to highlight the negative side of American life, from its racism to its pockets of extreme poverty.

Students and other visitors from the West, meanwhile, brought with them a different insight into life in their world and, through furtive deals on street corners, the opportunity to get hold of some of its forbidden fruits, from Levi jeans to Beatles records. In turn, the Western visitors returned home with impressions of a country every bit as exotic to them as America was to the Russians. The 1980 Olympic Games heralded the coming together of these two worlds. Despite an official sixty-five-nation boycott led by America in protest at the Soviet invasion of Afghanistan, some five million spectators visited Moscow and other cities in what turned into an enormous cultural exchange.

The impact of the Olympics was dwarfed by the changes that occurred after Gorbachev came to power in 1985; his policy of glasnost ('openness') loosened controls on the media and made it possible for them to speak freely not just about the outside world but also about the dark chapters in the Soviet Union's past. At last the truth could be told about the secret protocols attached to the Molotov-Ribbentrop Pact of August 1939, under which Stalin and Hitler carved up swathes of Eastern Europe between them, and about the massacre of twenty-two thousand Poles in Katyn in April–May 1940. The Soviet Union had always blamed Katyn on the Nazis, but now conceded that the massacre had been the work of the NKVD.* For the first time people were able to read books openly, such as Boris Pasternak's *Doctor Zhivago*, Vasily Grossman's *Life and Fate* and Anatoli Rybakov's *Children of the Arbat*. Osip Mandelstam, Vladimir Nabokov and Nikolai Gumilev were removed from the banned list.

Circulation of newspapers and literary journals soared to new heights, thanks in part to the serialisation of formerly banned works. Sales of *Ogonyek*, one of the more daring magazines, reached five million copies a week; *Literaturnaya Gazeta* sold eight million, *Izvestia* twelve million and *Komsomolskaya Pravda* twenty million. An unprepossessing weekly called *Argumenty I Fakty* – 'Arguments and Facts' – was read by twenty-five million.

At the same time, the strict laws governing economic activity were liberalised. Under Gorbachev, a form of private enterprise was allowed to emerge through the so-called cooperative movement; the name was chosen to maintain a veneer of socialist conformity. In the late 1980s, cooperative restaurants began to appear on the streets of Moscow, offering a tastier though more expensive alternative to the giant state-run eating establishments. Kiosks along the sides of streets and

---

* The NKVD was the forerunner of the KGB.

at railway stations began to sell Finnish beer and American chocolate. Cooperatives began to emerge in other sectors, too, such as small-scale manufacturing. It was here that the oligarchs of the future cut their teeth: Vladimir Gusinsky, the media tycoon, started out selling copper bracelets made with wire stripped from transformers; Mikhail Fridman's cooperative provided window-cleaning services to state companies; Boris Berezovsky, a mathematician by training, made his money in the car business; Roman Abramovich sold imported rubber ducks from his Moscow flat.

'These developments were shocking for people who lived in the USSR. Everything was completely new,' said Oslon. 'The West became a model and we wanted to emulate it. We wanted a great variety of products: sausages, computers, freedom, opportunities to work and become rich. And all this displayed how wrong everything was in the USSR and how well everything was settled in the West.

'This planet was still different, but it was nearer, it was in a zone within reach. We did not need a spaceship to fly to Mars, we could take a plane and arrive in the US. There were a few people who had been there, but the opportunity itself meant that the planet was closer. But it still remained a completely different planet.'

THE MAN TASKED WITH REBUILDING RUSSIA in the image of Planet America was Yegor Gaidar, a baby-faced economist from an old communist family. His grandfather, Arkady, was a war hero who later made his name as an author of children's books; his father, Timur, was a military correspondent for *Pravda* who had fought in the Bay of Pigs invasion. Although only thirty-five years old, Gaidar had already carved out a solid academic career as a researcher in several institutes and had been an editor of the ideological journal *Kommunist*. By 1991, contact with Western economics had convinced him that radical change was necessary, and he began to gather around him a group of like-minded thinkers. That November, during the dying days of the Soviet Union, he was named by Yeltsin as economics minister and deputy prime minister of the Russian Republic.

The economy Gaidar inherited was in a parlous state. The system of communist central planning, in which all means of production were owned by the state and directed through a succession of five-year plans, had run out of steam. Such a system had arguably allowed the Soviet

Union to mobilise the resources it needed to triumph over Nazi Germany, but it was ill-equipped to satisfy the needs of a sophisticated late twentieth-century society. The gap in living standards between the Soviet Union and the West was growing ever wider with each year that passed.

The economy had been stymied by a decline in the production of oil, the country's main export; old fields were being depleted and the development of new ones had slowed. Then, in the mid-1980s, the oil price had collapsed. The Soviet Union was not only selling less oil; it was now getting fewer dollars per barrel. Add a series of poor harvests and the industrial unrest that erupted in the more relaxed political climate, and it was clear that the economy was heading for crisis. The Kremlin initially reacted by borrowing abroad, but by 1990–1 its access to foreign credit had dried up.

Gaidar knew that drastic action was needed. Ending price controls was the first phase of his plan. The logic was simple: prices play a vital role in a market system by balancing supply and demand. They also determine the allocation of resources: at its simplest, if demand for a product surges, driving up its price, the company that makes it will increase its production and other competitors will enter the market. This does not happen under central planning, however, where prices are set by planners who, however skilled, could never simulate the effect of billions of individual decisions by consumers.

Gaidar's appointment caused surprise and was a tribute to Yeltsin's willingness to think radically. But while undoubtedly a brilliant theorist, Gaidar had never worked in government or industry. The same was true of the fellow thirty-somethings he brought with him. However, one of his advisers was Jeffrey Sachs, an American academic with hands-on experience. In 1985, as a professor of economics at Harvard, Sachs had helped the Bolivian government to tame hyperinflation of 24,000%; then, in 1989, he had played a key role in Poland's successful transition from central planning to a market economy. Now he took on his toughest challenge to date.

It was clear the process was going to be painful. As the Soviet Union had begun to fall apart, the Kremlin had faced growing demands from workers for wage rises. It had largely given in, printing more money and pushing up the budget deficit to almost twenty per cent of its gross domestic product (GDP). Yet there was no corresponding increase in the supply of goods and services. The result was that the economy was awash with money that could not be spent, leading to queues, shortages and a form of suppressed inflation known as the 'monetary overhang'. Once price controls were lifted at the start of 1992, the rouble inevitably plunged, further fuelling the inflationary spiral. Under communism, people had money but nothing to buy. Now the empty shelves were beginning to fill, but people couldn't afford what was on offer.

Gaidar was singled out as a particular target for loathing; he and his fellow reformers were derided by Aleksandr Rutskoi, Yeltsin's increasingly sceptical vice president, as 'the boys in pink trousers'. As their ideas came up against those of the old Soviet establishment, the battle lines were drawn. Far from supporting economic reforms, the parliament, dominated by communists, blocked Gaidar at every turn. The reformers also found themselves at odds with the Russian Central Bank, which was led by Viktor Gerashchenko, one of the Soviet faithful appointed by the parliament.

According to conventional economic theory, the way to combat hyperinflation is by cutting the money supply. Gerashchenko, by contrast, believed the problem was too little money in the economy. To the alarm of Jeffrey Sachs, he planned to increase the money supply by around thirty per cent a month to get the factories moving again. This, Gerashchenko claimed, would raise output, put more goods on the market and reduce prices. He was wrong: in December 1992 inflation hit an all-time high of 2,333.30%. Sachs would later famously describe Gerashchenko as 'the world's worst central banker'. Attempts to control the money supply were further complicated by the continued use of the rouble by the other fourteen former Soviet republics, which also went on printing money and, since it could be used to buy goods in foreign countries, had little incentive to stop.

It is difficult to fault the underlying logic of what Gaidar set out to do. Thanks to the introduction of the price mechanism, a link was established between consumption and production. Shops that for decades had been grim places with signs proclaiming 'shoes' or 'bread' began to look more like their Western equivalents as their role was transformed from distributors of scarce resources into commercial entities vying for consumers' roubles. Once there was only one kind of washing powder, which made only sporadic appearances on the shelves, provoking flurries of excitement as word got around of its arrival. Now there were several of them, all subtly different. The same was true of coffee, biscuits and breakfast cereal. Deodorant, hair conditioner and tampons began to appear. It was a whole new world, and Russians found themselves trying to understand its rules. How should they behave? And what should they buy? The advertising industry, until now a wing of official propaganda during the Soviet period, provided guidance.

The fastest, smartest and least scrupulous quickly learnt how to take advantage of the extraordinary economic opportunities. But the majority struggled, especially the older generations. Average living standards fell year after year as wages failed to keep up with prices and factories went out of business. Industrial production slumped. Those on pensions and other fixed state payments fared even worse; often they went for months without receiving any money at all. *Babushki* – elderly women – standing by the side of the road selling their meagre possessions soon became a feature of most cities.

Morality became optional: such were the spoils up for grabs that commercial rivals soon turned to violence and business shaded into organised crime. The vulnerable fell victim to tricksters determined to separate them from whatever wealth they had: people managed to 'privatise' the state apartment in which they had lived all their lives only to be persuaded to part with it for a fraction of its value. Others put their money into investment funds that promised returns too good to be true; these pyramid schemes soon collapsed, taking investors' savings with them. There was a geographical imbalance too. Initially most of the changes were concentrated in Moscow and St Petersburg, and to travel to the provinces in the first years of the new Russia was to travel back in time.

The hardships suffered by the majority of the population inevitably damaged the reformers' cause, especially when set against the wealth flaunted by the newly emerging business class. Modesty was an alien concept to the *novie russkie*, many of whom seemed straight out of school. Scarcely able to comprehend their good fortune, they cruised through the streets in their top-of-the-range BMW and Mercedes limousines, ate in upmarket restaurants where a single meal could cost more than an average worker's annual salary and drank champagne in nightclubs.

The effect of this on the majority still toiling for the state in return for a dwindling wage packet was understandable. The Soviet Union had been far from an egalitarian country, but the *nomenklatura*, its ruling class, had enjoyed their privileges discreetly behind closed doors. What rankled with many Russians was the manner in which the *novie russkie* had made their money: most had become rich through trade or finance – activities condemned as speculation in communist times – or through the misappropriation of state property.

Implementing such sweeping economic reforms would have been hard enough if there had been a broad political consensus, as had been the case in Poland when it started its transformation in 1989. Doing so in Russia, where the political class was sharply divided between reformers and communists, was far more difficult. 'Dismantling the Soviet-era system seemed to be a mission of great moral rightness,' Sachs recalled two decades later. 'I certainly hoped, and rather expected, that Russia would feel a wave of elation at the new freedom. In this I was somewhat mistaken. The period of elation was remarkably short, and the period of political civility was even shorter.'[5]

3

IN SEARCH OF A NEW MARSHALL PLAN

How much money would be required to turn post-Soviet Russia into a thriving economy? Ten billion dollars? Twenty? A hundred? After seventy years of looking-glass economics, Russia was a basket case. Factories churned out obsolete goods according to plans handed down from above; agriculture was a mess, while oil, gas and other plentiful raw materials were extracted in a brutal, slapdash manner that had turned the environment into a wasteland.

Viewed from Washington, Yeltsin and his team of young reformers led by Gaidar were taking Russia in the right direction with their pursuit of free market policies. Yet reforms alone were not enough: money was needed as well to oil the wheels of change and ease the pain of transition. After the Second World War, the United States welcomed Germany and Japan back into the international community, remaking its former enemies' political institutions in its own image and pumping a fortune into their reconstruction. Reborn as liberal democracies with thriving economies, they soon became model world citizens and America's most loyal allies. This was far from altruistic on Washington's part: it knew it needed the support of both countries in the developing Cold War with the Soviet Union.

Four and a half decades on, attitudes were very different. In July 1991 at the G7 summit in London, in the dying days of the Soviet Union, Gorbachev made a pitch for a Western aid package of $30-50 billion a year for at least five years. His request was turned down on the grounds that his economic reform plans were so vague the money would certainly be wasted. The Soviet leader was told to go away and come up with better proposals – but before he could do so, Gorbachev was out of a job.

The end of the Soviet Union – and accompanying fears of economic and political collapse – transformed the situation. American leaders now asked what they should do to help ensure the transformation of Russia and its former allies into peaceful, prosperous capitalist democracies, avoiding anarchy, an authoritarian backlash and mass emigration.

The immediate problem appeared to be a looming food crisis. Media reports of soaring prices, empty stores and hospitals without medicine, although often somewhat fanciful, prompted a mass outpouring of concern in the West. In what was known as Operation Provide Hope, a fleet of US air force C-5A and C-141 transport planes began to deliver thousands of tonnes of emergency food, medicines and medical supplies to Russia and the other former Soviet states – much of it drawn from stocks left over from the Gulf War. Churches, schools and community groups across America and Europe followed suit. However, getting these supplies to their destinations proved tricky, and much of the aid was stolen or left to rot. The Russian reaction varied from gratitude to amusement, though some were offended that their once-proud nation was being treated like a sub-Saharan African country suffering a drought. Their sense of humiliation was symbolised by the flooding of Russia with cheap American chicken pieces that were nicknamed *nozhki busha* ('Bush legs'), in honour of the US president.

There were also moments of farce, such as when a shipment of 120 tonnes of British beef was rejected by Moscow agricultural inspectors who feared it might be tainted with 'mad cow disease'. After hours of wrangling, it was dispatched to Murmansk, within the Arctic Circle, since there were no other cattle there to be infected by their dead brethren. Plans for further shipments were shelved. Lynda Chalker, the British overseas development minister, called the episode 'very embarrassing', adding: 'If they are going to react like this, we have lots of other things to do, not only with our beef but with our time.'[1]

Providing more concerted help for the Russian economy proved more problematic. Experts such as Sachs, who was advising Gaidar, and Lawrence H. Summers, chief economist of the World Bank, argued that Western governments should be ready to fund an IMF-approved programme to help the country survive its financial crisis and 'privatise, marketise and monetise' its economy. In a much-quoted article published in *The Economist* in December 1991, Sachs put the amount required for the entire former Soviet Union at $30 billion a year for several years. It was a considerable sum at a time when the American economy was also in the doldrums, but still a fraction of the hundreds of billions of dollars a year that Washington and its NATO allies had been spending on the military to combat the Soviet threat. The aim of such monetary assistance was to ease the squeeze on living standards and help establish foreign confidence, buying time for Gaidar and his beleaguered team to carry out their reforms.

Others, such as Marshall Goldman, another leading American Soviet expert, were not convinced. Russia's problem, he argued, was the lack of a proper legal framework, commercial code and property rights, which were needed to make markets function. Pump money in before this framework was established and it would be wasted or stolen or, worse, hit the growth of the nascent private sector by bolstering bureaucracy. The money could also ease the pressure on Russia to cut back on its military budget. 'Giving the Russians money is a dreadful mistake,' Goldman warned. 'This is not a dormant market system like Poland. We should not provide money until they have made major institutional changes.'[2]

Bush was not inclined towards any grand rescue package. The budget deficit that year was expected to exceed $350 billion and he was under pressure to rein in America's global commitments. With Pat Buchanan, his challenger in the Republican primaries, pursuing an isolationist 'America First' campaign, Bush could not be seen to be putting Russians ahead of his own compatriots. Sachs recalled a meeting in spring 1992 with Lawrence Eagleburger, deputy secretary of state. 'Jeffrey, you must understand,' Eagleburger told him. 'Assume for the sake of argument that I agree with you. It doesn't matter. Do you know what this year is? It's an election year. There will be no large-scale financial support.'[3]

The administration was prodded into action by an unlikely figure. Aged seventy-nine and well on the way to rehabilitation for the sins of Watergate, Richard Nixon warned in a strongly worded 'secret' memo – circulated to some fifty friends and top foreign affairs experts – that the United States and the West were missing a great opportunity to transform Russia and its neighbours into democracies by not providing enough aid.

The memo's contents found their way onto the front page of the *New York Times* on 10 March 1992, Super Tuesday in the presidential primary calendar, under the headline 'Nixon Scoffs at Level of Support for Russian Democracy by Bush'. Nixon, wrote Thomas Friedman, the newspaper's diplomatic correspondent, had sharply criticised Bush and James Baker, his secretary of state, for the administration's 'pathetic support of the democratic revolution in Russia'.

'The stakes are high, and we are playing as if it were a penny-ante game,' Nixon wrote. 'This is a pathetically inadequate response in light of the opportunities and dangers we face in the crisis in the former Soviet Union.' Nixon argued that America and its allies should provide far larger amounts of humanitarian aid, reschedule Soviet-era debts until the new market economy began to function and create a multi-billion-dollar fund to stabilise the rouble. 'What seems politically profitable in the short term may prove costly in the long term,' he added. 'The hot-button issue in the 1950s was "Who lost China?" If Yeltsin goes down, the question "Who lost Russia?" will be an infinitely more devastating issue in the 1990s.'

The (not so) secret memo was to form the basis of a speech that Nixon delivered at a two-day policy conference in Washington sponsored by the Nixon Library, at which Bush also spoke. Bush agreed that Russia needed more aid, but he did not make the strong public appeal for billions in new money that Nixon had declared was vital. Washington was considering a contribution to a fund to stabilise the rouble, Bush said, but he added that 'we're living in a time of constrained resources' and claimed 'I don't have a blank check' for foreign aid.

Nixon's intervention was as unwelcome as it was surprising for Bush. With his approval rating tumbling from the eighty-nine per cent it hit in the aftermath of his Gulf War victory, Bush was worried that all the foreign policy successes under his watch – from the collapse of communism to German reunification and the Gulf War – could be forgotten if Yeltsin were swept away by his hard-line foes. The administration's natural response was to play up the effectiveness of what little aid America had actually supplied, to refrain from asking Congress for anything more and hope that Yeltsin would somehow succeed in transforming his country without their support.

Having won his nomination in the primaries, Bush was eventually spurred into action by Bill Clinton, the Democratic front runner, who began to support calls for more help for Russia. With the Arkansas governor due to make a major address on world affairs on 1 April, Bush was in danger of being outbid and was under pressure to come up with a more substantial plan than the one he had originally intended to announce. Setting aside his customary caution, Bush scrambled into action, making his own speech just twenty minutes before Clinton was due to take the stage at New York's Waldorf Hotel. The G7, Bush told the audience, would make available $24 billion to support Russia – made up of $18 billion in loans, credits and direct aid from the allies and $6 billion in set-asides from the G7 for a much-needed rouble stabilisation fund.

'This isn't driven by election-year pressures,'[4] Bush added, insisting that he had instead been spurred on by an upcoming session of the Congress of People's Deputies, Russia's extended parliament, at which Yeltsin and his reformers were expected to be given a roasting. Although Bush's declared motivation was less than convincing, the statement did the trick: his announcement got the headlines, even though Clinton sold his own similar proposal rather more convincingly. Any aid package, Clinton insisted, should be seen 'not as a bailout, but as a bridge loan, much as a family gets from the bank when it's buying a new house before selling an old one'.

Bush's aid package was less concrete and less complete than his officials made it seem, and it was not clear how he had arrived at the $24 billion figure. The Japanese, locked with the Russians in an unresolved territorial dispute over a chain of Pacific islands, were angry that the deal was announced before there was final agreement on the details; officials from other donor countries were not clear about how much they would be expected to put in. Part of the confusion may have been deliberate, with the administration reluctant in election year to spell out precisely how much American taxpayers would have to contribute. Sceptical commentators argued that nothing like $24 billion would be paid, suggesting the real amount would be more like three or four billion. Having agreed the package, the administration went on the offensive to sell it to a sceptical Congress: the Freedom Support Act, as it was dubbed, would be the keystone of a post-Cold War American effort to 'build a democratic peace' with all the former communist lands.

An undertone of urgency came from the US–Russia summit that Bush was due to host in Washington a few weeks later on 16–17 June. Yeltsin had been to America briefly once since the end of the Soviet Union, visiting Bush at Camp David that February. The two leaders had got on well. Yet Yeltsin had been disappointed that Bush had still not given any firm promises on aid. When he travelled on to Canada that evening, he had complained that unspecified countries 'talk and talk' but 'for the past five months we have been asking for help, and it hasn't happened'. Now the Russian leader was to return, but for a much higher-profile official visit. When he arrived, Yeltsin would give a speech to both houses of Congress.

THE IMPENDING SUMMIT BROUGHT TO THE fore a question that had begun with Gorbachev's perestroika, the policy of 'restructuring' that accompanied glasnost, his policy of 'openness', and had now become urgent: what would be the nature of the relationship between the United States and the 'New Russia'?

The collapse of the Soviet Union had left America unchallenged in the world, both ideologically and militarily – a fact that Bush had pointed out in his State of the Union address in January 1992 with which he had set the tone for US–Russia relations. 'A world once divided into two armed camps now recognises one sole and preeminent power, the United States of America,' he declared. In rhetoric taken up by the next President Bush a decade later, he added, to sustained applause: 'As long as I am President I will continue to lead in support of freedom everywhere, not out of arrogance, not out of altruism, but for the safety and security of our children.'

Russia saw things differently: its new leaders were not prepared to give up their country's national interests, whether commercial or geo-political, and did not find it easy to come to terms with their sudden loss of superpower status – something America was slow to appreciate. Indeed, the 'Democrats' who were now in power had to be seen to be standing up for their country or risk being swept away. The summit, one commentator wrote, was being held 'in a weird twilight moment of Russian–American relations – a moment when the two countries have stopped being enemies but aren't quite allies yet'.[5]

Yeltsin did his best to drag relations out of this twilight zone with a triumphant joint address to both houses of Congress, which was the high point of his visit. Arriving at the podium to chants of 'Boris, Boris' from the assembled legislators, he declared that communism in the former Soviet Union was dead, that he would do everything necessary to find any US prisoners of war who might be alive in Russia and that he had already ordered that the SS-18 nuclear missiles due to be destroyed under a recent arms control agreement be taken off active status. He called on Congress to play its part in return and approve the aid package.

'For many years, our two nations were the two poles, the two opposites,' Yeltsin told legislators in a speech interrupted thirteen times by standing ovations. 'That evil scenario is becoming a thing of the past. Reason begins to triumph over madness. We have left behind the period when America and Russia looked at each other through gun sights, ready to pull the trigger at any time.'

Yeltsin also praised Bush for having been the first to call him and voice support during the abortive coup of August 1991. The American president 'was the first to understand the true meaning of the victory of the Russian people,' Yeltsin said. Bush's response was short and heartfelt: 'You leave with all of us feeling you are going to make it, somehow,' he said. 'We are at your side.'

With a single speech, Yeltsin had escaped the long shadow cast by Gorbachev. The bill passed the Senate on 2 July. The House proved more problematic but, on 6 August, it too followed suit.

That autumn, as the polls began to move against him, Bush again reached for the Russia card, trying to claim credit for ending the Cold War. This made him an easy target for Clinton. 'The notion that the Republicans won the Cold War reminds me of the rooster who took credit for the dawn,' Clinton declared.[6] 'We must never forget that in the end, communism rotted from the inside out, with heroes both famous and unknown leading the way.'

Gorbachev, meanwhile, took exception to Bush's depiction of him during the campaign as the ousted head of a defeated enemy power rather than as someone who had set out as an equal partner of the US president to try to establish a new world order. Humiliated by Yeltsin, who had taken his seat in the Kremlin, Gorbachev was acutely sensitive about his place in history. If Bush had 'won' the Cold War, then he was the one who lost it. He expressed his irritation in an interview with David Remnick in *The New Yorker* published in November 1992.[7] 'Bush warned me privately not to pay attention to what he would say during the presidential campaign,' said Gorbachev. 'I suppose there are necessary things in a campaign. But if the idea [that the US brought about the collapse of the Soviet system] is serious, then it is a very big illusion.'

The former Soviet leader's words were seized on by a jubilant Clinton. 'If Gorbachev shouldn't pay attention to him [Bush], you sure shouldn't pay any attention to him,' he told a rally in Jackson, Missouri.

WHILE BUSH WAS PONDERING WHETHER TO reach for his cheque book, the Russian government was already moving on to the next stage of its economic reform. Freeing prices had been only part of it. The government now intended to transform the fundamental structure of the economy by privatising the state-owned enterprises that accounted for all but a fraction of business activity. The scale of the task was enormous. Poland and the other former Soviet satellites had already gone down this path. Russia was many times bigger, however, and had spent more than twice as long under communism. No one still alive had lived or worked under any other system in Russia. Matters were further complicated by the break-up of the Soviet Union, which meant that some enterprises straddled what were now international borders.

The way privatisation was carried out was to a large extent responsible for the shape of the new Russia. The impetus was political as much as economic: ending state control of the economy and doing so as quickly as possible was seen as a way of diluting the power of the 'red directors' who controlled the state-owned enterprises, thereby preventing a return to communism. Considerations that should have been driving the process, such as maximising the amount of money raised or increasing the efficiency of privatised enterprises, were only secondary.

Initially the government decided to privatise around one-third of all industry. The scheme, presided over by Anatoly Chubais, a young reformer, was simple: each citizen was given a voucher that could be used to buy stakes in state industry. In keeping with the scheme's free market principles, people could either use the vouchers themselves or sell them on to someone else. Many chose the latter course: the vouchers changed hands at an average of $20, though some people sold theirs for as little as $7, the price of two bottles of cheap vodka. Others put them into voucher funds, which, largely unregulated, often turned into pyramid schemes.

On the face of it, the voucher scheme seemed the perfect way of creating a share-owning democracy that would, in turn, help underpin the foundations of a democratic Russia. Yet reality did not correspond with theory. At $20 a voucher, Russia's entire industrial and natural resource wealth, including its massive reserves of oil, natural gas and other minerals, would be worth just $10 billion – about one-sixth of the value of Walmart. This discrepancy inevitably opened up massive arbitrage opportunities: small-scale entrepreneurs would tour villages buying up vouchers for a modest mark-up and sell them on at a profit to larger-scale dealers. So the process would continue until blocks of tens of thousands of shares were being bought and sold at the Moscow voucher exchange, set up near Red Square.

This was only the first stage, as the vouchers had to be exchanged for shares in specific companies. This took place at so-called voucher auctions, but these were auctions unlike any other: if only one person turned up at a given auction bearing a single voucher, then it could be used to buy the entire block of stock being auctioned. If more people turned up, it would be divided between them.

With the organisation of these auctions left to the company managers, the scope for abuse was considerable, especially in the energy industry, one of the few parts of the Russian economy that held its value on world markets. Stories abounded of companies trying to rig auctions by restricting access to outsiders. Surgutneftegaz, a large Siberian energy producer, was rumoured to have been responsible for the closure of the local airport the night before an auction of its shares. Another oil company was said to have set up a roadblock of burning tyres to stop potential bidders getting through.

One of the most egregious tactics was used by the energy giant Gazprom, which owns one-third of global reserves of natural gas. Those who wanted to buy shares could do so only in the tiny Siberian and Arctic villages where the company had its energy deposits. The management also reserved the right to buy outsiders' shares at a price it dictated. The result was that only Gazprom people ended up buying the company, with the managers, who were the only ones with any money, benefiting from the auction.

As a result, the price at which Gazprom was privatised in 1994 through the vouchers scheme was $250 million; three years later, the Russian stock market would value it at $40.48 billion – rewarding its shareholders with a 16,192% profit. Even this was cheap: valued per cubic metre of its reserves, as a Western energy company would be, it would have been worth several hundred billion dollars. Other companies such as Unified Energy Services (electricity), Lukoil (oil), Rostelecom (telecoms), Yuganskneftegaz (oil) and Surgutneftegaz (oil), would also go on to trade at massive mark-ups.[8]

The voucher method proved, in retrospect, to have been one of the most unfair that could have been chosen. The state effectively sold off a large chunk of its assets for a fraction of its market price and the beneficiaries, in many cases, had been the very same 'red directors' whose power the government had wanted to break. The result was not just a massive redistribution of income and wealth. It also ultimately undermined the case of the liberals within the government by making economic reform synonymous with unfairness and the enrichment of an elite minority.

The problem was compounded by the paucity of Western aid, which meant a continued squeeze on pensions and other government spending, adding to the unpopularity of the reforms. 'During the critical months from January to April 1992, even a few hundred million dollars of freely convertible currency reserves would have allowed us substantially to extend our freedom of economic manoeuvre, but even these sums were not available to us,' Gaidar noted ruefully. 'By the time the bureaucratic procedures were at last complete, the stabilisation programme was already disintegrating before our eyes.'[9]

4

STOCKHOLM SYNDROME

A NEW AMERICAN PRESIDENT WAS ABOUT TO enter the White House. Bill Clinton won the November 1992 election by capitalising on George Bush's poor economic record. 'Read my lips: no new taxes', the phrase spoken by Bush as he accepted the Republican nomination four years earlier, became his political obituary. Foreign policy, an area in which Clinton, a former governor of Arkansas, lacked experience, had not been an issue, with the exception of the brief flurry of interest in Russia prompted by Nixon's memo. In the weeks after his victory, however, Clinton became increasingly preoccupied with the world beyond America and with Russia in particular.

Bush, the pragmatist, had not proposed any grand re-evaluation of the United States' relations with Russia and the other former Soviet republics. His priorities had instead been preventing the proliferation of the Soviet Union's vast nuclear arsenal and encouraging economic reform. Clinton was more of an idealist – and he did not like what he saw. As he pondered his role as president, he was struck by the extent to which the optimism that had accompanied the break-up of the Soviet Union a year earlier had been replaced by pessimism and fear. As Clinton put it in his memoirs: 'The "new world order" President Bush had proclaimed after the fall of the Berlin Wall was rife with chaos and big, unresolved questions.'[1]

Developments within Russia gave further cause for concern: Yeltsin's relationship with the Congress of People's Deputies, the parliament, was deteriorating rapidly. The main battle was over economic reform, which many deputies thought was being pushed too fast and without sufficient consideration for the living standards of ordinary people. But the disagreement had also turned into a broader power struggle between the two branches of government. The new independent Russia was still governed by the constitution drawn up when it was a Soviet republic, with a relatively limited role for the president. Yeltsin wanted more executive powers, but the Congress, elected during the days of the USSR, was unwilling to see its influence curbed.

During a stormy two-week session that December, its members agreed to hold a referendum the following April on enhancing the powers of the presidency, but Yeltsin was forced to pay a heavy price in return: he agreed to abandon Gaidar, the young reformer, whose appointment in June still hadn't been approved by parliament. On 14 December, Yeltsin replaced him with Viktor Chernomyrdin, a fifty-four-year-old former Communist Party apparatchik, who made clear his intention to slow the pace of economic change. Many of Yeltsin's reform-minded supporters in the Congress spoke of betrayal.

That same day, in Stockholm, Andrei Kozyrev, the Russian foreign minister, rose to address representatives of the fifty-one-member Conference on Security and Cooperation in Europe (CSCE). Aged forty-one, Kozyrev was an urbane character with a reputation as one of the more liberal-minded members of Boris Yeltsin's team – in short, the representative of a new Russia with which the West could do business. A product of the prestigious Moscow State Institute of International Relations, he had joined the Soviet ministry of foreign affairs in 1974. It was during a visit to New York as a junior member of his country's delegation to the United Nations General Assembly, his first trip abroad, that Kozyrev's beliefs in Soviet ideology were challenged. Visiting a supermarket, he was struck not just by the vast array of produce on offer but by the fact that the customers were all ordinary people – the kind who, according to communist propaganda, were exploited by the country's elite. Equally formative was his encounter with Boris Pasternak's *Doctor Zhivago*, still banned in his homeland. The young Kozyrev spent an entire day reading it on a bench in Central Park, too worried to take it back to the Soviet compound where he was staying.

In October 1990, at the age of thirty-nine, he became foreign minister of the Russian Federation and had kept the job in the new independent

Russia. At his confirmation hearing, he set out his vision: 'Democratic Russia should and will be just as natural an ally of the democratic nations of the West as the totalitarian Soviet Union was a natural opponent of the West,' he said.[2] His positive attitude was to earn him the nickname 'Mr Yes' – a play on the old 'Mr Nyet' tag applied to Andrei Gromyko, the grim-faced Soviet foreign minister in office for almost three decades during the Cold War.

Kozyrev's background made the speech he proceeded to give in Stockholm all the more surprising. Announcing 'some changes in the concept of Russian foreign policy', he declared that Russia's rapprochement with Europe and the norms of the CSCE could not be applied fully to the territory of the former Soviet Union. He also accused NATO and the European Community of 'interfering in Bosnia and the internal affairs of Yugoslavia' and demanded the lifting of sanctions that had been imposed against it. If this did not happen, he warned, 'we will reserve the right to take all necessary unilateral measures to protect our interests'.

'We clearly recognise that our traditions in many respects, if not fundamentally, lie in Asia, and this sets limits to our rapprochement with Western Europe,' Kozyrev added, accusing NATO and the nine-nation Western European Union Defence Organisation of drawing up plans to strengthen their military presence in the Baltic and other regions 'on the territory of the former Soviet Union'.

When Kozyrev had finished his tirade, there were stunned expressions across the hall – including on the faces of members of his own delegation, who had been kept in the dark about what their boss was planning to say. Lawrence Eagleburger, the US secretary of state, hustled his Russian counterpart into a side room and demanded an explanation.

What Kozyrev said next was every bit as surprising: the speech, he told Eagleburger, had been a charade, a wake-up call for the world of what would happen if Yeltsin lost to the conservative forces ranged against him in the Russian parliament. The speech, he said, was 'a fairly accurate compilation of the demands of what is by no means the most extreme opposition in Russia'. He added: 'I did it for the most serious reasons, so that you should all be aware of the real threats on our road to a post-Communist Europe.'

Three-quarters of an hour later, Kozyrev returned to the stage and made another speech explaining his trick. His statement, he told delegates, had been merely a 'rhetorical device' to warn them what things would be like if conservative forces returned to power in Russia. 'Neither President Yeltsin, who remains the leader and the guarantor of Russian domestic and foreign policy, nor I as minister of foreign affairs will ever agree to what I read in my previous speech,' he declared.

The audience was not impressed. 'An international forum is not the place for such behaviour,' complained Klaus Kinkel, the German foreign minister. Anatoliy Zlenko, the Ukrainian foreign minister, said: 'Maybe Mr Kozyrev has a sense of humour, but it is dangerous to use such tactics.'

WHEN IT CAME TO RUSSIA, PRESIDENT CLINTON placed a lot of faith in Strobe Talbott, a journalist at *Time*, who had been his house-mate at Oxford University a quarter of a century earlier. Talbott, a fluent Russian speaker who had translated and edited Khrushchev's memoirs, had 'known and cared about Russia and the Russian people' more than anyone else Clinton knew. Clinton also valued his fine analytical mind and fertile imagination, and trusted both his judgement and his willingness to tell him the unvarnished truth. Talbott was initially named as ambassador-at-large and special adviser to the secretary of state on the new independent states of the former Soviet Union. He was later appointed deputy secretary of state. Whatever his title, he was the administration's go-to man on Russia.[3]

During the transition period, Clinton spoke to Talbott often about the deteriorating situation in Russia. On 17 December, three days after Chernomyrdin's appointment and Kozyrev's Stockholm speech, Clinton called Talbott from Little Rock to say he was worried about 'this whole unbelievable mess in Russia'. If the situation in the country got completely out of hand, Clinton said, there was a danger of hundreds of thousands or even millions of refugees streaming westward. He could imagine Yeltsin being swept aside and Russia 'going bad on us', returning to a policy of confrontation with the West. During his presidency he said he wanted to do 'good stuff with Russia and really take advantage of what's new in a positive sense over there'. The first job, though, was 'averting disaster'.[4]

A few weeks later, Clinton reiterated his concerns. What was happening in Russia, he told Talbott, was 'the biggest and toughest thing out there. It's not just the end of communism, the end of the cold war. That's what's over and done with. There's also stuff starting – stuff that's new. Figuring out what it is, how we work with it, how we keep it moving in the right direction: that's what we've got to do.'[5]

Clinton had met Yeltsin for the first time when he had come to Washington in June 1992 for his summit with Bush. Clinton had been a great admirer of Yeltsin since he faced down the August coup, but Yeltsin had been initially reluctant to see him. It was traditional in election years for visiting leaders to meet the presidential challenger, but Yeltsin was advised by the Russian embassy in Washington that if he met anyone it should be Ross Perot, the businessman who was running as an independent. Clinton persisted and was given his half-hour with Yeltsin at Blair House, the official visitors' residence across Pennsylvania Avenue from the White House. Yeltsin was polite and friendly, but it was clear to Clinton that he preferred Bush and expected him to be re-elected.

Clinton did not hold this against him, and when Yeltsin called him a couple of days after his electoral triumph to invite him to meet and reaffirm America's support, Clinton was inclined to agree. There was a lot at stake for the Russian leader: on 25 April, the country would vote on whether it had confidence in him as president and agreed with his reforms. 'Yeltsin was up to his ears in alligators,' Clinton wrote in his memoirs. 'And I wanted to help him.'[6] Their meeting was set for 3–4 April in Vancouver. On 8 March, Nixon had called Clinton at the White House urging him to support Yeltsin. Nixon told him he would be remembered more for what he did for Russia than for his economic policy. Clinton concurred. During conversations with his foreign policy team in the weeks that followed, he 'pushed them to think bigger and do more'.[7]

The Vancouver summit provided a foretaste of the rapport that would develop between this unlikeliest of couples. At a first meeting, accompanied by only their closest advisers, Clinton tried to win over Yeltsin by expressing admiration for his attempts to transform Russia and asked what America could do to help. The proud leader of a once-mighty country, Yeltsin objected to the implication that the United States was coming to Russia's rescue. He needed outside assistance, but not too much, he said, since 'a dramatic increase' would allow the opposition back in Moscow to say Russia was 'under the US's thumb'.[8] Once Yeltsin had that off his chest, he was happy to accept Clinton's offer of $6 million to help house Russian army officers being withdrawn from the Baltic states – though he said he would prefer more, even if he could not be seen asking for it in public. Clinton agreed. Having banked the American offer, Yeltsin then went on the attack, demanding the removal of various pieces of Cold War-era legislation from the statute book – among them the Jackson–Vanik amendment passed in 1974 that had denied free trade with countries that restricted emigration. Such rules were offensive to him as a democrat, Yeltsin said.

Talbott, who took part in the meeting, was struck by Yeltsin's 'jabbing and wheedling' tone and his attempts to push Clinton into approving public statements that would look like American concessions. But Clinton took it all in his stride. 'He's not so much trying to make me look bad as trying to make himself look good with his real enemies back home,' he told Talbott.[9]

Yeltsin adopted a similar approach during the more formal parts of the summit, which concluded with little agreement on arms control and other security issues but a promise by Clinton of a $1.6 billion package – described as 'cooperation' rather than 'assistance' – which would be made available at that July's G7 summit in Tokyo. For Yeltsin, facing a referendum in three weeks' time, that was not soon enough: as Lloyd Bentsen, the treasury secretary, was speaking, Yeltsin passed him a scribbled note that said in capitals: 'It would be good if we could receive $500 million before April 25', the date of the vote. Clinton could not give him half a billion dollars on the spot, however, and Yeltsin had to make do with supportive words for his reform programme at their closing press conference.

The summit also gave Clinton an insight into Yeltsin's alarming fondness for alcohol. When the US and Russian delegations set off for a boat ride around Vancouver Island, Yeltsin downed three scotches within a few minutes of leaving the dock. He followed up with four glasses of wine and barely a bite to eat at dinner, and his speech became increasingly slurred. Warren Christopher, the secretary of state, passed one of his colleagues a note: 'No food, bad sign. Boat ride was liquid.' Keeping count of Yeltsin's alcohol intake was 'to become a standard feature of summitry', observed Talbott.[10]

When Talbott, Christopher and Anthony Lake, Clinton's national security adviser, complained that evening in the presidential hotel suite about the prospect of having to conduct high-stakes diplomacy under such conditions, Clinton told them to relax. 'I've seen a little of this problem in my time,' the president said, noting his own experience growing up with an alcoholic stepfather. 'At least Yeltsin's not a mean drunk.'[11]

Clinton's own memoirs reflected a similar sentiment. 'Whenever anyone made a snide remark about Yeltsin's drinking, I was reminded of what Lincoln allegedly said when Washington snobs made the same criticism of General Grant, by far his most aggressive and successful commander in the Civil War: "Find out what he drinks, and give it to the other generals".'[12]

Yeltsin did not receive the same understanding at home. Although he won the April referendum handily, his opponents in the Congress of People's Deputies refused to back down and the political crisis worsened. The months that followed were the most fraught of his presidency; on 21 September, Yeltsin tried to dissolve the parliament, even though the constitution did not give him the power to do so. The Congress responded by declaring Yeltsin's decision null and void, impeached him and named Aleksandr Rutskoi, the vice president, who had sided with his opponents, as acting president.

The roots of the crisis lay in the incomplete nature of the 'revolution' of 1991. While the perpetrators of the failed August coup were put on trial, most of those people who had loyally served the former communist regime clung to political power or had reinvented themselves in the private sector, making good use of their connections. Many – especially the young – wanted Russia to evolve as a 'normal' country in which they could live peacefully, make money and get on with their lives, but others mourned the loss of its status as a great power.

Many of those who had been responsible for abuses in government were still alive and in some cases held the same posts. Yet no attempt had been made to bring them to justice, as had been the case with those implicated in the Nazi regime. Nor was there a Truth and Reconciliation Commission of the sort set up in South Africa. There were calls for such a process, but who in the ruling class would have wanted such a reckoning? Certainly not Yeltsin himself, who had made his career in the Soviet system and served for decades under Brezhnev, Andropov, Chernenko and Gorbachev. Nor any of the others in positions of political power – even his opponents.

Setting aside questions of historical justice, Yeltsin faced a more immediate and concrete problem. The new independent Russia was still governed according to the constitution of 1978. Although the document had been amended in April 1992 to reflect the demise of the Soviet Union, Yeltsin was still forced to share power with the

Congress of People's Deputies, eighty-six per cent of whose deputies had been members of the Communist Party.

In retrospect, it would have been more logical to have held new elections for parliament and president as soon as possible after January 1992 and Russia's emergence as an independent state. A new constitution would also have helped. Instead, Yeltsin muddled on and, by autumn 1993, his stand-off with the parliament was beginning to spill over onto the streets, with mass demonstrations in Moscow and other cities. On 28 September came the first clashes between the special police and anti-Yeltsin protesters. Deputies barricaded themselves into the White House, the seat of the parliament on the Moscow river, and hundreds of fighters were reported to be joining them. The conflict finally erupted into open warfare on the morning of 4 October, when tanks fired on the White House in the deadliest street fighting Moscow had seen since the Bolshevik revolution. By that afternoon it was all over. The government put the death toll at 187; the opposition claimed it was several times higher.

By using tanks to blow his opponents out of the Moscow White House, Yeltsin had made clear that compromise and coalition building were not important elements of the political process. His right to continue to be considered a 'Democrat' seemed in doubt. However, political reform did follow. Yeltsin followed his bloody victory over parliament with elections and the adoption of a new constitution. Passed by referendum on 12 December 1993, the new document represented a break with Soviet practice by, among other things, abolishing the leading role of the Communist (or indeed, any other) Party and guaranteeing a pluralistic political system. In a nod to Russia's imperial past, the new lower house was called the State Duma, the name given to the first Russian legislature set up by Tsar Nicholas II in 1906.

The authors of the constitution had been inspired, in part, by the American political system, but their creation lacked the same checks and balances. The result was instead the creation of a political system that concentrated considerable power in the hands of one man and his entourage. During the communist years, Stalin's successors had to carry fellow members of the Politburo with them. The ousting of Khrushchev in 1964 and his replacement by Brezhnev showed the perils of failing to do so. Now all power was vested in the president.

It would have been difficult to imagine Yeltsin and his allies devising anything different, given the ferocity of the resistance they had faced from the parliament. The challenges involved in holding together such a large and ethnically diverse country – and preventing Russia from splintering as the Soviet Union had before it – made it easy to see the appeal of strong executive power. As long as Yeltsin was in power, the implications of such a concentration of power did not seem dangerous.

CLINTON'S POLICY WAS PREDICATED ON THE belief that it would be possible to create a partnership with the new and democratic Russia that he hoped would emerge from the wreck of the Soviet Union. Together, Washington and Moscow would hold a special global responsibility, now as allies rather than opponents – even though it was clear that America was the senior partner in the relationship. Ensure Russia's transformation into a friendly, democratic and economically successful state, so the argument went, and the rest of the Soviet Union would take care of itself.

Like Bush before him, Clinton was concerned about the fate of the Soviet Union's nuclear arsenal: its strategic weapons were divided between Russia, Ukraine, Belarus and Kazakhstan, while its tactical nuclear weapons were scattered even more widely.* America wanted Russia to be the only nuclear power, which meant working closely with Moscow to persuade Ukraine, Belarus and Kazakhstan to give up their arms.

Moscow quickly secured the return of all tactical nuclear warheads to Russia during the first half of 1992. It also soon reached bilateral understandings with Belarus and Kazakhstan on the removal or elimination of the strategic nuclear weapons systems on their territory. However, inducing Ukraine to give up the third-largest nuclear arsenal in the world was to prove more complicated. The Ukrainians realised the value of their bargaining chip and tried to extract the highest price: when Talbott met Leonid Kravchuk, the Ukrainian president, in Kiev on 10 May 1993, he demanded billions of dollars in 'compensation' and an American promise that it would treat an attack on Ukraine as if it were an attack on the US – the kind of security guarantee Washington gave its closest allies.[13]

The dispute highlighted the dilemma that Washington faced in its relations with the former Soviet republics. The Bush administration had swiftly opened embassies in the 'newly independent states' as a sign of its determination to treat them as fully independent countries.

---

* Strategic weapons are designed to target infrastructure and military installations, whereas tactical weapons are designed to be used in a direct military conflict.

Clinton reiterated this policy after coming to office, sending Talbott around their capitals to convince their leaders of America's support for their sovereignty and its willingness to assist them in disputes with each other and with Moscow.

Yet Russia's size and strategic importance led Washington to accept Russia's claim to a 'special role' in the former Soviet republics. Long before Kozyrev made his Stockholm speech, Russia had begun to show its determination to assume such a role. Yeltsin made no attempt to challenge the borders of the newly independent Russia, but it was also clear that the Kremlin struggled to accept Ukraine, Belarus and the other former Soviet states as fully independent. Russian officials coined a term for them: *blizhneye zarubezhye*, 'the near abroad', which carried with it connotations of a right of influence over their affairs.

During a difficult stage in the negotiations over Ukraine's nuclear arsenal, Vladimir Lukin, the Russian ambassador to the United States, told Talbott that Russia's relations with Ukraine were 'identical to those between New York and New Jersey', and that America should treat what happened within the former USSR as the contents of a 'black box'.[14] Some of Russia's neighbours, Talbott ruefully noted, wished they were 'less near' and 'more abroad'.

Yeltsin had set out his attitude towards the 'near abroad' in a speech in February 1993, in which he pressed for more integration among the newly independent states and, more controversially, set out Russia's right – and responsibility – to serve as a regional peacekeeper. 'Stopping all armed conflicts on the territory of the former USSR is in Russia's vital interest,' Yeltsin said. 'The world community sees more and more clearly Russia's special responsibility in this difficult undertaking . . . I believe the time has come for distinguished international organisations, including the UN, to grant Russia special powers as a guarantor of peace and stability in the former regions of the USSR.'[15]

Seen in such a context, the views expressed by Kozyrev in his spoof Stockholm speech were not a world away from what was now actual Russian policy. Indeed, by autumn 1993, Kozyrev was beginning to express similar sentiments himself. In a speech to the United Nations that September, he not only demanded international recognition of Russia's peacekeeping efforts in the 'near abroad' but asked the international community to support these efforts with financial and material help.[16]

Kozyrev fleshed out his thoughts in an interview with the newspaper

Izvestia that October, in which he warned that if Russia did not intervene in conflicts on the territory of the former Soviet Union it would
risk 'losing geographical positions that took centuries to conquer', and
may have to accept 'neighbours in Asia' – presumably China – stepping
in 'to force Russia out of the region and restrict its influence'.[17]

Such views were codified in the new Russian Military Doctrine
signed off by Yeltsin on 1 November, which set out, for the first time,
the principles according to which its armed forces should operate in
the post-Soviet world. The doctrine identified the former Soviet Union
as the main arena for Russian military activity and said 'the main
source of military danger to Russia is no longer any single nation or
alliance, but small regional conflicts'.[18] Russia would act in local wars
and armed conflicts near its borders and would also intervene in any
suppression of the rights, freedoms and legitimate interests of Russian-
speaking citizens in foreign states, it said.

In response to such perceived threats, the doctrine sanctioned the
use of troops beyond Russia's borders to protect national interests and
to quell conflicts 'in cooperation with other former republics'.[19] It also
abolished its 'no first use' policy on nuclear weapons. In its place was
a pledge not to use them against non-nuclear states that had signed
the Nuclear non-Proliferation Treaty – unless they were operating 'in
an alliance' with nuclear states.

The doctrine was, in a sense, confirmation of what was happening
already. In the years after 1991, Russia exerted economic and political
pressure on those countries that initially kept out of the Commonwealth
of Independent States to persuade them to join. Azerbaijan, Georgia
and Moldova eventually complied. Russia's economic weakness and
need to maintain good relations with the West meant the use of military force was not an option; nor did Yeltsin plan any foreign adventures.
Yet despite the parlous state of its economy, Russia was still a giant
compared to its neighbours, while its huge energy resources, on which
many of them depended, gave it considerable bargaining power.

Further leverage came from the Russian soldiers that remained
stationed in other republics for several years after the end of the Soviet
Union. Although the Kremlin gradually withdrew them, it accelerated
or slowed the pace according to the behaviour of the host country. In
some cases, the military presence was cloaked in terms of peacekeeping.
Yet there was little doubt about the real motivation.

Relations with Ukraine became especially fraught. As Serhii Plokhy wrote in his history of Ukraine: 'Whatever Yeltsin's intentions, Ukraine took its independence seriously and planned to use the forum to negotiate the terms of divorce, not remarriage.'[20] Tensions came to a head in January 1993 when Ukraine refused to become a full member of the Commonwealth of Independent States that it had itself helped to set up at the Belavezha meeting at which the Soviet Union was dissolved. Although ready to take part in the organisation's economic cooperation, it refused to sign up to any military commitments.

One of the biggest battles was over the 800,000 Soviet soldiers and officers left on Ukrainian territory. The Baltic states, like their counterparts in Central Europe, had simply asked the Soviet forces to leave. But the numbers there were far smaller. This was not an option for Ukraine, since there was nowhere for the 800,000 to go. The result was a compromise: officers were given a choice of swearing allegiance to the newly created Ukrainian army, retiring or being transferred. Soldiers and non-commissioned officers were sent home. The first group of officers swore allegiance to independent Ukraine on 3 January 1992; by spring, the overwhelming majority of their comrades had followed suit.

Determining ownership of the Black Sea Fleet – headquartered at Sevastopol on the Crimean peninsula – proved more complicated, especially when Admiral Igor Kasatanov, its commander, defied an attempted takeover by Ukraine and ordered his men to take to the sea instead. This prompted a crisis in Russo–Ukrainian relations that was defused only when Yeltsin and Kravchuk agreed at a summit that August to postpone any decision until the end of 1995, in the meantime putting the fleet under their joint personal control.

Resolving the fate of Ukraine's nuclear missiles was more complicated, but by late 1993, after months of patient diplomacy punctuated by much brinkmanship on all sides, a deal emerged. Under its terms, Russia would get the warheads and American money to help dismantle them, while Ukraine would receive US financial assistance too, as well as relief on its debts to Russia and some international assurances on its sovereignty. The deal's provisions were set out in a Trilateral Statement and accompanying annex, which was signed by Clinton, Yeltsin and Kravchuk in Moscow on 14 January 1994. The final act was played out that December when Ukraine formally acceded to the Treaty on the Non-Proliferation of Nuclear Weapons (NPT) as a non-nuclear weapons state.

In return, Ukraine, together with Belarus and Kazakhstan, signed the Budapest Memorandum on Security Assurances, according to which America, Russia and Britain agreed to respect their independence, sovereignty and existing borders and refrained from using force or threat of force against them. The agreement was hailed by all sides, though the security guarantees fell short of Ukraine's initial demands. Crucially it did not set out what would happen if any of the countries' territorial integrity was compromised.

THE CLINTON ADMINISTRATION, MEANWHILE, was formulating its approach to the former Soviet territory. Talbott set out Washington's broad policy goals in testimony to the House and Senate Foreign Relations Committee in September 1993. They were essentially fourfold: the attainment of democracy; the transition to a market economy; the non-proliferation of nuclear, chemical and biological weapons; and the resolution of regional conflicts. Clinton remained convinced that the only way to do this was in cooperation with Russia, or more specifically, with Yeltsin, whom he considered the only guarantor of reform and democracy. Speaking to a congressional committee two months later, Secretary of State Warren Christopher described the former Soviet republics as 'a long, long ways from the United States' and said he was happy to see Russia act to guarantee regional stability provided it respected 'international norms'. Christopher also refrained from criticising the Kremlin's new military doctrine, saying: 'What we are seeing here is Russian military doctrine trying to catch up with the new reality in Russia.'[21]

For some critics, though, by turning a blind eye to Russia's activities, Washington was acquiescing in the Kremlin's attempts to use its economic and military muscle to pursue its imperial ambitions and reconstitute the Soviet Union. The future dangers of this policy were highlighted by Zbigniew Brzezinski in a withering critique of US policy in the March/April 1994 edition of the journal *Foreign Affairs*:

> Implicit in these notions is the view that Russia's major geostrategic concern is regional stability. That makes Russian and American goals basically compatible. Moreover, since Russia is the only power capable of generating stability within the former Soviet Union, and since the independence of some of the new states is precipitating regional conflicts, the pacifying role of Russia is thereby enhanced . . .

President Clinton, addressing the Russian people, not only described the Russian military as having been 'instrumental in stabilizing' the political situation in Georgia, but even added that 'you will be more likely to be involved in some of these areas near you, just like the United States has been involved in the last several years in Panama and Grenada near our area'.

It follows that concerns regarding the alleged Russian threat expressed by states like Ukraine or Georgia are not to be taken too seriously, and as much has been said by top administration figures. In any case, the Ukrainians should blame their own intransigence regarding nuclear weapons for their international isolation and their resulting sense of vulnerability.

The other non-Russian states would be well advised to eschew excessive nationalism and to make their own accommodations with Moscow, thereby relieving Washington of excessive burdens or awkward pangs of conscience.

IT WAS NOT JUST THE KREMLIN'S attitude to the 'near abroad' that caused concern. Yeltsin was also taking a tough line against those minorities within Russia's borders who had been inspired by the break-up of the Soviet Union to try to secure their own independence. Chief among them was Chechnya in the North Caucasus. In September 1991, Chechen militants, led by Dzhokhar Dudayev, a former Soviet air force general, stormed a parliamentary session of the Chechen–Ingush autonomous republic, which lay within the Russian Federation, dissolving its government. A charismatic figure, Dudayev made himself president and declared independence. In the years that followed, the republic degenerated into chaos, turning into a centre of organised crime, and tens of thousands of non-Chechens fled.

Something had to be done. The Kremlin did not see independence for Chechnya as an option, not least because that would encourage other ethnic-based autonomous areas within Russia to follow its example. Yeltsin instead went for the military option, and in December 1994 Russian forces carried out heavy aerial bombardments of Chechnya. Ten days later, they entered the republic to 'establish constitutional order in Chechnya and to preserve the territorial integrity of Russia'. General Pavel Grachev, the Russian defence minister, boasted of a blitzkrieg that would end in victory by 20 December.

But the Kremlin's hope of a quick surgical strike followed by swift regime change proved illusory: it turned instead into a bloodbath. The capital, Grozny, was subject to the heaviest bombardment since the Allies' Second World War attack on Dresden, but the Chechens refused to yield. Several senior military figures – among them the deputy minister of defence, General Boris Gromov, the hero of the Soviet Union's equally ill-fated Afghan war – resigned in protest rather than be involved in a war against their own people. Morale among Russian troops was low and atrocities common on both sides. By the time an inconclusive agreement ending the conflict was signed on 31 August 1996, anything from 3,800 to 14,000 Russian soldiers had been killed and as many as 100,000 Chechens, most of them civilians.

The conflict presented the Clinton administration with a dilemma: it was shocked by reports of Russian brutality, but it also wanted to support Yeltsin and the territorial integrity of his country. Just as Bush had spoken out – albeit in vain – against the unravelling of the Soviet Union, so Clinton was alarmed at the prospect of Russia breaking up too. The arrival of Vice President Al Gore on a prearranged visit to Moscow four days after the start of the all-out invasion forced the administration to confront the issue. Gore set the tone with his reply: America hoped the conflict could be solved by negotiation but considered it 'an internal matter' for Russia.

Gore's remarks sounded like an endorsement by Washington of what was rapidly becoming a savage military campaign. Matters were made worse when Mike McCurry, the state department spokesman, appeared to draw parallels between Yeltsin's fight against the Chechens and the American Civil War, prompting one journalist to ask sarcastically whether the administration was calling Yeltsin 'the Russian Abraham Lincoln'. As further details of Russian atrocities emerged, Talbott, one of the architects of the policy, began to realise how the Chechen war was bringing to the surface one of the worst characteristics of the former communist regime: 'a reliance on raw force as the solution to all problems'.[22]

Russian society was divided by the conflict. While the nationalists lined up behind Yeltsin, liberal opinion was appalled by the carnage. Elena Bonner, the widow of the Nobel peace laureate Andrei Sakharov, who was continuing her husband's human rights work, told Talbott she feared the war could lead to a return to totalitarianism in Russia. America risked finding itself on the wrong side of an increasingly bitter debate.

5

EASTWARD BOUND

Václav Havel and Lech Wałęsa made an odd couple. The former, a Czech writer and philosopher turned president, was a very different character from his Polish counterpart, a one-time shipyard worker and the driving force behind the Solidarność trade union. Yet both had played a decisive role in freeing their respective countries from communism. And both wanted America to ensure they would never lose their freedom again. An invitation to the official opening of the Holocaust museum in Washington in April 1993 gave the two men, together with Árpád Göncz, their Hungarian counterpart, a chance to make their case to Bill Clinton.

During a meeting in the Oval Office that afternoon, they attempted to convince the president that the only way to maintain peace in Europe and prevent a return to authoritarianism was to allow their countries to join the West's democratic institutions – NATO in particular. Clinton, who greatly respected the pair for the persistence with which they had tackled Soviet power, found their argument convincing.

Sandwiched between Germany and Russia, in what Timothy Snyder, the Yale historian, has called Europe's 'bloodlands', Havel and Wałęsa's nations had always been vulnerable to attack by their powerful neighbours. Other countries had stood by as Czechoslovakia was dismembered by Hitler in 1938 and, less than a decade later, incorporated into the Soviet bloc. Britain had gone to war against Germany in 1939 for the sake of Poland, but when the Second World War had been won it had acquiesced in the country's banishment behind the Iron Curtain.

Germany, now anchored in the European Union, no longer appeared a threat, even if many in Europe had viewed the prospect of its reunification with some trepidation. Russia was a different matter. Since 1945, Moscow had exercised firm control over its satellites: their enforced adoption of a Soviet-style political system went hand in hand with membership of the Warsaw Pact, the military alliance established in 1955 as a counterweight to NATO. When Hungary attempted to leave the Warsaw Pact after the 1956 uprising against communist rule, Moscow sent in the tanks. It did the same in 1968 in response to the Prague Spring, the attempt by Alexander Dubček, the Czechoslovak communist leader, to build 'socialism with a human face'. Soviet forces would undoubtedly have gone in once again to Poland during the unrest in 1981 if its leader, General Wojciech Jaruzelski, had not imposed martial law.

The accession of Mikhail Gorbachev in 1985 had changed the rules. The Kremlin stood by when Jaruzelski allowed partially free elections in June 1989, which, three months later, produced Poland's first non-communist government since the 1940s. Nor did it attempt to intervene when Hungary began dismantling its border fence with Austria, allowing East Germans holidaying there to make their way to West Germany. Calls on Moscow to act by the hard-line East German leader, Erich Honecker, who rightly feared for the future of the GDR, fell on deaf ears.

This, declared Gennadi Gerasimov, the wisecracking Soviet foreign ministry spokesman, was the 'Sinatra doctrine'. 'He has a song, "I Did It My Way",' he told reporters in Helsinki that October as the Soviet bloc began to crumble. 'So every country decides on its own which road to take.' Asked whether this would include an acceptance by Moscow of the end of communist rule in the Soviet Union's satellites, Gerasimov replied that 'political structures must be decided by the people who live there'.

Gorbachev's motives are open to dispute. Did he really want to 'set these people free', to paraphrase Ronald Reagan? In fact, steeped as he was in communist ideology, did he conceive of them being enslaved in the first place? Or was it ultimately a realisation that, with the Soviet Union now dependent on Western credit, he could not risk a bloody crackdown?

Either way, he was surprised by the speed and determination with which Moscow's allies distanced themselves from its grip. On 9 November 1989, a few weeks after Gerasimov spoke, the Berlin Wall came down, heralding the end of communist rule there and elsewhere in Central Europe. Change was largely peaceful, except in Romania, where, after mounting protests, the dictator Nicolae Ceauşescu and his wife, Elena, were shot by an impromptu firing squad on Christmas Day.

The most immediate problem during this time was the future status of the two Germanys. Margaret Thatcher was among those who feared that a unified German state would be far too powerful. She was also concerned that a backlash against reunification might destabilise Gorbachev, the man of whom she had famously claimed 'we can do business together' when he visited Britain in December 1984, three months before he became Soviet leader.

'We do not want the unification of Germany,' Thatcher told Gorbachev in 'a very confidential manner' during a private meeting in September 1989, two months before the fall of the Wall. 'It would lead to changes in the post-war borders, and we cannot allow that because such a development would undermine the stability of the entire international situation, and could lead to threats to our security.'[1]

Thatcher knew how potentially explosive her remarks were and insisted they should not be recorded. A transcript of the conversation in the Kremlin archives nevertheless includes them, noting drily: 'The following part of the conversation is reproduced from memory.' It would be several years before Thatcher's words would come to light.

François Mitterrand, the French president, was also wary of a reunified Germany, but he and Thatcher failed to win over EU leaders to their side in the face of a determined push by Helmut Kohl, the West German chancellor. Crucially, America did not share the Europeans' and Russians' historical fears of German expansionism and saw the country instead as a good friend and reliable ally. 'Any issues that had existed in 1945, it seemed perfectly reasonable to lay them to rest,' said Condoleezza Rice, President H. W. Bush's adviser on Eastern European issues.[2] 'For us, the question wasn't should Germany unify? It was how and under what circumstances? We had no concern about a resurgent Germany, unlike the British or French.'

The breakthrough came after Kohl flew to Russia on 14 July 1990, for meetings with Gorbachev first in Moscow and then in the Soviet leader's holiday dacha in his home region of Stavropol. Kohl convinced Gorbachev, if he still needed convincing, that a unified Germany would not be a threat to the Soviet Union. Three days later, Kohl announced that the Soviet leader had given the go-ahead for the two Germanys to unite. Kohl's place in history was assured. On 3 October East Germany, the most affluent part of the Soviet empire, was effectively absorbed into West Germany. On the stroke of midnight the black, red and gold flag of the Federal Republic flew above the Brandenburg Gate.

One of the most crucial questions that had to be resolved before the two Germanys joined together was to which military alliance – if any – the new unified state should belong. Washington insisted that it should remain in NATO, as did Kohl, even though polls suggested that fewer than twenty per cent of West Germans agreed. Like the Americans, Kohl feared a neutral Germany could destroy NATO, cause the United States and Canada to pull their forces out of Europe and potentially turn Britain and France against his country.

Gorbachev disagreed. Speaking at a press conference in March 1990, he declared any form of participation of a unified Germany in NATO to be 'absolutely out of the question'. The Alliance, he argued, was a symbol of 'a dangerous and confrontational past'[3] – both NATO and the Soviet-led Warsaw Pact should be replaced by new 'permanent security structures', based perhaps on the thirty-five-nation Conference on Security and Cooperation in Europe (CSCE).

If Gorbachev had been serious about creating such structures, this was his opportunity: Germany had needed the Soviet Union's assent before reunifying, giving Moscow considerable leverage over the government in Bonn and over the West. Yet Gorbachev failed to play his ace.

ACCORDING TO NATO's FIRST SECRETARY GENERAL, Lord Ismay, the aim of the Western Alliance was 'to keep the Russians out, the Americans in and the Germans down'. Now, just over four decades later, a new question arose: what was to be the status of Moscow's former satellites and of the new states that emerged on the territory of the Soviet Union?

There were suggestions in Moscow after the fall of the Berlin Wall that the Warsaw Pact might continue in a new form, transformed from an instrument of Soviet control into a political institution that represented the interests of its member countries. Surprisingly, despite painful memories of 1956 and 1968, this was not rejected out of hand by other Pact members. The idea did not go anywhere, however, and in February 1991, the alliance was finally wound up, even though the last Russian troops did not leave Hungary or Czechoslovakia until that June, Poland until October 1992 and eastern Germany until August 1994.

Some in the 'emerging democracies', as the former satellite states became known, argued that they should become a neutral buffer between West and East, perhaps grouped together into a regional alliance. Yet by the middle of 1992, opinion in Poland, the largest of them, was warming to the idea of applying for NATO membership. Hanna Suchocka, Poland's first female prime minister, who came to power that July at the head of a centre-right coalition, believed that joining the Western Alliance would not just free her country from dependence on Russia, but underline its 'return' to Europe.

The Poles' resolve was strengthened by increasingly threatening noises from Moscow. These were partly a by-product of the battle between Yeltsin and the parliament, which was increasingly dominated by hard-line former communists. Victory for the hardliners, it was feared, could lead to attempts to reconstitute not just the Soviet Union, but also perhaps the Warsaw Pact. Such concerns were heightened by the publication in January 1993 of *The Concept of Foreign Policy of the Russian Federation*. 'Eastern Europe retains its significance for Russia as a historically evolved sphere of interest', it argued. 'The strategic task at the present is to prevent transformation of Eastern Europe into a kind of buffer zone isolating us from Europe. On the other hand, dislodgement of Russia from the Central European region by the Western states – which is now becoming a perfectly realistic prospect – cannot be permitted.'[4]

The Poles tried as best they could to assuage Russian concerns without at the same time allowing Moscow the power of veto over their future. For that reason, they argued that any eventual pursuit of NATO membership should be combined with greater involvement for Moscow in European security arrangements. Yet whatever attempts were made to sugar the pill, any eastward expansion of NATO looked set to antagonise the Russians, as many on the Polish left pointed out. 'A policy of tickling the Russian bear's nose, of playing off our eastern neighbours' interests, is dilettantish', wrote one commentator. 'It is on the level of a playground game.'[5]

But what of NATO's existing European members? In the euphoria
of the early 1990s, there were suggestions that the Western Alliance
should go the same way as its Eastern counterpart. Winding up NATO
would send a clear signal that the world was entering a new post-Cold
War era. Some even backed the idea, floated by Gorbachev, of replacing
it with a new security structure based on the CSCE. Yet would the
West, still celebrating its 'victory' in the Cold War, really dissolve an
alliance credited with achieving this victory? Manfred Wörner, who
became NATO's first German secretary general in 1988, was among
those who thought not. 'The classical threat has disappeared,' he said
in an interview with the *New York Times* in October 1991.[6] 'The risk is
in uncertainty – about the future political structure of the Soviet Union,
the bad economic situation, and all its consequences, in a country
which still has more than three million people under arms and tens
of thousands of nuclear weapons . . . The Soviet Union, or even just
Russia, is such an enormous land mass that it needs a geopolitical
counterweight. I don't think that Europe alone can provide it.'

It was another German, Volker Rühe, the defence minister, who was
one of the first to argue that NATO should not only continue but also
expand into the security void opening up to its east. In March 1993,
the month before Havel and Wałęsa's trip to Washington, Rühe made
a landmark speech in which he argued that Germany should support
the eastward expansion of NATO, both as a strategic buffer against
instability in Central and Eastern Europe and to reward the people of
Poland, the Czech Republic and Hungary for their popular protests,
which had helped make German reunification possible. Anchoring
their countries in the West would also help turn them into lucrative
new markets for German exports.

Rühe's comments, made at the International Institute for Strategic
Studies in London, were received with enthusiasm by many of the
Central Europeans in the room. Others were sceptical. Britain was
hostile, largely out of concern at the influence it would accord the
newly unified Germany. There was also the question of how the
Russians would react to the prospect of Alliance forces moving closer
to their border.

Such concerns undoubtedly weighed on Clinton, who was fresh
from his April 1993 Vancouver summit with Yeltsin when he met
Wałęsa and Havel. Clinton did not want to endanger the new spirit

of cooperation with Moscow, which he needed to further American goals on arms control and other global problems. The Kremlin played on this concern: Kozyrev repeatedly warned that NATO enlargement would go down so badly with Russian public opinion that it would strengthen support for the communists and nationalists.

The White House also had to deal with misgivings about enlargement at home – including from the Pentagon. Les Aspin, Clinton's first, short-lived defence secretary, believed that the end of the Cold War would allow America to cut its military commitments in Europe; enlarging NATO risked reversing this. There was scepticism among senior officers too. First, the largely Soviet-made weapons systems and the doctrines and command structures of Central Europe did not easily fit with NATO's. Second, enlargement risked embroiling existing Alliance members in minor conflicts of the sort already breaking out across the Balkans. Lieutenant General Barry McCaffrey, the military adviser to the state department, warned Talbott that if America did not take care we could 'get ourselves sucked into some godforsaken Eurasian quagmire' that would lead it stumbling into a shooting war with Russia.[7]

It was nevertheless clear to Clinton that Washington had to formulate a coherent approach towards Central and Eastern Europe, which was still seen by many Americans 'as a mysterious collective entity characterised by medieval castles, spicy sausages, and insufficient supply of vowels', according to Czech-born Madeleine Albright, who was Clinton's ambassador to the United Nations and later secretary of state.[8] In June 1993, therefore, the administration approved a new policy towards the region intended to bolster democracy, reduce trade barriers and reward countries that carried out economic reform.

According to Albright, it was decided that the Alliance should open its doors to membership, but do so gradually, country by country, and only provided that the aspiring members satisfied conditions such as ensuring civilian command of their armed forces and respecting minorities. 'An open and deliberate process,' she hoped, 'would help reassure Moscow that NATO's enlargement to the east would be a step toward Russia, not against it.'

The task of turning these ideas into practice was given to General John Shalikashvili, who in October succeeded Colin Powell as chairman of the Joint Chiefs of Staff. Like Albright, he had been born in Central

Europe – in his case in Warsaw – and fled as a child with his family
to Germany in 1944 ahead of the advancing Red Army. Shalikashvili
understood the region well and came up with a compromise: the former
communist countries, Russia included, would be invited to join a new
organisation to be called the Partnership for Peace (PFP). This would
give them an office in NATO's headquarters in Brussels. They would
take part in military training exercises alongside NATO countries,
during which they would learn how to work with existing members
and also with each other. Those that did the most to upgrade their
armed forces, establish peaceful relations with their neighbours and
solidify their democratic institutions would become eligible for full
membership of the Alliance. The idea was proposed at a meeting of
NATO defence ministers in Travemünde, Germany, that October.

For its backers, the PFP was a neat way of squaring the circle: it left
open the possibility of some of NATO's former foes joining the Alliance,
while putting off knotty questions such as which of them were to be
admitted as a full member, when and on what terms. By allowing Russia
to join, it also avoided the narrative of encirclement. As one US official
put it: 'The "partnership for peace" proposal was a very skilful compromise between people who said we should do nothing to offend the
Russians and people who said we should let the Eastern Europeans in
now. But the Eastern Europeans are not ready for that yet. The beauty
of the proposal is that it's a frame on whose canvas we can paint whatever we want.'[9]

Talbott broke the news to Yeltsin during a visit to his presidential
dacha in Zavidovo, in the forest outside Moscow, which had once been
Stalin's hunting lodge. They met in an overheated solarium filled with
stuffed game and potted plants. The Russian leader was delighted that
enlargement appeared to have been delayed. '*Genialno! Zdorovo!*
[Brilliant! Terrific!] Tell Bill this is a wonderful decision,' Yeltsin
boomed.[10] Indeed, the following June, Russia would become one of the
first members of the Partnership for Peace.

The Central and Eastern Europeans, by contrast, were disappointed,
as the new body failed to offer the security guarantees they craved.
The Lithuanians demanded immediate NATO membership. Wałęsa
called it 'blackmail' and 'too little'. The case for full membership, meanwhile, was made in a much-quoted article in the September/October
edition of *Foreign Affairs* by Ronald D. Asmus, Richard L. Kugler and

F. Stephen Larrabee. It was time, they argued, for a new 'transatlantic bargain' for the post-Cold War era, one that would project democracy and stability into the newly independent countries, which could otherwise slip back into chaos, instability and even spark regional wars. The best way of achieving this would be to extend NATO gradually. The Alliance, they said, should either 'go out of area or out of business'.[11] The authors accepted that NATO should remain sensitive to Russia's security interests and not give the impression that a new Iron Curtain was being erected along its western border. Yet Moscow should not be granted a right of veto over expansion. 'To hold the future of NATO hostage to the outcome of Russian politics is a recipe for the demise of the Alliance,' they argued.

Such arguments were strengthened by the results of election to the State Duma held on 12 December. For the first time in their history, Russians had a truly free vote for their parliament. Yet almost one-quarter used it to back the populist firebrand, Vladimir Zhirinovsky, and his ironically named Liberal Democratic Party of Russia. Gaidar's Russia's Choice, the party most closely identified with his 'shock therapy' economic reforms, came a distant second with just 15.5%.

Positioning himself on the nationalist right, Zhirinovsky had railed against the collapse of the Soviet Union and fought an outrageous electoral campaign during which he demanded the forcible reconquest of Alaska, urged nuclear waste to be piled up along the border with the Baltic states and claimed to dream of a time when Russian soldiers would be able to 'wash their boots in the warm water of the Indian Ocean'. Zhirinovsky was dismissed as a clown, a tool of the Kremlin and a creation of the KGB – a claim he denied. Clinton called his victory a 'protest vote' and claimed not to find it surprising, given the Russian people's 'high level of anger because they've been through a lot of tough times'.

Although Yeltsin's position as president was secure, there were concerns that he would have to modify his administration's policies in the light of the results: Zhirinovsky's posturing was absurd, but his views undoubtedly struck a chord with millions of Russians disappointed that their leaders' embrace of Western ways had not apparently borne fruit. Their main concern was plunging living standards. Yet national pride was also at stake: during the Cold War the Soviet Union had been America's main adversary, and as such was treated with respect; under

Gorbachev it had been gradually transformed into a partner. Following the break-up of the Soviet Union and the collapse of the economy, Russia had been reduced to a supplicant, while NATO enlargement looked like a brazen attempt by the West to exploit its weakness to take over countries formerly part of Moscow's sphere of influence.

'Today's Russia appears to be but a pale shadow of its powerful and influential predecessor,' wrote Alexei Pushkov, deputy editor-in-chief of the *Moscow News*, in an article published in the February 1994 edition of the *NATO Review*. 'Having rejected confrontation with the West, which had been at the centre of Soviet policy since the inception of the Cold War, Russia has not managed to find a new international role for itself.'[12]

Part of the problem, Pushkov argued, was the Russians' unrealistic level of expectations about their country and its future place in the world. Despite – or perhaps because of – Russia's vast size and military might, it was not possible for the country instantly to become part of the Western world or be accepted into the G7. Yet the West had also failed to fulfil its side of the bargain: for all the talk of a new Marshall Plan, promise of large-scale financial and economic assistance had not materialised. 'Some Russians tended to believe that all the fuss about the foreign economic aid campaign was a huge hoax, or at least that the rich West did not care at all about Russia after it became weak and stopped representing a military threat,' Pushkov argued.

At the same time, the 'loss' of the other former Soviet republics was also beginning to rankle. It was not just a matter of lost territory; Yeltsin had also failed to pay attention to the interests of ethnic Russians in the near abroad. This omission, which he only began to address in mid-1993, had 'created a huge "black hole" in Russian foreign policy, a vacuum that was just waiting to be filled by Zhirinovsky's slogans'.

MATTERS CAME TO A HEAD a few weeks after the Senate's Christmas/ New Year recess during confirmation hearings for Talbott, who had been appointed deputy secretary of state. Appearing before the Senate Foreign Relations Committee, he faced a grilling from Republicans over the PFP.

Senator Richard Lugar of Indiana, hitherto a champion of bipartisan support for Russia, reproached the Clinton administration for pursuing a 'Russia-first' policy, and described PFP as a 'Band Aid offered in place of corrective surgery'. Critics of the policy were encouraged by the powerful Polish-American community, which drew comparisons with the Yalta conference in 1945, at which Roosevelt and Churchill allowed Stalin control of Poland. In a letter to the *Washington Post* published on 7 December, Jan Nowak, national director of the Polish-American Congress, attacked what he saw as the 'prompt acceptance' by the United States and its allies of Moscow's 'veto'. The Kremlin, he warned, might feel it had been given 'a "green light" for ambitions to restore the Russian empire and to regain its sphere of influence in East Central Europe'.

Henry Kissinger, who had been secretary of state under Nixon and then Ford, joined in the assault on the PFP, claiming that it would 'dilute what is left of the Atlantic alliance into a vague multiculturalism'. Poland, the Czech Republic and Hungary, 'the historical victims of Russian aggression', would be obliged under the arrangement to 'consult with the very country that is causing their discomfort,' he thundered in an op-ed column, also written for the *Washington Post*.[13]

While Talbott was being grilled, Albright and Shalikashvili set off on a gruelling tour of Central and Eastern Europe, trying to sell the PFP to the countries' leaders. They met with a mixed response: in Poland, Wałęsa greeted them with scepticism, but agreed to say at a joint press conference that although he would prefer to 'leap' into NATO, he was willing to accept 'small steps'. The Hungarians and Czechs were more enthusiastic. It became clear to Albright, however, that their various hosts really wanted security guarantees, fearing 'that the Russian bear might not remain gentle for long'. Careful not to make a pledge that America could not honour, Albright was authorised to say merely that the security of each country was 'of direct and material interest' to the United States.[14]

When Clinton and other NATO leaders formally approved the PFP at their Brussels summit on 10 January 1994, they made it clear that they saw it as a staging post to membership of the Alliance. 'We expect and would welcome NATO expansion that would reach to democratic states to our East, as part of an evolutionary process, taking into account political and security developments in the whole of Europe,' the invitation document declared.[15] 'Active participation in the Partnership for Peace will play an important role in the evolutionary process of the expansion of NATO.'

The American hawks' fears – and the Kremlin's relief – proved unfounded. It was no longer a question of whether NATO would expand eastward but when it would do so and how far it would go. For the time being, no one wanted to commit to a timetable. Deciding how many new members to take in was even more difficult. Should NATO expand up to the borders of the former Soviet Union, effectively shifting the old Iron Curtain that once ran from Stettin in the north to Trieste in the south, by a few hundred miles to the east? Or should it go further, right up to the borders of Russia itself, taking in not just the Baltic states but the other former Soviet republics such as Ukraine, Georgia and Moldova? For all the talk, the question of NATO enlargement had not been settled, and it cast a long shadow over relations between Russia and the West in the years that followed.

6

BILL AND OL' BORIS

Boris Yeltsin sent tanks into the middle of Moscow to open fire on his own parliament, killing dozens of people. He used the air force to kill Russian civilians in Chechnya, and through his drunken antics he came close to reducing himself – and his country – to a laughing stock. Yet Yeltsin was still the best bet the West had. And as the June 1996 presidential election approached, the West was worried that it was going to lose him.

The stage had been set by parliamentary elections in December 1995, in which the communists won 157 seats, compared to just 55 for Our Home – Russia, the pro-Yeltsin group derided as the 'party of power' – and 51 for the LDPR. In the run-up to the presidential vote, polls showed support for Yeltsin at just eight per cent, embarrassingly low for an incumbent leader, all but guaranteeing victory for Gennady Zyuganov, the communist leader.

The popular enthusiasm that Yeltsin had inspired in the late 1980s and early 1990s was ancient history. Now the population was pre-occupied by falling living standards and the increasingly unpopular war in Chechnya, coupled with nostalgia for Russia's lost superpower status. Then there was Yeltsin's own increasingly erratic behaviour. In August 1994, during a visit to Berlin, at a lunch event he had jumped onto the stage and started to conduct the military band. The following month, on an official visit to Ireland, he was deemed too 'unwell' to get off his plane at Shannon airport, leaving Albert Reynolds, the Irish premier, to wait in vain at the end of the red carpet. On another occasion, during a trip to Washington, Clinton was later to reveal, Yeltsin was discovered by the Secret Service standing drunkenly in his underpants outside the White House trying to hail a cab to go and buy a pizza.

Given the odds, Yegor Gaidar proposed to Yeltsin that another member of the 'Democrat' camp should run in his place. Yeltsin was indignant. 'Can you imagine Zyuganov as president of Russia?' he retorted. 'Which one of you can beat Zyuganov? Go on, propose a candidate.'¹ There wasn't one: Yeltsin's ratings may have been low, but those of the other reformers were lower still. Even put together, they could barely match the support enjoyed by the communist leader.

A mathematics teacher turned Communist Party apparatchik, Zyuganov, a beefy figure with pale, thinning hair, emerged in the late 1980s as one of Gorbachev's harshest critics. In the early 1990s he helped form the new Communist Party of the Russian Federation, becoming its chairman in 1993. Zyuganov's views were difficult to pin down. In his contacts with the West he tried to portray himself as a European-style Social Democrat and urged foreign businesspeople to invest in Russia. Yet out on the stump back home he called for the restoration of the Soviet Union and the protection of 'prized' industries, and demanded an end to privatisation. His party's programme for the parliamentary election had been filled with nostalgia for the good old days of communism, supplemented by a large dollop of nationalism (and a whiff of anti-Semitism).

Zyuganov explained this apparent contradiction to a group of journalists over lunch in a smart restaurant during the parliamentary campaign. 'Anybody hears what he wants to hear,' he said. 'You should understand that a clever propaganda worker and a skilled politician will never talk in the same language with different audiences.'²

That February at the World Economic Forum in Davos, Switzerland, the outside world had the opportunity to get the measure of the man who looked set to become Russia's first post-communist communist leader. When Zyuganov appeared at the Sunstar Parkhotel, he was besieged by autograph hunters in the lobby and feted by Western money men. True to form, Zyuganov told his audience what they wanted to hear. Ruling out a return to old Soviet ways, he promised to safeguard private property and continue attempts to build a market economy. Privatised companies, he insisted, could still operate 'if they work well and are being run properly'. He also vowed to 'create a climate of confidence' in place of the chaos created by the unpredictable Yeltsin. 'In our country, it's the mafia and corrupt bureaucrats who have power,' Zyuganov added. 'We believe in a regulated market where every type of ownership – state, collective, partial, private – is allowed to have its place in the sun.'[3]

With the polls still strongly in Zyuganov's favour, the mood in the Yeltsin camp was one of alarm. That March, Rodric Braithwaite, who had been British ambassador to Moscow from 1988 to 1992, met Gaidar at an event they were both addressing. 'Gaidar was very gloomy and said "we have got to win this election or the Communists will come back and that will be the end of civilisation as we know it", Braithwaite recalls.[4] Braithwaite suggested to him a different possible outcome: Zyuganov would win but then 'fall flat on his face', which would mean the communists would be discredited, as had been the case when they had been voted back into power elsewhere in Eastern Europe. 'But he was not prepared to take that risk and neither were Chubais and Yeltsin.'

The White House was working to prevent a victory for Zyuganov, too. In the eyes of the Clinton administration, Yeltsin's survival had become inseparable from Russia's transition to democracy. There was also a strong personal chemistry between the US leader and 'Ol' Boris', as Clinton referred to him in conversation with Talbott. During the course of twenty meetings with the Russian leader, Clinton came to appreciate the struggles that Yeltsin faced with his enemies at home. He also genuinely seemed to like him. During one lunch together, Clinton recalled fondly, Yeltsin 'served roast pig and told me real men hack off the ears and eat them. And once he served twenty-four courses, including moose lips.'[5]

Encounters between the two men had by now begun to follow a familiar course: anxious to convince his political foes at home that he was no pushover, Yeltsin would first rail in public over the latest indignity heaped on his country by the West. Then, once he and Clinton were behind closed doors, he would adopt a far more conciliatory tone. Clinton suffered such tirades in silence: relations between Washington and Moscow had moved on since the days of the Cold War. Both knew that America held all the cards.

The looming Russian presidential election again put a focus on the pair's relationship, and how best to play it. If Clinton appeared in

Russian eyes to cosy up too much to Yeltsin, he risked making the Kremlin leader look like a Western stooge. But if he did not offer Russia enough assistance, there was a danger Yeltsin might lose the vote. To complicate matters, Clinton had his own re-election just a few months later to consider.

That April, in an attempt to give Yeltsin a pre-election boost, Clinton visited Russia. They flew first to St Petersburg, where arrangements were handled with characteristic efficiency by the first deputy mayor, Vladimir Putin, known in the city for the help he gave Western companies trying to navigate the local bureaucracy and for his loyalty to his mentor, Mayor Anatoly Sobchak. Then it was a short hop in Air Force One down to Moscow.

While out jogging with Talbott early the next morning on the birch-lined paths of Sparrow Hills, near Moscow University, Clinton reflected on Yeltsin's predicament and wondered aloud if it was being made worse by American policy. 'We haven't played everything brilliantly with these people; we haven't figured out how to say yes to them in a way that balances off how much and how often we want them to say yes to us,' he said.[6] 'We keep telling Ol' Boris, "Okay, now here's what you've got to do next – here's some more shit for your face". And that makes it real hard for him, given what he's up against and who he's dealing with.'

Later at the Kremlin, Clinton had to endure the usual tongue-lashing from Yeltsin, this time for 'going it alone' and 'sidelining Russia' by sending Warren Christopher, the secretary of state, on a peace mission to the Middle East without first consulting the Kremlin. When Yeltsin had finished, he had the press ushered out before Clinton could respond. This time, once they were alone, Clinton did not suppress his anger but let rip; after all, the only real reason he had come to Russia was to help Yeltsin's campaign. As ever, the Russian leader soon backed down.

Over lunch Yeltsin expressed concern that Zyuganov might get some reflected glory from a meeting with Clinton scheduled for later that day. 'It's okay to shake hands with Zyuganov, Bill, but don't kiss him,' Yeltsin said, speaking in a joking tone.[7] 'Don't worry,' Clinton replied. 'We've spent fifty years rooting for a different result than that guy represents.' Yeltsin's tone then became more serious. 'I'm warning you: if the Communists win, they'll go after Crimea and Alaska. We won't permit that.'

Yet Washington alone could not ensure Yeltsin's victory – a truth Yeltsin's supporters understood only too well. One group, the so-called 'faction of war', led by Aleksandr Korzhakov, a former KGB general who headed Yeltsin's Presidential Security Service, urged him to post-pone the vote or cancel it altogether. Oleg Soskovets, his official campaign chief, suggested a different tactic: the vote should still go ahead but with the communists banned.

Yeltsin came close to going down this path, ordering aides to draft a presidential decree banning the Communist Party, dissolving the newly elected parliament and putting off elections for two years. Appalled, they leaked the plans to *Itogi*, a highly influential television current-affairs programme. Yeltsin's younger daughter, Tatyana Dyachenko, a leading figure in his re-election campaign, urged him to rethink. So did Anatoly Chubais, now first deputy prime minister, who warned that this would effectively be a coup. At a stormy meeting, Yeltsin agreed to let the vote go ahead. 'I reversed a decision I had almost made,' he recalled opaquely in his memoirs.[8]

The challenge now for Dyachenko and 'the family' – Yeltsin's closest advisers, some of them actual family, some not – was to ensure that he won. Aleksandr Oslon, the pollster, was one of those to whom they turned for advice on running the campaign. 'I proposed creating a new Yeltsin,' Oslon recalls. 'A Yeltsin that people wanted to see, who was cheerful, humane, kind, who knew what the problems were and tried to solve them, who looked after the weak and supported the average and who gave opportunities to the strong.'[9] A group of adver-tising and PR experts charged with coming up with an advertising campaign surprised the president's advisers with their proposals. The slogan was simple and positive: 'I believe, I love, I hope'.

'This had nothing to do with Yeltsin: he was a huge bear of a man, gloomy, a drinker, with an angry voice,' says Oslon. 'This image of him was formed and suddenly there was this "I believe, I love, I hope".'[10]

An important role was also played by some of Russia's richest busi-nesspeople. Putting aside their personal and commercial differences, they made use of their vast wealth and their control of the media to ensure that Yeltsin would remain in the Kremlin. The extent of their influence was noted by Bill Browder, a swashbuckling young American fund manager who made a fortune in Yeltsin's Russia before ultimately falling foul of Putin. Browder had been in Davos to hear Zyuganov speak. Walking through the lobby of the Sunstar he came across Boris Fyodorov, a leading reformer who had been Russia's finance minister from 1993 to 1994 and was now the chairman of a Moscow stockbroking firm. When Browder asked about the wisdom of investing in Russia in the light of what looked like a Zyuganov victory, Fyodorov put him straight. 'Don't worry about the election, Bill,' he told him. 'Yeltsin is going to win for sure.'[11] Seeing Browder's disbelief, Fyodorov stuck out his hand and swept his finger over the lobby. 'These guys will fix that,' he continued.

Browder followed his hand and recognised three men in an intense huddle in the corner: the tycoons Boris Berezovsky and Vladimir Gusinsky, together with Anatoly Chubais, who had just left the government and was running Yeltsin's campaign. As Browder and his business partner, Marc Holtzman, went round the room, various other oligarchs and 'minigarchs' told them the same thing. Browder was struck by their confidence, though he could not help wondering if it was merely wishful thinking.

The businessmen had been offered a sweetener for their support. It became known as the 'loans for share' scheme and was arguably the biggest scandal of the Yeltsin era. The idea had been floated at a meeting of the cabinet in March 1995. Vladimir Potanin, the thirty-five-year-old president of Onexim bank, proposed that a consortium of banks could help plug the budget deficit by lending the government $2 billion. In return they would be given the chance to buy shares in a dozen of the country's leading exporters. In theory, the stakes would be put up for auction and anyone interested would be free to bid. In reality the auction was rigged. No foreigners were allowed to bid and even Russians were excluded, other than the handful of banks with close ties to the Kremlin.

The favoured few picked up these companies for just three to ten per cent of their market value. The shares were meant to be held by the winning bank in a trust. The loans were due to expire in autumn 1996, after the election, at which point the state should have been able to repay the money, take back the shares and resell them on the open market. In practice, it was clear the government would never try to repay the loans, allowing its friends to take control of the companies for a fraction of their true value. In a further twist, the state effectively lent the businessmen the money in the first place.

The businessmen dutifully carried out their side of the bargain, pouring money into the effort to get Yeltsin re-elected. Under campaign finance rules, each candidate could receive a maximum of just over $3 million in private contributions. In the event, Yeltsin received as much as one to two billion dollars. Private television stations provided blanket coverage of his campaign; the state-run channels were already doing the same as a matter of course.

The scheme was variously condemned as a 'Faustian bargain' or 'Frankenstein's monster' and became a symbol of all the sins of Yeltsin's reformers. Subsequent analysis has suggested that, as least as far as the results were concerned, the deal was not as bad as it was portrayed: after the oligarchs consolidated control, their new firms actually performed better than comparable state enterprises or companies that had been sold to incumbent managers. (Indeed, their success would later contribute to Russia's rapid growth after 1999.)[12]

Yet it was still deeply unjust. It was also not clear why the oligarchs deserved such a reward for supporting Yeltsin. After all, they, more than anyone else, had reason to fear a communist victory. Nor did they need to order their television stations to run positive coverage, since most of those in the media were supporters of Yeltsin. Whatever the rationale, the result was a massive transfer of resources into the hands of a small group of businessmen who, during the earlier stages of privatisation, had already secured considerably more than their fair share.

When the results of the first round came in, Yeltsin led Zyuganov by 35% to 32%, with a further 15% for Aleksandr Lebed, a charismatic army general brought in by the Kremlin to split the communist vote. Yeltsin was still not home and dry, though. A few days after the vote, long-running tensions between a group of reformers centred on Chubais and a rival Kremlin faction grouped around Korzhakov, Yeltsin's security chief, turned to open warfare. Two of Chubais' staff were arrested by Korzhakov's men as they left the White House in Moscow carrying $500,000 in cash in a cardboard box. Korzhakov knew full well that government money was being used to finance Yeltsin's campaign; indeed, he was meant to have been providing security for the men carrying it. By revealing the practice, he hoped to undermine the second round of the poll and increase his influence over the president.

His ploy backfired badly, however: news of the arrest was leaked to the media, who interpreted it as a coup. The next day, Chubais went

to Yeltsin and demanded he sack Korzhakov. It was a difficult decision
for Yeltsin. Korzhakov had been loyal to him for more than a decade;
appointed as Yeltsin's bodyguard in 1985, he had stood next to him on
the tank during the failed coup of August 1991 and supported him
through the many and various crises of his presidency. Yet Yeltsin was
also beginning to have his misgivings as Korzhakov started foisting
documents on him, telling him to appoint certain people and sack
others. 'Apparently he had started putting together some sort of a
group,' Yeltsin recalled later. 'But I caught on to what was going on.'[13]
Korzhakov was shown the door.

Yeltsin's health, meanwhile, had taken a sharp turn for the worse. With
less than two weeks to go before the second round of voting he suffered
a heart attack – his fifth – on the day he had been due to record an
election broadcast. Too sick to go to the Kremlin, he had to record the
broadcast at his dacha. Office furniture and wood panelling were
brought from his office to convey a spurious sense of normality.
Rumours spread of the illness, but the television channels, desperate
for a Yeltsin victory, revealed nothing. Too much was riding on his
re-election.

As the second round, set for 3 July, approached, the advertising
campaign was changing. The soft and sentimental television commer-
cials aired in the run-up to the first round of the election were replaced
by something much darker: Bolshevik-era documentary footage of
summary executions and starving children. Vote for Zyuganov, voters
were warned, and you risk taking Russia back to the days of famine,
civil war and purges. It was, of course, a huge exaggeration. As one of
Yeltsin's advisers put it, the latter stages of the campaign were based
on 'the myth of the terrible Bolshevik with a knife in his teeth who
will come to take away your property, your apartment and so on' when
in reality there was a consensus between the democrats and Zyuganov's
communists on 'the basic liberal package', namely: 'freedom to travel
abroad, free trade, freedom of economic activity, rallies, demonstrations
and elections. None of that was under threat.'[14]

Conjuring up a 'red scare' nevertheless did the trick, even though
Yeltsin's health had barely improved by polling day. Accompanied by
two doctors in white coats, he managed only with difficulty to push his
ballot paper into the slot. The doctors were edited out of the picture.
The cover-up was reminiscent of the days of Gorbachev's short-lived

predecessor, Konstantin Chernenko, for whom a fake polling booth was erected in the hospital where he lay dying in order for him to be shown on television voting in the March 1984 elections to the Supreme Soviet.

In a result that surprised no one, Yeltsin was elected, winning 54.4% of the vote to Zyuganov's 40.7%. The presidential inauguration on 9 August was understandably short. Struggling to walk to the microphone, Yeltsin slurred his way through the oath of office, which had been shortened to just thirty-three words. The oligarchs quickly moved to claim their reward: not content with the considerable spoils of the 'loans for shares' scheme, they also obtained political power. Vladimir Potanin, the man behind the scheme, became a deputy prime minister. A few months later, on 30 October, Boris Berezovsky was appointed deputy secretary of the Security Council and, in an interview with the *Financial Times*, boasted of the oligarchs' role in winning the poll. 'We hired Chubais and invested huge sums of money to ensure Yeltsin's re-election,' he said. 'Now we have the right to occupy government posts and enjoy the fruits of our victory.'[15]

Clinton was quick to welcome Yeltsin's victory. During a visit to Independence Day celebrations in Ohio, he praised Russians for turning out in such large numbers in what he described as a 'free and fair election', and congratulated 'President Yeltsin and the people of Russia for their commitment to the freedom that we love'.

'With a decisive voice, the Russian people chose democracy,' Clinton told the crowd, to applause. 'They deserve enormous credit for the remarkable progress they have made, for democracy and toward a free economy. And yesterday they said, "We want to keep on moving forward. We choose freedom. We choose democracy. We choose hope. We choose the future".'

7

A FATAL ERROR?

Yᴇʟᴛꜱɪɴ'ꜱ ʀᴇ-ᴇʟᴇᴄᴛɪᴏɴ ʙʀᴏᴜɢʜᴛ ꜱɪɢʜꜱ ᴏꜰ ʀᴇʟɪᴇꜰ from Washington to Warsaw. Yet rather than usher in a new period of cooperation between America and Russia, Yeltsin's victory in June 1996, followed by Clinton's re-election that November, set the stage for a new and more serious row over the enlargement of NATO. The Partnership for Peace (PFP) in June 1996 had got off to a successful start: all of the former Soviet republics and satellites – with the exception of Tajikistan – had signed up. Yet, as Russia had feared, this did not quiet the clamour for full membership of NATO. At its Brussels summit in 1994, the Alliance had formally pledged to take in new members. Official invitations to join were issued when NATO leaders met in July 1997 in Madrid.

America's arms makers were also emerging as enthusiastic backers of enlargement, anticipating the profits to be made as would-be new members bought US weaponry to replace their old Soviet-made kit. Among their more colourful advocates was Bruce P. Jackson, a former US military intelligence officer turned businessman who by the mid-1990s was working for Lockheed Martin. In 1996 he formed a non-governmental organisation called the Committee to Expand NATO. Media reports suggested it was funded by arms manufacturers; the committee denied this, saying that while it had the 'political support of the industry', its by-laws forbade it from accepting corporate contributions.

Between 1996 and 1998 alone, America's six biggest military contractors spent $51 million lobbying Congress and public opinion, according to analysis published by the *New York Times*.[1] They also helped ethnic groups of Eastern European descent to campaign for their countries to be allowed to join the Alliance. As the newspaper pointed out, it was a potentially good investment, given the amount of money at stake: a single F-16, made by Lockheed Martin, cost about $20 million; a Boeing F-18 closer to $40–60 million. Poland alone wanted to buy 100 to 150 fighter planes and was weighing offers from Lockheed and Boeing as well as from companies in Britain, France and Russia. In the event, the Warsaw government finally decided at the end of 2002 to buy forty-eight state-of-the-art F-16s in a deal worth an estimated $3.5 billion in total.

'There was clearly a sense that these could be potentially lucrative markets,' said Jamie Shea, a veteran NATO official who was at that time the Alliance's spokesman.[2] 'American defence manufacturers realised that these countries, in order to show their credentials as being serious about NATO, would have to buy in advance F-16s and other American equipment to demonstrate that they were prepared to assume a burden; then afterwards, once they were in NATO, even more American equipment for the sake of interoperability.' Shea, in fact, found himself undoing much of the arms manufacturers' work. 'I remember going around the countries assuring them that they did not have to order American equipment in order to qualify for NATO membership,' he said. He told them it was far more important to reform their defence and intelligence establishments and meet the various democratic objectives for membership.

Russia remained alarmed at the prospect of the Alliance's advance towards its border. So, too, was Jacques Chirac, the French president: determined to create a European position that differed from that of the Americans, he argued that NATO should not press ahead with enlargement without Moscow's approval. During a meeting with Talbott in January 1997, Chirac accused America of mishandling the issue and failing to appreciate Russian sensitivities. He suggested that he and Helmut Kohl should negotiate with Yeltsin. But the German leader rebuffed him; he was keen to have Poland in NATO since it would mean his own country would no longer lie on the Alliance's eastern border.

Clinton was also becoming jittery. At a cabinet meeting on 17 January 1997, he asked what was in it for Yeltsin. He was told Russia would be offered membership of a joint consultative body with NATO and some modification to the terms of the Conventional Forces in Europe (CFE)

Treaty. Clinton was sceptical. 'What the Russians get out of this great deal we're offering them is a chance to sit in the same room with NATO and join us whenever we all agree to something, but they don't have any ability to stop us from doing something that they don't agree with,' he said. 'They can register their disapproval by walking out of the room. And for their second big benefit, they get our promise that we're not going to put our military stuff into their former allies who are now going to be our allies, unless we happen to wake up one morning and decide to change our mind.'[3]

Commentators weighed into the battle. Old Cold Warriors such as Kissinger and Brzezinski came out in support of enlargement. 'Now that Soviet power has receded from the centre of the Continent, the North Atlantic Treaty Organization needs to adapt itself to the consequences of its success,' said Kissinger.[4] Others in America were warier, warning of the danger of provoking Russia and questioning why the proposal had not been the subject of congressional hearings. Just because former Soviet bloc countries wanted to join NATO didn't mean it was in the Alliance's interests to admit them, they argued, nor would it necessarily enhance America's own security. The West was about to 'make perhaps the biggest mistake of the post-Cold War period: rushing to expand NATO without satisfactorily resolving our relationship with Russia first', Susan Eisenhower, chairwoman of the Center for Political and Strategic Studies, wrote in the *Washington Post* in March 1997, four months before the summit at which invitations were to be issued to the newcomers.[5] On the other side of the Atlantic *The Times* also joined the critics, attributing Clinton's enthusiasm for enlargement to his desire to please the Polish constituency in Michigan. 'European and American leaders are but months away from implementing a plan that risks undermining the credibility of NATO, weakening the hand of reformers in Russia, and reducing – not enhancing – the real security of the countries in Central and Eastern Europe,' it thundered.[6]

Opponents of enlargement also found a powerful champion in George Kennan, the doyen of US foreign policy, whose Long Telegram, written in February 1946, set out the principle of the Cold War strategy of 'containment' of the Soviet Union. By then in his nineties, Kennan did not mince his words. 'Expanding NATO would be the most fateful error of American policy in the entire post-Cold War era,' he wrote in an opinion piece for the *New York Times*, entitled 'A Fateful Error'.

'Such a decision may be expected to inflame the nationalistic, anti-Western and militaristic tendencies in Russian opinion; to have an adverse effect on the development of Russian democracy; to restore the atmosphere of the cold war to East–West relations, and to impel Russian foreign policy in directions decidedly not to our liking.'

Kennan's article, which appeared on 5 February, on the eve of a visit to Washington by Viktor Chernomyrdin, had considerable impact. Talbott had been tipped off about it by Kennan before it appeared and a clipping of it was lying on Clinton's desk in the Oval Office when Talbott joined a meeting there. 'Why isn't Kennan right?' Clinton demanded. 'Isn't he a kind of guru of yours going back to when we were at Oxford?'[7] Talbott was unfazed, pointing out that the veteran diplomat, despite his reputation as a Cold War warrior, had been opposed to the creation of NATO in the first place. So why take his comments seriously? Clinton, he felt, was convinced. 'Just checking, Strobe. Just checking,' the president smiled.

Meanwhile the Kremlin continued to make its displeasure felt. Russian hardliners were angry because it confirmed their impression of NATO as an offensive alliance directed at them; liberals were worried because they feared it would bolster support for the hardliners. Speaking at that year's World Economic Forum in Davos, Chubais warned that enlargement would draw a 'new line across the whole of Europe.'[8]

When Chernomyrdin arrived in Washington with his delegation, Yuri Mamedov, the deputy foreign minister who had long been Moscow's chief interlocutor with America, told Talbott with a smile: 'We just gave our prime minister a copy of George Kennan's brilliant article. Your hero has saved us having to write talking points on your NATO folly.'[9] That particular train had already left the station, however, and there was little that Chernomyrdin could do about it. Although during plenary sessions he warned an audience of Russian and American officials of the disastrous consequences of enlargement, he was more conciliatory in private.

'I understand that the decision [on enlargement] has been made, and we know you can't reverse it,' Chernomyrdin told Gore as they flew on Air Force Two to Chicago for an event intended to promote US investment in Russia. 'But we need help on managing our own domestic politics on the issue.' 'Viktor,' Gore replied, 'we'll do that, as long as you can find a way to declare victory in what we can offer.'[10]

The issue looked set to dominate a summit between Clinton and Yeltsin the following month in Helsinki. The Clinton administration was determined to push on with enlargement but was prepared to come up with ways of what Albright, who had just been promoted to secretary of state, called 'minimising Russian heartburn'.[11] It aimed to do so through the creation of a NATO–Russia charter that would give Moscow a voice (but not a veto) in European security discussions.

Negotiating terms proved to be a painful process. During the next few weeks, Russia continued to insist on a ban on both the deployment of NATO forces and the establishment of permanent military infrastructure in the new member states. Almost on the eve of the Helsinki summit, the Russians added a new condition: Yevgeny Primakov, the former foreign intelligence chief who had taken over as foreign minister from Kozyrev in January 1996, insisted that none of the former Soviet republics be allowed to join the Alliance – which meant excluding Estonia, Latvia and Lithuania, since they were the only ones to have formally expressed an interest. This was anathema to the Americans: Washington did not accept Russia's right to block its neighbours from joining any international organisation or alliance. In any case, as Talbott noted, the United States had never recognised the Baltic states' incorporation into the Soviet Union in the first place.

The stage was set for a difficult summit. Clinton's strategy was to make it clear that enlargement was going to happen but to look for ways to sweeten the pill and make it easier for Yeltsin to sell the results at home; he aimed to do so by setting a target date for Russian accession to the World Trade Organization and turning June's Denver G7 Summit into something more like a G8. 'We've got to use this thing to get . . . [Yeltsin] comfortable with what he's got to do on NATO,' Clinton told Talbott.[12]

The meeting, which began on 20 March, was dubbed the Summit of the Invalids: Clinton had ripped a tendon in his right knee a few days earlier after tripping on a step at the Florida home of the golfer Greg Norman. He rolled into the meeting aboard what became nicknamed Wheelchair One. Yeltsin was recovering from heart surgery, although Clinton was alarmed to see he still managed to polish off four glasses of wine and one of champagne at a dinner thrown by Martti Ahtisaari, the Finnish president. 'He put down a lot more than a guy in his shape with his background should have had,' Clinton, normally tolerant of Yeltsin's drinking, told Talbott. 'Every time I see him I get the feeling that it's part of my job to remind him that the world really is counting on him.'[13]

The summit ended with the inevitable: a grudging acceptance by Yeltsin of enlargement, though not before the Russian leader had made one last attempt to persuade Clinton to agree that NATO would not 'embrace' any of the former Soviet republics. This need not be something formal, Yeltsin suggested: a secret 'gentleman's agreement' would suffice. Clinton insisted, however, that there could be no question of a veto on any country's eligibility for NATO, especially not in the form of a secret deal, details of which were bound to leak out to the press. He did not want to stand accused of agreeing to a modern-day version of the Molotov-Ribbentrop Pact under which Hitler and Stalin had divided up Central Europe.

Once they were alone, Yeltsin revealed to Clinton that he was concerned about a backlash at home. 'Boris, do you really think I would allow NATO to attack Russia from bases in Poland?' Clinton asked. 'No,' Yeltsin replied, 'I don't, but a lot of older people who live in the western part of Russia and listen to Zyuganov do.'[14] Clinton realised that Yeltsin was deadly serious. As he later explained to Tony Blair, who became British prime minister that May, it was important to understand the Russian mentality. 'They are still affected by Napoleon, Hitler and the way the Cold War came to an end, and about the way the Soviet Empire collapsed,' he said. Yeltsin 'wound up mortally hating communism but still believing in Mother Russia. All these guys do, and we've got to be sensitive about that.'[15] Yet Clinton pressed on, although he offered a commitment not to station troops or missiles in the new countries prematurely and pledged to back Russian membership in G8, the World Trade Organization and other international organisations. Yeltsin finally had no alternative but to give up. 'Well, I tried,' the Russian leader said.[16]

Two months later, after more weeks of painstaking negotiations with the Russians, likened by Talbott to 'root canal work', agreement was finally reached on a NATO–Russia Founding Act, which provided an institutional means for Russia to take part in transatlantic security discussions. 'NATO and Russia do not consider each other as adversaries,' the document declared. 'They share the goal of overcoming the vestiges of earlier confrontation and competition and of strengthening mutual trust and cooperation.' This, it said, marked the beginning of a fundamentally new relationship between Russia and the Alliance, which they intended to develop based on 'common interest, reciprocity and transparency'. The document was signed on 27 May.

In an attempt to reassure Russia that enlargement did not mean moving NATO's conventional or nuclear forces closer to its borders, the document also said that 'in the current and foreseeable security environment, the Alliance will carry out its collective defence and other missions by ensuring the necessary interoperability, integration, and capability for reinforcement rather than by additional permanent stationing of substantial combat forces'. James Rubin, an assistant secretary of state, claimed the wording had been carefully crafted by Albright not to rule out such a move for all time, since she 'understood that the relatively benign Russia of President Boris N. Yeltsin might revert to a more dangerous foe'.[17]

Clinton had squared the Russians, but now he faced the equally difficult challenge of getting the NATO allies on board. While enlargement was widely backed within the Alliance, there was no agreement on how many countries should be invited to join in the first wave. Washington wanted to limit it to Poland, the Czech Republic and Hungary, not just because they were the most prepared, but also because the more members there were, the more complicated the problem of assimilating them would be. But a majority of NATO members wanted a larger number: Chirac, having swung round to accept enlargement, lobbied hard for the inclusion of Romania. Others wanted Slovenia or Slovakia.

An insight into Clinton's thinking came from a conversation he had over lunch with Blair in Downing Street that May.* During it, he dismissed as a 'silly argument' suggestions by critics of enlargement in Congress that it could provoke a nationalist backlash in Russia. When Sandy Berger, Clinton's newly appointed national security adviser, noted that polling data showed NATO was not a 'grass roots' issue for Russians, Blair chipped in, saying: 'What a surprise – they are just being normal and caring more about the economy.'

Clinton was adamant, however, that the first wave of enlargement

---

* A transcript of the conversation, which took place on 29 May 1997, was released to the BBC under the Freedom of Information Act.

should be limited to three countries. 'Our first concern is that the first shall not be the last – we have said that all along,' he told Blair. 'If there are five, no one will believe in a second round and we will be under pressure to reassure them [the countries not admitted] publicly . . . The open door must be credible.' A larger group would also 'turn up the heat on the Baltic issue' – the even more contentious matter of NATO membership for Estonia, Latvia and Lithuania – 'and we are not prepared to handle that yet. This is a problem that needs time to sort itself out; we need to give it a few years.'[18]

The issue came to a head at a meeting of NATO foreign ministers in Sintra, Portugal on 30 May, the day after Clinton's meeting with Blair. Although backed by just Britain and Iceland, Washington ultimately prevailed, not only because of its undue weight within NATO but also because of the principle of consensus on which the Alliance worked. Invitations were extended only to Poland, the Czech Republic and Hungary, but the communiqué established the principle of the 'open door', a process for the consideration of future applicants. When Clinton travelled to Warsaw he was greeted by a crowd of thirty thousand jubilant people, accompanied by marching bands, red carpets, balloons and banners, at an event they called 'Yalta's funeral'. NATO was heading east, whether Russia liked it or not.

IN TRYING – IN VAIN – TO PREVENT the eastward expansion of NATO, Yeltsin had been hampered by the same problems that Gorbachev had faced a decade earlier when confronted with the fall of the Berlin Wall and the break-up of the Soviet Union: the weakness of the economy and dependence on the West. As a result of the reforms that had begun with the liberalisation of prices in January 1992, the nature of the Russian economy had been transformed beyond recognition. Yet its macroeconomic performance was disappointing: between 1992 and 1995, GDP fell by almost a quarter in real terms, real wages by almost one-third and employment by eight per cent, hitting living standards, which had already been depressed by the chaos that accompanied the break-up of the Soviet Union. By mid-1995, the economy had finally begun to stabilise, with the introduction of a fixed exchange rate for the rouble and the first big credit from the International Monetary Fund (IMF). Yeltsin's victory in the election encouraged a flood of foreign investment. In 1997, it grew for the first time in a decade.

It proved to be a false dawn. A financial crisis that had started in South-East Asia that summer sent a shock wave through global financial markets and drove down the price of crude oil and non-ferrous metals, exports of which were the mainstay of the Russian economy. The government attempted to support the rouble, which it saw as the key to preserving the fruits of stabilisation, but the international loans started to dry up and Russian banks got into trouble. One of the achievements of reform since the end of Soviet Union had been the integration of a closed economy into the wider world. Now this very integration was threatening it with collapse.

In March 1998, in one of his characteristic mercurial flashes, Yeltsin sacked Chernomyrdin, his loyal and unassuming long-time prime minister. He replaced him with a virtual unknown, Sergei Kiriyenko, a thirty-five-year-old former banker who had been minister of fuel and energy for less than four months. The appointment came as a surprise to everyone – Kiriyenko included, who claimed to have been told about his new job the same morning. Yeltsin said his aim was to make reforms 'more energetic and effective'. Commentators suggested it was Kiriyenko's weakness and lack of power base that commended him to Yeltsin, who was still mulling a change in the rules to allow him to run for a third presidential term in 2000. Chernomyrdin had upset his boss by playing an increasingly prominent role while Yeltsin had been off sick, turning him into a potential threat.

Despite Kiriyenko's lack of experience, he seemed to the Clinton administration to be pursuing the right policies. But this was not enough. By July 1998, it was clear to both Washington and Moscow that Russia was in urgent need of financial help. On 13 July the IMF and the World Bank weighed in with a $22.6 billion financial package in return for a pledge from Moscow to cut spending and raise its tax take. But after the Russian government had burnt through $10 billion of its reserves, its attempts to prop up the rouble looked doomed to fail. On Friday 14 August there was a run on several banks. The following Monday, the government finally took action: it reneged on the service of domestic public debt, declared a moratorium on private foreign debt and let its currency float freely. The results were dramatic: the rouble, stock exchange and external debt market collapsed, the domestic payment system was temporarily paralysed and most of the big banks collapsed under the weight of their debts. Real incomes plunged, inflation reached eighty-six per cent and many members of Russia's newly emerging middle class found themselves out of a job.

Yeltsin himself was nowhere to be seen. Rumours circulated that he was ill or had gone on an alcoholic binge or both. His staff said he was away 'working with documents'. Clinton, meanwhile, was pre-occupied by other, more personal matters: after months of speculation about the nature of his contacts with Monica Lewinsky, a White House intern, he went on television the same Monday to admit finally that he had indeed had a relationship with her – contrary to his notorious assertion ('I did not have sexual relations with that woman').

Events in Moscow moved quickly. On 23 August, the evening tele-vision news announced tersely that Yeltsin had dismissed Kiriyenko and was bringing back Chernomyrdin. It was a baffling move even by Yeltsin's standards, given that it was only five months since he had sacked him, deriding him as a spent force. The Duma looked almost certain to refuse to confirm his appointment.

The Clinton administration watched on in horror. It had staked a lot on its relationship with Yeltsin and now the country was falling apart before its eyes. Clinton was due to fly to Moscow on 1 September for a summit with Yeltsin. The Russians, keen for a sign of American support, were desperate the meeting should go ahead. Clinton was wavering, however. His political advisers warned that if he went abroad just before Congress was due to come back in session, it would look as if he were trying to divert attention from the Lewinsky scandal as talk of his impeachment reached its height. There were also persistent rumours that Yeltsin might suddenly step down while Clinton was in Moscow, dragging him into the country's political crisis. Talbott was dispatched to find out what was going on.

Clinton, who was vacationing in Martha's Vineyard, voiced his despair in a telephone call with Blair on 27 August. 'Now, what the hell do you think is going on over in Russia?' he asked. 'We're watching it closely. Yeltsin's in the dacha, Chernomyrdin's working on confirma-tion. There are rumours that Yeltsin would resign once Chernomyrdin is confirmed. I don't know, but I know this: they are absolutely insistent that I come. I can't initiate my not going. It's kind of a mess . . .

'Their economy is still rapidly deteriorating,' Clinton continued. 'The Central Bank is still under pressure to inject liquidity into the banking sector. The problem is, when they do, the banks turn around and take the money out of the country, and so there's no control over that money. There's no clear economic policy.'

Underlying the short-term crisis, Clinton argued, was the broader question of Russia's struggle to make the transition from communism. Central European countries such as Poland and Hungary had succeeded despite suffering the same challenges. Yet Russia had failed to create the institutions required for a democracy and a market economy. 'I'm quite concerned now that a working majority of the populace is for the suspension of some democratic freedom just to have a strong leader who'll get the damn show on the road again and make the trains run on time,' he said.[19]

In the end, Clinton went ahead with his trip to Moscow, although only after Talbott secured an assurance from Yeltsin that he would not embarrass his guest by staging a sudden departure from the Kremlin during the visit. Talking with his team on the flight to Moscow, Clinton reflected on the extent to which a Russian collapse might be blamed in part on the failure of his own policy towards the country. When he was fighting for election in 1992 he had echoed Nixon's criticism of Bush for not putting enough 'real money' into Russia. He now wondered if his own administration had gone on to make the same error. 'We're giving them a big, tough reform message, but there ain't no dessert on the menu we're showing them,' he told Talbott. 'Hell, I'm not sure they can even see the main course.'[20]

The summit itself was a strange affair. The two leaders covered the usual issues from international terrorism to the spread of nuclear weapons and disarmament, but there were no important decisions or announcements. Yeltsin was more preoccupied with what to do about Chernomyrdin, whom the Duma had already rejected: should he insist on his appointment and risk a full-blown political crisis, or appoint someone else in his place? The journalists covering the summit were more interested in Lewinsky, while ordinary Russians were not much concerned with geopolitics and were just getting on trying to cope with a plunging rouble and surging prices. 'Maybe I did some good by just showing up,' Clinton told Talbott on the flight home. 'At least I didn't do any harm – which with these ol' boys can sometimes be a trick all by itself.'[21]

A few days later, the Duma rejected Chernomyrdin's reappointment for a second time. Under the rules of the constitution, Yeltsin could have nominated him for a third time and, if his candidacy were again turned down, dissolved the Duma. Instead, in what was seen as a conciliatory gesture, he turned to Yevgeny Primakov, a holdover from the Soviet era who was more acceptable to parliament.

The choice did not go down well in Washington. Primakov was scathing about the efforts of the reformers and reluctant to accept Western advice – though not shy about asking for Western financial help. In the event, nothing more than a small IMF loan was forthcoming, but the Russian economy began to bounce back far more strongly than economists had expected as the effects of the weaker rouble fed through. Between 1998 and 1999, government revenue rose by almost twenty per cent and the budget deficit fell from 5.2% of GDP to just 1.1%.

On 12 May 1999, Primakov, too, was fired by Yeltsin and replaced by Sergei Stepashin, a forty-seven-year-old veteran of the security services. Primakov's departure was ostensibly prompted by his failure to come up with a plan to revive the economy. In reality, Yeltsin, in poor health and increasingly isolated, was jealous of Primakov's popularity and unhappy with his ties to the communists. To add to his woe, Yeltsin also faced an attempt by the communists in the Duma to impeach him. He survived comfortably, just as Clinton had survived the attempt to impeach him over the Lewinsky affair. The charge that had appeared most likely to succeed against Yeltsin, condemnation of his role in the war in Chechnya, fell sixteen votes short of the three hundred votes required. Yet even questioning his mandate in this way contributed to the existing sense of disarray. Overshadowing everything was the next presidential election, due in June 2000.

WHILE GRAPPLING WITH RUSSIA'S ECONOMIC CRISIS, Clinton was also pushing NATO enlargement through the Senate, and on 30 April 1998, the measure eventually passed by a healthy eighty votes to nineteen. 'This vote is a major milestone on the road to an undivided, democratic and peaceful Europe,' Clinton said in a statement. 'The addition of these three democracies to our alliance will strengthen NATO, expand the zone of stability in Europe and reduce the chances American men and women will ever again be called into Europe's fields of battle.'

Kennan for one was not impressed. 'I think it is the beginning of a new Cold War,' he declared the following month in an interview with Thomas Friedman of the *New York Times*.[22] 'There was no reason for this whatsoever. No one was threatening anybody else . . . Our differences in the Cold War were with the Soviet Communist regime. And now we are turning our backs on the very people who mounted the greatest bloodless revolution in history to remove that Soviet regime . . . Of course there is going to be a bad reaction from Russia, and then [the NATO expanders] will say that we always told you that is how the Russians are – but this is just wrong.'

The act of accession was signed by the foreign ministers of Poland, the Czech Republic and Hungary on 12 March 1999. Albright was deeply moved at seeing the country of her birth confirmed back in the Western fold, and it was at her insistence that the ceremony was held not in Washington but at the Truman Presidential Library in Independence, Missouri, in honour of the president under whom the Alliance had been founded.

'NATO enlargement is not an event, it is a process,' Albright declared in her speech.[23] 'Over time, NATO will do for Eastern Europe what it has done for the West. Steadily and systematically, we will continue erasing, without replacing, the line drawn in Europe by Stalin's bloody boot.'

The three foreign ministers rose to the occasion. 'Poland forever returns where she has always belonged: the free world,' said Bronisław Geremek, the country's foreign minister, a dissident during the communist era. He had brought along some appropriate mementoes for the library, among them a campaign poster from 1989, the year Solidarność won against the communists. It showed a picture of Gary Cooper's Marshal Will Kane from *High Noon* striding proudly towards his destiny, ballot rather than gun in hand. 'It helped us to win,' Geremek added. 'For the people of Poland, high noon comes today.'

His Czech counterpart, Jan Kavan, who had fled Czechoslovakia after the Prague Spring, having been a student leader, said he had never dreamt his country would join the Alliance. 'Accession to NATO is a guarantee that we will never again become powerless victims of any foreign aggression,' he said. The Hungarian foreign minister, János Martonyi, who experienced the 1956 uprising as a thirteen-year-old, declared that his homeland was returning 'to her natural habitat'.

But what should be done about those aspiring members who had not made it into the first group? At the Washington summit on 24–5 April at which Hungary, Poland and the Czech Republic officially joined, NATO issued new guidelines for membership with individualised 'Membership Action Plans' not just for Slovakia and Romania, but also for Albania, Bulgaria, Estonia, Latvia, Lithuania, Macedonia and Slovenia. The Continent's post-Soviet structure was beginning to take shape – and it excluded Russia.

The reaction from Moscow was predictably hostile: Yeltsin, in hospital for the previous two weeks suffering from what was described as a stomach ulcer, said nothing, but others did not mince their words: 'We consider the expansion of NATO a dangerous historic mistake that can entail grave circumstances,' said General Leonid Ivashov of the Russian defence ministry.[24] It even brought criticism from Boris Nemtsov, a former deputy prime minister considered one of the most pro-Western politicians. Nemtsov decried the move as a strategic mistake that would help unite communists and other opponents of democracy in coming parliamentary and presidential elections.

It was too late: despite Moscow's protests, NATO was edging eastward. On the plane taking them back to Europe, the foreign ministers of the Alliance's three newly minted members were asked whether they could foresee Russia ever becoming a member of NATO. There was a long pause before Martonyi finally replied: 'Silence is your answer.'

IN THE YEARS SINCE 1999 THERE has been much discussion about NATO enlargement and whether the West broke a promise by pressing ahead with it. Each stage in the deterioration of relations between East and West has been marked by new claims of pledges made and broken. Attention has focused in particular on a conversation between Gorbachev and James Baker, Bush's secretary of state, in February 1990, during which Baker pledged that if Soviet forces were withdrawn from Eastern Europe, NATO would not move in to replace them. The 'military presence or jurisdiction of NATO would not be expanded even one inch in an easterly direction', Baker had told Gorbachev, according to transcripts of the conversation. Helmut Kohl, the West German leader, gave similar assurances. This idea of NATO's 'broken promise' became a cornerstone of Russia's post-Soviet identity.

NATO itself has conceded that some statements by Western leaders, especially those by Baker and by Hans-Dietrich Genscher, his German counterpart, 'can indeed be interpreted as a general rejection of any NATO enlargement beyond East Germany'. John Major, the British prime minister, was even more explicit, telling Dmitri Yazov, the Soviet defence minister, in March 1991, that he 'did not himself foresee circumstances now or in the future where East European countries would become members of NATO', according to the then British ambassador, Rodric Braithwaite, who was present at the meeting.[25] Yet, despite the opening of countless records and releases of archival material, it is clear that the assurance remained just that. No legally binding written guarantee has ever emerged.

In any case, such statements were made in the context of the negotiations on German reunification, and the Soviet side never specified their concerns. Nor was the issue raised during the crucial '2+4' negotiations that finally led Gorbachev to accept a unified Germany in NATO in July 1990. At that time the Warsaw Pact still existed, and Poland, Hungary and the then Czechoslovakia, among others, were still members. As Gorbachev's foreign minister, Eduard Shevardnadze, put it, the idea of the Soviet Union and the Warsaw Pact dissolving and NATO taking in former Warsaw Pact members was beyond the imagination of the negotiators at the time.[26]

According to this argument, the disbanding of the Warsaw Pact in February 1991 and the break-up of the Soviet Union at the end of the year created a completely new situation: freed from Soviet control, the countries of Central and Eastern Europe were finally able to choose their destinies again. Given that they were all set on integration with the West, refusal by NATO to accept them would have meant a de facto continuation of Europe's Cold War division and a denial of the provision, enshrined in the 1975 Helsinki charter, for a country's right to choose its own alliance.

Within Russia, criticism has inevitably focused on Gorbachev himself and his failure to secure a binding guarantee that ruled out any eastward expansion of the Alliance. So many other minor issues that came up during negotiations were addressed in formal documents. Why did he not demand the same for something as important as enlargement?

The charge clearly rankles with the former Soviet leader. In the years since, Gorbachev has condemned enlargement as a blunder and contrary to the spirit of the undertakings that he was given. Europe's long-term security would have been better served by the creation of new institutions that would have united the Continent rather than preserved its division, he claims. Yet he has also dismissed as absurd any suggestion that he was outwitted by the West.

'German reunification was completed at a time when the Warsaw Pact was still in existence, and to demand that its members should not join NATO would have been laughable,' Gorbachev wrote in his book *The New Russia*, published in 2016. 'No organisation can give a legally binding undertaking not to expand in the future. That was a purely political question, and all that could be done politically in the condition of time, was done.'[27]

8

KOSOVO

THE RAIN WAS POURING DOWN AT Pristina airport in Kosovo on 12 June 1999, when General Sir Mike Jackson, the British commander of K-For,* ducked into one of the few buildings still left standing after weeks of allied bombardment. His Russian counterpart, Viktor Zavarzin, joined him. Jackson reached into his map pocket, pulled out a bottle of whisky and offered him a swig. Zavarzin, a burly man, willingly accepted. 'Relations warmed up after that,' Jackson recalls in his memoirs.[1]

This impromptu display of East–West camaraderie came at the end of a day that could have had a very different conclusion. The Kosovo war was ending with the defeat of President Slobodan Milošević. After more than two months of the relentless NATO bombing of Yugoslavia, Russia had grudgingly accepted the demise of its Orthodox Slav ally. But now it wanted to ensure it would be allowed to play its part in patrolling the peace. Insisting that its forces would be answerable only to Russian commanders, the Kremlin had sent two hundred of its troops that were stationed in Bosnia to occupy the airport.

Wesley Clark, NATO's supreme commander, feared the Russian move might mean the partition of Kosovo into an Albanian south and a Serbian north, and ordered five hundred British and French paratroopers to stop them before they could reach the airport. Jackson defied him: 'I'm not

---

* The NATO-led international peacekeeping force for Kosovo.

going to start the Third World War for you,' he reportedly told Clark during a heated exchange. It was eventually agreed that Russian peace-keepers would deploy throughout Kosovo, but independently of NATO.

The bloody, slow-motion disintegration of Yugoslavia during the 1990s had been a matter of contention between Russia and the West, showing the ability of the two sides to see the same events from very different perspectives. Their dispute centred largely on the role of the Serbs and their leader, Milošević. For the West, he was the villain of the piece. Russian attitudes, however, were coloured by their historical, cultural and religious links with the Serbs. While often exasperated by Milošević himself, they were not so ready to give up on his country. Yeltsin repeatedly warned Clinton that any support he gave to the Alliance against the Serbs was at great domestic cost to his position and could be used against him by his political enemies.

America had worked hard to keep Russia on board during the Bosnian crisis of the early 1990s. Richard Holbrooke, the architect of the Dayton Accords, which had put an end to the three-and-a-half-year war, understood that for Moscow it was a matter of respect and a desire to be seen as one of the 'big boys'. What Russia wanted most, Holbrooke said, 'was to restore a sense, however symbolic, that they still mattered in the world. Behind our efforts to include Russia in the Bosnian negotiating process lay a fundamental belief that it was essential to find the proper place for Russia in Europe's security structure, something it had not been part of since 1914.'[2] America largely succeeded in its aim, even if Kozyrev, while foreign minister, complained during a private meeting with Talbott: 'It's bad enough having you people telling us what to do whether we like it or not. Don't add insult to injury by also telling us that it's in our interests to obey your orders.'[3]

After the Bosnian conflict ended, Russian forces served under an American commander in IFOR, the NATO-led multinational implementation force. But by early 1998, international attention began to turn again to Serbia, or more specifically to Kosovo, a province in its south that is home to two million people. It is a region rich in historical enmities and ethnic conflict dating back to 1389 when Serb forces were defeated by the Ottomans near Pristina. During the communist years after the Second World War, Kosovo had the status of an autonomous province within Serbia, but much of that autonomy had been swept away by Serb nationalists in 1990. Kosovo Albanians began to resist, peacefully at first. By the middle of the decade, however, their resistance had turned violent with the emergence of the Kosovo Liberation Army (KLA), an armed pro-independence group that carried out attacks on police, security forces and government officers, as well as on ethnic Serb villages. The Serbs retaliated, plunging the province into chaos.

Reports in late February and early March 1998 that Serb paramilitaries had massacred scores of ethnic Albanians in Prekaz convinced Madeleine Albright of the need to 'lay down a marker'. 'We are not going to stand by and watch the Serbian authorities do in Kosovo what they can no longer get away with in Bosnia,' she declared.[4] Earlier in the decade, the international community had ignored the first signs of ethnic cleansing in the Balkans before finally acting. America, Albright hoped, had learnt from its mistake. 'The violence in Kosovo was recent, but the problem created by Milošević's ruthless ambition was not,' she believed.[5]

In a series of meetings over the months that followed, Albright – backed by Robin Cook, the British foreign secretary – tried to step up pressure on the Serbs to back down. It proved a struggle: both France and Italy were suspicious of the KLA. Russia was even more of a problem: Yeltsin insisted that attempts be made to find a negotiated solution rather than merely respond to violence with more violence. He also questioned the outside world's right to intervene in the internal matter of a sovereign state.

Talks continued through 1998 – but so too did the violence. Kosovo was degenerating into civil war and the Serbs, thanks to their superior forces, were winning. Albright, meanwhile, was pushing for forces. On 23 September, the UN Security Council adopted a resolution declaring the situation in Kosovo a threat to peace and security and listing a series of actions that Milošević had to take. Crucially the resolution fell far short of authorising military action. Nor could the Americans hope to get such a resolution through the United Nations: Igor Ivanov, who had just taken over from Primakov as Russian foreign minister, made clear that Moscow would veto it. If NATO was going to act, it had to do so on its own and without a UN mandate.

As the Western media filled with fresh reports of Serb atrocities, Albright kept up the pressure for action. Washington was increasingly coming to believe that the only solution was regime change and the toppling of Milošević. On 13 October, NATO formally authorised the use of force against the rump Yugoslavian state, allowing it just four days to come into line. The threat worked: a few hours later, Holbrooke announced that he and Milošević had a deal that would give back the province its autonomy. Yet over the winter the agreement began to unravel as both Milošević and the KLA hardened their stance. Convinced that NATO's relevance and effectiveness was at stake, Albright decided to tighten the screws on the Serbs. News of another massacre, this time of forty-five people in Račak on 16 January, proved the final straw. After some extensive lobbying of Washington, of America's European allies and of Russia, Albright secured approval for the convening of peace talks at Rambouillet in France starting on 6 February. Both sides would be asked to accept a plan that would give autonomy to the people of Kosovo. But in what looked certain to be rejected by the Serbs, the proposed deal, it was stipulated, would be implemented by a 28,000-member NATO peacekeeping force.

The talks proved complicated, not least because of divisions within the Kosovo Albanians, some of whom were unwilling to back any deal that promised autonomy rather than independence. On 18 March, together with the Americans and the British, they finally signed the accords. Milošević, however, continued to baulk at the idea of having NATO peacekeepers on his territory and refused to sign; the Russians backed him.

During a last meeting with Milošević in Belgrade on 22 March, Holbrooke warned the Yugoslav leader that failure to go along with the Rambouillet agreement would mean his country would face 'swift, severe, and sustained bombing'. Milošević appeared resigned to his fate; Holbrooke found him 'cool and almost contemptuous'.

'You're a great country, a powerful country,' Milošević said. 'You can do anything you want. We can't stop you.' Defiant to the end, the Yugoslav leader added: 'Go ahead and bomb us, but you will never get Kosovo.'[6]

On the evening of 23 March, just over a week after the foreign ministers of Poland, the Czech Republic and Hungary signed the NATO accession document, Holbrooke returned to Brussels. He announced that peace talks had failed and that he was formally handing the matter over to NATO for military action. The next day Primakov, now prime minister, boarded a flight to Washington to meet Gore. When he was told by Gore that a NATO attack on Yugoslavia was imminent, Primakov ordered his plane to turn around, mid-Atlantic, and take him back to Moscow.

That same evening the bombing started. In a statement published the next day, Yeltsin denounced the action. 'This is essentially an attempt by NATO to enter the twenty-first century in the uniform of the world policeman,' he declared. 'Russia will never agree to this.'⁷ As Russian television showed a steady diet of pictures of suffering Serbs, crowds gathered outside the US embassy in Moscow. Demonstrators hurled paint, stones and eggs. They burnt American flags, broke windows and urinated. Then, on 28 March, at the culmination of several days of protests, a masked gunman jumped out of a four-by-four and tried to fire a grenade launcher at the building. When it failed to work, he raked the walls with sub-machine-gun fire. It was the most serious attack of its sort ever to have been carried out against the American embassy in Russia.

In the Duma, nationalists and communists passed resolution after resolution condemning the bombing and negotiated with Milošević on creating a military strategic union of the two states. Even liberal young Muscovites brought up on a diet of American music and films were shocked by what seemed to be an unwarranted attack on fellow Slavs. Some declared themselves ready to go to Serbia to fight. Coupled with the economic crisis, which had shattered confidence in Western ideas, the backlash threatened to do serious damage to relations with America and its allies. Criticism came even from pro-Western liberals such as Nemtsov. 'If America behaves like an elephant in a china shop in Europe and other parts of the world, then anti-American sentiment will not only dominate Russia but other countries as well,' he warned.⁸

The strikes continued for eleven weeks and were extended to central Belgrade, hitting the interior ministry, the headquarters of Serbian state television, Milošević's party headquarters and even his home. On 7 May, five guided bombs struck the Chinese embassy, killing three reporters and outraging the Chinese. When Bill Clinton telephoned Jiang Zemin to apologise, the Chinese leader declined to take the call.

The war presented Yeltsin with a serious problem: although he had little love for Milošević, he was worried that the nationalist backlash in Russia could undo his attempts to turn his country towards the West. Determined to find a peaceful solution to the crisis, he sent Chernomyrdin as an envoy to Belgrade to put pressure on Milošević, and lobbied Blair and Chirac to stop the bombing. He failed on both counts. Milošević was 'a man from the past, the bad past', the French leader told him.⁹

NATO forces, making more than a thousand flights a day, pummelled Yugoslavia's power stations, bridges, factories and roads. The violence between the Serbs and the Kosovo Albanians was escalating, and the atrocities the bombing was meant to have prevented were multiplying. Finally, after seventy-nine days, Milošević capitulated and the bombing campaign ended.

Despite Russia's opposition to the war, it had never come close to interfering on the Yugoslav side. Yeltsin was not going to risk a Third World War for the sake of Milošević. It is difficult, however, to overestimate the damage that Kosovo did to relations between Moscow and Washington, and the campaign negatively influenced broader Russian perceptions of America. 'The bombing of Yugoslavia caused a big reaction against the West,' said Oslon, the pollster. 'Firstly, because this represented the use of military force not somewhere far away but here in Europe. And secondly because we had always had close relations with the Serbs.'

Almost two decades later, Igor Ivanov, the then foreign minister, remains convinced that, given time, it should have been possible to find a way of persuading the Serbs to grant wide autonomy to the Kosovo Albanians without going to war. NATO's air campaign, coinciding with the eastward enlargement of the Alliance, he argued, was part of a broader American drive to take advantage of Russian weakness to rewrite the rules of international relations.

'It was clear that NATO wanted to take military action, but it was a premeditated violation of the UN charter,' Ivanov recalls.¹⁰ 'I said to Madeleine [Albright]: "You are creating a very dangerous precedent for the future."

'But it was their decision to impose the new world order. They started this policy in the last years of the Clinton administration. Yugoslavia was the first practical demonstration of their intention to create a unipolar world led by the US and their allies and with a strong military presence of NATO.'

IN A SPEECH TO STANFORD UNIVERSITY in September 1997, Strobe Talbott insisted that America's policy towards Russia should contain an indispensable feature: 'strategic patience'. 'That means a policy not just for coping with the issue or the crisis of the moment or the week or even of the season, or for getting through the next summit meeting,' he said. 'Rather it means a policy for the next century.'

Yet as the 1990s drew to a close, such patience was running out, and both Russians and Americans could look back and wonder what had become of the hopes that had been raised by the fall of the Berlin Wall. True, Germany had been reunited, while the former Soviet satellites, liberated by Gorbachev's 'Sinatra doctrine', had largely lived up to their label of 'new democracies' and were well on their way to rejoining Western Europe. Just as importantly, the worst fears that had accompanied the break-up of the Soviet Union had not been realised. With the exception of some violence in the Caucasus and Central Asia, the fifteen republics of the former Soviet Union had gone their separate ways peacefully. Nor were there any 'loose nukes': the massive Soviet nuclear arsenal was now entirely in Russian hands.

Anyone visiting Moscow or St Petersburg from London or Washington at the end of the 1990s would have found themselves in what seemed to be a 'normal' city – unlike a decade earlier. The shops looked like they did back home, with lavish window displays and well-stocked shelves. Some of their names were familiar too. The cavernous old state restaurants with their surly staff and unappetising fare had been replaced by new eateries offering European food or sushi. (Everyone wanted sushi.) Billboards urging citizens to build socialism or extolling the virtues of the five-year plan had been replaced by advertisements for cars or shampoo. Most businesses were now in private hands rather than owned by the state. Elections offered a genuine choice of candidates. The press was vibrant, often iconoclastic and free. Foreign travel, once a privilege bestowed by the state, was now a right.

Yet the upheavals of the 1990s had created more losers than winners, and it took years before living standards drew level even with the last years of the Soviet era. Many people, especially members of the older generations, still felt a sense not so much of liberation but rather of disorientation after so much of what they had been brought up to believe in had been denounced as a lie. There was a feeling of wasted lives, of humiliation and wounded pride.

Attitudes to the West had changed too. Russians had become used to drinking Italian wine or German beer and eating French cheese or American hamburgers. Yet the East and West had not come together in any more profound way. The enlargement of NATO to include

Poland, Hungary and the Czech Republic had merely shifted the Iron Curtain several hundred miles to the east. Kosovo had been the last straw. Did Russia's views count for nothing?

'Russia is a humiliated country in search of a direction without a compass,' wrote Charles Gati, a senior research professor of European and Eurasian Studies at Johns Hopkins University, in 1995.[11] 'It is smaller than it has been in three centuries. Both the outer empire in Central and Eastern Europe and the inner empire that was the Soviet Union are gone, and Moscow must now use force to keep even Russia itself together. As its pitiful (and shameful) performance in Chechnya has shown, the military has been reduced to a ragtag army, with presumably unusable nuclear weapons. Worse yet, Russia is deprived of pride and self-respect.'

Gati went on to invite Americans to imagine themselves in the place of the Russians. 'To appreciate the present mood of letdown and frustration, imagine that our currency became all but worthless,' Gati wrote. 'That our stores identified some of their wares in the Cyrillic rather than the Roman alphabet, showing prices in roubles; that our political and economic life were guided by made-in-Moscow standards; and that our leaders were lectured by patronising foreign commissars about the need to stay the course in order to join their "progressive", which is to say the communist, world.'

Gati's commentary, published in the *Washington Post*, was entitled 'Weimar Russia'. He was not the only one to liken the Soviet Union's 'loss' of the Cold War with imperial Germany's defeat in the First World War. Both countries had had to rebuild political institutions from scratch and had struggled to do so; both had suffered from hyperinflation and economic hardships. Both had found it difficult to come to terms with their lost territories and had begun to make threatening noises towards their neighbours. Both had blamed their woes on democrats who had stabbed them in the back and, perhaps most worryingly of all, their people were easy prey for demagogues promising to re-establish their lost imperial grandeur.

So what had gone wrong? There is little doubt that in the early 1990s America had genuinely wanted to welcome Russia into the West; yet not, as Gorbachev had proposed during his last summit with Bush in July 1991, as an equal partner. If Russia were to be a partner, it would have to be a junior one. Yet Russia, by virtue of its size, history and arsenal of doomsday weapons, was not prepared to be treated like a larger Poland. It had been granted the status of a superpower during the Cold War, and insisted this should continue.

It failed to appreciate, however, that this status had been tied to its ideological pull as the centre of an alternative socialist worldview, and by the sense of menace it exuded. Take these away and Russia was no longer able to claim to be an equal of the United States, whose economy was so many times larger. The sense of gloom was compounded by the 'loss' of the Soviet republics, which, to many Russians, now that the euphoria that accompanied the fall of communism had long since faded, seemed a senseless partition of the country in which they had grown up.

Could the West have acted differently during the 1990s? In the years that followed, a Russian narrative emerged, according to which America and its allies had not just deliberately destroyed the Soviet Union but contrived to keep the new independent Russia weak and divided thereafter – a view encouraged by triumphalist American claims to have 'won' the Cold War. According to such a view, the West did its utmost to turn the other former Soviet republics against Russia, thwarted every attempt by Moscow at economic and political reinte-gration in the post-Soviet space and failed to make good on its promises of financial aid.

The academic Sergei Karaganov summed up the sense of humiliation and encirclement felt by Russians during the 1990s in an article published in *Izvestia* in 2014. In it he berated the West for its refusal to end the Cold War either de facto or de jure after the end of the Soviet Union. 'The West has consistently sought to expand its zone of military, economic and political influence through NATO and the EU', Karaganov wrote. 'Russian interests and objections were flatly ignored. Russia was treated like a defeated power, though we did not see ourselves as defeated. A softer version of the Treaty of Versailles was imposed on the country. There was no outright annexation of territory or formal reparations like Germany faced after World War I, but Russia was told in no uncertain terms that it would play a modest role in the world. This policy was bound to engender a form of Weimar syndrome in a great nation whose dignity and interests had been trampled.'

Such a criticism has been compounded by claims that the West was at fault for not providing enough aid to Russia – and failing to share with it the 'peace dividend' brought by the end of the Cold War. While the US saved an estimated $1.3 trillion from reduced military spending by scaling back its armed forces, US aid to Russia between 1993 and 1999 was no more than $2.50 per person. This, Lila Shevtsova of the Brookings Institution has noted, was an amount equal to just one per cent of the US defence budget for a single year, 1996, or a quarter of the price of a Nimitz-class aircraft carrier.[12]

Rodric Braithwaite, British ambassador to Russia from 1988 to 1992, believes this was a missed opportunity. 'Determined Western leaders could have tapped into the general sympathies for Russia and put together a genuine stabilisation scheme which would have mitigated the pain of transition and relieved much of the distress which ordinary Russians were to suffer over the next few years,' he wrote in his memoirs.[13]

Yet perhaps, on the contrary, the West's mistake was not to have been tough enough. Garry Kasparov, the chess grand master who has become one of the most virulent critics of the present Russian regime, has argued that the West should have set tighter rather than looser conditions for its economic assistance. And he faults Western leaders, acting out of 'a combination of apathy, ignorance and misplaced goodwill', for showing Russia too much – rather than too little – respect, tolerating a continued role for its former communist leaders and thereby denying its people the clean start enjoyed by its former satellites.[14]

Such failures were exemplified by the reliance placed by Clinton on Yeltsin as the sole guarantor of democracy and bulwark against the return to communism. Even as Yeltsin unleashed a brutal war on Chechnya in 1995 and moved in an increasingly authoritarian direction, the administration continued to back him wholeheartedly. This short-sighted policy contributed very little to Yeltsin's stature in Russia, and ensured that America and the West effectively acquiesced in Russia's retreat from democratic principles.

To blame outsiders for the economic hardship and massive inequalities of the 1990s, as some Russians have, is absurd. The West may have provided the economic model, but it was Russia's own leaders – either out of ignorance or self-interest – who contrived to implement such ideas in an unfair way. This was especially the case with the rules governing the sell-off of state industry, which seemed calculated to help insiders at the expense of the population as a whole. And while the army of Western consultants and businesspeople who descended on the country were well rewarded for their efforts, it was Russians who amassed obscene fortunes at the expense of their compatriots. After seventy years of communism, it was not just a matter of creating a whole new set of institutions; people's moral values had been eroded by living in a system that was based on cheating and dishonesty.

Underlying the Russians' disquiet was their inability to come to terms with the 'loss' of the former Soviet republics, and, to a lesser extent, the satellites beyond, which quickly became a cause for concern, not just in Kiev and Almaty but also in Warsaw, Budapest and Prague. The impression of Russia as a revanchist power was confirmed by the results of the December 1993 election when almost one in four voters backed Vladimir Zhirinovsky, who argued for the forceful reconstitution of the Soviet Union. Against this threatening backdrop, it made sense to satisfy the demands of the Central European states to join the EU and NATO while there was still a relatively benign regime in the Kremlin.

Yet Weimar Germany was not the only possible model that Russia could have adopted. As Gati argued in a follow-up to his 'Weimar Russia' article, published two decades later, it could instead have followed the path of West Germany after the Second World War.[15] Under Konrad Adenauer and his successors, West Germany accepted its lost territories and made peace with its neighbours, transforming itself not just into an economic success story but also into a mature and responsible member of the international community.

As long as Russia remained weak and economically dependent on Western help, the simmering resentment felt by many of its people would remain just that. Yet as the veteran American commentator Walter Laqueur argued at the time, it was wishful thinking on the part of the West to assume that a country that had been a great power for centuries would meekly accept a lesser role – any more than Germany had seventy years earlier. 'The belief among Russian nationalist ideologues that their country cannot exist except as a great empire is deeply rooted and goes back a long time,' he wrote. 'To many Russians, a number of regions that were lost (such as Ukraine) are still considered to be parts of Russia proper.'[16]

All that was needed now was a figure able to harness this sense of grievance and thirst for revenge; a leader who would promise to restore pride and impose order. Russia – and the world – would not have to wait for long.

II.

REBIRTH

9

A NEW START

BY THE STANDARDS OF POLITICAL BOMBSHELLS, this one was nuclear. On midday on New Year's Eve, 1999, Boris Yeltsin appeared on Russian television to announce to a stunned public that he was stepping down from the presidency. His second and final term was not due to expire for another six months, but it was time to bow out and make way for a new generation.

'I have made a decision. I have contemplated this long and hard. Today, on the last day of the outgoing century, I am retiring,' Yeltsin told viewers. 'Many times I have heard it said: "Yeltsin will try to hold onto power by any means, he won't hand it over to anyone." That is all lies. Russia must enter the new millennium with new politicians, new faces, new, intelligent, strong and energetic people. As for those of us who have been in power for many years, we must go.'[1]

Rubbing his eye, Yeltsin finished with a personal appeal inspired by the difficult transition from communism that Russia had undergone in the years since he had come to power.

'I want to ask you for forgiveness, because many of our hopes have not come true, because what we thought would be easy turned out to be painfully difficult,' he said. 'I ask you to forgive me for not fulfilling some hopes of those people who believed that we would be able to jump from the grey, stagnating, totalitarian past into a bright, rich and civilised future in one go . . . I myself believed in this. But it could not be done in one fell swoop. In some respects I was too naive.'

Yeltsin said he would hand power over to Vladimir Putin, a former KGB officer who had been a virtual unknown until his appointment as prime minister that August. The next presidential election, scheduled for June 2000, would be brought forward to March.

For a man whose time at the helm of Russia had been marked by turbulence and uncertainty, it was a characteristic piece of theatre. It was also a demonstration of Yeltsin's determination to control his own destiny. No Kremlin leader before him had voluntarily given up power; all had succumbed either to death or to a palace coup. The memory of Mikhail Gorbachev, driven from office almost exactly eight years earlier when his country was taken away from beneath him, will have been fresh in his mind.

It is not clear precisely when Yeltsin had taken the decision to step down. He nevertheless kept his intentions to himself until the very end, even going ahead with the recording of his annual presidential New Year's Eve address on 28 December, only to scrap it afterwards, telling the crew they needed to have another attempt later because he was not happy with the text or with his croaky delivery.

It was time to tell the 'family', who had effectively been running Russia since securing his re-election in 1996. The first to know were Aleksandr Voloshin, his chief of staff, and Valentin Yumashev, a close aide who in 2001 was to marry Yeltsin's younger daughter, Tatyana Dyachenko. That evening Yeltsin summoned the two men to his official residence at Gorky 9, a heavily guarded complex on the Rublyovo-Uspenskoye Road on the western outskirts of Moscow. They were both stunned. Yeltsin then told Dyachenko. Yeltsin's long-suffering wife, Naina, only learnt the news on the morning of New Year's Eve.

After recording a new speech, this time announcing his resignation, Yeltsin had a final meeting with Patriarch Alexy, head of the Russian Orthodox Church, and handed over the nuclear suitcase to Putin. While his bombshell was being broadcast to the nation, he was sitting down for a boozy farewell lunch with leading members of the so-called 'power ministries' responsible for defence and security. Then at 1:00P.M., now an ex-president, Yeltsin left his office in the Kremlin for the last time and his driver took him home. Dozens of people called wanting to speak to him, among them Bill Clinton. They were all told to call back later. Yeltsin was now a free man and wanted to have a nap.

That evening it was Putin, now acting president, who made the

.ional New Year's Eve address in Yeltsin's place. It was short, to the
.t and intended to assuage the traditional Russian fear of instability.
.i assure you that there will be no vacuum of power, not for a
.inute,' Putin declared. 'I promise you that any attempts to act
.ontrary to the Russian law and constitution will be cut short.' The
state, he said, would stand firm to protect freedom of speech, of
conscience and of the mass media and ownership rights – 'these
fundamental elements of a civilised society'.

Putin ended with a few words of gratitude to his predecessor, which
today sound tinged with irony. 'We will be able to see the true importance
of what Boris Yeltsin has done for Russia only after some time has passed,'
he said. 'However, it is clear already now that it was thanks to the president that Russia has opted for democracy and reform and is moving
towards these goals, and has become a strong and independent state.'

The world's airwaves began filling with tributes to Yeltsin soon after.
One of the most effusive was from Clinton, who had managed to have
a twenty-minute conversation with him after he woke from his nap.
Clinton praised the outgoing Russian leader for 'dismantling the
communist system' and 'building new political institutions under
democratically elected leaders within a constitutional framework'. He
largely glossed over the serious problems that had begun to emerge in
relations between America and Russia in the late 1990s over NATO
enlargement, Kosovo and corruption, which had now been joined by
concerns over the brutality of the second war in Chechnya.

Asked by reporters why he admired Yeltsin, Clinton struck a more
personal note. 'I liked him because he was always very forthright with
me,' he said. 'He always did exactly what he said he would do. And he
was willing to take chances to try to improve our relationship, to try
to improve democracy in Russia.'[2] Writing later in his memoirs of the
Russian leader's departure, Clinton said: 'It was both a wise and a shrewd
move, but I was going to miss Yeltsin . . . For all his physical problems
and occasional unpredictability, he had been a courageous and visionary
leader . . . I could tell he was comfortable with his decision. He left
office and lived as he had governed, in his own unique way.'[3]

But what of Putin? Yeltsin had assured Clinton that the man he had
selected as his successor would remain committed to democracy, open
markets and arms control. But what would Putin's elevation mean for
US–Russia relations? And how did he see America: as an ally and

partner, or a rival and maybe a foe? Clinton knew better than anyone how personalised power could be, especially in Russia.

IF WASHINGTON INITIALLY STRUGGLED TO GET the measure of Putin, it was understandable. His path to the Kremlin had been extraordinary both for its speed and its unexpectedness. At the end of 1991, as the Soviet Union broke up, Putin had been in his native St Petersburg, where he held a relatively minor post in the mayor's office as head of the committee for external relations. It was not until June 1996 that he had come to Moscow to become a deputy chief of the presidential property management department. Yet by July 1998 he was head of the Federal Security Service (FSB), one of the successor services of the KGB. In August 1999 he was named prime minister.

A flurry of biographies has been written about Putin, starting with his poor upbringing in Leningrad, as his home city was then known. The only child of a stern father, who was the Communist Party representative in a factory making railway carriages, he grew up in a run-down communal apartment in a once-elegant nineteenth-century apartment building in the centre of town. Amusement came from chasing rats around the courtyard. Accounts of his childhood have undoubtedly been coloured by his later career, yet he seems to have been an unremarkable boy and young man, who briefly went off the rails before finding redemption in martial arts. A film, *The Shield and the Sword*, about the exploits of a Soviet spy in Nazi Germany, which was released in 1968 when he was sixteen, appears to have inspired him to join the KGB.

After studying law at Leningrad State University, Putin was accepted into the KGB and posted to East Germany – although he would never become the secret agent of his childhood dreams. He was sent instead to Dresden, a backwater that lay in what was known mockingly as the Tal der Ahnungslosen ('Valley of the Clueless') because it was out of the range of television broadcasts from West Germany. Just a handful of officers worked there – an enormous contrast with the KGB's operation in East Berlin, the largest in the world. It was nevertheless certainly a step up, both in terms of career and lifestyle, from his life in Russia.

The German Democratic Republic (GDR), a communist state created out of what had been the Soviet-occupied zone of post-Nazi Germany, was on the front line with the West. It was also one of the most affluent parts of the Soviet empire, with living standards substantially higher than in the Soviet Union itself. 'We had come from a Russia where there were lines and shortages, and in the GDR there was always plenty of everything,'[4] recalled Putin. It was one of the most repressive too: between 1950 and 1989, some 274,000 people worked for the Stasi, the ministry for state security. Many ordinary people regularly reported their friends, family and neighbours to the authorities. Erich Honecker, who had led the country from 1971, refused to follow Gorbachev and liberalise East Germany, rightly seeing in such a move the seeds of destruction of his artificial state, whose only reason for existence was its communist political system.

Home for Putin and his wife, Lyudmila, a former air stewardess, was a serviced apartment block shared with KGB and Stasi families. Everything down to the dishes was provided for them. All they had to buy was food. Salary was paid partly in dollars and partly in East German marks. They also had use of a Lada for weekend excursions, which was a step up from the two-stroke Trabant that was the height of most East Germans' motoring dreams. Work was a five-minute walk away. They and their German counterparts would socialise with each other in the evenings and at weekends. Vladimir Usoltsev, a former KGB colleague, recalled how Putin spent hours leafing through Western mail-order catalogues in an attempt to keep up with fashions and trends.[5]

Putin developed a taste for the local beer, Radeberger, and had a three-litre keg of it sent every week, with predictable consequences for his waistline. Lyudmila, who became pregnant with their second daughter shortly after they arrived, was struck by the contrast with Russia: how the streets were clean, the windows of their apartment block washed every week and how her German counterparts would hang out their laundry in neat lines behind the block every morning. She was jealous, too, of the fact that their counterparts in the Stasi were better paid than they were.

It was here in Dresden, far from home, that Putin lived through the collapse of the political system in which he and other Russians of his generation had grown up. Much has been made in his biographies of the fact that, by spending the second half of the 1980s in Honecker's East Germany rather than in the Soviet Union, he failed to be caught up in the spirit of intellectual excitement as glasnost challenged old taboos and revealed the truth about the communist past. Instead he experienced the negative effects of Gorbachev's actions on the Soviet empire. As a young patriotic KGB officer, there seems little doubt that it made a deep impression on him.

Most telling were the events of 5 December 1989, a few weeks after the fall of the Berlin Wall. As a process of score-settling against the discredited East German communist regime gathered pace, a crowd stormed the headquarters of the Stasi, who seemed helpless to resist. A small group then crossed the road to the large house where Putin and his KGB colleagues worked.

'The guard on the gate immediately rushed back into the house,' recalled one of the group, Siegfried Dannath. But shortly afterwards Putin emerged. He was 'quite small, agitated'.

'He said to our group, "Don't try to force your way into this property", Dannath added. '"My comrades are armed, and they're authorised to use their weapons in an emergency".'[6]

Aware of how dangerous the situation could become, Putin called the headquarters of a nearby Soviet army tank unit to ask for protection. He was shocked by the answer he received. 'We cannot do anything without orders from Moscow,' the voice at the other end replied. 'And Moscow is silent.'

As Putin put it: 'Nobody lifted a finger to protect us.' Worried that details of their intelligence work would fall into enemy hands, he and his KGB colleagues began frantically to destroy their files. 'I personally burned a huge amount of material,' he recalled in his autobiography, *First Person*. 'We burned so much stuff that the furnace burst.'

The feared storming never took place, but those who have studied Putin claim the incident – and his experience of the collapse of East Germany – nevertheless taught him important lessons that would inform his later attitudes: in particular, the frailty of political elites and the ease with which they can be toppled by 'people power'. Two weeks later Helmut Kohl, the West German chancellor, visited Dresden and was greeted by jubilant crowds demanding the reunification of the two Germanys. 'That's it. It's in the bag,' Kohl told Rudolf Seiters, one of his ministers.[7] Soon afterwards, the Soviets began to pull out.

Putin was recalled to the Soviet Union in early 1990, ending up back in his home town, which the following year reverted to its old name of St Petersburg. The KGB gave him a post at the university, his alma mater, as assistant to the rector for international affairs, which gave him responsibility for watching students and visitors. It was not much of a job for an ambitious thirty-seven-year-old lieutenant general. The country was in chaos: the euphoria of the early glasnost years had given way to disorder and economic collapse. Lyudmila was appalled to see that the queues for food were even longer than they had been before they left. The Soviet Union was rapidly going the same way as East Germany.

A decade later, Putin reflected on the tumultuous events he had witnessed in Dresden. 'Actually I thought the whole thing was inevitable,' he said of the collapse of East Germany. 'To be honest, I only really regretted that the Soviet Union had lost its position in Europe, although intellectually I understood that a position built on walls and dividers cannot last. But I wanted something different to rise in its place. And nothing different was proposed. That's what hurt. They just dropped everything and went away . . . We would have avoided a lot of problems if the Soviets had not made such a hasty exit from Eastern Europe.'[8]

YELTSIN'S ILL HEALTH IN THE LATE 1990s had made it unlikely that he would attempt to serve for a third term. But Western powers had little idea who might replace him. In the United States, such a question is answered through a succession of primaries in which candidates fight it out in the public eye; in European democracies leaders are generally selected by their party. Russia is different. Yeltsin understood that his position as president effectively gave him the chance to choose a successor, someone who would not just continue his political legacy but also protect his own interests and those of his extended political family.

Yeltsin had initially plumped for Boris Nemtsov, one of the most charismatic of the young reformers, who served from 1991 to 1997 as governor of the Nizhni Novgorod region, which included Russia's eponymous third-largest city, before moving to Moscow and becoming first deputy prime minister. Yeltsin even introduced him to Clinton as his successor. Opinion polls in the summer of 1997 put likely support for Nemtsov at well over fifty per cent.

Yet their relationship began to sour. Yeltsin thought Nemtsov 'a bit of a guerrilla' who had a habit of forcing through decisions on policy without first discussing them with him. And so he changed his mind: 'I took a good look at him and realised he was not ready to be the country's president,' Yeltsin recalled.[9] In any case, Nemtsov's chances of being considered for the top job were ended by the Russian financial crisis of 1998, during which Yeltsin dissolved the government in which

Nemtsov was serving. Also spoken of as a potential successor was Sergei
Stepashin, who became prime minister in May 1999 after Yeltsin fired
Primakov. Stepashin's chances faded almost as quickly as they had begun,
however. Yeltsin quickly saw that his appointee was not up to the job
of prime minister, let alone president, and in August, he too was fired.

And then along came Putin. In his memoirs, Yeltsin writes that by
late 1998 he had been sensing the Russian public's need for a new quality
in the state, for a steel backbone that would strengthen the whole
government. 'We needed a person who was intellectual, democratic and
who could think anew but who was firm in the military manner.'[10]
Yeltsin claimed in one interview to have been keeping an eye on Putin
for some time – and not just from his personnel dossier. 'I had a pretty
good understanding of his performance in St Petersburg under Sobchak,'
Yeltsin said. 'And when he moved to Moscow, I started watching him
especially closely. I could see that he was not just an intelligent and
well-educated person but also decent and self-controlled.'[11]

Yeltsin did not reveal who had drawn Putin to his attention, but the
oligarch Boris Berezovsky, who served briefly as deputy chief of the
National Security Council after Yeltsin's re-election in 1996, claimed
the credit. He and his fellow oligarchs knew that Yeltsin's days were
numbered and they were on the lookout for a potential replacement
whom they could bend to their will. Putin had reportedly helped
Berezovsky years earlier when he was setting up a car dealership.
Courteous and respectful of their interests, he seemed like their man.
What especially appealed to the 'family' was Putin's reputation for loyalty
– which he had demonstrated in 1997 when he reportedly helped to
spirit Sobchak out of Russia and into exile in Paris to escape a corruption investigation after he lost the mayoral election the previous year.

On 9 August Yeltsin announced that he was nominating Putin as
prime minister – his fifth in less than eighteen months. In the Russian
system, the prime minister has largely administrative functions, nominating members of the cabinet and implementing domestic policy. The
president appoints him – subject to approval by the Duma – and can
fire him at will. Under Yeltsin it had become something of a scapegoat
position: when things went wrong, he was quick to pin the blame on
his prime minister.

This appointment seemed different. Yeltsin made it clear that he
wanted Putin as his successor and saw the post of prime minister as

a springboard for the top job. 'Next time, for the first time in the country's history, the first president of Russia will hand over power to a newly elected president,' Yeltsin announced, reading from a prepared statement. 'I have decided to name a man who, in my opinion, is able to consolidate society. Relying on the broadest of political forces, he will ensure the continuation of reforms in Russia.'[12]

Yeltsin's appointment of a virtual unknown not just as prime minister but also as his choice of future president was greeted with surprise both in Russia and abroad. Putin would have the advantage of incumbency, but how would a relative unknown be able to beat one of the 'big beasts' of Russian politics such as Yevgeny Primakov, the former prime minister, or Yury Luzhkov, the powerful mayor of Moscow? Putin's approval rating, according to Aleksandr Oslon, the pollster, was just three per cent. Oslon told Yumashev that it did not look as if the plan was going to work. 'Podozhdite, podozhdite [Wait, wait],' Yeltsin's aide replied. 'Maybe we will succeed.'[13]

In Washington, Yeltsin's choice of Putin was greeted with incredulity. For Talbott, it was further proof that Yeltsin had 'lost his grip on reality'. It was not just a matter of Putin's lack of relevant experience and connections; he did not even look the part. Most of Russia's leading political figures, such as Yeltsin, were bearlike, bulky men with booming voices. Putin, by contrast, 'was slightly built and had the manner of a disciplined, efficient, self-effacing executive assistant'.[14]

Putin's chances were transformed by events more than a thousand miles away in the North Caucasus. Following the end of the first Chechen war in 1996, an uneasy peace had descended on the region. The next year Yeltsin had signed a peace treaty with Aslan Maskhadov, the Chechen president, who predicted it would eliminate 'any basis to create ill feelings between Moscow and Grozny'.

Yet around the time of Putin's appointment, the conflict burst back into life when forces headed by Shamil Basayev, a Chechen warlord, crossed the border into neighbouring Dagestan, driving thousands of people from their homes and killing a number of Russian soldiers. When Basayev proclaimed a jihad to liberate nearby Muslim areas of the North Caucasus from the Kremlin's rule, he transformed what had hitherto appeared to be a conflict in a faraway place into a potential threat to the Russian heartland. This fear was confirmed by a series of mysterious blasts in Moscow and in the provincial towns of Buynaksk and Volgodonsk in the course of less than two weeks in September 1999 that killed 307 people and injured more than 1,700.

These explosions have been the subject of many a conspiracy theory: Basayev, who had proudly claimed responsibility for previous terrorist attacks on Russian soil, denied they were anything to do with him, prompting some to assert – albeit without firm evidence – that they had been the work of the security services, presumably on the orders of Putin.

Such suspicions grew after the discovery of three bags marked 'sugar' and a detonator in the basement of an apartment block in Ryazan, 120 miles south-east of Moscow. The device appeared to have been set to go off at five thirty the next morning. The contents of the bags were identified by a local explosives expert as hexogen, a military explosive of the same type as that used in one of the Moscow bombings. Amid growing panic in the town, the local police mounted a massive operation involving 1,200 officers. Two men who answered the description of those who had been seen lurking outside the building were arrested, but the pair turned out to be members of the FSB. The next day, the FSB director, Nikolai Patrushev, a close associate of Putin since his Leningrad days, claimed it had been a training exercise – albeit one that had been carried out without the knowledge of his local officers.

The strange goings-on in Ryazan were seized upon during the election campaign by Putin's opponents, who suspected foul play. Putin himself indignantly rejected such suggestions. 'No one in the Russian special services would be capable of such a crime against his own people,' he said. 'The very supposition is immoral. It's nothing but part of the information war against Russia.'[15]

Whatever the truth, there is no doubt as to the impact of the blasts on Russian public opinion. 'These explosions [in Moscow] were a crucial moment in the unfolding of our current history,' recalled Sergei Kovalev, a member of the Duma. 'After the first shock passed, it turned out that we were living in an entirely different country . . . How, it was asked, can you negotiate with people who murder children at night in their beds? War and only war is the solution! What we want – so went the rhetoric of many politicians, including Vladimir Putin – is the merciless extermination of the "adversary" wherever he may be, whatever the casualties, no matter how many unarmed civilians must die in the process.'[16]

Putin's actions lived up to his fighting words. The first Chechen war had been a national humiliation that merely postponed the question of the republic's independence. By tying his own fate so closely to a second conflict, Putin was taking a considerable political gamble. Taking personal charge of the crisis, he unleashed a ferocious bombing campaign against Chechnya that killed thousands of civilians and added to a mass flow of refugees into neighbouring Ingushetia. Then, in early October, Russian forces began an all-out ground assault.

The extent and brutality of the response was enormous; Chechnya was, after all, part of Russia. It was as if the British government had launched air strikes against Belfast at the height of the Troubles in Northern Ireland. Putin pressed on, however, coupling the military response with high-profile media appearances designed to hone his macho image. Most striking were the comments he made the day after the mysterious explosives find in Ryazan, when he resorted to prison slang to underline his determination to strike hard at his Chechen foes. 'We will pursue the terrorists everywhere. If it is in the airport, then in the airport,' he declared. 'You will forgive me, but if we catch them in the toilet, we will rub them out in the outhouse.'

A decade later, Putin claimed to have regretted his words, saying, 'I should not have been wagging my tongue like that.' Yet his earthy tone went down well with the Russian public, as did a trip he took the following month to Chechnya, the last stretch of which he spent aboard a Sukhoi-25 jet. During his brief visit he handed out medals to pilots at an airbase and met village elders in Znamenskoye, a Chechen village 'liberated' by the Russians. The aim of the military campaign, he said, was to rid Chechnya 'of those bandits who are not only up to their elbows but up to their shoulders in blood'.[17] Such words helped reinforce Putin's image as a man of action. 'After that appearance, people noticed him and it became clear that there was something to him,' says Oslon.[18]

According to Oslon's analysis, however, Putin's real success came in dealing with another more prosaic issue: the state's failure to pay pensions. Pensioners were one of the groups hardest hit by the collapse of the old communist system. Pensions were small and often not paid at all; the result was suffering not just for the elderly but often for their extended families, with whom they shared the money. Payment was handled by the increasingly independent-minded regional governors, many of whom had other priorities. That October, Putin ordered the governors to pay up. It was a sign of his growing influence that they did as they were told.

Observing the contest from the other side of the world, Talbott began to appreciate that Yeltsin's judgement was not so flawed, after all. It was not just that the war in Chechnya was going in Putin's favour. There was something more fundamental at work, namely the future president's difference from the man he was to replace: while Yeltsin's ill health made him seem older than his sixty-eight years, Putin was a forty-seven-year-old who made great play of his vigour and athletic prowess, whether playing judo or ice hockey. He also let it be known that, unlike Yeltsin, he drank little. While Yeltsin behaved like a Tsar, Putin seemed more like a manager who could make the system work.

Putin's ratings, by then, had jumped to forty per cent. Oslon watched as his support – which had initially been largely confined to the poorest, the uneducated and rural voters – spread to the more affluent. By December, Moscow and the intelligentsia were swinging behind him as well. Yeltsin, hedging his bets to the last, was finally ready to take the plunge: rather than serve out the remaining few months of his term, he would step down early in favour of his protégé. On 14 December, he summoned Putin to Gorky 9 for a secret meeting.

According to Yeltsin's own account, Putin was less than enthusiastic when Yeltsin told him of his plan. 'I'm not ready for that decision, Boris Nikolayevich,' he told him.[19]

Putin's reaction made Yeltsin's heart sink, but he persisted. 'I want to step down this year, Vladimir Vladimirovich,' he continued. 'This year. That's very important. The new century must begin with a new political era, the era of Putin.'

Putin was still not convinced, but Yeltsin's mind was made up. Any remaining doubts he had would have been dispelled by the results of parliamentary elections held five days later on 19 December. In September the Kremlin had set up a new party, Unity, largely to counter the threat from Primakov and Luzhkov's Fatherland–All Russia alliance. Despite blanket coverage from the state media and generous donations from oligarchs, the party got off to a poor start, barely registering in the polls. Then on 24 November, Putin's one-hundredth day in office, he gave it his endorsement: it would be inappropriate for him as prime minister to back any party, he said, but as an 'ordinary voter' he would support Unity at the ballot box. It seemed a risky move, but it paid off:

when the election results came in, Unity took twenty-three per cent of the votes, one point fewer than the communists, but way ahead of the Luzhkov–Primakov alliance, which won just thirteen per cent.

Yeltsin felt vindicated by the trust he had placed in his protégé. Putin, too, finally seemed to be relishing the prospect of his own new role, as Talbott noted when he called on the leader-in-waiting in his vast office in the White House, the seat of the Russian government, three days after the election. 'There was an aura of power settling around him,' Talbott recalled. 'I could see it in the deference of the other Russians in the room, in the frenzied interest of the press and in the cockiness of the man himself.'[20]

Yeltsin, too, noticed the change in Putin when he summoned him back again a fortnight after their initial meeting to discuss the details of the handover of power. 'I immediately had the impression that he was a different man,' he recalled. 'I suppose he seemed more decisive. I was satisfied. I liked his demeanour.'[21]

They worked through the various details of how everything was to unfold over the next few days, with Putin making various changes. Then it was all over. 'There was a lot I wanted to tell him,' Yeltsin recalled, 'I think he had a lot to say to me, too. But we didn't say anything. We shook each other's hand. We hugged good-bye. Our next meeting was to be on December 31, 1999.'[22]

Putin did not betray the trust Yeltsin had placed in him. Hours after taking over on New Year's Eve, he signed his first decree: seven pages long, and prepared by Yeltsin's aides, it granted the former president a series of benefits and privileges, including a salary, staff and use of the dacha at Gorky 9. Most importantly, it gave Yeltsin a guarantee of immunity from prosecution over his involvement in any of the murky deeds, such as the loans for shares scheme, that had taken place during his time in office.

Yeltsin would later boast that he had manoeuvred Putin from obscurity into the presidency over fierce resistance. 'It was really very hard, getting Putin into the job,' his daughter Tatyana admitted. 'One of the hardest things we ever pulled off.'[23]

PUTIN WAS STILL ONLY ACTING PRESIDENT; one of his first tasks was to win a popular mandate to perform the job that Yeltsin had gifted him. The election was set for 26 March 2000 and the result a foregone conclusion. By the end of December 1999, Putin's approval rating had jumped to 47%; a month later, it had reached an astonishing 57%. Although it subsequently dropped back, Putin won 53.4% of the vote, sufficient to give him victory without even having to go to a run-off. Gennady Zyuganov, the communist leader whom Yeltsin had beaten in 1996, trailed on 29.5%.

Putin made it clear that his aim was to rebuild the machinery of state power and create an orderly society. The goal was the establishment of what the Russians call a 'vertical of power' that put the president firmly in charge of the federal government and the government in charge of everything else. It also meant reining in the competing sources of power that had got out of hand under Yeltsin: the regional leaders, the oligarchs and the independent media.

Yet the watchword of the first few years of Putin's rule was also continuity. He was still surrounded by most of Yeltsin's aides, including Aleksandr Voloshin as chief of staff, and he paid frequent visits to his predecessor at his dacha. 'At that time, all of us – me, Voloshin and all the other people – believed he wanted to continue Yeltsin's vision of building a Democratic Russia, a fair market economy and so on,' said Mikhail Kasyanov, who was Putin's first prime minister but later became one of his fiercest critics.[24] 'We all supported Putin at that time. And in fact Putin, to be fair, implemented his promises given to me in terms of supporting economic reform.'

First to feel the effects of Putin's attempt to create his 'vertical of power' were the oligarchs, many of whom had backed him in the expectation that he would be their puppet. Instead, after winning the presidential election, Putin vowed to 'rid Russia of the oligarchs as a class'. In a warning shot that June the media mogul Vladimir Gusinsky was thrown into jail for three days on corruption charges. The charges were dropped, but not before the heavily indebted oligarch agreed to transfer Media-Most, his media conglomerate, to Gazprom for $300 million. He later claimed to have done the deal only under duress.

Putin's real coup de théâtre came on 28 July, however, when he summoned leading oligarchs to a gilded hall in the Kremlin and effectively offered them a bargain: they could keep the vast wealth that they had accumulated through the privatisations and other dubious deals of the 1990s, but only on condition that they stayed out of politics. They had little choice but to fall into line: the government had piles of *kompromat* ('compromising material') that it could use against them.

When it came to foreign policy, Putin saw it as his 'mission' to improve Russia's ties with America. 'Russia under Yeltsin had not formulated its interests and, in any case, in the 1990s we had so many domestic problems that we did not have time to think about issues such as NATO enlargement,' recalled Voloshin.[25] 'Millions of people were unemployed, millions of people could not receive their pensions, people did not know how to get medical attention for their mothers or feed their children.

'Putin believed relations with the West could and should be improved so that we could be partners. He considered the problem was that they did not understand us or the difficulties that we were facing: we needed to explain our situation, discuss it with them and they would help us and it would lead to a different relationship.'

The first prominent Western figure to meet Putin after he came to power was Lord Robertson, the former British defence secretary, who in October 1999 had taken over as secretary general of NATO. While attending the Organisation for Security and Co-operation in Europe (OSCE) summit in Istanbul the following month, he received a message saying that Igor Ivanov, the Russian foreign minister, wanted to meet. 'We chatted and talked, hoping we could get things moving, but that was about it,' Robertson recalls.[26] 'Then in February 2000 I got a phone call from Igor Ivanov to say, "If you were to make a request to come to Moscow, you might get a favourable response".' Although surprised by the odd form of words, Robertson seized the opportunity, and the invitation duly appeared.

Later that month, Robertson flew to Moscow – courtesy of the German air force. He was surrounded by television cameras as he gave an impromptu late-night news conference at the airport in his fur hat. Visible behind him on the fuselage of the plane was the word 'Luftwaffe'.

Robertson was received in the Kremlin. Flanked by Ivanov and Marshal Igor Sergeyev, the defence minister, Putin told him he wanted a step-by-step resumption of relations with NATO. 'He said he believed that Russia should be part of Western Europe, that it was Russia's destiny and he wanted to work towards that, even though not everyone agreed with him,' says Robertson. 'The legacy of Kosovo was still there but he thought it was a distraction. We would work together and cooperate. The atmosphere clearly changed.'

Robertson was also struck by his host's manner. 'The word "shy" is maybe not appropriate for a former KGB colonel but he was slightly unsure of himself,' he recalls. 'His head was down, but he was making it clear that he was the boss and that he knew what he wanted to do, and building relationships was part of that. I could see the EU was a mystery to him, but at the same time he recognised that Western Europe was stable and prosperous and maybe for once Russia had predictable and safe western boundaries.

'At the end of the meeting, he joked that maybe I should come in a British plane the next time. He was smiling as he said it. There were flashes of humour.'

It was Tony Blair, Robertson's former boss, who championed Putin's entry onto the world stage. Blair had found Yelstin 'very weird' and 'unpredictable'. In his memoirs he described a bear hug from the Russian leader that left him gasping for breath and in need of a stiff drink. Putin seemed refreshingly normal and modern in comparison. Blair's chief of staff, Jonathan Powell, and John Sawers, his foreign affairs advisor, suggested the prime minister steal a march on the rest of Europe by being the first to establish a relationship with him.

In March Blair set off to meet Putin in St Petersburg, even though the election in which he was to be confirmed as president was still two weeks away. Putin was delighted by the boost the visit gave his campaign. They held talks at Peterhof, the 'Russian Versailles' built by Peter the Great outside the city. On the way there, Putin pointed out to Blair the shabby block of flats where he grew up. He also gave him a personal tour of the Hermitage. That evening they and their wives saw Prokofiev's opera *War and Peace* at the Mariinsky Theatre. The only sour moment came when Sir Roderic Lyne, the British ambassador, leant back too heavily on one of the antique eighteenth-century chairs in the Peterhof and broke its back. As Powell recalled, "Putin demanded compensation, only half jokingly".[28]

Blair was an appropriate partner for Putin's international debut: the two men were both young, dynamic lawyers. Putin seemed to consider him something of a role model. Their meeting also had a historical resonance: after all, it was Mikhail Gorbachev's 1984 encounter with Margaret Thatcher – and her comment afterwards: 'I like Mr Gorbachev. We can do business together' – that had helped established the future Soviet leader's reputation abroad.

The following month, Putin – now elected but still not yet inaugurated

– travelled to Britain for his first foreign trip as president, which included tea with the Queen at Buckingham Palace. At a joint press conference, Blair praised Putin as a leader 'ready to embrace a new relationship with the European Union and the United States, who wants a strong and modern Russia and a strong relationship with the West'. Challenged over Chechnya, Blair said he had discussed the issue, but made it clear he would not let it hinder relations. The two leaders were to meet five times over that year, including once in Moscow in November, when they went out for beers in a fake German Bierkeller and Blair said of his host: "He is someone who wants to do the right thing by himself and the world."

Putin's first months in the Kremlin also saw an improvement in relations with America. On 14 April, less than three weeks after his election as president, the Duma ratified the START II treaty, the most comprehensive arms control agreement to be concluded between the two states. Already ratified by the US Senate in 1996, it required both countries roughly to halve their respective nuclear arsenals by 2007, restricting each to no more than 3,500 nuclear warheads. A week later, the Duma ratified the Comprehensive Test Ban Treaty.

It was also announced that Clinton would meet Putin for what would be the two presidents' first and last summit. It was set for Moscow in June. Clinton had already met Putin twice the previous year when he was still Yeltsin's prime minister and nominated successor: first in September at the APEC summit in Auckland and then in November in Oslo at a tribute to Yitzhak Rabin, the late Israeli prime minister. Clinton was impressed by what he saw, contrasting Putin – measured and precise, compact and extremely fit from his years of practising martial arts – with the large, stocky and voluble Yeltsin.

'Putin has enormous potential, I think,' he told Blair in a telephone conversation. 'He's very smart and thoughtful. I think we can do a lot of good with him.'[29]

Clinton had only a few months left in the White House, but set off to Moscow with a number of goals: reaching agreement on allowing America to deploy a national missile defence system, bringing an end to Russian military assistance to Iran and attempting to coordinate Russian and Western diplomacy in the Balkans. He was also under pressure to draw attention to Russian backtracking on human rights.

Missile defence was probably the most contentious. It was almost two decades earlier, in March 1983, that President Ronald Reagan had unveiled his Strategic Defense Initiative, an ambitious network of ground-based and orbital anti-missile defences intended to protect the United States from a strategic nuclear strike. It quickly became nick-named the 'Star Wars' project after George Lucas' film franchise. What worked in the movies did not necessarily work in reality, however, and it soon became clear that it would need years, perhaps decades of more work to create such a global shield.

Reagan's enthusiasm for the project had been prompted by his dislike of the doctrine of Mutual Assured Destruction (MAD) which he likened to a stand-off in the Wild West with 'two westerners standing in a saloon aiming their guns to each other's head – permanently'.[30] Reagan wanted America instead to develop a shield that such weapons would be unable to penetrate, thereby rendering them obsolete. He even, optimistically in hindsight, envisaged that such a system could be built in conjunction with the Russians.

Yuri Andropov, the then Soviet leader, had been suspicious: he feared it would make it possible for America to carry out a first strike against Soviet missiles, confident that the shield would deal with retaliation from the remnants of Moscow's forces. The Strategic Defense Initiative, they claimed, was also inconsistent with America's obligations under the 1972 Anti-Ballistic Missile Treaty, which restricted both countries to two sites at which they could base a defensive system, one for the capital and one for intercontinental ballistic missile silos.

Clinton had arrived in office sceptical about missile defence, but, as the Republicans used the issue against him, he responded by bolstering spending on research. Since the end of the Cold War, the justification for the system had been changed: initially intended to protect America against a deliberate Soviet missile strike, it was now meant to stop missiles fired accidentally by Russia – or China – or intentionally by rogue states such as Iraq or North Korea. This did not make it any more palatable to the Kremlin.

At the summit, however, little progress was made on nuclear issues. He and Putin pledged to destroy another thirty-four metric tons each of weapons-grade plutonium, but they could not reach agreement on amending the ballistic missile treaty to allow American deployment of the missile shield. Clinton was not overly concerned; he doubted the system would actually work and feared that, even if it didn't, it would encourage other countries to build more missiles to maintain their deterrent capacity. He also understood that, with a new US president about to be elected, Putin would prefer to wait before committing himself.

Also hanging over the summit was the matter of NATO enlargement. Despite the Alliance's relentless march eastward, the Russians clung to the idea that the organisation could be transformed from a purely military one into something far more political in nature – one that might even include Russia as a member. In an interview with the BBC's David Frost, screened on 5 March, a few weeks before his election, Putin reiterated Yeltsin's concern about NATO's eastern expansion but said he was prepared to discuss 'more profound' integration with the Alliance, provided Russia was regarded as an equal partner. Asked if Russia could ever join NATO, he replied: 'I don't see why not. I would not rule out such a possibility.'*

Indeed, Putin seemed to have warmed to the idea. According to Voloshin, there had been a number of discussions in the Kremlin about the possibility of NATO membership, though only provided it shifted away from its old Cold War focus to concentrate on terrorism, piracy and other contemporary issues. Putin suddenly brought up the idea at the summit during a meeting at which Clinton was joined by Sandy Berger, his national security adviser, and Madeleine Albright, the secretary of state. During what Voloshin described as a 'semi-philosophical' discussion, Putin asked: 'How would you react if Russia joined NATO?'

'Clinton was a bit surprised,' recalled Voloshin. 'He looked at Albright who was next to him and she pretended that she was looking at a fly on the wall. Then Clinton looked at Berger, who did not react at all. Clinton realised that his advisers would not help him so he answered: "As far as I am concerned, personally" – and he repeated "personally" three times – "then I would support it".'[31]

At the summit, Clinton seemed to have missed the bonhomie that had characterised his many meetings with Yeltsin, though Putin tried to re-create the atmosphere, even trying out his English, in which he

---

* The idea was not an entirely new one: in March 1954, twelve months after Stalin's death, the Soviet Union sent a note to America, France and Britain saying it would be prepared to join NATO under certain conditions. 'To put it very bluntly, the Soviet request to join NATO is like an unrepentant burglar requesting to join the police force,' retorted Lord Ismay, the Alliance's secretary general. His memo can be read at http://www.nato.int/

had been taking lessons. After the formal talks, the two men repaired to a wood-panelled theatre for a jazz tribute to Louis Armstrong conducted by Oleg Lundsrem, one of Russia's best-known bandleaders. Although the meeting was cordial, it lacked the first-name familiarity of previous Clinton–Yeltsin summits.

The lack of progress was predictable given the disconnect between the American and Russian electoral calendars: Putin, fresh from his election triumph, was on the way up, and Clinton, well into the eighth and final year of his presidency, was on the way out. 'Clinton felt patronised,' wrote Talbott, who accompanied him. 'Putin had given Clinton what was calculated to seem a respectful hearing, but Clinton knew a brush-off when he saw one . . . Putin had, in his own studied, cordial and oblique way, put US–Russian relations on hold until Clinton, like Putin's predecessor, Boris Yeltsin, had passed from the scene.'[32]

After the meeting, Clinton drove north-west out of Moscow through what Talbott described as 'the capital's high-rent exurbia, where modern redbrick cottages had sprouted amid leftovers of the old power structure – sprawling VIP dachas, rest homes and clinics behind stucco walls or high green wooden fences'.[33] They slowed to travel down a narrow potholed road and arrived at Gorky 9.

Yeltsin, his wife, Naina, and their daughter, Tatyana, were waiting at the door of the dacha. Yeltsin embraced Clinton for a full minute, repeating in a low voice, '*moi drug, moi drug* [my friend, my friend]', before leading him by the arm into the living room. The scene that followed, as Talbott described it, was a remarkable tribute to the closeness of the personal relationship that had – for better or for worse – set the tone of US–Russia relations for much of the previous decade.

As the two men sat in gilt oval-backed chairs next to a traditional Russian sky-blue stove, drinking tea and eating a rich, many-layered cake that Naina had been up half the night baking, Yeltsin eschewed the small talk Clinton had expected and instead delivered a message from Putin: his successor had just called him and asked him to make clear to Clinton that Russia would continue to pursue its interests as it saw them and resist pressure to acquiesce in any US policies it considered a threat to its security.

For Clinton, the sight of Yeltsin, his face stern, posture tense and fists clenched, was one familiar to him from the many meetings they had held over the previous eight years. As Talbott put it, Clinton 'took the browbeating patiently, even good-naturedly'. He knew that 'a session with Yeltsin almost always involved some roughing up before the two of them could get down to real business'.[34] Yeltsin followed by singing Putin's praises as 'a young man and a strong man', as if these were the essence both of what Russia needed and what he, by selecting Putin, had hoped to preserve as his own legacy.

When Yeltsin had finished, it was Clinton's turn to speak his mind, albeit more gently: he wasn't sure, he told Yeltsin, how 'this new guy of yours' defined strength, either for himself or for the country. Clinton also expressed doubts about Putin's values, instincts and convictions. 'You've got the fire in your belly of a real democrat and a real reformer. I'm not sure Putin has that,' Clinton told him. 'You'll have to keep an eye on him and use your influence to make sure that he stays on the right path. Putin needs you . . . Russia needs you.'[35]

Clutching Clinton by the hand, Yeltsin leant into him, muttering: 'Thank you, Bill. I understand.'

Running late, they all went outside for a group photograph, followed by some hurried goodbyes and a bear hug. As they got into the car, Clinton fell silent and stared at the birch trees lining the road. Talbott found his mood more sombre than it had been on the way out. 'That may be the last time I see Ol' Boris,' Clinton said. 'I think we're going to miss him.'[36]

THE RUSSIANS, BY CONTRAST, WERE WARMING to their new leader. After the wild swings of the Yeltsin era, Putin brought political stability. The economy was also powering ahead, thanks to rising oil prices and the after-effects of the devaluation of the rouble. It was now growing at an annual rate of seven per cent, regaining ground lost in the previous decade. Consumer spending and investment were rising even faster. The government was also able to record post-Soviet Russia's first budget surplus. This was largely due to factors beyond Putin's control. Yet he also laid out an economic programme that won praise from Western governments and introduced a new flat tax of just 13 per cent. In pursuit of his 'vertical of power', he also began a major reorganisation of Russia's unruly regions, dividing the country into seven large new administrative areas and putting his own allies in charge of them. Underlying his efforts was an attempt to create a new state structure that melded freedom and order. Liberal critics feared that Putin, with his KGB background, would err too far towards the latter, but most ordinary Russians appeared to give him the benefit of the doubt.

The new regime nevertheless suffered one major setback when the *Kursk*, a nuclear-powered Oscar-class submarine, sank in August 2000 during a naval exercise in the Barents Sea, after a torpedo on board malfunctioned and exploded. All 118 personnel on board perished. The Russian response was the same mixture of denial, misinformation and eventual acknowledgement that had characterised the Chernobyl disaster fourteen years earlier. Putin himself was on holiday on the Black Sea and made no immediate move to return; instead he was filmed enjoying himself, shirtsleeves rolled up, hosting a barbecue. Russian media were scathing about the approach taken by the authorities: had pride prevented them from seeking Western help to save the submariners? Some of the harshest criticism was reserved for Putin himself. Why could he not find time to comfort the families of those who had lost loved ones?

Yet, despite what was widely acknowledged as a public relations disaster for the new president, his ratings did not particularly suffer, according to Oslon. Putin appeared to draw a different lesson from the *Kursk*, moving in the months that followed to tighten his control over the media. Just as he had gone for Gusinsky, now he took on another oligarch, Boris Berezovsky. Despite having helped bring Putin to power, Berezovksy had begun publicly to criticise him, and his ORT network had been especially condemnatory of his handling of the *Kursk* disaster. Berezovsky fought hard to hold onto ORT, but the following February bowed to pressure. He and his long-standing partner, Badri Patarkatsishvili, sold their stakes to Roman Abramovich, who promptly ceded editorial control to the Kremlin. That April, the government also took control of NTV from Gusinsky.

As part of Putin's reassertion of Russian statehood, he also made significant symbolic moves. That December, the Soviet-era national anthem, which had fallen into disuse, was revived, albeit with new words, in place of the little-loved piece by the composer Mikhail Glinka, which had been used by Russia during the 1990s. The Soviet red banner – without the hammer and sickle – was restored as the official flag of the armed forces. The white-blue-red flag and the double-headed eagle coat of arms, which had existed in a kind of limbo, were also given legal approval. Putin declared the restoration of the anthem to be part of a process of healing of Russia's past and fusing the Soviet period with Russian history – but the move brought a rare intervention from Yeltsin, who joined liberal critics in labelling it a mistake.

Putin, meanwhile, was continuing his diplomatic offensive. Less than a fortnight after hosting Clinton in Moscow, he went to Berlin for a summit with Gerhard Schröder – who was to become a firm ally – and in July attended his first G8 summit as president, in Japan, where he was the star of the gathering. He made pre-summit visits to North Korea and China and returned to Japan in September for a meeting with Yoshiro Mori, the Japanese leader. In October he went to see President Chirac in Paris.

The West was still willing to give Putin the benefit of the doubt. Blair and Clinton discussed their impressions of the Russian leader in a phone call on 23 November after Blair went to Moscow for a working visit. 'He feels that he is not understood about the problems he is facing there,' said Blair. 'He was very anxious to impress me. He wanted to see America as a partner, I think.'[37] Clinton was also optimistic on the basis of his contacts with Putin: 'I think he is a guy with a lot of ability and ambitions for the Russians. His intentions are generally honourable and straightforward, but he just hasn't made up his mind yet,' he said, before adding prophetically: 'He could get squishy on democracy.'

Putin himself, when asked by the Russian media about foreign policy during a long interview that December intended to sum up his first year in office, declared that his country had to find a middle way between the 'imperial ambitions' of the Soviet era and the need to 'understand clearly our own national interest[s] . . . to formulate them clearly and to fight for them.'[38]

Oslon, the pollster, asks Russians every December to look back on the year that is just ending, compare it with the previous one and with their expectations for the one that is to follow. For most years since the end of communism, their answers suggested that they saw things getting worse and worse. Asked the question in December 2000, however, a majority declared the year drawing to a close to have been better than 1999 and thought 2001 would be even better still. 'A remarkable change had taken place by the end of 2000,' said Oslon. 'During the course of the year the population became convinced that a new epoch was beginning. The epoch of chaos – "the sick decade" – had ended. The period of recovery had begun.'[39]

10

A SENSE OF PUTIN'S SOUL

IF US–RUSSIA RELATIONS IN THE 1990S were dominated by the personal relationship between Clinton and Yeltsin, then the decade that followed belonged to George W. Bush and Vladimir Putin. Bush had beaten Al Gore, the outgoing vice president, to the White House in one of the closest and most controversial presidential elections in modern times: the final outcome depended on Florida, where the vote was so close it went to a series of recounts. On 12 December 2000, more than a month after the poll, the US Supreme Court ruled five to four in Bush's favour.

The campaign was largely dominated by domestic issues, which suited Bush. His career, initially in the oil industry and then as governor of Texas, had given him little experience of foreign policy, save for the affairs of neighbouring Mexico. Campaigning early in the race in Boston in November 1999, he was ambushed by a local television reporter, who asked him to name the leaders of Chechnya, Taiwan, Pakistan and India; Bush managed the surname of just one – Taiwan's Lee Teng-hui.

Bush's team of supporters tried to laugh off the interview. 'The person who is running for president is seeking to be the leader of the free world, not a *Jeopardy* contestant,' retorted Karen Hughes, his communications director. Yet coming after other gaffes earlier in the campaign – during which Bush had confused Slovenia with Slovakia, described the inhabitants of Greece as 'Grecians' and of Kosovo as 'Kosovarians' – it confirmed the popular impression of him as someone who, in stark contrast to Gore, did not know enough about the world to become president.

Bush was undaunted. Conceiving the role of president as akin to that of chief executive officer of a giant corporation, he vowed to surround himself with experts on world affairs and other policy areas. His role, he believed, would be to set the broad goals and strategies of his administration, leaving it to experts to fill in the detail. 'Nobody needs to tell me what to believe, but I do need somebody to tell me where Kosovo is,' he said while campaigning.[1] For the latter he turned to Condoleezza Rice, a glamorous and high-powered African-American who had dazzled all those who crossed her path.

On the face of it, Rice was an unlikely expert on Russia. Aged forty-five, she had grown up in a segregated, middle-class neighbourhood in Birmingham, Alabama in the last days of Jim Crow. Her father, a high-school guidance counsellor and Presbyterian minister, and her mother, a high-school teacher, were ambitious for her: she began learning the piano at the age of three, was tutored in French and Spanish while at elementary school and enrolled at the University of Denver at just sixteen. Although she initially majored in music, she realised she would probably not be good enough to make it as a professional pianist and switched to political science. After graduating aged nineteen, she took a master's degree at Notre Dame and returned to Denver for her PhD on military policy and politics in Czechoslovakia. Her inspiration was the Dean of the Graduate School of International Studies, Josef Korbel, a Czech-born former diplomat (who was also the father of Madeleine Albright).

Rice went on to become associate professor of political science at Stanford, but her career changed direction in 1984 when she attended a dinner with Brent Scowcroft, then chair of President Ronald Reagan's Commission on Strategic Forces. She challenged the substance of his talk and, impressed by 'this little slip of a girl', Scowcroft decided 'that's someone I've got to get to know'.[2] They stayed in touch and she went to Washington on a fellowship for the Council on Foreign Relations. When Scowcroft became Bush Senior's national security adviser, he made Condi, as everyone called her, his adviser on Soviet and Eastern European affairs. Bush was said to have been 'captivated' by Rice, relying on her advice in his dealings with both Gorbachev and Yeltsin. Yet after just two years in the job she returned to Stanford, where, aged just thirty-nine, she rose to become not only the university's youngest provost, but also the first woman or African-American to hold the job.

The seeds for Rice's return to Washington were sown in August 1998 when Bush Senior invited her to his house in Kennebunkport. George W. was considering a run at the White House if he won re-election as Texas governor convincingly that November, and his father wanted him to meet Rice to talk about foreign policy. As she admitted in her memoirs, Rice did not much rate the younger Bush's chances, but was happy to talk to him. They kept in touch over the next few months, emailing back and forth about the conflict in the Balkans and NATO enlargement. After Bush won his landslide victory in the gubernatorial contest in Texas, he invited Rice to join the 'exploratory committee' for his presidency.

Rice took a one-year leave of absence from Stanford to become Bush's foreign policy adviser. She knew she would have her work cut out. 'Foreign policy would be the governor's Achilles heel against more seasoned candidates in the primaries and the general election,' she predicted.[3] 'I knew that George W. Bush would look to me to help answer the inevitable questions about his readiness to assume the mantle of commander-in-chief.' For his part, Bush was conscious of the important contribution Rice would make to his campaign. She 'can explain to me foreign policy matters in a way I can understand,' he told an interviewer during the campaign. She was 'both a good manager and an honest broker of ideas . . . a close confidante and a good soul'.[4]

Rice set out to assemble a small group of foreign policy specialists to develop policy for Bush. Her first call was to Paul Wolfowitz, who had been ambassador to Indonesia under Reagan and undersecretary for policy in the Pentagon in Bush Senior's administration. Other members of the team included Richard Armitage and Stephen Hadley, who had both worked for the previous Bush, and Richard Perle, assistant secretary of defence under Reagan. They nicknamed themselves the Vulcans in honour of Rice's hometown of Birmingham, Alabama, a steel city that has as its symbol the Roman god of fire. The team's aim was to help prepare the younger Bush for the potentially treacherous foreign policy issues that Gore already knew well.

Rice set out her ideas on US foreign policy in an article published at the beginning of 2000 in *Foreign Affairs*, 'Promoting the National Interest'. Rice argued that America had considerable power and should not be afraid of using it directly in its own interests rather than feeling it had to act through the United Nations and other multinational bodies. Rice was scathing about the Clinton administration's 'romantic' policy towards Russia. It was in America's interest to have a strong and stable Russia, particularly one that was democratic and prosperous, she said, but 'if we have learned anything in the last several years, it is that a romantic view of Russia, rather than a realistic one, did nothing to help the cause of stability in Russia.

'Pouring IMF funding into an unreformed and corrupt economy in fact weakened Russia and helped to lead to the 1998 crash,' she added. 'So realism with Russia is the best way to encourage a stable and prosperous Russia. We must support real economic reform, not pretend economic reform, and ultimately Russia has enough resources including a highly educated population to be able to create conditions to attract private investment, but the hard work of creating a fair tax code and rooting out corruption really is up to the Russians. They understand this and I think resent the United States for having failed to speak up when economic reform was not taking place.'[5]

This argument was the perfect stick with which to beat Gore, whose membership of a joint commission with Viktor Chernomyrdin, the former prime minister, appeared to embody everything that was wrong with Democratic policies. Gore was a specific target of a polemical attack on the outgoing administration's policy, 'Russia's Road to Corruption: How the Clinton Administration Exported Government Instead of Free Enterprise and Failed the Russian People', published by congressional Republicans in September 2000. The West's victory in the Cold War 'presented America with its greatest foreign policy opportunity since the end of World War II', the report argued, and the US–Russia relationship that Clinton inherited 'could only have been dreamed of by his predecessors from Truman to Reagan'. Yet Clinton had failed to take charge of Russian policy, the report claimed, delegating it instead to Gore, Talbott and Summers, who had concentrated on bolstering the Russian government and did not do enough to encourage the country's transformation into a free and democratic society.

Gore, in particular, the report argued, was guilty of turning a blind eye towards the corrupt practices of Chernomyrdin, citing his personal friendship with the Russian prime minister. When CIA officials dispatched to the White House a secret report based on a large dossier from the agency claiming Chernomyrdin had accumulated billions of dollars while in office, it had been sent back by Gore to the agency marked 'Bullshit'.

All was not lost, though: the US–Russia relationship was of 'continued central importance in US foreign policy' and should be put on track through a combination of policies that included engaging Russians across the political spectrum, giving priority to private rather than government solutions, promoting the country's integration into the world economy but also forthrightly defending American interests by pushing ahead with national missile defence and the expansion of NATO. The future president and his secretary of state should take charge of policy towards Russia themselves rather than delegating it to subordinates.

These ideas came to constitute Bush's worldview, which he outlined on the campaign trail and implemented as soon as he came to office. At its broadest level, according to one analysis of his presidency, it came down to two beliefs: the first was the need for America to act unilaterally and in its own interests, 'shed[ding] the constraints imposed by friends, allies, and international institutions'. The second was that it should use its strength to change the status quo and act proactively against potential threats rather than simply react to events.[6] One commentator, writing in May 2001, described the Bush administration's policy as 'aggressive unilateralism' – a belief that the US 'should be more willing than in the past to do what is in its national interest, even when it knows that others will be unhappy, believing they will follow along over time'.[7]

Such policies did not preclude the development of a good working relationship with Russia. On the contrary: Thomas Graham, one of Bush's advisers on the country, believes the new president came to power determined to make a success of his relations with the Kremlin, even if he was hazy on the details. 'I don't think he had a lot of well-formed ideas about Russia beforehand,' says Graham. 'And I don't think he came to office with any major plan about how he was going to deal with it other than that this is a significant relationship that had soured at the end of the Clinton administration and that there were certain things you needed to do with Russia if you wanted to press forward on some of the other things that were important to the administration.'[8]

Yet for all the talk, the new administration sent out signals of its intention to treat Russia as a mid-ranking country rather than a super-power. It took Washington until July to appoint a new ambassador and the man they chose, Alexander Vershbow, the US envoy to NATO, had clashed with Russia over the Alliance's eastward expansion and its involvement in the Balkans. He had also been a consistent advocate of plans to put up an anti-missile shield over America. Russia also lost its special treatment within the state department bureaucracy: under Clinton, the former Soviet states had been handled by an Office of the Newly Independent States (S/NIS). They were now folded into the far larger Bureau of European and Eurasian Affairs. The much-derided Gore–Chernomyrdin Bilateral Commission was abolished.[9]

These moves coincided with increasingly tough rhetoric. In December 2000, before the new administration had started work, Rice had said: 'It would be foolish in the extreme to share defences with Moscow if it either leaks or deliberately transfers weapons technologies to the very states against which America is defending.' She followed that in February 2001 by declaring in an interview with *Le Figaro*: 'I believe Russia is a threat to the West in general and to our European allies in particular.'[10]

LESS THAN A MONTH INTO THE new administration, relations between Washington and Moscow were hit by a Cold War-style diplomatic spat over spying. On 18 February Robert Hanssen, a senior FBI agent who worked as a counter-intelligence supervisor at the agency's headquarters, was arrested and accused of passing highly classified information to the Russians. It later transpired that he had been doing so for twenty-two years in return for a total of $1.4 million, much of it paid in stacks of hundred-dollar bills left in plastic rubbish bags at clandestine drop-off spots in suburban Virginia. Caught in Foxstone Park, Fairfax County, after his last dead drop, Hanssen reportedly asked FBI agents: 'What took you so long?'

It was no surprise that the end of the Cold War had not brought an end to Russian spying on America. For their part, the Americans, of course, continued to spy on the Russians. Yet the scale of Hanssen's activities was especially humiliating, and his unmasking came after years of frustration within the FBI about a revival in the Russian intelligence presence in America, which was estimated to have gone back up close to Cold War levels.

The new administration was faced with a choice of how to respond.

When Aldrich Ames, the last high-profile American double agent, had been caught in 1994, Clinton had kept retaliatory measures to a minimum. This time it was different. The incoming administration appeared determined to make a point and ordered the departure of more than fifty Russian diplomats in the largest diplomatic expulsion since 1986. Moscow sent home the same number of Americans.

Donald Rumsfeld, Bush's defence secretary, accused Moscow of extensive involvement in spreading weapons to dangerous nations; his deputy, Paul Wolfowitz, said the Russians 'seem to be willing to sell anything to anyone for money'.[11] As if to confirm their concerns, Putin welcomed Mohammad Khatami, the Iranian president, to Russia in March 2001 to discuss arms sales and reiterated Russia's intention to help complete the country's long-stalled Bushehr nuclear power plant. He also stepped up military and political cooperation with China.

Another cause of tension with Russia was Bush's avowed aim to build a national missile defence system. During his election campaign, he had argued that it was imperative for America to develop such a system to protect itself not so much against Russia as against threats from rogue states. There were clear implications, however, for the Anti-Ballistic Missile Treaty. The Clinton administration had believed it might be possible to find a way of reconciling the two. By contrast Bush and his advisers rejected the treaty, signed by Nixon and Brezhnev in 1972, as a relic of the Cold War, based on a balance of terror that no longer existed. Furthermore, they argued the treaty's rigidity prevented either side from taking advantage of new technologies and, amid the proliferation of weapons of mass destruction, made them unable to respond to new threats.

In a major address to the National Defence University on 1 May, Bush set out his position. 'This treaty does not recognise the present, or point us to the future,' he said. 'It enshrines the past. No treaty that prevents us from addressing today's threats, that prohibits us from pursuing promising technology to defend ourselves, our friends and our allies is in our interests or in the interests of world peace.' America and Russia, he argued, should instead work 'to create a new framework for security and stability' that 'reflects a clear and clean break from the past, and especially from the adversarial legacy of the Cold War'. Perhaps, he added, 'one day, we can even cooperate in a joint defense'.[12]

Bush's first meeting with Putin was set for the following month at

Brdo Castle, a sixteenth-century villa outside the Slovenian capital, Ljubljana. Before leaving Washington, he had been briefed by a small group of Russia and Europe experts on what to expect. The summit was the culmination of a European tour that took Bush first to Spain and then on to Belgium, where he attended the NATO summit. While he was there he took the opportunity to ask Robertson for his impressions of Putin.

'I think you'll get on well,' Robertson told him.[13] 'Both of you came to politics late in life; both of you came from a distance from the capital city. You both had narrow majorities; both of you are running huge countries and both of you have high expectations riding on what you're going to do and both of you are unlikely to accept advice that says: "We always do it this way, Mr President." Finally,' Robertson added with a smile, 'a bit like myself, both of you seem to wonder how the hell you got there.'

Then it was on to Sweden and to Poland, where Bush surprised his audience by declaring that the 'new democracies, from the Baltic to the Black Sea and all that lie between' should have the same chance to 'join the institutions of Europe' – opening the way to a second wave of NATO enlargement that would extend the Alliance onto the territory of the former Soviet Union. Such a move was certain to be anathema to the Kremlin.

Bush was nevertheless determined to make the most of his encounter with Putin and to move on from the difficult first months of his presidency. 'When we come out of this meeting, what do we want to have accomplished?' he asked aides gathered in the conference room of Air Force One before launching a lengthy discussion of the issues he wanted to raise. Karen Hughes, a veteran Bush aide who had become his counsellor, remembers a sense of great anticipation. 'Even now, it's still *the* moment when the president of the United States meets the president of Russia for the first time,' Rice told her.[14]

As Bush and Putin sat together in the beautifully restored palace, with its formal gold drapes and huge flat glass prisms covering almost the entire ceiling, the two leaders seemed eager to try to defuse the tensions. Accompanied initially by a quorum of national security advisers and interpreters, they turned to the intelligence briefings that had been prepared by their respective security services. To Hughes' surprise, Putin noted that Bush had played rugby while at college. 'I did play rugby,' the American president replied. 'Very good briefing.'

Then it was Bush's turn. As Putin, looking tense and reading from a series of note cards, launched into the first item on his presentation, namely the debt that Russia had inherited from the Soviet Union, Bush interrupted him to ask: 'Is it true your mother gave you a cross that you had blessed in Jerusalem?'[15] A look of shock came over Putin's face as the interpreter delivered the line in Russian; but he recovered quickly as he recounted the story: his face and voice softening, he described how he had hung the cross in his dacha, which had subsequently caught fire. When the firefighters arrived, he told them that it was all he cared about. Bush was struck by how Putin dramatically re-created the moment when the firefighter unfolded his hand to reveal the cross. It was, Putin said, 'as if it was meant to be'.

'Vladimir,' Bush replied. 'That is the story of the cross. Things are meant to be.' At that moment Bush recalled feeling the tension draining from the room and noted the emotion in Putin's voice.

The two leaders looked much more relaxed as they emerged, laughing and talking easily with one another, Hughes recalled. In a later meeting in a bigger room, where the American delegation sat across a large glass table from their Russian counterparts, Putin spoke a lot about trade and investment and how he wanted the secretary of commerce to bring a delegation of American business leaders and investors to Russia.

At a joint press conference afterwards, Bush described their meetings as an important step towards building a constructive, respectful relationship between America and Russia. 'More than a decade after the Cold War ended, it is time to move beyond suspicion and toward straight talk, beyond mutually assured destruction and toward mutually earned respect,' he said, before adding of Putin: 'The president is a history major, and so am I. And we remember the old history. It's time to write new history in a positive and constructive way.'[16] In reality, however, their meeting had done little to resolve the fundamental divisions between the two countries, especially over the fraught issues of missile defence and NATO enlargement. Asked about the planned expansion of the Alliance, Putin replied: 'Look, this is a military organisation. It's moving toward our border. Why?'

The warmth between the two men nevertheless appeared to point to a new relationship. Unlike Clinton, Bush did not take Putin to task over the war in Chechnya or his attempts to curb freedom of speech.

Clinton had been focused on efforts to push Russia towards a liberal free market economy; with Bush it was different. 'It was clear that we would like to see democratic reforms, movement on opening up the economy, all those things, but the relationship was not presented that way,' says Graham. 'I heard more than once that the president did not want to hector the Russians.'[17]

The most memorable moment came when a journalist asked Bush if he trusted Putin. Seated in the audience, Condoleezza Rice began to panic. This was the one question for which they had not prepared the president, and it was fraught with pitfalls. Bush did not hesitate to answer. 'I looked the man in the eye. I found him to be very straight-forward and trustworthy. We had a very good dialogue,' he replied. 'I was able to get a sense of his soul: a man deeply committed to his country and the best interests of his country.' To emphasise the success of the meeting, Bush said he had asked Putin to visit him in Crawford, Texas, a privilege yet to be extended to many allied leaders. 'I wouldn't have invited him to my ranch if I didn't trust him,' he joked.

For Bush the meeting was the high point of his trip to Europe. 'I just feel that this is the start of something really historic,' he told Rice during the flight home.[18] But Bush's critics found it difficult to recon-cile the warm words that the two men had for each other with their policy differences. There was also concern that Bush may have sent the wrong signal to the hard-line political elites surrounding Putin by indicating that the United States was more interested in missile defence than human rights, press freedom and the sacking of Chechnya.

'I can understand the strategy on rapport, but it went too far,' said Michael McFaul, a senior fellow at the Carnegie Endowment for International Peace, who was among those who briefed Bush before his trip. 'I think there is plenty of good reason not to trust President Putin. This is a man who was trained to lie.'[19]

In the years to come, Bush's claim to have been able to see into Putin's soul was to come back to haunt him. 'It was an awkward way to get out of the predicament,' Rice recalled a decade later. 'We were never able to escape the perception that the president had naively trusted Putin and then been betrayed.'[20]

11

FROM 9/11 TO IRAQ

IT WAS 4:46P.M. ON 11 SEPTEMBER 2001 in Moscow when Mohamed Atta flew American Airlines Flight 11 into the North Tower of the World Trade Center in New York. In the hours that followed almost three thousand people were killed or fatally injured. It was the most serious terrorist attack in American history. It also marked the start of a new era in international relations. A decade after the collapse of its old foe, the Soviet Union, America had a new enemy: Islamic terrorism.

Vladimir Putin had spent the afternoon in the Kremlin meeting a group of forty-eight Russian journalists and handing out various state honours. In comments broadcast on state television he singled out special praise for those who had reported from Chechnya. The ceremony had just ended when his security summoned him to a conference room, where they were watching television reports of the attacks, which were still unfolding.

'What can we do to help them now?' Putin asked Sergei Ivanov, his defence minister and close friend from St Petersburg. 'What do they need?'[1] Ivanov pointed out that the previous day the Russian military had begun exercises in the northern Pacific in which they simulated a Cold War-style nuclear conflict with America. Putin ordered him to call off the exercises: the Americans already had problems enough to cope with.

At the time Flight 11 hit the tower, Bush had been on his way to the

Emma E. Booker Elementary School in Sarasota, Florida to highlight education reform. He pressed ahead with the event, reading a children's story, 'The Pet Goat', to a class of second-graders, even as Andrew Card, his chief of staff, whispered to him that a second plane, later identified as United Airlines 175, had struck the South Tower. Storming out would 'scare the children and send ripples of panic throughout the country', Bush claimed later. He intended instead to 'project calm'.

Afterwards he went swiftly to the school auditorium, where the audience had come expecting to hear a speech about education. 'Ladies and gentlemen, this is a difficult moment for America', Bush told them. 'Two airplanes have crashed into the World Trade Center in an apparent terrorist attack on our country.'

Bush then rushed to the airport and to Air Force One, which climbed to 45,000ft, well above its usual cruising altitude. Bush called Dick Cheney, his vice president, who was in PEOC, the President's Emergency Operations Center, an underground bunker beneath the East Wing of the White House, built for President Franklin D. Roosevelt and strong enough to survive a nuclear strike. 'We're at war,' Bush told him.

The president wanted to fly straight back to Washington as soon as possible, but, with reports of other hijacked planes and fears of an attack on the White House, he reluctantly allowed himself to be persuaded by aides to keep away from the capital. Instead, he flew first to Barksdale Air Force Base in Shreveport, Louisiana, home to the Eighth Air Force, where he recorded a short televised message vowing to 'hunt down and punish those responsible for these cowardly acts'. Then it was on to Offutt Air Force Base in Bellevue, Nebraska, home to Strategic Air Command, where the communications were better and Bush could convene a video conference with the National Security Council. 'We are at war against terror,' he told them. 'From this day forward, this is the new priority of our administration.' With all civilian air traffic now grounded and the chances of further attacks limited, it was deemed safe for Bush to return to Washington. He touched down at Andrews Air Force Base at 6:44P.M. and boarded Marine One bound for the White House. The helicopter flew an evasive pattern at treetop level, accompanied by two decoy craft.

As soon as Putin learnt of the plane strikes, he tried to telephone Bush, the first world leader to do so. With Bush out of touch in the air, the call was taken by Rice, who was in the PEOC bunker with

Cheney. Putin assured her that Russia would not raise its military readiness in response to any moves taken by America following the attacks, as it would have done during the Cold War years.

'Is there anything else we can do?' Putin asked Rice. She thanked him and the thought flashed through her head: 'The Cold War really is over.'[2]

'Russia knows directly what terrorism means,' Putin said later in a televised address. 'And because of this we, more than anyone, understand the feelings of the American people. In the name of Russia, I want to say to the American people – we are with you.' Russian television framed its coverage accordingly. Muscovites laid flowers outside the US embassy; the anti-American feeling that had flared after NATO's attacks on Serbia two years earlier had been replaced by shared sorrow.

The next day, Bush returned Putin's call. The mood was warm. Putin told him he had signed a decree ordering a minute of silence to show solidarity with America. 'Good will triumph over evil,' Putin said, ending the conversation. 'I want you to know that in this struggle, we will stand together.'[3]

America had ignored persistent Russian warnings of the dangers of Islamic terrorism – the last of them as recently as 9 September, when Putin telephoned the American president following the assassination of Ahmad Shah Massoud, the head of the Afghan Northern Alliance, which was fighting the Taliban government. Putin had been told by Russian intelligence of their fears that the killing of Massoud meant that something much more serious, and longer in preparation, was afoot. He passed this on to Bush but came away concerned that the American leader 'did not fully grasp the seriousness of the issue', as Primakov put it.[4]

'I didn't allow myself to say, "We did warn you about this"', Putin recalled after the attacks. 'It wasn't the moment. I frequently talked about the threat in Afghanistan. I said it's not only a threat to us because the training camps there are sending terrorists to Chechnya. It threatened the whole world.'[5] Putin appeared genuinely to relish the opportunity to help. As it became clear that Bush was preparing a retaliatory strike on Al Qaeda in Afghanistan, Putin not only offered words of support, he also vowed to provide America with intelligence information collected by Russia about the infrastructure, location and training of Islamic terrorists. After all, they were Russia's enemies as much as America's.

Putin was also the key to a greater prize: as part of his plans to strike back at the Taliban, Bush wanted to send ground troops into Afghanistan. To do so he needed logistical cooperation from neighbouring Uzbekistan and Tajikistan. Bush did not know the leaders of either of the two former Soviet states, but appreciated that Putin held enormous sway over them. On 22 September, Bush called him for help. During a long conversation that Saturday morning, Putin agreed to open his airspace to US military planes and to use his influence with the Uzbek and Tajik presidents to help American troops enter Afghanistan. Bush had worried that the Russian leader would have been opposed, fearing his country would be encircled by US forces. Instead Putin seemed more preoccupied by the threat from terrorism. He even ordered Russian generals to give their American counterparts a briefing on their own experiences in Afghanistan in the 1980s.

It was, Bush recalled, 'an amazing conversation'. He told the man he now referred to as Vladimir how much he appreciated his willingness to 'move beyond the suspicions of the past'.[6] Before long, Bush had the agreement he needed. On 7 October, the war against the Taliban – 'Operation Enduring Freedom' – was launched.

Putin's backing for Bush was dictated in large part by his own struggle at home with the Chechen rebels, whose battle for secession, which had begun in the early 1990s as part of the broader demand for self-determination across the former Soviet Union, had evolved from a secular movement to an increasingly Islamist one. By likening the Chechens to Al Qaeda, the Russian president was able to pose in American eyes as a victim of fundamentalist terrorism rather than as an autocratic leader crushing an oppressed minority. Even before 9/11, Western criticism of Russian brutality in Chechnya had been muted. Now it went even quieter.

Although this may seem like a cynical ploy, there seemed a genuine sense in the Kremlin that the attacks would bring home to America the reality of what Russia had been suffering at the hands of the Chechens. 'Everybody in the Kremlin thought that now the Americans finally realised what kind of problem this was,' says Voloshin, who had been in St Petersburg on 11 September and returned to Moscow that evening to find the Kremlin 'in a state of shock'. 'When this was our problem, they could not see it. But now they had to realise how horrible this was and that now we would have to remain close.'[7]

As a result, the Kremlin was pleased to see that Washington was at last moving against various US-based Islamic funds: Russia had long been pressing American authorities to close them down on the grounds that they had links with terrorism and were being used to buy arms for Chechnya, but Washington refused, claiming they were purely humanitarian. Now it took action against them. The move was welcomed in Moscow but was also seen as proof of America's double standards.

'After 9/11 we had a hope that now they had to understand us and we had to become partners in a fight against terrorism,' says Voloshin.[8] 'But then it turned out that the Americans did not need us as partners; they were worried only about their own problems and they did not care about ours. It was a period of some expectations and missed opportunities for cooperation.'

EVIDENCE OF THE NEW SPIRIT CAME that October when Putin announced that Russia would abandon its massive electronic eaves-dropping post at Lourdes, Cuba. Some 1,500 Russians were employed at the 28-square-mile complex, listening to phone calls, tracking US naval operations, monitoring launches from Cape Canaveral and providing communications support for spies in North America. Since its inception in 1964, the complex had been a major concern to American intelligence. Putin said he would also begin a long-planned withdrawal from Russia's other such centre at Cam Ranh Bay, Vietnam. The motivation was largely financial, with the hundreds of millions of dollars a year saved from the closures to be spent on re-equipping the Russian army. Yet the symbolism was clear.

Despite the warming relations with Moscow, the US administration was keen to press ahead with leaving the Anti-Ballistic Missile Treaty. The aim was to free America from what John Bolton, Bush's pugnacious new undersecretary of state for arms and international security, called a 'dangerous relic of the Cold War'.[9] During their summit in Slovenia, Bush had warned Putin that he planned to give him the required six months' notice of America's withdrawal, leaving both countries able to develop their own anti-missile defences; 9/11 did nothing to change his mind. On 13 December, Bush made his announcement.

Putin reacted calmly to the news: Bush's decision was mistaken, he argued, but the United States was within its legal rights to take the action and he was not going to use the announcement to encourage 'anti-American hysteria' in Russia. For the Kremlin, the Anti-Ballistic Missile Treaty and the various other arms control agreements concluded during the Cold War retained symbolic importance as a recognition of their status as America's equal. Dismantling this network of treaties, as the Bush administration seemed determined to do, was an attempt to erode this status. Putin had gone out of his way to help America over 9/11, but Bush did not appear prepared to reciprocate. However warm Putin's personal relationship with Bush, he could do little to influence his administration. The new era of cooperation clearly had its limits.

Despite such differences, Putin and Bush remained determined to find a way of improving relations. At a summit in Moscow in May 2002, they signed a new arms control deal – the Strategic Offensive Reductions Treaty (SORT, or Moscow Treaty) – that committed both countries to reduce their respective arsenals from about 6,000 warheads to no more than 2,200 at the end of 2012. The Bush administration had initially proposed an informal agreement between the two presidents. Putin wanted a formal treaty, however, and Bush acceded to his request. Rice said that the accord should not be considered the first Russian–American treaty of the twenty-first century but 'the last treaty of the last century'.[10] In contrast to the arms control treaties of old, the text ran to just three pages. It was hailed by Bush as paving the way to what he called 'an entirely new relationship' with Russia.

Divisions between the two sides persisted, however, especially over the nuclear plant that the Russians were helping the Iranians to build in Bushehr and which America thought could be misused by Tehran to help its clandestine nuclear weapons programme. Bush told reporters that he and Putin 'spoke very frankly and honestly' about the need to make sure 'a non-transparent government run by radical clerics doesn't get their hands on weapons of mass destruction'. For his part, Putin defended his country's cooperation with the regime in Tehran, saying it was 'not of a character that would undermine the process on non-proliferation'.

'It [Bushehr] was not a threat to anyone, but all our negotiations used to start and finish with this issue,' said Voloshin. 'We used to explain to everyone: "Do we look like people who want Iran to have nuclear weapons? Probably not." We figured out they could not construct a nuclear weapon with the help of this nuclear power plant. We told them [the Americans] this, tried to persuade them, specialists met them, but everything was quite useless.'[11] Rightly or wrongly, the Russians believed the Americans were motivated not by security fears but by commercial rivalry. (The Kremlin felt vindicated in this assumption when the plant was finally completed in 2011 and Iran seemed no closer to developing nuclear weapons.)

NATO enlargement was even more divisive. Since his summit with Clinton in June 2000, Putin had continued to send out mixed signals about the Alliance. In July 2001, during his first press conference as president, he had urged that NATO be disbanded, dismissing it as a relic of the Cold War. It would be better to replace it with a new pan-European security organisation, he said. Asked how Russia should react to a further expansion of the Alliance, Putin outlined a number of possible scenarios, one of which was Russian membership. 'We do not view NATO as a hostile organisation and do not see its existence as a tragedy,' he said. 'Although we don't see the need for it either.'

Putin was not the only one to talk about Russian membership of the Alliance; surprisingly, some members of the incoming Bush administration were also sympathetic to the idea. Russia was already a member of the Partnership for Peace. A review of Russian policy by the state department's office of policy planning suggested issuing an invitation to Moscow as part of the enlargement process. Richard Haass, the office's director, saw it as a way for the West to show Russia the respect that it craved.

'I thought it would take some of the sting out of NATO enlargement and it would remove the argument that the post-war order was somehow built against Russia,' Haass said more than a decade later. With NATO gradually becoming what he called an 'à la carte' organisation, he also did not think it would impair the Alliance's functioning. The idea did not go any further than Colin Powell, the secretary of state, however. 'Those who doubted the wisdom of it . . . worried that it would impair the continuing military effectiveness of NATO, that Russia, essentially as an insider, would become obstructive and would work against NATO's continuing viability,' recalled Haass.[12]

That October, in a reflection of the changed international situation since 9/11, Putin again raised the subject of Russian membership of

NATO during a private meeting with Robertson at Alliance headquarters in Brussels.

'Mr Secretary General. When are you going to invite us to join NATO?' he asked his host.[13] Robertson replied that no country was ever 'invited' to join the Alliance. They had to apply.

Putin was not impressed. 'Russia is not going to stand in a queue with other countries that don't matter,' he said. Robertson suggested they 'stop the diplomatic sword dance about membership and build the relationship between us'. 'And that's what we did,' he says. It was the last time Putin spoke about joining NATO.

It was tony blair who came up with a way of squaring the circle. His relationship with Putin remained close. Jonathan Powell, his chief of staff, recalls how the Russian leader called several times 'to have chat with Tony' on how to approach European issues, adding 'We thought we had created an interesting new relationship with a Russian leader who could be more like a normal leader.'[14] As Blair wrote in his memoirs, these contacts helped him to understand. Putin's determination that Russia should regain something of the role as a great power that the Soviet Union had enjoyed. In November 2001 he proposed a new relationship with NATO intended to reflect and enhance the new spirit of international cooperation brought about by 9/11.

The idea was to create a new body, to become known as the NATO–Russia Council, to replace the NATO–Russia Permanent Joint Council that had been set up in 1997. Despite the similarity between their names, there was a key difference between the two bodies: the old organisation was structured in such a way that Russia could express its opinion only after decisions had been taken by NATO. Its successor would allow Russia to discuss security issues as an equal with the Alliance's nineteen members before decisions were taken.

NATO foreign ministers agreed to create the council during a meeting with their Russian counterpart, Igor Ivanov, in Reykjavik in May 2002. Powell claimed the accord would open a new chapter in relations with Russia – and with the other former Soviet states – while preserving the Alliance's ability to act independently. For Jack Straw, the British foreign secretary, it marked the 'funeral of the Cold War'. He added: 'With this, Russia comes out of the cold as a partner, ally and friend of NATO.'

The idea may have been Blair's, but Silvio Berlusconi, the Italian prime minister, made it his own. In one of the more unlikely political partnerships, Berlusconi had become close to Putin since their first encounter at the G8 summit, which he had hosted in Genoa in July 2001, and tried to take over from Blair to become a kind of self-appointed mediator between the Russian leader and George W. Bush. The two men went on to hold more meetings than any Russian and Italian leaders before them, seeing each other on average twice a year, often in an informal setting: at Berlusconi's opulent villa in Sardinia or at Putin's sprawling dacha in the middle of the forest near Davidovo outside Moscow or his home in Sochi. They became close friends: Berlusconi would go each October to Russia for Putin's birthday party, and Putin would bring his family with him when he visited Sardinia. A large four-poster in Palazzo Grazioli, a grand building in Rome where Berlusconi rented a floor while prime minister, was jokingly known as 'Putin's bed', according to a tape leaked to the Italian media in 2009, although it was not clear why it got its name.

'Berlusconi believes that Putin, a fellow "tycoon", trusts Berlusconi more than any other European leader,' said Ronald Spogli, the US ambassador to Rome, in a cable published by WikiLeaks. 'Berlusconi admires Putin's macho, decisive, and authoritarian governing style, which the Italian PM believes matches his own. From the Russian side, it appears that Putin has devoted much energy to developing Berlusconi's trust.' The cables also quoted a contact in the Italian leader's office, who claimed that the two men exchanged lavish gifts and reported suspicions that Berlusconi was 'profiting personally and handsomely' from secret energy deals with Putin – a claim the Italian leader denied.

It was during one of their many encounters, in April 2002 in Sochi, that their conversation turned to the new NATO–Russia Council. According to Berlusconi's biographer, the American journalist Alan Friedman, the Italian leader played up the idea of the new body as a counterbalance to NATO enlargement, and suggested that Italy host a meeting at the end of May at which the treaty could be signed. The two men promptly called Bush, who went for the idea.

Berlusconi, the showman, was delighted at the prospect and set about organising the event as if it were one of the spectaculars for which his television companies were renowned. With security still tight in the aftermath of 9/11 and a guest list that included some of the most

)werful people in the world, it was decided that the summit, set for
May, should be held not in Rome but instead at the Pratica di Mare
base south-west of the capital. Ground-to-air missiles were installed
'rotect the airspace and commercial flights from nearby Fiumicino
ort were suspended. The Italian navy cleared a stretch of the
literranean coast.

was on the venue itself that Berlusconi really made his mark:
six thousand workers, toiling for twenty days, built something
:o a giant film set – 'a sort of Cinecittà for world leaders, made
wood painted to look like stone and with fake ancient Roman
ry constructed out of fiberglass',[15] as one commentator put it
ε ι)ugh the construction was almost destroyed by a massive rain-
he evening before the summit. The main area where the leaders
met and signed the treaty was decorated with arches reminiscent of
the Colosseum. Another, likened to an Aztec temple, was used for
news conferences, while the fifteen hundred journalists covering the
event worked in an area resembling an aircraft hangar decorated with
faux travertine marble. Ancient statues were brought in from
museums in Rome. Berlusconi's personal lighting engineer oversaw
the installation of a lighting system that could be used to show each
leader at his or her best, the way contestants are highlighted in a
game show. At the lunch Berlusconi sneakily tried to rearrange the
table settings so he could sit next to Putin, until Lord Robertson, the
NATO secretary general who was chairing the meeting, spotted what
he was doing and told him firmly that they had to stick to alphabet-
ical order.

That small setback apart, Berlusconi's efforts paid off: the day's
events proceeded in suitably over-the-top fashion, with the final shot
capturing the Italian leader, flanked by Bush and Putin, signing the
document, while Blair and Chirac looked across the table. The language
used at the summit was equally hyperbolic. The joint declaration
claimed NATO and Russia were 'opening a new page in our relations,
aimed at enhancing our ability to work together in areas of common
interest and to stand together against common threats and risks to
our security'.

At a press conference, Putin admitted differences with NATO on
'certain security questions' but insisted that 'what unites us is much
stronger and more serious'. The agreement, he said, was a 'very impor-

tant step towards the creation of truly partner-like relations between Russia and NATO, based on mutual respect of each other's interests'. For a long period of time, Russia had been on one side of global issues and 'practically the rest of the world' on the other, he said. 'No good came out of this confrontation between Russia and the rest of the world. And most of the citizens of my country understand this very well. Russia is now returning to the family of civilised nations.'

For his part, Robertson paid 'a particular tribute to President Vladimir Putin for his vision and courage in breaking the bonds of old policies and all politics', adding that the agreement 'shows that cold warriors can become partners in building a better world'. Berlusconi praised Putin's braveness. 'Mr Putin is a democrat, a liberal-minded politician, a Western man,' he said. 'He will manage to unite the destinies of his country, Europe and the West in the interests of all our countries and the whole of humankind.' Russia, he added, 'must join the European Union'.

Anders Fogh Rasmussen, the Danish prime minister, left Italy 'very optimistic, and convinced that we were now entering a new era of cooperation between Russia and our Western organizations, NATO and the European Union'.[16] Other leaders shared his belief that a new era was beginning. In a speech in Edinburgh that December, Robertson described the new relationship between Russia and NATO as 'a revolution' that marked the end of a dark century for Europe that had begun with the storming of the Winter Palace in 1917 and ended with the attacks of 11 September 2001. The agreement signed in Pratica di Mare had 'changed the world forever', he declared.[17]

In a recent interview, Berlusconi looked back with pride on his achievement. 'I guess of all the things I did in my life, this may be the one I am most proud of,' he told Friedman, his biographer.[18] 'This really was the moment that marked the end of the Cold War, you know.' Robertson agrees: 'There was a pragmatism about Putin,' he recalls. 'And I think it was for good calculated reasons. As he said, they had always been isolated and it had done them no good. If they were going to be part and parcel of this great enterprise, then fine. And in all the times I met him that seemed to be the sentiment.'[19]

Yet rather than marking the beginning of a new start for Russia and the West, the Pratica di Mare meeting looks, in retrospect, more like the high point in relations. Part of the problem was resistance within the US administration to allowing Russia genuinely to become a member of the NATO–Russia Council's decision-making process. Much was made by NATO of the difference between the old '19+1' set-up and the new arrangement under which Russia would now play a full part in making decisions rather than be presented with a fait accompli. But old attitudes die hard: in reality, NATO members continued to meet among themselves and would agree a common position on issues before they invited in the Russian representatives.

'There wasn't any issue, at least initially, that the US government was prepared to put before the NATO–Russia Council where the NATO position had not been worked out beforehand, which in a sense was really contrary to the spirit of the document,' says former Bush adviser Thomas Graham.[20] 'The Russians will have figured this out very, very quickly. They participated, but it wasn't really what it appeared to be on the surface.'

The old-style Cold War thinking was not confined to one side, however: according to Graham, when it came to selecting whom to send to Brussels, the Russians chose 'a bunch of intel types' who turned their mission to the organisation into a 'collection platform' for intelligence and set themselves the goal of 'burrowing out as many secrets as they could about NATO'. 'There was deep suspicion on both sides, but that was only natural because we had been enemies just ten years earlier,' he adds.

Putin appears to look back on the meeting as a lost opportunity. Creation of the NATO–Russia Council 'was a positive movement towards building a long-term partnership between Russia and NATO' that 'created the conditions for long-term cooperation,' he said in an interview more than a decade later. 'But, unfortunately, we – and I mean everyone, without shifting the blame onto anyone – we failed to take full advantage of the agreement that was reached in Italy. The Russia–NATO agreement itself is certainly a platform for building relations, but changes were needed in practical policies as well and, unfortunately, we have not seen those.'[21]

One of the greatest stumbling blocks was NATO's determination to continue its expansion eastward towards the Russian border. Enlargement had become an article of faith for the Alliance, as it was for the European Union, which was also growing. Potential new members, for their part, were clamouring to be admitted. The only question was how many should be let in, and when. The Alliance was again divided, but the roles were reversed: this time Germany and France were cautious and concerned about the Russian reaction – especially to the inclusion of Estonia, Latvia and Lithuania, which had been part of the Soviet Union itself rather than merely its satellites. Britain wanted a relatively small expansion. America, backed by the Nordic countries and the three new Central European members admitted in 1999, pushed for a 'Big Bang' solution that would redraw NATO's eastern flank all the way from the Baltic to the Black Sea.

The Russian reaction was predictable: Primakov reiterated Moscow's objections to a move that 'brings a military alliance right up to our borders for no real purpose'.[22] Yet that, in a sense, was the point. While repeating the mantra that expansion was no threat to anyone, US officials insisted that Russia could not be allowed a right of veto over the Alliance's membership.

At the Prague summit that November, a formal invitation was issued to Bulgaria, Romania, Slovakia, Slovenia and the three Baltic states. Croatia, next in line, was given its own Membership Action Plan. In a speech on the eve of the summit, Bush insisted, as Clinton had before him, that NATO membership was good not just for the Alliance and those countries that joined it, but for Russia as well because of the stability and security it would provide. 'Russia does not require a buffer zone of protection,' he declared. 'It needs peaceful and prosperous neighbours who are also friends. We need a strong and democratic Russia as our friend and partner to face the next century's new challenges.'[23]

Bush flew straight on after the summit to St Petersburg, apparently at Putin's request. 'My visit with Vladimir was my first stop after Prague,' he told reporters as he stood by Putin's side in the majestic setting of the Catherine Palace. 'The mood of the NATO countries is this: Russia is our friend. We've got a lot of interests together; we must continue our cooperation in the war on terror; and the expansion of NATO should be welcomed by the Russian people.'

Putin seemed as little convinced by such claims as Yeltsin had been. Like Russian leaders before him, he wanted weak, disunited countries along his borders rather than strong, united ones. Only this way could Russia have the strategic depth it needed for its defence. Putin spoke of 'the problem' of NATO expansion, saying publicly he did not consider it necessary. Privately, though, there was no repetition of the rancour that had accompanied the first wave of enlargement.[24] According to Robertson, the Russian leader appeared to be bowing to the inevitable. 'I met Vladimir Putin nine or ten times in the lead-up to 2002 and at no point did he raise in a negative way the enlargement of NATO,' he recalls.[25] 'Not once. I think Putin thought it was going to happen anyway.'

Bush also worked hard to portray America and Russia as allies fighting a common threat. His comments had a special resonance: Russia was still reeling from a brazen siege by Chechen terrorists of the Dubrovka Theatre in Moscow a month earlier, which had ended with the death of 128 hostages – most of them from the gas used by commandos during the rescue mission. The Russian authorities were widely criticised for their handling of the attack, but Bush went out of his way to be supportive. He compared the incident with 9/11, saying there was a 'common thread' running between them. 'Any time anybody is willing to take innocent life for a so-called cause, they must be dealt with,' Bush said.[26] 'People tried to blame Vladimir. They ought to blame the terrorists. They're the ones who caused the situation, not President Putin.'

12

MISSION ACCOMPLISHED

ONE OF THE FIRST QUESTIONS BUSH had asked aides after 9/11 was whether there was any evidence of Iraqi involvement in the attacks. 'See if Saddam did this. See if he's linked in any way,' he ordered Richard Clarke, the National Security Council counterterrorism chief on 12 September.[1] Clarke was baffled. 'I thought I was missing something here,' he told Colin Powell. 'Having been attacked by Al Qaeda, for us to go bombing Iraq would be like invading Mexico after the Japanese attacked Pearl Harbor.'[2] As the president was told unequivocally in his daily CIA briefing nine days later, there was 'no evidence' connecting Iraq to the attacks and no reason to assume Saddam Hussein had any ties to Al Qaeda. On the contrary, it was well known that the Iraqi leader viewed Bin Laden and other radical Islamists as a threat to his secular regime. Yet this did not dissuade Bush from pressing ahead with plans to finish the job his father had started during the Gulf War a decade earlier: to topple Saddam.

An important milestone on the road to war was Bush's State of the Union address of 29 January 2002, when he spoke of an Axis of Evil spanning North Korea, Iran and Iraq that was 'arming to threaten the peace of the world' and that, 'by seeking weapons of mass destruction . . . pose a grave and continuing danger'. 'Our war on terror is well begun, but it is only begun,' Bush continued. 'We can't stop short. History has called America and our allies to action, and it is both our responsibility and our privilege to fight freedom's fight.'

In the months that followed, Bush embarked on a charm offensive to win support from his allies for his coming war against Iraq. Tony Blair was an early convert. 'I will be with you, whatever . . . Getting rid of Saddam is the right thing to do . . . His departure will free up the region,' he wrote to Bush in July 2002, in one of a series of confidential letters examined by the inquiry led by Sir John Chilcot into Britain's role in the Iraq war and that was finally published fourteen years later.

The leaders of Australia and Japan were in favour of military action, as were some of the smaller Western European states and most of the Central and Eastern Europeans. It was revealing that 'some of the strongest advocates for confronting Saddam were those with the freshest memory of tyranny', Bush noted in his memoirs, citing approvingly comments by Siim Kallas, the Estonian prime minister, who likened failure to take action against Saddam to the appeasement of Hitler during the 1930s.[3]

Jacques Chirac, the French president, was sceptical, however. Gerhard Schröder, the German chancellor, appeared supportive at first but was facing parliamentary elections that September and, to Bush's dismay, declared at the start of the campaign that Germany would provide neither troops nor money. Dismay turned to fury days before the German poll when Herta Däubler-Gmelin, the justice minister, accused Bush of stirring up the prospect of war against Iraq to 'divert attention from domestic difficulties', adding: 'Hitler has done that before.' Bush was appalled. 'It was hard to think of anything more insulting than being compared to Hitler by a German official,' he wrote in his memoirs.[4]

Putin was far more measured in his comments, but nevertheless had serious misgivings about attempts to topple Saddam. Like Yeltsin before him, Putin believed in the maintenance of the status quo and opposed enforced regime change – a position that had already put Russia at odds with America over Kosovo. Nor did he see Saddam as a threat. Commercial considerations also played a part: Russia had long-standing ties with Iraq dating back to Soviet days. Russian oil companies had stakes in undeveloped Iraqi fields, and Russia bought much of the oil exported by Iraq under the United Nations 'oil for food programme', which was set up in 1995 to allow the country to sell oil on the world market in exchange for food, medicines and other essentials for ordinary Iraqis. It was also claimed that various top

Russian officials close to Putin personally benefited from kickbacks in connection with such oil sales.

With the US invasion looming, Putin attempted to mediate in the conflict, sending former prime minister Yevgeny Primakov, an Arabist who had acted as Gorbachev's envoy to Iraq during the Gulf War, to Baghdad to try to persuade Saddam to step down. The Iraqi leader refused, denouncing his visitor in front of his aides. 'Russia has turned into a shadow of the United States,' he growled.[5]

At the NATO summit in Prague the previous November, Bush had spoken of leading a 'Coalition of the Willing' to disarm Saddam if he refused to give up his weapons of mass destruction. In response, Putin, Chirac and Schröder formed a 'Coalition of the Unwilling'. On 10 February 2003 the Russian leader flew to Paris where the three issued a joint statement urging that Iraq be disarmed peacefully. 'There is still an alternative to war. The use of force can only be considered as a last resort,' they declared.[6]

In a final attempt to avert the conflict, Voloshin was sent to Washington to meet Bush, Rice and other members of the adminis-tration. On his arrival late on a Sunday evening, he was surprised to hear that his first scheduled meeting was with George Tenet, the head of the CIA. 'Some of the members of my delegation thought it was some kind of a provocation and told me not to do that,' recalls Voloshin.[7]

They met at eight the next morning in a large grey administrative building near the White House, where Tenet had an office. 'Tenet was a nice, decent person and he made a good impression on me,' says Voloshin. He was accompanied by several of his deputies, who told him they had found evidence of Iraqi links with extremists who had fought in Chechnya. To back up their claims, they provided the names of the fighters.

'They gave me a lot of details,' Voloshin said. 'The main aim was to show that Iraq wasn't just their enemy but our enemy too and we were making a mistake by communicating with them because they were supporting the terrorists.' Voloshin was not impressed. 'We realised that there were thousands of these terrorists. Some of them came here from Iraq, some of them went to the US, so what?'

Further meetings followed with Condoleezza Rice and her deputy. Then Bush arrived. After a few minutes of conversation, the president launched into a ten-minute monologue. 'He was very emotional. He was talking about totalitarianism, dictatorship, Islamic extremism, it was a real speech,' Voloshin recalls. 'When he finished there was silence. It was like a speech by Che Guevara or Fidel Castro; one of those very emotional speeches like you get in Latin American countries.' As they spoke afterwards, Bush told Voloshin that he had been expressing his 'honest point of view', adding: 'This is my responsibility before God.' Voloshin stayed on until the Tuesday evening and had other conversations with Powell, Evans and Cheney, but it seemed pointless. The administration had already made the decision to go to war.

On 20 March, US-led forces began their attack on Iraq with a 'shock and awe' bombing campaign. Iraqi forces were swiftly overwhelmed as the Americans swept through the country. Four days later, Putin called Bush. 'This is going to be awfully difficult for you,' Putin told him. 'I feel bad for you. I feel bad.' 'Why?' asked Bush. 'Because there's going to be enormous human suffering.' 'No,' Bush said, 'We've got a good plan. But thank you for your concern.'[8]

As they spoke, Bush realised that Putin, himself still embroiled in Chechnya, was talking about the personal toll that the conflict would have on him. 'It was a genuine call,' Bush recalled later. 'It wasn't a told-you-so. It was a friendship call. And I appreciated it.' It was, he added, 'the only call I got along those lines, by the way'.

ON 9 APRIL BAGHDAD FELL, AND with it – live on CNN – a 40ft iron statue of Saddam in Firdos Square. Bush, who did not have a television in the Oval Office, watched the spectacle in an area outside, gathered with his aides in front of a screen. For the previous twenty days he had been anxious about the outcome of his gamble. Now he was 'overwhelmed with relief and pride'.[9]

Bush was persuaded that it was time to signal that a new phase in the war had begun. He decided to do so in dramatic fashion by giving a speech on 1 May aboard USS *Abraham Lincoln*, an aircraft carrier that was returning home after ten months at sea, during which time it had supported operations in both Afghanistan and Iraq. In an elaborate piece of theatre, the president donned a flight suit and boarded a Lockheed S-3B Viking bound for the ship, even taking control of the plane for a few minutes over the Pacific. It was the first time in more than thirty years that the former F-102 pilot in the Texas Air National Guard had sat in a military jet.

'My fellow Americans,' Bush declared in his speech, 'major combat operations in Iraq have ended . . . The transition from dictatorship to democracy will take time, but it is worth every effort. Our coalition will stay until our work is done. Then we will leave, and we will leave behind a free Iraq.'[10]

Bush hedged his words, but they were overshadowed by the setting. Behind him on the bridge of the ship was a banner that read 'Mission Accomplished'. It had been intended as a tribute to the five thousand sailors, airpersonnel and marines who had just completed the longest deployment of an aircraft carrier of its class. Instead, as Bush noted ruefully in his memoirs, his speech came across as a premature victory dance, while the 'Mission Accomplished' banner, which he claimed not to have noticed, 'became a shorthand criticism for all that subsequently went wrong in Iraq'. The damage was done. 'All the explaining in the world could not reverse the perception. Our stagecraft had gone awry. It was a big mistake.'

In the weeks and months that followed, Iraq descended into a state of lawlessness, becoming a magnet for extremists. Toppling Saddam had been the easy bit; running a vast, religiously divided country proved a far greater challenge – rendered all the more difficult by America's determination to deny any future role to members of Saddam's Ba'athist regime.

The impact on America's relations with Russia was nevertheless not as damaging as it might have been. Bush felt badly let down by Chirac and Schröder, who were his NATO allies, but clearly had lower expectations of Moscow. Putin went out of his way to stress that his relations with Bush had not only survived their disagreement over Iraq but had even been strengthened by the crisis, and paid a visit to Camp David that September. At a press conference after their talks, Bush insisted that old suspicions between the two countries were 'giving way to new understanding and respect', adding: 'I respect President Putin's vision for Russia: a country at peace within its borders, with its neighbours, and with the world, a country in which democracy and freedom and rule of law thrive.'

Asked if their disagreement over Iraq would impact on the relationship, Bush admitted that he and 'Vladimir' had had some 'very frank discussions' over Iraq but insisted that both understood each other's respective positions. 'Because we've got a trustworthy relationship, we're able to move beyond any disagreement over a single issue,' Bush said, before adding, with a typical flourish: 'Plus, I like him. He's a good fellow to spend quality time with.'

WASHINGTON'S ACKNOWLEDGEMENT OF THE NEED TO work together with Russia on strategic issues was tempered by concern over Russia's gradual slide towards authoritarianism. Putin's first years in office were marked by a continuation of Yeltsin's policies and the ongoing presence in the Kremlin of many of his former aides. But Putin became determined to prove that he was his own man. Matters came to a head in the run-up to the December 2003 parliamentary elections, seen as a dress rehearsal for the presidential poll the following March.

The new mood was symbolised by the arrest that October of Mikhail Khodorkovsky, the head of the oil giant Yukos, who, with an estimated fortune of $15 billion, was believed to be the wealthiest man in Russia. Although charged with tax evasion, fraud and embezzlement, Khodorkovsky's real crime was his attempt to enter politics. He provided lavish financing for opposition parties and hinted at his own presidential ambitions. The last straw was in February 2003 when Khodorkovsky joined other wealthy businessmen at a meeting in the Kremlin which, unusually, was open to the media. There, against the advice of his aides, he launched an attack on corruption. Putin took it personally, responding with a barely veiled condemnation of the billionaire businessman's own affairs. 'Some companies, including Yukos, have extraordinary reserves,' he said, menacingly. 'The question is: how did the company get them?' The message was clear. Khodorkovsky was now in danger. He could have capitulated or gone abroad. Instead, he chose to stay and fight. In July, his long-term business partner, Platon Lebedev, was arrested. Khodorkovsky responded by going on a speaking tour. Three months later, while boarding his plane at Novosibirsk airport, he too was arrested. After a ten-month trial that was a clear travesty of justice, both men were found guilty in May 2005 and sentenced to nine years in prison colonies. Khodorkovsky was sent to a camp centred on a uranium mine near Krasnokamensk, in south-east Siberia near the Chinese border, reachable from Moscow by a nine-hour plane journey followed by fifteen hours on a train.

There were also important changes behind the scenes in the Kremlin. A few days after Khodorkovsky's arrest, Voloshin stepped down as Putin's chief of staff. He was replaced by Dmitry Medvedev, a baby-faced former law professor a decade his junior. Medvedev, still only thirty-eight, had been a close associate of Putin during his St Petersburg days and ran his 2000 presidential election campaign. He was very clearly the president's man. Voloshin was the last most influential remaining member of Yeltsin's 'family'. Underlying his departure was a desire by Putin to assert himself among those in the Kremlin he had inherited from his predecessor, many of whom had initially seen him as only a temporary figure. 'Putin didn't want to be a transitional president . . . he didn't like being controlled or having his ideology controlled,' said one adviser who observed him at close hand. 'That is why he entered into open conflict with Voloshin . . . The key issue for him were the relations within the Kremlin team. It was a way of getting rid of the "family".'

Putin also took a tougher line with the former Soviet republics, increasingly using their dependency on Russian energy as leverage against them. After a dispute over gas prices with Aleksandr Lukashenko, the Belarusian leader, escalated in January 2004, Putin ordered supplies to the country to be cut – despite temperatures often dropping below −20°C (−4°F). 'It was to punish Lukashenko,' recalls Kasyanov, who was coming to the end of his term as prime minister at the time.[11] 'Putin said: "Lukashenko doesn't respect me. He promised me he would sign the contract and then he didn't".'

Putin's new tougher stance paid off. United Russia, a pro-Putin party created in December 2001 out of two other parties, took a resounding first place in the December 2003 parliamentary election, winning 223 out of the 450 seats in the Duma. The presidential election three months later, which turned into a kind of 'referendum' on Putin's rule, was little more than a formality. Pitted against five nonentities, Putin secured more than seventy-one per cent of the vote in the first round, obviating the need for a run-off. His nearest challenger, Nikolay Kharitonov, the communist candidate, won just under fourteen per cent. It was a curious election: Putin refused to participate in any debates or make any policy statements, but still received blanket coverage on state media – a point noted by international observers, who also identified a slew of other irregularities, including a suspiciously high turnout of more than ninety per cent in Chechnya and other parts of the North Caucasus that voted solidly for the president.

There is little doubt that Putin would have won a landslide even in a fair fight, thanks largely to the economy, which was booming. Over the previous four years, Russia's GDP had been growing at an average annual rate of 6.5%; the average household was 53% better off in real terms than it had been when he first came to power and real wages were up by 86%. Much of this was due to the steady increase in the oil price, yet even Putin's critics did not dispute that he had provided conditions that had allowed the economy to flourish. After the chaos of the Yeltsin years, Russians were enjoying the fruits of political stability.

Yet Chechnya remained a serious problem. In September 2004, almost two years after the Moscow theatre siege, the terrorists struck again to even more disastrous effect, this time in Beslan in North Ossetia. More than 1,100 people – including 777 children – were taken hostage by a group of armed Islamists, mostly from nearby Chechnya and Ingushetia, who stormed School Number One in the town. Sent by Basayev, the Chechen warlord who had claimed responsibility for the Moscow theatre attack, they demanded recognition of the break-away republic's independence and the withdrawal of Russian troops. On the third day of the stand-off, Russian security forces stormed the school with tanks, incendiary rockets and other heavy weaponry. At least 385 hostages were killed, 186 of them children. Many more were injured or reported missing. The attack followed several other incidents blamed on Islamic terrorists: a few days before Beslan, two female suicide bombers destroyed two Russian airliners in flight, and both a Moscow metro station and a bus stop were bombed.

At a meeting with journalists and policy experts a few days later, Putin rejected accusations that the terrorists' action could be blamed in part on the brutality of Russian policies in Chechnya. He also dismissed suggestions that such violence showed the need to seek a political solution to the conflict. 'Why don't you meet Osama bin Laden, invite him to Brussels or to the White House and engage in talks, ask him what he wants and give it to him so he leaves you in peace? Why don't you do that?' he demanded with searing sarcasm. 'You find it possible to set some limitations in your dealings with these bastards, so why should we talk to people who are child killers?'[12]

Putin made clear that he saw the drive for Chechen independence

as part of a plan by Islamists, working in league with foreign funda-
mentalists, to undermine the whole of southern Russia and stir up
trouble among Muslim communities in other parts of the country too.
He also accused Western intelligence services of maintaining contacts
with the Chechen rebels, in what he claimed was an effort to weaken
Russia by keeping it tied up with domestic problems. He backed his
accusation by noting that both America and Britain had given political
asylum to some Chechen leaders.

In fact, Bush showed solidarity with Russia during and after the
Beslan attack – just as he had done after the Moscow theatre siege.
After signing a book of condolence at the Russian embassy in
Washington, he expressed sympathy for those who had 'suffered at
the hands of the evil terrorists' and declared that America 'stands
side-by-side with Russia as we fight off terrorism, as we stand shoul-
der-to-shoulder to make the world a more peaceful place and a free
place'.[13]

Beslan, some American commentators noted, was Russia's 9/11. They
urged Bush to seize on the horrors of what had happened at the school
as a reason to work more closely with Russia in the fight against global
terrorism. Yet such cooperation was complicated by Putin's own
response, which consisted largely of consolidating his 'vertical of power'.
Within a few days of the massacre, he announced a series of measures
to change the way in which Russia was governed: in the future, regional
leaders were to be appointed by Moscow rather than elected, and the
rules governing election to the Duma changed to reduce the chances
for independent-minded candidates. Voluntary people's patrols of the
sort seen in Soviet times would be established and work in tandem
with police to ensure the re-establishment of public order.

Such a policy would do little to tackle the root cause of the discontent in Chechnya and, in American eyes, risked a further erosion of
the democratic freedoms won since the end of the Soviet Union. There
was also the danger that an authoritarian Russia, deprived of its last
remaining democratic checks and balances, would pursue a more
aggressive foreign policy that would lead to greater friction with the
United States and its allies.

By the time of Beslan, the hopes of a new start that had been raised
by a shared revulsion at the carnage of 9/11 were slipping away. Buoyed
by his warm personal relationship with Putin, Bush had seemed

genuinely optimistic that Russia and the West would find a common cause not just in fighting Bin Laden and Al Qaeda but in facing the other security challenges of the twenty-first century. The aim, says Jamie Shea, a veteran NATO official, was 'to build coalitions of interest' to deal with such global issues in the hope that these would gradually overshadow residual Russian bitterness at the diminution of its influence in Eastern Europe.

Yet the West underestimated how badly the losses of the previous decade still rankled with Moscow, and how much the Kremlin continued to consider the former Soviet republics as part of its sphere of influence. 'In NATO the mistake we made was not realising just how seriously these European security issues were,' said Shea.[14] 'We saw them as a kind of legacy of the Cold War that didn't really matter any longer, that weren't important to Russian security. We thought the Russians would gradually get over it; that it was rhetoric for domestic consumption. Our mistake was that we should have taken it more seriously.'

The West would soon learn quite how seriously the Kremlin took such issues. A new front in the post-Cold War rivalry between Russia and America was about to open up.

13

THE COLOUR REVOLUTIONS

'UKRAINE, A NEW AND IMPORTANT SPACE on the Eurasian chessboard, is a geopolitical pivot, because its very existence as an independent country helps to transform Russia,' wrote Zbigniew Brzezinski, the ultimate Cold Warrior, in 1997. 'Without Ukraine, Russia ceases to be a Eurasian empire. However, if Moscow regains control over Ukraine, with its fifty-two million people and major resources as well as access to the Black Sea, Russia automatically regains the where-withal to become a powerful imperial state, spanning Europe and Asia.'

Russia had accepted Ukraine's independence in 1991 – albeit reluctantly – and in the intervening years the two countries had learnt to live with one another. Ukraine had been run since 1994 by Leonid Kuchma, a former aerospace engineer who served as prime minister under Leonid Kravchuk, the first president of independent Ukraine, before standing against his patron and winning the top job. Kuchma came to power pledging to speed up economic reform and improve relations with Russia. He scored some initial successes, solving the dispute with the Kremlin over the Black Sea Fleet, securing Crimea and persuading Russia to accept Ukraine's borders. He also began to orientate his country towards the West and pushed on with privatisation even though, as in Russia, the main beneficiaries were the oligarchs.

Kuchma won re-election in November 1999 with 57.7% of the vote by presenting himself as the only candidate capable of defeating the communists, who drew support largely from those suffering as a result of the country's precipitous economic decline, which was worse even than Russia's. He was also helped by the death that March in a conveniently well-timed car accident of his main rival, Viacheslav Chornovil, a former dissident who had played a key role in the drive for Ukrainian independence.

Once re-elected, Kuchma attempted to create his own version of the 'managed democracy' that Putin was establishing in Russia, but failed, not least because he lacked Putin's popularity. Instead, he became embroiled in accusations of corruption and censorship of the media. 'Just as William the Conqueror used to distribute the land to his barons, so Kuchma handed out land, factories and so on to those whom he trusted,' said one observer of the Ukrainian scene. 'They could do anything they wanted. But again, like William the Conqueror, he was very strict at collecting taxes from them.'[1]

Then in September 2000 came the murder of Heorhii Gongadze, a journalist who had been critical of Kuchma. His mutilated headless corpse was found in a forest outside Kiev. Tapes of conversations in Kuchma's office, made secretly by one of his bodyguards, were leaked to the opposition. In one, Kuchma was heard ordering his police minister to 'take care of Gongadze'. Kuchma conceded later that it was indeed his voice on the tapes, but said the meaning of his words had been distorted by selective editing. In any case, under the terms of the constitution that he had himself written, Kuchma was allowed only two terms in office and so was unable to stand in the next presidential election, the first round of which was set for 31 October 2004.

Like Yeltsin, Kuchma set about selecting a successor he could trust to look after his interests. After some consideration, he plumped for Viktor Yanukovych, his Russophile prime minister. Born in Donetsk, in the industrial east, of mixed Russian, Polish and Belarusian origin, Yanukovych had not got off to an auspicious start in life: he had lost both his parents by the time he was a teenager and had been jailed twice for robbery and assault before he turned twenty. Yet he had managed to turn his life around, enrolling at the Donetsk Polytechnic Institute when he was in his mid-twenties and going on to become a regional transport executive. He moved into politics in 1996 when he was appointed deputy head of the Donetsk region. In November 2002, Kuchma made him prime minister, which gave him a stepping stone to the top job.

But Yanukovych was not a natural presidential candidate: he was almost completely lacking in charisma and had the disadvantage of being up against Viktor Yushchenko, leader of Our Ukraine, a Europhile political coalition that had the most seats in parliament. Yushchenko had an impressive CV: he had run the Ukrainian Central Bank for most of the 1990s and then in December 1999 became prime minister, lowering taxes and presiding over rising government revenues. Although he was ousted seventeen months later after falling foul of Ukraine's tangled parliamentary politics, he continued to be ranked consistently as the country's most popular politician in opinion polls. As the presidential election loomed, he formed an alliance with Yulia Tymoshenko, a colourful businesswoman turned politician who agreed to support his candidature as long as he named her as his prime minister.

The contest was more than just a fight between the two Viktors. It was also a battle between the two halves of the country: the largely agricultural, Ukrainian-speaking west, once part of the Habsburg empire, which backed Yushchenko, and the more industrialised, Russian-speaking south and east, which has been ruled by the Tsars, which was Yanukovych's power base. Voters in the south and east had been markedly less enthusiastic about breaking with the Soviet Union in 1991, and in subsequent parliamentary elections backed groups such as Yanukovych's Party of the Regions, which were conservative and pro-Russian. People in the north and west, by contrast, tended to vote for reform-minded parties that saw Ukraine's place as in Europe. The United States, influenced in part by its powerful Ukrainian community, looked more favourably on such parties, in the hope that they could help push the country along the same path as Poland and its neighbours, which were rapidly leaving Ukraine behind economically. For this reason, they were rooting for Yushchenko. The Kremlin was wary of anything that looked like an attempt to pull Ukraine away from Russia and its sympathies were consequently with Yanukovych.

Underpinning this was a feeling among some Russians that Ukraine was in a sense not a separate country at all but an artificial construct. Their shared roots stretched back more than a millennium to Kievan Rus', a federation of Slavic countries centred around Kiev and spanning the whole region. The Ukrainian language, to the extent that it is spoken, was dismissed as little more than a dialect of Russian. 'All the talk of a separate Ukrainian people existing since something like the ninth century and possessing its own non-Russian language is a recently invented falsehood,' wrote Alexander Solzhenitsyn in 1990.[2] 'We all sprang from precious Kiev.' Putin spoke for many Russians when he told George W. Bush: 'You have to understand, George, that Ukraine is not even a country. Part of its territory is in Eastern Europe and the greater part was given to us.'

A FORETASTE OF THE STRUGGLE THAT was about to erupt in Ukraine had been provided the previous year in Georgia when that republic's president, Eduard Shevardnadze, had been driven from power in a popular uprising. Shevardnadze had led Georgia for more than a decade during communist times before Gorbachev, newly installed in the Kremlin, summoned him to Moscow in 1985 to become Soviet foreign minister, where he played an important role in the rapprochement with the West that led to the end of the Cold War. The end of the Soviet Union meant he was suddenly out of a job and he returned to the land of his birth.

There, Shevardnadze fought and won a civil war against supporters of Zviad Gamsakhurdia, a charismatic if crazed former dissident who had led Georgia to independence in 1991, and in 1995 became Georgian president. He had a turbulent time, surviving three assassination attempts and grappling with separatists in Abkhazia and South Ossetia, who were becoming bolder and angrier, egged on by Russia. Accusations of corruption and nepotism grew after Shevardnadze won a second term as president in 2000 in a contest condemned as rigged. All eyes were on the parliamentary elections set for November 2003, which were not expected to be either free or fair.

Both Russia and America watched developments in Georgia closely. Shevardnadze had hitherto been seen fondly in Washington for his time at Gorbachev's side. Now, according to Rice, a man she remembered for his dignified air, shock of white hair and delightful sense of humour had turned into 'an ageing and somewhat pathetic figure surrounded by corrupt family members and associates who were dragging Georgia into a downward spiral of stagnation and decline'.[3] James Baker, who had worked with Shevardnadze as the first George Bush's secretary of state, was dispatched in the summer of 2002 to Georgia to suggest gently that it was time to step down with dignity. But

Shevardnadze was determined to cling on. In the meantime, the American government and other groups such as the billionaire George Soros' Open Society Foundation were pouring money into fledgling Georgian non-governmental organisations opposed to Shevardnadze.

As expected, the Georgian elections were rigged, and several thousand people took to the streets of Tbilisi, the capital, to protest. These demonstrations reached a peak on 22 November 2003 when Shevardnadze, in defiance of the protesters, attempted to open the session of the new parliament. But he met his match in Mikheil Saakashvili, a charismatic young politician almost four decades his junior. At just thirty-five, Saakashvili had already made a name for himself in Georgia. After reading international law in Kiev, he had won a US state department fellowship and studied at Columbia University Law School in New York before being elected to parliament in 1995 for Shevardnadze's Union of Citizens of Georgia. In October 2000, Saakashvili became Shevardnadze's justice minister, but he lasted just under a year before resigning in protest at corruption. A year later he formed the United National Movement, a centre-right party intended to provide a focus for those pressing for reform.

Now, while Shevardnadze was speaking, Saakashvili burst into parliament at the head of a crowd of supporters and demanded that his former patron resign. He held above his head a long-stemmed red rose that would become the symbol of the revolution. Shevardnadze responded by declaring a state of emergency and mobilising troops and police near his residence in Tbilisi, but the military refused to support him and the next evening he stepped down. Saakashvili was elected president in January 2004; when parliamentary elections were rerun two months later, his party swept the board. The Rose Revolution was notable for having been completely bloodless.

For Washington, the toppling of Shevardnadze and his replacement by a young, freedom-loving pro-Western leader was a rare and welcome success for Bush's 'freedom agenda', which had begun to feel hollow at a time when the security situation in Iraq was deteriorating rapidly. Russia, sensitive to any kind of regime change in the 'near abroad', saw things differently.

MEMORIES OF EVENTS IN GEORGIA WERE fresh as Ukrainians prepared to vote for a new president. For all the symbolic importance of the Rose Revolution, Ukraine was of a far greater significance because of the country's size, strategic importance and the extent of its ties with Russia. As in Georgia, a host of Western non-governmental organisations (NGOs) descended on the Ukraine in the run-up to the election, the first round of which was set for 31 October. The biggest youth group, Pora (meaning 'it's time'), drew inspiration from Kmara, the Georgian civic youth resistance movement. Millions of dollars were pumped into the country by the US Agency for International Development (USAID) to promote civil society, free media and awareness of democracy.

So was America trying to ensure a level playing field, or was this a cynical attempt to ensure victory for Yushchenko, the West's preferred candidate? John Herbst, the US ambassador to Kiev, who held regular meetings with all interested international and Ukrainian NGOs, insisted the aim was 'a free and fair election, not any particular winner'.[4] Thomas Graham, by then at the National Security Council, likens the tactics to those pursued by Ronald Reagan in Nicaragua in the 1980s when he pushed Daniel Ortega, the Sandinista leader, to hold popular elections, knowing that he would lose them. 'The public posture was all we want is fair and free elections, but I think we were being a bit disingenuous about what we were really trying to achieve,' says Graham.[5] 'We had some confidence that if the elections were free and fair then Yushchenko would win. But I could see why the Russians thought it was an attempt to prevent someone entering office who would have had more pro-Russian leanings.'

The Kremlin was watching the contest even more closely. Yushchenko's pro-Western sympathies did not endear him to Russia, and there were attempts to portray his Chicago-born wife as a spy. 'Putin knew Mr Yushchenko's statements and opinions. And he did not have a great desire that he come to power,' Kuchma told the British journalist and writer Angus Roxburgh, looking back at the elections.[6] And so the Kremlin backed Kuchma's choice, even if there was little enthusiasm for Yanukovych himself as a candidate.

In order to ensure that the right man won, an army of Russian political strategists – or 'political technologists' as they called themselves – descended on Ukraine to practise the dark arts they had perfected during regional election campaigns at home. Among them was Gleb Pavlovsky, the founder of an organisation called the Foundation for

Effective Politics. Pavlovsky was an unlikely Kremlin spin doctor. Born in 1951 in the Ukrainian city of Odessa, the self-styled former hippy had joined the dissident movement and was sent into exile in 1982 for anti-Soviet activity, spending three years in the Komi Republic, an inhospitable part of northern Russia. The Gorbachev years brought a new beginning: he took advantage of the more liberal climate to campaign for human rights and became involved in various media projects.

By the turn of the millennium Pavlovsky had become part of the campaign to elect Putin in 2000 and to re-elect him in 2004. In May that year, two months after Putin won his second term, he turned his talents to Yanukovych's campaign. Based in Ukraine until the election, Pavlovsky flew back to Moscow every week to report to his masters in the Kremlin. He quickly realised that Kuchma had not chosen the best successor and understood why Putin was supporting him only reluctantly. 'Kuchma's big mistake was that he thought Yanukovych was rough, strong and ruthless and could suppress any disorder that might arise, as well as support his interests,' says Pavlovsky. 'But he just didn't look like a candidate who could win.'[7]

More than a decade later, Pavlovsky chuckles as he recalls a university rally in the western city of Ivano-Frankivsk, when someone threw a hard-boiled egg at Yanukovych and he passed out for a few moments. 'He lost consciousness and then tried to justify it by saying that it was a stone,' he says. 'But it wasn't a stone. It was a boiled egg and he was just scared.'

The Kremlin had no choice but to work with the candidate it had. But in an attempt to hedge its bets, it also reached out to Yushchenko's team. Oleh Rybachuk, his campaign chief and future chief of staff, recalled receiving strange overtures from an old school friend he had not seen for more than twenty years. The man suggested he come to Moscow to meet people close to Putin. Rybachuk assumed the man was working for Russian intelligence, but took him up on his offer out of curiosity. As he described it to Roxburgh, over the next month and a half he visited Moscow every week, where 'in dimly lit restaurants and speaking in whispers', his host tried to establish what Yushchenko would do if elected. Rybachuk's answer confirmed the Kremlin's worst fears: 'Our policies are simple,' he told them. 'We want to be a democratic country, a European country. We want to be a NATO member for European security. When we come to power we won't be a problem because you'll know what to expect from us.'[8] His candour did not make the prospect of victory for Yushchenko any more acceptable to the Kremlin.

On 5 September, after a dinner with the head of the Ukrainian security services, Yushchenko was suddenly taken ill. Ukrainian doctors were unable to determine what was wrong with him – except that it was potentially life-threatening – and he was sent to hospital in Vienna. Doctors there eventually found that he had been poisoned with dioxin, a toxin produced in a handful of countries that included Russia and excluded Ukraine. The diagnosis saved Yushchenko's life, but the poisoning left his face horribly disfigured.

Yushchenko was out of action for two weeks at a crucial moment in the campaign, during which time his deputy, Yulia Tymoshenko, kept the flag flying, addressing rallies around the country at which she accused the opposition of trying to poison him. Heavily sedated against the excruciating pain, Yushchenko marked his return with a televised interview that was broadcast live to squares across the country. The station was owned by Petro Poroshenko, a wealthy businessman and supporter of Yushchenko who, a decade later, would become president himself.

Inevitably Yushchenko's illness – and the suspicion of foul play – strengthened his standing and hurt his rival, prompting the Kremlin to deploy the most powerful weapon in its armoury: Vladimir Putin. The Russian leader still enjoyed considerable popularity with the Ukrainian population, and Yanukovych's team hoped some of it would rub off on their lacklustre candidate. On 9 October, Kuchma and Yanukovych were invited to Moscow to join Putin in celebrations for his birthday. Reflecting on the choice faced by Ukraine, Kuchma wondered aloud whether his compatriots would opt for a 'tried and tested' path that would bring results or one 'that will scupper everything that's been done these past ten years'. Their meeting with Putin would, he hoped, 'help to push things in the right direction'. With just five days to go before the poll, Putin reciprocated with a three-day visit to Ukraine. After a live interview, broadcast simultaneously on all three of the country's state television channels, he accompanied Yanukovych to ceremonies marking the sixtieth anniversary of the country's liberation from the Nazis. The anniversary actually fell on 6 November, but that would have been after the first round of the election, so it was brought forward to 28 October. Putin sat alongside Kuchma and Yanukovych in a reviewing stand on Khreshchatyk, Kiev's main street, as hundreds of performers dressed in Second World War uniforms marched past in a giant patriotic carnival intended as a reminder of how Russians and Ukrainians had fought side by side against the Nazis. Yushchenko, by contrast, was portrayed in propaganda dreamt up by the Kremlin's spin doctors as anti-Russian and an heir to the nationalists who teamed up with the German occupying forces to betray the Soviet Union.

The result of the first round of the vote showed that there was everything to play for. Although Yushchenko headed a crowded field with 39.9% of the vote, Yanukovych was a very close second on 39.26%. With the communists and socialists likely to swing behind Yanukovych in the second-run round-off, Moscow's plan appeared to be working. The only television debate of the campaign was held on 15 November, six days before the second round. Pavlovsky, who had helped Yanukovych prepare, felt that his man had won it.

The polls nevertheless showed Yushchenko ahead, with around 53% compared with Yanukovych's 44%. Yet when the official results of the second round came in, Yanukovych romped home with 49.5% against his rival's 46.9%. Telephone intercepts of conversations between members of Yanukovych's staff revealed they had tampered with the state electoral commission's server in order to falsify the results.

Despite sub-zero temperatures, some 200,000 people descended on Maidan Nezalezhnosti, Kiev's Independence Square, erecting a tent city and vowing to stay there until the injustice was corrected. Their protest became known as the Orange Revolution, after the colour of Yushchenko's campaign. Over the next week, a million people joined, laying siege to government buildings. Protests were echoed in Lviv and elsewhere in the west of the country where support for Yushchenko was strongest; by contrast, demonstrations in favour of Yanukovych erupted in the south and east. Ukraine's historical division was reasserting itself, peacefully, but in great numbers.

Putin, who was on an official visit to Brazil, called Yanukovych to congratulate him, but American and European leaders refused to follow suit. Images of the young protesters on the Maidan were broadcast around the world. The message was clear: the people of Ukraine, a country until then largely neglected by the outside world, wanted freedom and justice – but were being denied it by their rulers. And still the demonstrators kept on coming to the Maidan. It was the biggest display of people power since the end of communism.

The Kremlin wanted the Ukrainian authorities to act decisively and disperse the crowds, but Kuchma knew that this would lead to a bloodbath and was unwilling to risk it; after all, it was Yanukovych's future rather than his own that was at stake. Indeed, a contested election could work in his favour by giving him an excuse to stay on. Kuchma had also reportedly been warned by Richard Lugar, the influential US senator who headed the election observers, that he could suffer the same fate as Slobodan Milošević, on trial for war crimes in The Hague, if the situation turned violent. So he held off doing anything, hoping the bitter cold would persuade the protesters to give up and go home. But they were made of sterner stuff. In the early hours of 23 November, Kuchma called Aleksander Kwaśniewski, the Polish president, asking him to mediate. Kwaśniewski knew Kuchma well and also understood the political situation in Ukraine. He agreed to put together a European Union mission.

In the meantime, Ukraine's central election commission upped the stakes by proclaiming Yanukovych the victor. Colin Powell responded with a statement in which he refused to accept the result as legitimate 'because it does not meet international standards and because there has not been an investigation of the numerous and credible reports of fraud and abuse'. The US secretary of state added: 'We're not looking for a contest with the Russians over this. We're looking for a way to make sure that the will of the Ukrainian people is respected.'9

For the next few days, Ukraine teetered on the edge of violence. Some forty thousand miners from Yanukovych's home region of Donetsk were reported to be marching towards Kiev to do battle with the Maidan protesters. Warned by Kwaśniewski that this would lead to a bloodbath that would be laid at his door, Kuchma called them off. A few days later, interior ministry troops were reported to be massing on the edge of the capital. Again, it proved to be a false alarm. Despairing of a way to break the impasse, Kuchma finally agreed to a rerun of the poll, although only after flying to Moscow on 2 December to obtain the grudging approval of Putin. A settlement was agreed six days later. It included a new election and an agreement on constitutional reform that would transform Ukraine from a presidential-style republic like Russia into one in which the parliament had more powers – including the right to appoint the prime minister, hitherto the prerogative of the head of the state.

When the new vote took place on 26 December, Yushchenko won by fifty-two per cent to fourty-four per cent – a result that mirrored the exit polls. Despite the clear margin, a majority of voters in the east still backed his rival. After several court challenges by Yanukovych were rejected, Yushchenko was inaugurated as president on 3 January. The next day the parliament approved his choice of Tymoshenko as prime minister by a vote of 373 to 0.

RUSSIA AND THE WEST DREW RADICALLY different conclusions from the events of those weeks. For many in the Bush administration, the Orange Revolution was part of a wave of democratisation that would continue to sweep through the former Soviet states, eventually reaching Russia itself. It also had serious geopolitical implications: Yushchenko indicated that he wanted his country to join both the European Union and also eventually NATO, effectively detaching Ukraine from Russia's sphere of influence for the first time in centuries and allowing it to take its place alongside Poland, Hungary and the other new democracies of Central and Eastern Europe.

In a show of Western support, Yushchenko was invited to the Alliance's summit in February 2005. Then, during a visit to the United States in April, he was welcomed by Bush in the White House and addressed a joint session of Congress, the first leader of a former Soviet republic other than Russia to be accorded such a privilege. His face still pockmarked by the effects of the poisoning he suffered during the campaign, he made the most of the platform. Greeted with applause and chants of 'Yushchenko, Yushchenko' like those that filled the streets of Kiev during the Orange Revolution, he thanked lawmakers for the 'clear and unambiguous' support that Washington had given during the crisis and called for help for Ukraine to deepen its integration with the West and to 'live in peace and accord with all of its neighbours, whether in the East or in the West'.

Russia saw things very differently. Yanukovych's defeat was a slap in the face for the Kremlin, given the effort and prestige it had invested in him. Taken together with the events in Georgia and in Kyrgyzstan, whose leader was toppled in the 'Tulip Revolution' of March 2005, it suggested the 'near abroad' could no longer be taken for granted by Moscow. That impression was further reinforced by the reception Yushchenko was given in Washington. The United States, it seemed to Putin, was trying to detach Ukraine from Russia's orbit, and its professed concerns for democracy and human rights were little more than a cover for America's geopolitical interest. In so doing, it believed, Washington was going against the interests not just of the Kremlin but also against those of the millions of people who had voted for Yanukovych and wanted to continue to have close ties with Russia. Since independence, Ukraine had maintained a uniquely delicate balance between Russia and the West, but that balance was now in danger of being upset.

The Orange Revolution was all the more alarming because of the existential threat it posed to the Kremlin: the Ukrainians, like the Georgians before them, had provided a compelling model of how ordinary people could mobilise in a post-Soviet society to prevent a discredited regime from clinging to office – with more than a helping hand from the CIA, in Putin's view. Putin's concern was that Bush, with his determination to promote democracy around the world, might now try to encourage similar such forces in Russia to challenge Putin's own hold on power.

Russian concerns were enhanced by Bush's re-election on 2 November, three days after the first round of the Ukrainian election: not only did he increase his share of the vote, but the Republicans also upped their representation in both houses of Congress. In Bush's second inaugural speech on 20 January, he declared a belief in America's duty to promote democracy around the world as the only way of preserving its security – and preventing a repetition of the 9/11 attacks. 'As long as whole regions of the world simmer in resentment and tyranny – prone to ideologies that feed hatred and excuse murder – violence will gather, and multiply in destructive power, and cross the most defended borders, and raise a mortal threat,' Bush declared. 'The best hope for peace in our world is the expansion of freedom in all the world. America's vital interests and our deepest beliefs are now one.'

Bush's words were an explicit rejection of the pursuit of international stability, which had been the basis of US policy since the end of the Second World War. During the Cold War, America had backed the

existing global order and the Soviet Union had preached world revolution. Now Washington preached intervention, while Russia called
for maintenance of the status quo and non-interference in the affairs
of sovereign countries.

What to Bush seemed like a neat coincidence of morality and
national self-interest looked very different from Moscow. For Russia,
Washington appeared to be following up its war in Iraq by giving
itself a licence to support regime change wherever it wished in the
world. To Putin's fury, the countries at the top of its hit list were those
with which Russia had the closest economic and business ties. This
was coupled with disappointment at what Russia had achieved from
its new relationship with America. On a personal level, Putin had
come to like Bush, as well as to admire him as a strong leader. Yet
for all the backslapping bonhomie whenever they met, he was affronted
by Bush's unwillingness to treat Russia as an equal. Furthermore, since
coming to power he had made a string of concessions – ranging from
support for the 'war on terror' to acceptance of a second wave of
NATO expansion – but had received nothing in return. The cooperation with Washington that had characterised his first years in office
was replaced by wariness at the West's malign intentions towards his
country. Putin began to see conspiracies everywhere. He feared Russia
itself could be next.

'Putin began to realise that this fellow Bush had quite a few opportunities and that technically it was possible that after Iraq and
Afghanistan he might focus on Russia,' said Pavlovsky. 'Suddenly the
old Russian pattern was resurrected: to hell with it, we've been best
friends with America and they're going to do a 22 June [1941, when
Hitler's army attacked the Soviet Union in breach of their treaty] on
us. Of course, it was after Ukraine that the Kremlin started feeling this
way. And Bush's new programme – to spread democracy around the
world – helped to intensify it.'[10]

The Finnish president, Tarja Halonen, met Putin in St Petersburg on
14 December, in the middle of the Ukraine crisis, and found him 'frus-
trated, stressed and anxious' about Russia's relations with the West.
According to a member of Halonen's staff, Putin spent much of the
meeting complaining about the way his country had been misunderstood
and mistreated. He directed particular criticism towards US support for
the Saakashvili government, which had come to power in Georgia 'in

an illegal way', and implied that Washington was actively fostering regime change in the 'near abroad', with the EU providing political cover.

'Putin is in a state of mind where he can't decide what to do,' said Olli Perheentupa, director of the Finnish foreign office's Russia unit. 'He goes from one summit to the next, just reacting to the outside world, not moving forward according to any strategy or vision.' That was soon to change.

14

MUNICH

In February 2007 Vladimir Putin stood in front of the Munich Security Conference, the first Russian leader to do so since the event's inception more than four decades earlier, at the height of the Cold War, as a forum for discussing foreign policy. There was a great sense of anticipation among the audience in the Bayerischer Hof hotel, which included the German chancellor Angela Merkel and Robert Gates, the newly appointed US defence secretary. Before beginning his speech, Putin said he would avoid 'excessive politeness and the need to speak in roundabout, pleasant but empty diplomatic terms', adding: 'If my comments seen unduly polemical, pointed or inexact to our colleagues then I would ask you not to get angry with me.' He hoped the moderator wouldn't try to cut him off after two or three minutes.

Putin proved to be as good as his word, proceeding to launch a broadside against America and what he saw as its determination during the years since the collapse of the Soviet Union to create, and dominate, a 'unipolar world'. 'The United States has overstepped its borders in all spheres – economic, political and humanitarian – and has imposed itself on other states,' Putin declared. Such a formula had led to disaster. 'Local and regional wars did not get fewer, the number of people who died did not reduce but increased. We see no kind of restraint – a hyper-inflated use of force.' Only the United Nations – not NATO nor the European Union – could authorise the use of military force around the world, Putin said, and even then it should be as a last resort.

For many of those in the audience it sounded remarkably like the declaration of a new Cold War. Jaap de Hoop Scheffer, the NATO secretary general, called Putin's remarks 'disappointing and not helpful'; John McCain, who was to announce his presidential run that April, accused him of making the 'most aggressive remarks by a Russian leader since the end of the Cold War' and insisted that it was autocratic Russia – rather than America – that needed to change its behaviour. In his response the next day, Gates, a former CIA director, tried to defuse the tension with humour, noting that 'as an old Cold Warrior', Putin's speech 'almost filled me with nostalgia for a less complex time'.

A decade later, Igor Ivanov, who at the time of the speech was a member of Putin's Security Council, denies it was confrontational. 'That speech was not, as some people wanted to present it, the intention of Russia to restore the Soviet Union or something,' he says.[1] 'It was a cry from the soul of someone who could no longer accept and tolerate what [the West] was doing.' It also very much represented the Kremlin leader's own thoughts: various drafts of the speech had been prepared by the foreign ministry and the presidential administration, but the final version was all Putin's. 'What he said was a surprise for all of us because it was very personal,' recalls Ivanov. 'It was his own speech.'

PUTIN'S WORDS REFLECTED HIS GROWING ASSERTIVENESS since the Colour Revolutions. He consolidated political and economic power in his hands and marginalised his opponents. A pro-Kremlin youth group, *Nashi*, was created to organise demonstrations and take on opposition protesters. Fundamental elements of democracy such as the separation of powers, an independent judiciary, the rule of law and freedom of the press, which had been established during the Yeltsin era, were being eroded. Elections continued to be held, but the shifting multiparty system of the 1990s was giving way to one in which there was a single dominant governing party, United Russia, and a few smaller parties that could be presented as opposition but without challenging the Kremlin's hold on power.

The new mood had been reflected in Putin's State of the Union address in April 2005, in which he described the demise of the Soviet Union as 'the greatest geopolitical catastrophe of the last century', adding: 'As for the Russian people, it became a genuine tragedy. Tens

of millions of our fellow citizens and countrymen found themselves
beyond the fringes of Russian territory. The epidemic of collapse has
spilled over to Russia itself.'² Putin's comments, apparently timed to
coincide with the sixtieth anniversary of the end of the Second World
War the following month, provoked alarm and condemnation from
some of the leaders of neighbouring countries. In the years since, they
have been repeatedly quoted against him and offered as evidence of a
master plan to re-create the USSR. In reality, his words were not so
extraordinary: Putin was looking back, as many ordinary Russians did,
and regretting the loss of territory and superpower status that his
country had once enjoyed.

United Russia's dominance looked certain to be enhanced by new
electoral rules – due to come into force for the Duma election of
December 2007 – that stipulated all candidates should be elected on the
basis of party lists and increased the minimum share of the vote required
for a party to enter parliament. Those who took to the streets to protest
against the changes found themselves on the wrong side of the law. In
the run-up to the July 2006 G8 summit, held on Russian soil for the
first time in St Petersburg, more than a hundred people were intimidated,
harassed or beaten by the police, or had their passports taken away for
no legal reason. A large number were young activists linked to an alternative event, timed to coincide with the summit, entitled The Other
Russia. Foreign delegates were told by a high-ranking Kremlin official
that attendance at the event would be treated as an 'unfriendly gesture'.
Many ignored the warning and went anyway.³

The Kremlin even came up with a new term to define how Russia
was run. It was no longer a matter, as it had been in the early 1990s,
of attempting – albeit with only limited success – to rebuild the country's political institutions along Western lines. Russia was instead to
be a 'sovereign democracy'. The term was coined by Vladislav Surkov,
Putin's deputy chief of staff and one of his most influential aides, in a
speech to the United Russia Party in February 2006. According to
Surkov's opaque definition, it was 'a society's political life where the
political powers, their authorities and decisions are decided and
controlled by a diverse Russian nation for the purpose of reaching
material welfare, freedom and fairness by all citizens, social groups
and nationalities, by the people that formed it'.

Commentators devoted many column inches to pondering the

nature of the system that Surkov was describing. Masha Lipman, of the Carnegie Moscow Center, put it more pithily in a commentary in the *Washington Post*: "'Sovereign democracy" is a Kremlin coinage that conveys two messages: first, that Russia's regime is democratic and second, that this claim must be accepted, period. Any attempt at verification will be regarded as unfriendly and as meddling in Russia's domestic affairs.'[4]

Russia was also flexing its muscles abroad. It blocked a strong United Nations Security Council move against Iran, and alarmed both America and Israel by inviting a delegation from Hamas to Moscow in March 2006 after the militant group won the Palestinian elections. Russia was also quick to re-establish its former strong ties with Uzbekistan after Washington fell out with its leader, Islam Karimov, over his bloody suppression of an Islamist uprising in Andizhan in the east of the country in May 2005. The United States demanded an international inquiry into the massacre. Karimov refused and in July, amid an escalating war of words, told America it was no longer welcome to use the military base it had set up there after the 9/11 attacks. Putin, by contrast, had no interest in scrutinising Karimov's human rights record. That November, Russia and Uzbekistan signed a mutual cooperation agreement.

Russia was also making greater use of gas as a political weapon: friendly powers henceforth would be rewarded by investment in joint projects, while uncooperative neighbours would be punished with price hikes or even denial of supply – a fate suffered by Ukraine on New Year's Day 2006, when a long-running dispute with Russia culminated in the cutting off of all gas running through its territory.

Underpinning its actions was a changed attitude to the West. Gorbachev and Yeltsin had been constrained by the weakness of the economy; the need to keep on good terms with Western creditors limited Russia's ability to stand up to America over policies it did not like. Putin, by contrast, presided over a growing Russian economy, which had jumped in size by two-thirds since 1999. His arrival on the scene had, in itself, led to an improvement in confidence and with it the first signs of an upturn. Matters were helped by economic reforms carried out by Mikhail Kasyanov, the prime minister for his first four years. A rise in the global oil price did the rest: from an average $23 or so per barrel in 2001 and 2002, it jumped to $50 in 2005, just over

$58 in 2006 and more than $64 in 2007. Oil production, meanwhile, had risen by a half during the course of the new millennium.[5] This, in turn, allowed the Kremlin to put money into a domestic 'stabilisation' fund, which contained $100 billion by the time of the Munich speech. In 2006 the Kremlin paid off its entire $22 billion debt to the IMF ahead of schedule.

Russia and its wealthy elite did not want to be isolated from the rest of the world, but they also expected recognition of their country's standing and respect for its economic and geopolitical interests. And they were no longer prepared to put up with being lectured about how far their country and its practices fell short of the American ideal.

Putin's new-found assertiveness – coupled with Bush's so-called 'freedom agenda' – prompted a rethink of America's attitude towards Russia. Talk of Russia's integration into the West and of a 'strategic partnership' between Moscow and Washington that had prevailed since the days of Gorbachev no longer seemed appropriate. The question now was how best to cope with a newly assertive Russia. As part of this, Western policymakers began to accept that Russia would not necessarily ever embrace democracy. For that reason, it should be considered as different from Central European countries such as Poland and Hungary and even some of the other former Soviet republics such as Ukraine. It should be placed instead in the same category as China, geopolitically important but essentially competitive.

Within the US administration there were growing calls from the beginning of 2006 for a 'recalibration' of policy towards Russia, with a split emerging in the White House between what one official described as 'the Putin lovers' and the 'democracy lovers'.[6] Minds were further concentrated by the G8 meeting that July in St Petersburg. In the run-up to the event, Putin's critics warned that it risked granting legitimacy to an increasingly undemocratic administration. McCain urged Bush to boycott it completely.

'The G8 summit in St Petersburg is becoming the focal point for everybody to reconsider where we are in terms of Russia,' claimed Anders Åslund, a Russia specialist at the Institute for International Economics. 'Is this really where we want to be? Should we change policy?'[7]

The new tougher line was championed by Dick Cheney, the US vice president, who advocated the pursuit of a 'values-centred' policy towards Russia,[8] rather than a more pragmatic one based on national interest. That January, he had summoned Russia scholars – Åslund among them – to his office and tasked John Negroponte, the national intelligence director, with providing further information about Putin's intentions.

Like many of those around Bush, Cheney never understood the president's personal warmth towards Putin; he always saw him as the KGB officer he had once been. Cheney's dim view of the Russian leader had been reinforced by an experience that January when he had led the US delegation to Poland to mark the sixtieth anniversary of the liberation of Auschwitz. In his memoirs, he describes how Putin turned up late for his speech, bursting into the ornate nineteenth-century Juliusz Słowacki Theatre in Kraków's Old Town when proceedings were already under way. As burly security guards cleared the way, the Russian leader strode up the aisle and, ignoring the fact that someone else was speaking, began to deliver his own speech. Cheney saw Putin's action as a calculated snub to Kwaśniewski, his host, who had earned the Kremlin's displeasure by championing the cause of Yushchenko in the Orange Revolution. 'Watching his behaviour that day reminded me why Russia's leaders are so disliked by their neighbours and why we were right to expand NATO and offer membership to former Soviet client states like Poland and Romania,' Cheney recalled.[9]

Yet Rice, who responded to Cheney by summoning her own group of experts, remained sceptical. She feared that if America pushed the Kremlin too far on human rights, it risked complicating cooperation over other issues such as Iran's nuclear programme, where America was trying to persuade the Kremlin to back tougher action against Tehran. There was also a reluctance to abandon Putin completely, especially in the light of his decision to allow US forces into Central Asia. Bush, too, was haunted by his earlier claim to have got a sense of his interlocutor's soul. To shift from such backslapping bonhomie to open hostility would have made the president look like a poor judge of character.

Matters came to a head in May 2006, when Cheney met European leaders in Vilnius, the Lithuanian capital. In a speech he combined praise for the political and economic progress made by many of the former communist countries of Central and Eastern Europe with his strongest rebuke to date of Russia's record. 'In Russia today, opponents of reform are seeking to reverse the gains of the last decade,' Cheney declared.[10] 'In many areas of civil society – from religion and the news media, to advocacy groups and political parties – the government has unfairly and improperly restricted the rights of her people. Other actions by the Russian government have been counterproductive, and could begin to affect relations with other countries. No legitimate interest is served when oil and gas become tools of intimidation or blackmail, either by supply manipulation or attempts to monopolize transportation. And no one can justify actions that undermine the territorial integrity of a neighbour, or interfere with democratic movements.'

Russian anger at Cheney's criticism was compounded by the very different approach that Washington adopted towards two other former Soviet republics, whose records on human rights and democracy were far poorer even than Russia's. When Ilham Aliyev, the leader of oil-rich Azerbaijan, had visited Washington that February, he had been feted by Bush. In Washington's eyes, the country's strategic location between Russia and Iran and its willingness to provide logistical support for the war in Afghanistan and the broader fight against terror outweighed concerns about the manner in which Aliyev had succeeded his father as president in 2003.

America displayed similar tolerance towards Kazakhstan, which Cheney flew on to after Lithuania. Like Azerbaijan, it has considerable energy resources, and it is strategically located between Russia and China. Its leader, Nursultan Nazarbayev, who has run the country since 1989, first as Communist Party leader and then since 1991 as president, won another seven-year term in December 2005 with more than ninety-one per cent of the vote – a suspiciously impressive performance even for a man beloved by his people.

Standing alongside Nazarbayev in the marble hall of the magnificent presidential palace in Astana, the capital, Cheney praised the country's economic achievements and made no mention of the banning of opposition parties, shutting down of newspapers or intimidation of advocacy groups. When asked about the country's human rights record, Cheney expressed 'admiration for all that's been accomplished here in Kazakhstan', coupled with confidence that such 'accomplishments' would continue.[11]

Such inconsistency played into the hands of America's critics. Bush's freedom agenda, far from being prompted by genuine concern for human rights, was merely a stick with which to beat Russia, they claimed. Putin took a swipe at US policy in his State of the Union address a few days later. 'As the saying goes, Comrade Wolf knows whom to eat, it eats without listening and it's clearly not going to listen to anyone,' he said, adding: 'Where is all this pathos about protecting human rights and democracy when it comes to the need to pursue their own interests?'[12] There was more of the same at the G8 in St Petersburg, where Putin used a joint press conference to compare the state of Russia's democracy unfavourably with that in Iraq following the US invasion. 'I'll be honest with you: we, of course, would not want to have a democracy like in Iraq,' Putin retorted, prompting laughter from the press corps.[13]

It was more than just verbal sparring. Something more fundamental was happening, according to Dmitry Trenin, a leading Russian analyst at the Carnegie Moscow Center. His article, 'Russia leaves the West', which appeared in the July/August 2006 edition of *Foreign Policy*, foreshadowed the points Putin made in his Munich speech the following February. The Kremlin's new approach to foreign policy, Trenin argued, assumed that Russia, as a big country, was essentially friendless: none of the great powers wanted it to be strong, since it would be a competitor, and many instead wanted it to be weak so that they could exploit and manipulate it. This meant Russia was left with a choice between accepting subservience and reasserting its status as a great power. It was clear which of the two Putin would choose.

'Until recently, Russia saw itself as Pluto in the Western solar system, very far from the centre but still fundamentally a part of it,' Trenin wrote. 'Now it has left that orbit entirely: Russia's leaders have given up on becoming part of the West and have started creating their own Moscow-centred system.

'The United States and Europe can protest this change in Russia's foreign policy all they want, but it will not make any difference. They must recognise that the terms of Western–Russian interaction, conceptualised at the time of the Soviet Union's collapse fifteen years ago and more or less unchanged since, have shifted fundamentally. The old paradigm is lost, and it is time to start looking for a new one.'

AT THE TIME OF PUTIN'S MUNICH SPEECH, he had just over a year to serve of his second and – under the terms of the Russian constitution – final term. Yet Putin was not yet ready to give up power, and he was not going to allow constitutional niceties to stand in his way. A solution had to be found: the simplest would be to engineer a change in the constitution to allow for a third or fourth term, a tactic followed by the leaders of Kazakhstan and Uzbekistan, whose presidents were still in power after almost two decades. However, this would hand further ammunition to his critics.

As the date of the presidential election, set for 2 March 2008, approached, other more inventive solutions presented themselves. Talks scheduled for December between Russia and Belarus to discuss a long-term merger of their countries prompted speculation that Putin might become president of what, in strict constitutional terms, would be a new nation, thereby resetting the electoral clock. Yet the talks proved fruitless – and even before they had started, Kremlin sources had dismissed the idea as mere speculation.

Putin had another solution: in October, during the conference of the United Russia Party, he announced that he might become prime minister the following year. Putin had often said he intended to remain involved in politics after his second term expired and that he might seek re-election after someone else took his place as president. With this statement, however, he made it clear that there would be no break in his influence. Implicit in this was a reinterpretation of the Russian constitution to turn the prime minister into a powerful figure in his own right, rather than merely a tool of the president, as had hitherto been the case.

But who would take Putin's place in the Kremlin? For much of the year, speculation centred on three men: Dmitry Medvedev, the first deputy prime minister and chairman of Gazprom; Sergei Ivanov, a deputy prime minister and defence minister; and Vladimir Yakunin, head of the Russian railways. All were members of Putin's St Petersburg circle. There was also some speculation about Viktor Zubkov, who was appointed prime minister that September. Another Putin associate from St Petersburg, he had been involved in the fight against money laundering and financial crime, initially in that city and then in Moscow. Soon after taking the job, Zubkov spoke publicly of the possibility of standing for president.

It was not to be: on 10 December 2007, Putin appeared on television alongside the leaders of the four political parties allied with the Kremlin to announce that he was formally endorsing Medvedev. 'I've been very close to him for more than seventeen years,' Putin declared. 'I fully and completely support this candidate.'

Medvedev, with his background in the law rather than in the state security services, had virtually no independent power base in the Kremlin. Nor had he ever stood for popular election. Yet this weakness was, in a sense, his strength, as far as his suitability to Putin was concerned. Putin also knew that he could trust him; the two of them had worked together under Mayor Sobchak in St Petersburg, and Medvedev had gone on to be Putin's legal adviser, as well as running his election campaign in 2000 and spending two years as his chief of staff.

In his first speech after being endorsed as candidate, Medvedev announced that, if elected, he would appoint Putin as his prime minister. Election posters underlined his promise to work closely with the outgoing president, portraying the two men side by side with the slogan: '*Vmeste Pobedim*' ('Together We Win'). This 'Vote Medvedev – get Putin' policy had the desired effect. Medvedev stormed home with seventy-one per cent of the vote, compared to just eighteen per cent for his nearest rival, Gennady Zyuganov, the veteran Communist Party leader, who had taken a break from the 2004 presidential contest but was back to try his hand again. The other perennial post-Soviet candidate, Vladimir Zhirinovsky, came a distant third.

Precisely as had happened in 2000, a man virtually unknown to the public a few months earlier had been catapulted into the leadership of one of the most powerful countries on earth. As Medvedev moved into the Kremlin and Putin went back to his old office in the White House, analysts were left to ponder the nature of the political tandem that would rule Russia for the next four years. Would Putin – in defiance of the spirit if not the letter of the constitution – continue to wield absolute power? Or would his young protégé, reputed to be more moderate and open to the West, take advantage of his new role to make his mark?

15

THE TRAP

L OOK AT A MAP OF THE former Soviet Union and try to find South Ossetia. You may need a magnifying glass. Lying in the north of Georgia on the southern slopes of the Caucasus, it covers a mere 1,500 square miles – making it just one-third of the size of Yorkshire – and is home to just over fifty thousand people. The Ossetians are a people divided: travel just over two miles through the Roki Tunnel, which cuts its way through the mountains, and you will enter North Ossetia, an autonomous republic within the Russian Federation, which is double the size in land terms and has thirteen times the number of people. Yet South Ossetia's small size belies its significance. In August 2008 this poor, mountainous territory found itself at the heart of a war between Russia and Georgia that threatened to draw in the West, causing the most serious strain in relations between Washington and Moscow since the end of the Cold War.

South Ossetia's difficult relationship with Georgia was the result of long-standing enmity between the two that had flared up periodically over the centuries, most dramatically in 1990, during the dying days of the Soviet Union, when the region had declared independence from Georgia. About a thousand people were killed and more than 120,000 were driven from their homes in the conflict that followed, but an uneasy calm had prevailed with a Russian-brokered ceasefire in June 1992. South Ossetia had since been placed under the control of a peacekeeping organisation known as the Joint Control Commission for Georgian–Ossetian Conflict Resolution, which was made up of representatives from Georgia, South Ossetia, Russia and North Ossetia.

The region's 'frozen' status was similar to that of Abkhazia, Georgia's other separatist ethnic enclave, which had been embroiled in war for the previous two decades. Both regions received support from Russia, but Moscow held back from granting formal recognition to either for fear the move would undermine its own refusal to allow Chechnya, which was in an analogous position, to secede from Russia. The Georgian authorities believed the Kremlin was using the conflicts to undermine the integrity of their state. Yet as always with these stories of Russia's 'meddling' in the near abroad, its activities were carried out in the context of long-running ethnic grievances.

Mikheil Saakashvili, Georgia's young president, was determined to bring both regions to heel. Since his election in January 2004 following the Rose Revolution, he had made it clear where he saw his country's place in the world. During his inauguration ceremony, the European flag had flown over the parliament building, and the Georgian national anthem was followed by Beethoven's 'Ode to Joy', the EU's anthem – somewhat to the consternation of some of Brussels' representatives who were present. Heike Talvitie, the EU special representative for the South Caucasus, voiced concern over Saakashvili's unrealistic expectations of membership for Georgia, which was poor and located on the far side of the Black Sea, more than a thousand miles from the union's existing eastern border.[1]

Conscious of the importance of maintaining good relations with his powerful northern neighbour, Saakashvili made Moscow his first foreign trip the following month. Surprisingly, given the differences in their respective outlooks, he and Putin appeared to hit it off – even though their meeting got off to an inauspicious start after Saakashvili turned up at the Kremlin half an hour late, claiming to have lost track of time while swimming laps in the pool. Saakashvili declared he would do everything in his power to get on well with Russia, but once they were alone Putin warned his young guest of the perils of getting too close to America, which, he believed, had not just supported but actually planned the Rose Revolution. Putin also expressed unease about America's modest military presence in Georgia: a group of several hundred troops had been sent to the Pankisi Gorge, near the border with Chechnya, under a programme launched two years earlier to help the Georgians drive out any Islamist militants who had crossed the frontier.

According to Saakashvili's own account, after listening patiently for more than twenty minutes to Putin's tirade, he politely stopped his host. 'Do you really believe that what happened in Georgia is an American plot?' he asked. 'Do you really believe that our government is paid by Americans, or George Soros or, you know, that we are directed by them?'[2] Putin conceded that he did not – but made clear his belief that some people in Saakashvili's government might be working closely with the Americans.

The Moscow trip, nevertheless, appeared to have been a success. 'Actually, I liked him,' Saakashvili said of his meeting with Putin. 'I cannot blame George Bush for looking into his soul because my first impression was that I liked him. I thought, well, yeah, he comes from this KGB kind of background, he is very different from what I come from and what I believe in, but this seems to be a pragmatic guy . . . And you know, he was basically also trying to show, by the end of our conversation, that he could go a long way to solving some issues.'[3] The Kremlin seemed to reciprocate. In Saakashvili, Russia saw 'a politician who has taken responsibility for what happens in Georgia', Sergei Prikhodko, the deputy head of Putin's administration, told the ITAR-TASS news agency.

With Russia's help, Saakashvili took his first step towards reasserting control over the entire territory of Georgia: that May he persuaded Aslan Abashidze, the independent-minded leader of Ajaria, which lies on the Black Sea coast in the south-west of the country, to step down. Igor Ivanov, secretary of Putin's Security Council, flew down to Georgia and offered Abashidze asylum in Russia if he left quietly. He accepted the offer and hitched a ride back to Moscow in Ivanov's plane.

Saakashvili had won victory without firing a shot and the success quickly went to his head: he vowed to his jubilant supporters that he would now take Abkhazia and South Ossetia as well. In the weeks that followed, he heightened his war of words with the two regions. During a military parade to mark Georgian Independence Day on 26 May, he addressed Abkhazians and Ossetians in their own respective languages and urged them to reintegrate with Georgia. Troops were sent towards the South Ossetian border ostensibly on an anti-smuggling operation; the deployment sparked the worst skirmishes for a decade.

Despite the need to keep on good terms with Russia, Saakashvili's real aim was to tilt his country towards the West, ideally joining both NATO as well as the European Union. He and his young cabinet ministers impressed their hosts when they travelled to Washington shortly after Saakashvili's trip to Moscow. When Bush visited Tbilisi in May 2005, tens of thousands of cheering Georgians packed into the city's Freedom Square to greet him. Bush demonstrated a 'sophisticated knowledge of local issues', Saakashvili told a visiting US diplomat the following January. Russia, by contrast, saw other countries in black and white, dividing the world into 'their friends and "America's stooges"'. Saakashvili then laughed: 'And we are the most outspoken American stooges.'[4]

There was certainly no love lost between Saakashvili and Moscow. During a meeting with William Burns, the US ambassador to Russia, a couple of weeks later, Igor Ivanov launched a tirade against the Georgian leader, denouncing him as a 'very emotional and impressionable' person who had been 'unready' when he came to power.[5] In March 2006, Burns summed up Georgia's dilemma in a cable that was subsequently leaked: 'Georgia has a concrete short-term goal: recovery of South Ossetia, the key to which is in Moscow,' he wrote. 'Georgia also has a concrete medium-term goal: recovery of Abkhazia, the key to which is also in Moscow. And Georgia has a long-term goal: joining NATO, a prospect that makes Russia want to throw away both keys.'[6]

As part of its pursuit of NATO membership, Saakashvili increased his country's military presence in Iraq. Georgia already had 850 troops in Iraq, and in March 2007 announced plans to more than double that figure to two thousand, making it America's second largest ally after Britain – an extraordinary level of contribution given the country's population and level of poverty. Georgian officials play down any quid pro quo with the Americans, even informally, though it was difficult to see the move as anything other than a down payment on its own security.

Although Washington was impressed by Saakashvili's pro-Western stance, there was also concern at his often reckless behaviour. Richard Miles, the US ambassador to Georgia, saw Saakashvili as needlessly provocative towards Russia and urged caution. But the Georgian leader remained determined to rein in the wayward regions of South Ossetia and Abkhazia. During his successful re-election campaign in January 2008, he likened the South Ossetian capital, Tskhinvali, to 'a loose tooth ready for removal' and vowed to seize it 'within months at the most'. Any such move looked certain to bring Georgia into conflict with Russia, but Saakashvili pressed on regardless.

The issue was further complicated by the question of NATO membership not just for Georgia but also for Ukraine. Both were next in line to be granted a Membership Action Plan, the programme intended to prepare countries to join the Alliance. Their candidacy was set to be discussed in Bucharest that April, along with that of Albania, Croatia and Macedonia. Bush remained a great believer in strengthening and expanding the Alliance and was determined that its enlargement in 2004, which had brought in seven new members, should not be its last. Any further expansion was bound to be anathema to Russia, but the administration tried to insist, as it had the last time and the time before that, that the move was not directed against Moscow. NATO, alongside the European Union, was 'a vital instrument in the stabilisation of post-Communist Europe', Condoleezza Rice said. 'It gave aspirant states from the former Eastern bloc a lodestar as they sought to reform and to end old rivalries between them.'[7]

At a meeting on the margins of the World Economic Forum in Davos that January, Yushchenko had virtually begged Rice for Ukraine to be granted a Membership Action Plan – failure to do so would be a 'disaster, a tragedy', he told her.[8] Struggling to make good on the promises of the Orange Revolution and locked in a difficult coalition with Tymoshenko, who had previously been a rival, Yushchenko had turned this into a litmus test of his ability to deliver greater integration with the West. Saakashvili felt much the same. As Rice saw it, both Georgia and Ukraine saw the process as 'an essential affirmation of their pro-Western orientation and – though unsaid – a shield from Moscow's pressure'.[9]

It was precisely this that made the prospect of the two countries' membership so unwelcome to Russia. The Kremlin had accepted the previous rounds of enlargement through gritted teeth; the accession of Estonia, Latvia and Lithuania had been hard to stomach, as it had brought the Alliance for the first time onto former Soviet soil. Yet in Moscow's eyes, the three Baltic states were not as integral as the other former Soviet republics and their 'loss' was therefore easier to bear.

Georgia and Ukraine were a different matter, and the idea of them becoming members of the Alliance was completely unacceptable.

America's European allies drew the opposite conclusion: Poland and its Central European neighbours saw NATO's further expansion as a demonstration of the organisation's commitment to their own security and enthusiastically backed it. Shifting the Alliance's border eastward meant they would no longer be front-line states. Merkel, by contrast, was wary of both Saakashvili and Yushchenko, and had no desire to provoke Putin unnecessarily.

Matters were further complicated by the re-emergence of the Kosovo question. NATO's intervention a decade earlier on behalf of the Kosovars, which coincided with the first wave of the Alliance's enlargement, had marked a low point in Russia's relations with the West under Clinton and Yeltsin. Now the issue was back. Although freed from Serb rule, the province had remained in the years since in a legal limbo and its leaders were pressing for full independence. Martti Ahtisaari, the former Finnish president entrusted by the UN with sorting out Kosovo's status, inclined towards backing them. But Russia remained opposed, not just out of solidarity with its traditional Serb ally, but also out of concern at the precedent it might set. Spain and other EU countries with restive minorities were also wary.

On 17 February 2008, Kosovo went ahead and unilaterally declared its independence anyway. America recognised the declaration, as did twenty-two of the EU's twenty-seven members, but Russia declared the move illegitimate. 'The Kosovo precedent is a terrible precedent,' Putin declared. 'Essentially it is blowing up the whole system of international relations which has evolved over the past not even decades but centuries . . . Ultimately this is a stick with two ends, and one day the other end of this stick will hit them on their heads.'

Yet Putin was not above using the declaration for his own purposes. In fact, the Kremlin had promised the leaders of Abkhazia and South Ossetia that it would support their separatist ambitions if Kosovo declared its independence and was recognised by the West. In March, the Russian government lifted the remaining sanctions against them, while the Duma held hearings on recognition of the two breakaway republics. Moscow made it clear that what happened next would be linked directly to Georgia's bid to join NATO.

Condoleezza Rice had no doubt as to how controversial it would be to admit Georgia and Ukraine. When the National Security Council met before the Bucharest summit to decide a position, she outlined the pros and cons of granting the two countries a Membership Action Plan but did not come down firmly on one side or the other. Bush, with his usual disregard for diplomatic nicety, did that for her. 'If these two democratic states want MAP, I can't say no,' he declared.[10] Rice admired the president's clarity of vision, but she was the one left with the problem of pushing through the policy in Bucharest.

When the summit opened on 2 April, it had still not been decided which countries were going to be invited to join NATO – unusual for an issue of such importance, which would normally have been settled long in advance. The leaders left it to their foreign ministers to start the ball rolling. They did so at a dinner that, according to Rice, produced one of the most pointed and contentious debates among allies that she had ever experienced. Frank-Walter Steinmeier of Germany spoke first and, as expected, outlined his country's objections to allowing in either of the countries: Ukraine because of the weakness of its government and Georgia because of the 'frozen conflicts' in Abkhazia and South Ossetia. The French, too, were sceptical. Like the Germans they were worried that admitting Ukraine and Georgia into NATO risked drawing the Alliance into the two countries' squabbles with Moscow.

The Central Europeans, who saw the issue as a litmus test of the West's will to defend the interests of the former Soviet states, piled in furiously. 'If NATO had taken that view, West Germany wouldn't have been admitted in 1949,' said one. 'You were one big frozen conflict until 1990,' said another. Radek Sikorski, the Polish foreign minister, twisted the knife, reminding Steinmeier that it was Germany's fault that Poland and its neighbours had spent forty years under Soviet domination.

In the end a compromise was struck – albeit a curious one. Ukraine and Georgia were not granted the MAP status they sought, but Alliance members agreed by acclamation that 'Ukraine and Georgia will become members of NATO'. Asked by the press to comment on the decision, Rice replied: 'It's a matter of when, not whether.'[11] Yet the answer to that 'when' was left deliberately vague. 'In a way, it was a paradox,' commented Anders Fogh Rasmussen, the Danish prime minister. 'A MAP is no guarantee of future membership of NATO, but having denied them a MAP, we nevertheless stated that they will become members of NATO in the future.'[12]

Putin, who joined the summit on its second day for bilateral talks with NATO, left no doubt over where he stood, angrily accusing the Alliance of encircling Russia. 'A powerful military bloc appearing near our borders will be perceived as a direct threat to the security of our country,' he declared. 'Statements claiming this process is not directed against Russia are not satisfactory to us.' Moscow would take 'necessary measures' if NATO continued approaching Russia's borders, he added.

According to Rasmussen, Putin pointed out that Georgia was involved in a centuries-long ethnic conflict with the Abkhazians and South Ossetians and warned that if Georgia joined NATO then Russia would approach these breakaway territories in the same way as the West had handled Kosovo – by eventually recognising their independence. On Ukraine, he was even more aggressive: the country was made up of lands received from Russia in the East and from Poland and Romania in the West, and joining the Alliance might lead to its disintegration, he warned. He sounded a particular warning about Crimea, noting that it was 90 per cent Russian and that its transfer to Soviet Ukraine in 1954 had been illegal. Those present failed to appreciate the seriousness of his warning.[13]

Yet Putin was not closing the door on the West completely. In the second part of his speech, he called for cooperation with NATO on Iran and Afghanistan and spoke about the Russian Black Sea Fleet taking part in Operation Active Endeavour, NATO's antiterror operations in the Mediterranean. He also said that Russia was ready to resume the Treaty on Conventional Armed Forces in Europe, which it had suspended the previous December. During a press conference in the grandiose palace built by the late Romanian dictator, Nicolae Ceauşescu, Putin insisted that the world's problems could not be solved without Russia and appealed for the West to give due consideration to his country's own security concerns, adding, through his interpreter: 'So let's be friends, guys, let's be frank and open.' The spirit of cooperation that had been in evidence six year earlier in Pratica di Mare was still not completely dead.

There was the same mixed message from Putin when he and Bush continued on to the Black Sea resort of Sochi for what was to be their last summit. The formal high point of the meeting was the signature of an agreement on the 'strategic framework' of US–Russia relations, which was aimed at encapsulating the legacy that the two men would bequeath to their successors. 'We reaffirm that the era in which the United States and Russia considered one another an enemy or strategic threat has ended,' they declared. 'We reject the zero-sum thinking of the Cold War, when "what was good for Russia was bad for America" and vice versa. Rather, we are dedicated to working together, and with other nations, to address the global challenges of the twenty-first century, moving the US–Russia relationship from one of strategic competition to strategic partnership.' The warm words could not obscure the long list of subjects of disagreement between them. Their different views over NATO expansion were only part of it. The thorniest issue was Bush's plan for a US missile shield based in Eastern Europe, a system that Washington said was needed to provide protection against Iran, but which Russia said threatened its security.

Yet after more than forty meetings, there were still signs of the chemistry between Bush and Putin that had been evident during the two men's first encounter in Slovenia seven years earlier. They shared a hug as Bush arrived at Putin's dacha and exchanged jokes as they were briefed on the Russian leader's pet project: the 2014 Winter Olympic Games, which had been awarded to Sochi in July 2007. Putin joked about how Bush was a 'brilliant dancer' after he and other members of the American delegation were plucked from their seats by a Russian folk group and made to take the stage for what seemed to Bush like a combination of square-dancing and jitterbug. Bush praised his host as a strong leader. 'You're not afraid to tell me what's on your mind. And when it's all said and done, we can shake hands,' he said.

Putin, Bush recalled in his memoirs, was 'sometimes cocky, sometimes charming, always tough.'[14] He had come to know the Russian leader well over the years, even if they were never as close as Clinton and Yeltsin had been before them. Bush had hosted Putin at his ranch in Crawford and taken him fishing with his father in Kennebunkport. For his part, Putin had invited Bush to his dacha outside Moscow, where he showed him his private chapel and let him drive his classic 1956 Volga. Their respective wives joined them on several of the visits. When Putin got his first glimpse of the Oval Office early one morning with the light streaming through the windows, he blurted out, 'My God . . . This is beautiful.' It was 'quite a response for a former KGB agent from the atheist Soviet Union', quipped Bush.[15] Putin was less impressed by Bush's beloved Scottish terrier, Barney, when he encountered him at Camp David. Bush found out why on his next trip to Russia, when Koni, Putin's big black labrador, came charging through the birch-lined grounds of his dacha. 'Bigger, stronger and faster than Barney,' Putin told him.[16] The incident told Bush a lot about how Putin saw the world.

Over the years Bush had watched Putin change, becoming more aggressive abroad and more defensive of criticism of his increasingly authoritarian policies at home. Bush was in no doubt that it was all down to the surging oil price: during their first encounter in 2001, oil was selling at $26 a barrel and Putin was still worried about paying off the debt that had been run up in the last years of the Soviet era. By the time the two men met in Sochi it had passed $100 a barrel and was to peak that July at $145. Russia's new-found wealth had gone to the Kremlin leader's head, removing the need to seek approval from the West for his actions.

'Putin was a proud man who loved his country,' Bush recalled.[17] 'He wanted Russia to have the stature of a great power again and was driven to expand Russia's spheres of influence. He intimidated democracies on his borders and used energy as an economic weapon by cutting off natural gas to parts of Eastern Europe.' Bush also took advantage of the Sochi meeting to meet Medvedev, who was due to take over as president the following month. Bush was impressed by a speech he gave outlining his commitment to the rule of law, liberalising the economy and reducing corruption, but was not convinced he would actually be running the country after his job swap with Putin.

THROUGHOUT THAT SPRING, TENSIONS ROSE BETWEEN Georgia and Russia. Each accused the other of being poised to attack. Initially, Abkhazia seemed the more likely of the two flashpoints: Russia sent in reinforcements, vowing to protect its citizens there. In early May, Rice expressed concern about Moscow's growing military presence. Russia's announcement a few weeks later of plans to send four hundred supposedly unarmed troops to Abkhazia to repair a railway line added to fears of invasion and prompted some in the Saakashvili camp to contemplate a pre-emptive strike.

Saakashvili decided instead to try a diplomatic solution and appeared to make progress that June during a meeting with Medvedev at a summit of post-Soviet states in St Petersburg. The Georgian leader was impressed by the change of style in the Kremlin: Medvedev, who had assumed the presidency in May, was much warmer towards him than Putin had been and gave the impression of being more accommodating. Yet the two sides remained far apart, primarily over Moscow's insistence that Georgia conclude a no-use-of-force agreement with the Abkhaz and the South Ossetians. Medvedev tried to get Rice to persuade Saakashvili to sign, describing his refusal as 'playing with fire'.[18] Rice, in turn, attempted to reassure Medvedev that Saakashvili would not use force, though she also blamed the Russians for making things more difficult through their own involvement.

A meeting on 5 July between Saakashvili and Medvedev in Kazakhstan to celebrate the birthday of President Nazarbayev was inconclusive but appears to have left the Georgian leader with the impression that Russia was preparing to attack. America, too, was worried that a conflict was about to break out, and four days later Rice travelled to Tbilisi. Saakashvili met her on the terrace of the Kopala restaurant, which afforded breathtaking views of the capital. As they sat there, the Georgian president pointed out the beautiful restoration work that had been carried out since he had come to power and boasted of his success in developing the economy and cutting corruption.

Rice was concerned that Saakashvili's pride and impulsiveness could put all these gains at risk. She also feared that he had learnt the wrong lesson from his battle with Abashidze, the Ajarian leader. On that occasion, Saakashvili had deliberately provoked a stand-off and had won. That precedent, she feared, might prompt him to take a hard line elsewhere, even though Abkhazia and South Ossetia's location made them much more important to Russia. Steering the conversation round to the matter at hand, she told the Georgian leader that he would have to sign a no-use-of-force pledge. Saakashvili was reluctant, blaming the Kremlin for stirring up the situation and suggesting he would sign only if he was offered something in return. An exasperated Rice finally put it to him more forcibly.

'Mr President,' she said, 'whatever you do, don't let the Russians provoke you. You remember when President Bush said that Moscow would try to get you to do something stupid? And don't engage Russian military forces. No one will come to your aid, and you will lose.'[19]

Saakashvili finally got the point, looking to Rice 'as if he'd just lost his last friend'.[20] She tried to soften what she had said by pledging that America would defend Georgia's territorial integrity and agreed, at her host's request, to repeat that pledge publicly. Rice made it clear, though, that such a defence would be verbal and would not commit America to defend Georgia with arms.

Matters moved quickly: a few days later, the Russian 58th Army began military exercises across the North Caucasus. American and Georgian forces, meanwhile, staged military exercises entitled 'Immediate Response 2008'. Skirmishes continued between the Georgians and the Ossetians. Late on the evening of 7 August, these long-simmering tensions erupted into war: Georgian forces responded to an escalating series of attacks by South Ossetian rebel forces by launching a full-blown offensive against Tskhinvali, the South Ossetian capital. A senior Georgian military official vowed to restore 'constitutional order' and its forces destroyed large parts of the city, killing not just Russian peacekeepers but also hundreds of Ossetian civilians. Many of the dead were Russian citizens, thanks to a controversial policy that made them, together with citizens of Abkhazia, eligible for Russian passports.

Within hours, hundreds of Russian tanks came rolling through the Roki Tunnel from North Ossetia, helped by massive air support. Over the next five days, some forty thousand Russian troops entered Georgia, half of them through South Ossetia and the other half through Abkhazia. They drove the Georgians from South Ossetia and then made for Tbilisi, rampaging through Gori, the birthplace of Joseph Stalin, along the way.

The crisis erupted as world leaders were in Beijing for the opening ceremony of the Olympic Games. Bush and his wife, Laura, were standing in line to greet President Hu Jintao when James Jeffrey, Bush's deputy national security adviser, whispered to him news of events in Georgia. Bush saw Putin a few seats ahead of him, but decided this was not the appropriate place for heated diplomacy. Bush thought he should respect the new order in the Kremlin and instead contact Medvedev, since he was now the president. 'My strong advice is to start de-escalating this thing now,' Bush told him, according to his own account. 'The disproportionality of your actions is going to turn the world against you. We're going to be with them.'[21] Medvedev responded by comparing Saakashvili with Saddam Hussein and accusing him of launching an unprovoked 'barbarian' attack that had killed more than 1,500 civilians. 'I hope you're not going to kill 1,500 people in response,' Bush shot back.

Bush then called Saakashvili, whom he found understandably shaken by the ferocity of the Russian counter-attack. The Georgian leader urged Bush not to abandon his country. 'I hear you,' Bush replied. 'We do not want Georgia to collapse.'

Bush's biggest concern was that the Russian forces would continue all the way to Tbilisi, which lay only seventy miles or so from South Ossetia, and overthrow Saakashvili. Yet he was determined the conflict should not turn into an open dispute between Russia and America. Rice issued a statement calling for an immediate ceasefire and urged Russia 'to cease attacks on Georgia by aircraft and missiles, respect Georgia's territorial integrity, and withdraw its ground combat forces from Georgian soil'. Sergey Lavrov, who had become foreign minister in 2004, accused the Georgians of driving Ossetians from their homes in what he condemned as a policy of ethnic cleansing – a term widely used a decade earlier during the wars in the Balkans.

A flurry of urgent diplomacy followed, with President Nicolas Sarkozy of France, who held the EU's rotating presidency, taking the lead. By 11 August the Georgians claimed they had withdrawn their forces from South Ossetia, though the claim was difficult to verify. That afternoon, Lavrov called Rice to tell her that the Russians had three demands. The first two were relatively straightforward: the Georgians would have to sign the no-use-of-force pledge and send their troops back to their barracks. Saakashvili would not like it, but he had no alternative, Rice thought. Lavrov's third demand, however, appalled her: 'Just between us, Misha Saakashvili has to go,' he said.[22]

For Rice, this was reminiscent of the Kremlin's behaviour during the Soviet period, when it had replaced the puppet leaders of its client states at will. 'Sergei, the secretary of state of the United States does not have a conversation with the Russian foreign minister about over-throwing a democratically elected president,' she retorted. To Lavrov's fury, Rice said she would tell the world – the UN Security Council included – what he had just said.

America's anger at the Kremlin's behaviour was evident at a meeting of the National Security Council the next day, where, according to Rice, there was 'a fair amount of chest beating about the Russians' and 'all kind of loose talk about what threats the United States might make'.[23] The belligerent mood was defused by Stephen Hadley, Bush's national security adviser, who asked: 'Are we prepared to go to war with Russia over Georgia?'[24] America was not, which meant there was no alternative but to negotiate a settlement. It was not easy. A ceasefire framework was hammered out by Sarkozy, but a dispute soon followed over one of its provisions, which the Russians had interpreted as allowing them to retain a military presence on Georgian territory outside South Ossetia and Abkhazia.

It was up to Rice to try to find a solution. She flew first to the south of France to meet Sarkozy and then on to Georgia, where she found Saakashvili and his aides in a very different state from when she had last seen them: the stress of the previous few days was written on their sleepless faces.

Rice finally managed to obtain an agreement, which she and Saakashvili went to announce to the press. She told him to be brief and careful with his words. Instead, exhausted and furious, he launched into a tirade against the Russians, condemning them as 'twenty-first century barbarians' who had raped his country. He then turned on the Europeans, talking of Munich and appeasement. Saakashvili's words were especially ill-advised given that a column of Russian vehicles was now just twenty-five miles from Tbilisi. Rice was livid and could not get out of Tbilisi fast enough. 'He's blown it,' she told Eka Tkeshelashvili, the young foreign minister, as they travelled to a hospital to visit victims of the war.

A meeting of the Alliance's foreign ministers in Brussels a few days after the signature of the peace agreement issued a declaration of support for Georgia and urged Russia to remove its troops from the country. The Alliance reiterated its intention 'to support the territorial integrity, independence and sovereignty of Georgia and to support its democratically elected government and to deny Russia the strategic objective of undermining that democracy'. Yet the events of the previous few weeks had demonstrated why it would have been unwise to have given Georgia a formal path towards NATO membership.

In a sign of the extent to which relations had deteriorated, ministers announced the suspension of the NATO–Russia Council. At its launch during Berlusconi's lavish Pratica di Mare summit, the organisation had been hailed as ushering in a new era of cooperation between East and West. Now, just six years later, it seemed an ineffective and naive relic of an earlier age.

Russia announced it was calling back its NATO representatives and cancelling all planned manoeuvres with NATO for the year. The next day, Rice went to Poland to sign a missile defence agreement; although the date had long been fixed, it added to the tensions. Poland marked the occasion by staging a parade to celebrate the eighty-eighth anniversary of its defeat of Russian forces during the Polish–Soviet war. Colonel General Anatoly Nogovitsyn, Russia's deputy chief of staff, said that by signing the pact, Poland was exposing itself 'a hundred per cent' to a potential Russian nuclear strike.

Merkel adopted a more conciliatory tone during talks with Medvedev on the Black Sea near Georgia. Though condemning some of Russia's action as disproportionate, she said negotiations already under way with Moscow on a number of issues should continue. 'It is rare that all the blame is on one side,' she said. 'In fact, both sides are probably to blame. That is very important to understand.'[25]

On 26 August Russia recognised Abkhazia and South Ossetia as independent republics, separate from Georgia, something it had hitherto declined to do. The Georgian government responded by severing diplomatic relations with Russia. It was not until October that Russia had largely withdrawn its forces. The conflict had claimed the lives of hundreds of people and displaced almost 200,000.

A three-volume, 1,500-page report issued by the European Union in September 2009 pinned responsibility for the war on both the Georgians and the Russians. It is a sobering thought that the consequences could have been graver: at the time of the conflict, US troops were in Georgia training the country's soldiers for Iraq and Afghanistan. At a meeting of White House principals, Hadley raised the issue of limited military response in support of Georgia, though there was no support for it.[26]

Opinions differed within NATO on the lessons to be drawn from the war and its implications for Georgia and Ukraine's membership of the Alliance. America, the Central Europeans and, to a certain extent, Britain, saw the conflict as proof of the need to extend the Western security umbrella, but other members drew the opposite conclusion: they blamed Georgia for provoking the conflict and considered Saakashvili untrustworthy. In a setback for the Bush administration,

NATO foreign ministers refused US demands to hasten Georgian and Ukrainian membership and further angered Washington by agreeing 'conditional and graduated re-engagement with Russia', reopening contacts that had been frozen in protest at the war.

Russia, meanwhile, was celebrating a victory of sorts. Thanks to its policy of provoking Saakashvili and then deploying overwhelming force when he rose to the bait, the Kremlin had achieved its aims: the Georgian leader had been humbled and his country's membership of NATO postponed, perhaps indefinitely. Russia had laid down a marker of its 'privileged' interests in its neighbourhood. Yet the five-day campaign had also revealed the weaknesses of the Russian army, which was still largely unreformed since the Soviet days, with insufficient training and poor equipment. Two months later, Russia embarked on an ambitious programme of defence modernisation and military restructuring intended to transform the military from the massive standing force of the Cold War era into a lighter, more mobile force better suited to small-scale conflicts. The country's defence industry began to turn out modern weapons systems and equipment and in 2009 its forces began to stage large-scale military exercises for the first time in two decades.

In an article published in the *New York Times*, Mikhail Gorbachev blamed the conflict on Saakashvili's recklessness and warned against calls in the West to rearm Georgia and punish Russia by expelling it from the G8, disbanding the NATO–Russia Council or keeping it out of the World Trade Organization.[27] Bemoaning the failure to develop a serious agenda for genuine, rather than token, cooperation between Russia and America, the former Soviet leader went on to rail against a series of indignities perpetrated by the West, from the expansion of NATO and the recognition of Kosovo's independence to abrogation of the Anti-Ballistic Missile Treaty and America's decision to station missiles in Eastern Europe. 'All of these moves have been set against the backdrop of sweet talk about partnership. Why would anyone put up with such a charade?' Gorbachev complained. 'If our opinion counts for nothing in those institutions, do we really need them? Just to sit at the nicely set dinner table and listen to lectures?'

The Bush administration disagreed. In a landmark speech that September at the German Marshall Fund in Washington, Rice condemned Russia's 'premeditated' invasion of Georgia but also criticised Saakashvili for falling into the Kremlin's trap. 'We warned our Georgian friends that Russia was baiting them, and that taking this bait would only play into Moscow's hands,' she said. With only a few more months remaining for the Bush administration, Rice also allowed herself some broader thoughts about the deterioration in relations between Russia and America since the early 1990s. 'The legitimate goal of rebuilding the Russian state has taken a dark turn,' she said, 'with the rollback of personal freedoms, the arbitrary enforcement of the law, the pervasive corruption at various levels of Russian society, and the paranoid, aggressive impulse, which has manifested itself before in Russian history, to view the emergence of free and independent democratic neighbours – most recently, during the so-called "colour revolutions" in Georgia, and Ukraine, and Kyrgyzstan – not as a source of security, but as a source of threat to Russia's interests.'

Rice put it more succinctly in her memoirs: the US–Russia relationship had not fallen apart over Iran, North Korea or arms control; the two countries had cooperated well over the fight against terrorism in the aftermath of 9/11 and nuclear proliferation. The problem, as she saw it, was instead Russia's inability to come to terms with the realities of the new post-Cold War order on its western border and its continued insistence on a sphere of influence there. 'Moscow believed that it still had special privileges on the territory of the former Soviet Union and the Warsaw Pact,' she wrote.[28] 'We believed that the newly independent states had the right to choose their friends and their alliances. That had turned out to be an irreconcilable difference.'

AND SO A DECADE THAT HAD begun with the promise of so much drew to an end with Russia and the West further apart than they had been since the last days of the Soviet Union. George W. Bush may have quickly come to regret his claim to have seen into Putin's soul, but he had not been alone in hailing the arrival of the new Kremlin leader as a chance for a fresh start after the chaos of the late 1990s. Clinton, too, had been impressed by Putin, even if he had had no time to build the same rapport he had enjoyed with Yeltsin. Blair, Berlusconi and the other European leaders had been equally positive.

The chances of a new era of cooperation were greater after the 11 September 2001 attacks on Washington and New York, which prompted a genuine acceptance that both sides had more in common with each other than divided them. America, it seemed to the Kremlin, had finally accepted the seriousness of the threat posed by militant Islam. A new partnership beckoned. And this cooperation bore fruit. America sought – and was granted – access to Central Asia, Russia's backyard, in order to carry out its attack on the Taliban in Afghanistan. But Putin wanted something in return. Just as Gorbachev, during his last summit with Bush Senior in July 1991, had outlined a vision according to which the two erstwhile Cold War foes would move on from past enmity and sort out the world's problems between them, so Putin saw Russia not as a junior partner, but as an equal. The Kremlin's demands could be summed up in a single word: 'respect'.

Yet America had become rather too fond of a unipolar world, and Russia waited in vain for its reward. Its commercial and political ties with Iran and other Middle Eastern regimes remained a matter of discord with Washington. Then, in 2003, Bush ignored Russian objections and attacked Iraq. For Igor Ivanov, who had been Russian foreign minister at the time, it is difficult to overestimate the damage this caused to US–Russia relations. 'A really strong, anti-terrorist international coalition was created after September 2001,' he says.[29] 'It was destroyed in 2003 when the Americans decided to start their war in Iraq.'

The emergence of Bush's freedom agenda added an almost messianic dimension to US foreign policy, providing a justification for invasion and 'regime change'. It was not just a matter of Iraq: Georgia's Rose and Ukraine's Orange Revolutions brought the threat closer to home. Only the most paranoid of Russians would suggest either event was orchestrated by America. Yet the financial and organisational support given to the pro-democracy demonstrators played an important part in the success of both uprisings. The second wave of NATO enlargement, which extended the Alliance onto the territory of the former Soviet Union, was a further blow.

Such humiliations were no worse than those suffered by Russia under Yeltsin during the 1990s. But Russia had become a very different country. After a cautious start, Putin had become increasingly assertive and determined to pursue his country's national interests. Crucially, thanks to the surge in the oil price, he had the economic wherewithal to do so. No longer was Russia's freedom constrained by its need to go, begging bowl in hand, to its Western creditors.

Yet change was in the air. Medvedev's accession in May 2008 was followed that November by Barack Obama's victory over fellow senator John McCain. These two new leaders, both in their forties and lawyers by training, represented a new generation. Their arrival in power seemed to hold out the possibility of a new start.

III.

THE HOT PEACE

16

OVERLOAD

W HEN HILLARY CLINTON, THE NEWLY APPOINTED US secretary of state, met Sergey Lavrov, the Russian foreign minister,
in Geneva in March 2009 it appeared to promise a turning point in
superpower relations. Barack Obama, who had moved into the White
House two months earlier, wanted to put ties with the Kremlin back
on a friendlier footing after the frostiness of the late Bush years.
Washington called it a 'reset'. To underline the point, Clinton presented
Lavrov with a small box, inside which was a red plastic button on a
yellow base that carried the word 'reset' in both English and Russian.
Or rather, that was what it was meant to say.

'We worked hard to get the right Russian word. Do you think we
got it?' asked Clinton in front of reporters invited to watch the first
few minutes of their meeting.

'You got it wrong,' replied Lavrov, to Clinton's surprise – and laughter
from the audience. *Peregruzka*, the word chosen, which had been
written inexplicably in Latin rather than Cyrillic characters, translated
as 'overcharge' or 'overload'. The word they should have chosen was
two letters longer: *perezagruzka*. Clinton's predecessor, Condoleezza
Rice, a fluent Russian speaker, would not have made such an elementary linguistic error.

The term 'reset' had been first used by Obama in an interview with
Tom Brokaw on *Meet the Press*, NBC News' weekly television show,
the previous December. 'I think that it's going to be important for us

to reset US–Russian relations,' Obama said. He defined this as continuing to send a clear message to the Russians 'that they have to act in
ways that are not bullying their neighbours', while at the same time
cooperating with them on a 'whole host of areas, particularly around
non-proliferation of weapons and terrorism'.

The idea was fleshed out the following February by Joe Biden,
Obama's vice president, shortly after the inauguration. Appropriately
enough, he did so at the Munich Security Conference, the same venue
at which Putin had shocked the world with his cri de cœur in 2007.
'The last few years have seen a dangerous drift in relations between
Russia and the members of our alliance,' said Biden. 'It's time to press
the reset button and to revisit the many areas where we can and should
be working together with Russia.'

This meant, in particular, nuclear issues – cooperating to secure
'loose' weapons and materials and negotiating deeper cuts in arsenals
– but also dealing with the rising threat from the Taliban and Al Qaeda,
both of which Russia had warned America about a long time earlier,
Biden conceded. The two countries would not see eye to eye on
everything, he admitted: for example, Washington rejected Russia's
claim to a sphere of influence in Georgia and elsewhere in the near
abroad. 'But the United States and Russia can disagree and still work
together where our interests coincide,' he added. 'And they coincide in
many places.'

Given the nadir in relations under Bush and Putin, the policy offered
a new start. As for the plastic button, that was down to Philippe Reines,
one of Clinton's most senior advisers. Fiercely loyal and often acerbic,
Reines had come up with the idea for the stunt, reportedly sourced
the plastic box from Geneva's Intercontinental Hotel and taken charge
of the translation. Although the Clinton camp tried to laugh it off, the
result was recriminations, especially when Reines reportedly tried to
pin the blame on members of Obama's team – a claim he denied.

Several weeks later, a senior member of the administration received
an email from a Russian friend. 'You know how you really translate
"reset" in Russian?' the friend wrote. "Reset".'[1]

LIKE MANY PRESIDENTS BEFORE HIM, Barack Obama came to
office with little direct experience of foreign policy. In Chicago, where
he had worked as a community organiser, he was preoccupied with

issues closer to home such as schools, the welfare system and health-care. Yet his was a generation for which the issue of nuclear weapons always had a special resonance: as Obama wrote in his biography, *The Audacity of Hope*, he came of age during the Reagan era, at a time when America was railing against the 'evil empire' while embarking on a trillion-dollar arms build-up and carrying out nuclear tests under the Nevada desert. Obama was too young to 'remember having to do drills under the desk', but as a student 'interested broadly in foreign policy', he recalled in an interview with the *New York Times*, he focused on how the United States and the Soviet Union could manage their nuclear arsenals and 'dial down the dangers that humanity faced'.[2]

In 1983, at the height of the Cold War, Obama, then a senior at Columbia University, wrote an essay for *Sundial*, a campus magazine, in which he outlined a vision of a 'nuclear-free world' and denounced 'the relentless, often silent spread of militarism in the country'. In an academic paper at about the same time, he analysed how a president could go about negotiating arms reduction deals with the Russians. Obama had the chance to become involved with nuclear issues for real after he became a senator in January 2005 and established contact with Richard G. Lugar, the Indiana Republican who was chairman of the Senate Foreign Relations Committee and a long-time campaigner against nuclear proliferation. That August he accompanied Lugar on a trip to Russia and Ukraine to monitor the success of efforts to scrap nuclear arms and prevent materials from going astray.

The visit made a strong impression on Obama. They travelled to nuclear facilities at Saratov, on the Volga, where Russian generals proudly showed off their fencing and security systems, before treating their guests to a lunch of 'borscht, vodka, potato stew and a deeply troubling fish Jell-O mold'.[3] Then it was on to Perm, in the Urals, where the delegation witnessed SS-24 and SS-25 tactical missiles being dismantled, and to Kiev, where they visited Ukraine's equivalent of the Centers for Disease Control and Prevention, a modest three-storey building that reminded Obama of a high-school science lab. As the American delegation watched aghast, a middle-aged woman in a lab coat and surgical mask pulled a couple of test tubes from the freezer, the door of which was secured with string, and began waving them around. One of the test tubes contained anthrax, their translator announced matter-of-factly; the other was filled with plague.

Obama's experiences provided him with an insight into the implacable Soviet mixture of old and new: in Perm he was transported back to the days of the Cold War, when their delegation was held for three hours by a young border officer after they refused to let him search their plane. In Moscow they caught a glimpse of the new Russia as they drove past the Calvin Klein store and a Maserati dealership and saw a motorcade of SUVs pulling up outside a swanky restaurant, disgorging an oligarch's bodyguards. For Obama, what he saw 'underscored the seemingly irreversible process of economic, if not political, integration between west and east'.[4]

In his first foreign policy speech, delivered to the Chicago Council on Foreign Affairs in April 2007, just over two months after he announced his candidacy, Obama set out a worldview in sharp contrast to George W. Bush's. 'We all know that these are not the best of times for America's reputation in the world,' he began. 'We know what the war in Iraq has cost us in lives and treasure, in influence and respect. We have seen the consequences of a foreign policy based on a flawed ideology, and a belief that tough talk can replace real strength and vision.'

Obama wanted an end to US involvement in Iraq, but he was not calling for American withdrawal from the world. He was arguing instead for a different form of engagement, based less on big power politics and more on international cooperation and institutions in order to tackle problems such as terrorism, nuclear proliferation and climate change. 'The threats we face at the dawn of the twenty-first century can no longer be contained by borders and boundaries,' he said. 'We must neither retreat from the world nor try to bully it into submission. We must lead the world, by deed and example.'

Obama made only a brief reference to Russia – and that, predictably, was on the subject of nuclear proliferation. 'We know that Russia is neither our enemy nor close ally right now, and we shouldn't shy away from pushing for more democracy, transparency, and accountability in that country,' he said. 'But we also know that we can and must work with Russia to make sure every one of its nuclear weapons and every cache of nuclear material is secured.'

By the time of the speech, Obama was already well on his way to assembling his foreign policy team, which would eventually count several hundred members: it was headed by Anthony Lake, Bill Clinton's first national security adviser, and Susan Rice, who had held several jobs in the same administration, rising to become assistant secretary of state for African affairs. The team was called the Phoenix Initiative; the name was chosen to show that foreign policy under the new president would rise from the ashes to which it had been reduced by Condoleezza Rice and the Bush administration's Vulcans.

To devise a policy on Russia, they turned to Michael McFaul, a professor of political science at Stanford University. McFaul's links with Russia went back more than a quarter of a century: he had first visited the Soviet Union as an undergraduate in 1983, spending a summer at the Leningrad State University at a time when Brezhnev's era of 'stagnation' was at its height. In 1990, as the Soviet Union was falling apart, he had returned, this time to Moscow. McFaul was there to write his doctoral dissertation on Soviet–African relations, but he was more interested in the dramatic developments unfolding around him. Determined to play his part in establishing liberal values and building civil society, he attended demonstrations, handed out leaflets and organised seminars on democracy. It was 'like being in a movie', he recalled later.[5]

As McFaul forged his career in academia, political transition became his dominant interest and he established links with the Bush administration. Although a convinced liberal interventionist, he found common ground with the neo-conservatives when it came to the pursuit of democracy in the former Soviet states. In the 2004 presidential election, he worked on John Edwards' unsuccessful attempt to win the Democratic nomination.

McFaul turned down Lake when he called in late 2006 to sign him up to Obama's Phoenix team, according to an account in the *New Yorker*. Half an hour later, Susan Rice, who knew McFaul from Stanford and Oxford, made a follow-up call to McFaul. 'I am part of this thing, too, so get your shit together and join,' she told him. 'That's Susan's personality, and so I said, "Yes! Of course!"' McFaul told the magazine.

The Phoenix Initiative set out their ideas in a blandly named document, 'Strategic Leadership: Framework for a 21st Century National Security Strategy', published in July 2008. The report, Susan Rice wrote in her preface, aimed to offer 'bold and genuinely new thinking about America's role' on five top 'strategic priorities': counterterrorism, nuclear proliferation, climate change and oil dependence, the Middle

East and East Asia. While Bush's policy had been based on maintaining US military and political primacy, their report spoke about 'intercon- nectedness' and 'diffuse power'. The day it appeared, Obama was in Berlin giving a speech to 200,000 people in which he presented himself as the antithesis to everything the Germans (and indeed most non-Americans) disliked about the Bush presidency. The loudest cheers came for his vow to end US military involvement in Iraq, to 'save this planet' from climate change and to strive for a world without nuclear weapons.

The more immediate foreign policy issue that Obama had to face was a more traditional one: the crisis in Georgia, which erupted during the last months of the campaign. John McCain, who had won the Republican nomination, placed much more emphasis on maintaining America's role as the world's most powerful nation than on fuzzy ideas about cooperation. A supporter of the Colour Revolutions, McCain was also deeply suspicious of Putin's Russia, which he believed was being run by a group of KGB apparatchiks determined to reassemble the Soviet Union.

The differing worldviews of the two men were evident that August when Russian troops rolled into South Ossetia: while McCain imme- diately denounced the Kremlin for crossing an internationally recognised border and demanded an immediate withdrawal, Obama initially urged both sides to show restraint and 'avoid an escalation to full-scale war' – although he did later harden his rhetoric.[6] The contrast was even more pronounced that October during their first televised debate on foreign policy, when McCain accused his young rival of being naive for having urged restraint in Georgia when it was clear that the war was the result of Kremlin aggression. Obama shrugged off the charge and talked tough himself, claiming a 'resurgent and very aggressive Russia is a threat to the peace and stability of the region'. It was absolutely important, he said, 'that we explain to the Russians that you cannot be a twenty-first-century superpower, or power, and act like a twentieth-century dictatorship'. There were going to be areas of common interest, Obama conceded, such as nuclear proliferation, highlighting his own work in the area. But he added, in a swipe at Bush's famous comment after his first encounter with Bush in Slovenia, that America had to have a president 'who is clear that you don't deal with Russia based on staring into his eyes and seeing his soul'.[7]

OBAMA'S VICTORY ON 4 NOVEMBER WAS greeted with almost unanimous enthusiasm around the globe. Bush had divided the world with his aggressive pursuit of American national interests. His place in the White House had been taken by a new leader who was young, intelligent and a great orator – and also the first African-American to hold the post. Commentators depicted Obama's election as a clarion call for hope and peaceful change that held out the prospect of a better world. His slogan of 'Yes we can' seemed to be a rebuttal of Bush's 'I will, whether you like it or not'.

The Kremlin, by contrast, seemed reluctant to acknowledge the significance of Obama's election. When Medvedev delivered his own State of the Union address hours after news of the US result broke, he did not even mention Obama by name, let alone congratulate him. He instead threatened to respond to America's plans to install a missile defence system in Poland and the Czech Republic by deploying mobile Iskander missiles around Kaliningrad, a Russian exclave sandwiched between Lithuania and Poland, both of them now NATO members.

'These are forced measures,' Medvedev said. 'We have told our partners more than once that we want positive cooperation, we want to act together to combat common threats. But they, unfortunately, don't want to listen to us.' In other tough words, Medvedev blamed the war in Georgia on the 'arrogant course of the US administration' and said American regulators were to blame for the global financial crisis that was now taking its toll on Russia, because of the way they had inflated the financial bubble in the preceding years.

Yet the speech was not entirely negative: in a sign of his growing determination to differentiate himself from Putin, Medvedev sounded more liberal on domestic policy. And during a meeting with President Nicolas Sarkozy of France in Nice the following week, he appeared to back down from his missile threat, saying merely that all countries 'should refrain from unilateral steps' before their scheduled discussions on European security the following summer. The next day, Medvedev travelled on to Washington for a summit of G20 leaders on the financial crisis. Making his first visit to America as president, he struck a conciliatory tone. Although reiterating his threat to deploy missiles in Kaliningrad, Medvedev said he had no immediate plans to do so. He also expressed the hope that relations would improve under Obama.

'There is no trust in the Russia–US relations, the trust we need,'

Medvedev said. 'Therefore we have great aspirations for the new administration.' He also tried to make light of his failure to congratulate
Obama publicly on his election, saying, somewhat unconvincingly, that
he had simply forgotten. 'There's nothing personal here,' he added.

Obama, meanwhile, was preparing to come some way to meeting
the Russians over the fraught issue of missile defence, which in one
form or another had been bedevilling relations since the Reagan days.
Obama did not share Bush's enthusiasm for the project and said he
would support it only if it could be proved to be technically effective
and affordable. But how best to convey the message to Medvedev?
William Burns, the undersecretary of state and until May 2008 ambassador to Moscow, suggested the administration should set out its
proposals in a letter that he would personally deliver to the Kremlin.
He would be accompanied by McFaul, who had become senior director
for Russian and Eurasian affairs at the National Security Council.

McFaul was sceptical. 'I thought it was a silly idea,' he recalled.[8] 'I live
in the Silicon Valley. We don't deliver letters, ever. There is no such thing
as a paper letter any more, let alone you would fly across the other side
of the earth to deliver it. I just proposed we should send an email.'

Obama was impressed by the idea, however, and so McFaul dutifully
accompanied Burns to Moscow. In the letter, Obama directly addressed
the contentious subject of missile defence, saying America would have
no need to proceed with it if Iran halted its efforts to build nuclear
warheads and ballistic missiles. Although not offering a direct quid
pro quo, it was intended to give the Russians an incentive to join
America in a common front against Tehran. The letter also touched
on other issues such as a new treaty to reduce nuclear stockpiles.
'Essentially, it was the template for the reset,' wrote Mark Landler in
his study of US foreign policy under Clinton and Obama.[9] Medvedev
was impressed, and McFaul finally understood the effect that his presence had had. 'Bill [Burns] was right. I was wrong. The symbolism of
the two of us coming together to the first resetting of the relationship
was very dramatic,' he said.

There was more positive mood music when Obama and Medvedev
encountered one another for the first time at that April's G20 meeting
in London. The main business at hand was tackling the global reces-
sion, but the American and Russian leaders managed to meet in
Winfield House, the grand official residence in Regent's Park of the

US ambassador to the Court of St James. To Obama's surprise, Medvedev proposed allowing US military forces to fly over Russia on their way to and from Afghanistan. 'It was quite shocking,' said McFaul. 'We didn't expect it. I took it as a sign for him to also want to reset the relationship.' The Russians appeared to show some flexibility over Iran too.

Less easy to resolve was the question of nuclear weapons and how to reduce America and Russia's massive nuclear arsenals. Obama was pressing for a number of practical measures, including securing a follow-up agreement to the Strategic Arms Reduction Treaty (START), which was due to expire that December. But he remained wedded to the utopian idea of eliminating them completely, as he argued three days later in a speech in Prague that he considered one of the most important of his presidency. As Obama saw it, America, as the only power to have used such a weapon in war, had a moral responsibility to lead the march to a nuclear-free future.

'I'm not naive. This goal will not be reached quickly. Perhaps not in my lifetime,' he told a cheering crowd of twenty thousand people in Hradčanské Square, in front of the stunning backdrop of Prague Castle. 'But now we too must ignore the voices who tell us that the world cannot change. We have to insist: "Yes we can".'

THE FIRST REAL TEST OF OBAMA'S 'reset' was at the Moscow summit that July. Events in the run-up to the meeting were not promising. Georgia, in particular, remained a source of tension between Washington and Moscow. The administration was worried that Russia might be preparing a further assault on its southern neighbour. Washington was sending mixed messages too: in May, despite Russian objections, America went ahead with long-planned small-scale military manoeuvres in Georgia.

Obama also faced the ticklish problem of how to deal with the 'tandem', as the Putin–Medvedev double act was known within the administration. Since Yeltsin's day, it had been clear that the president was the one with real power over both domestic and foreign policy, with the prime minister's responsibilities confined largely to economic matters. Yet Putin's considerable influence meant this was unlikely to continue to be the case. How should Washington behave – in accordance with the Russian constitution or with political reality?

The administration was as clueless as everyone else about who was really in control, judging by cables sent back to Washington from the embassy in Moscow, which were subsequently leaked by WikiLeaks. They make for amusing reading – and suggest the paucity of the diplomats' sources. In one cable dated November 2008, Eric Rubin, the US deputy chief of mission in Moscow, set out three different possible versions of the relationship between the two men, including one that suggested 'Medvedev continues to play Robin to Putin's Batman'. Rubin admitted, though, that a definitive answer was impossible because of the 'impenetrable nature of Kremlin politics and the fertile field of speculation and rumour that the information vacuum creates'.

In another dispatch, 'Why Medvedev Matters', sent the following February, John Beyrle, the US ambassador to Moscow, dismissed reports of a power struggle between Putin and Medvedev, insisting that Putin remained the 'linchpin' of the leadership and the 'indispensable player in resolving inter-clan disputes'. The real battle, Beyrle argued, was instead between Medvedev, seen as a reformer who was more sympathetic to the West, and the hardliners of the security services and the power ministries. For Beyrle, it was therefore in America's interest to act to bolster Medvedev. 'How we structure our dialogue with Russia will play a role in reinforcing Medvedev's authority and ability to implement his calls for a politically and economically more modern Russia,' he wrote. 'Medvedev should be seen as the primary interlocutor for President Obama, and the earlier Medvedev's stewardship of the US account can be demonstrated to the Russian elite, the faster he can move to shore up his foreign policy credentials.'

Beyrle insisted that this should be possible 'while managing Putin and his ego'. It was to prove a difficult balancing act, though – as Obama made clear in an interview a few days before the Moscow summit during which he described Putin as having 'one foot in the old ways of doing business and one foot in the new'. The message was clear: Medvedev, like Obama, was a man of the future, while Putin, like Bush, should be consigned to the past. The strategy risked backfiring, given that when it came to national security, as on so many other issues, Putin was still wielding the real power. Belittling him in this way would not make Obama's task easier.

Obama's meeting with Medvedev in Moscow nevertheless appeared to provide evidence of the 'reset' in action: the two presidents agreed to slash their nuclear arsenals, resume military contacts suspended after the war with Georgia and allow up to 4,500 flights of US troops and weapons across Russia to Afghanistan each year. 'They're real things. It is not fluff,' McFaul told reporters who travelled with them to Russia.[10] 'I dare you to think of a summit that was so substantive.' On a personal level, the two men also seemed to get on. 'Those two presidents are a different generation,' said Pavel Palazhchenko, a long-time interpreter for Mikhail Gorbachev, whom Obama also met while in Moscow. 'Many of the dogs in the old fights are really not their dogs. And they will be willing to take a fresh look at some issues.'

The atmosphere at Obama's al fresco breakfast meeting with Putin – their first encounter – did not prove so warm. The American president began by asking his host what he thought had gone wrong with their relationship. Putin responded with a lengthy lecture in which he noted that missile defence was one of the main issues dividing them because it threatened the power of Russia's strategic nuclear forces. The meeting had been scheduled to last an hour. By the time the sixty minutes were up, Obama had barely had the chance to say anything and asked for an extension. They ended up talking for two hours.

'I found him to be tough, smart, shrewd, very unsentimental, very pragmatic,' Obama said afterwards. 'On areas where we disagree, like Georgia, I don't anticipate a meeting of the minds anytime soon.'[11]

For McFaul, Putin was expressing exasperation at the way past presidents – not just Bush, but also Clinton before him – had not so much worked with Russia as dictated to it. 'It was as if Putin were saying: "I know your reset and all that. But I've been through this before and I know how this movie ends and it doesn't end well",' McFaul said. 'But the president pushed back. He said, "I'm different. This is a new time. Whatever the past of the Cold War and whatever your experience in the 1990s we are going to reset this relationship".'

Many in Central and Eastern Europe nevertheless remained sceptical about Russia's intentions and feared their own countries' interests might be sacrificed to Obama's drive to improve relations with the Kremlin. On 16 July, just over a week after the summit, two dozen senior politicians wrote to Obama warning him not to forget the lessons of recent history. The former leaders of nine EU states, they included Lech Wałęsa and Aleksander Kwaśniewski of Poland, Václav Havel of the Czech Republic and Mart Laar of Estonia. 'Russia is back as a revisionist power pursuing a nineteenth-century agenda,' they wrote. 'There is nervousness in our capitals. NATO today seems weaker than when we joined . . . The danger is that Russia's creeping intimidation and influence-peddling in the region could over time lead to a de facto neutralisation of the region. There are differing views within the region when it comes to Moscow's new policies. But there is a shared view that the full engagement of the United States is needed.'

To assuage such concerns, Biden was dispatched on a four-day visit to Ukraine and Georgia. The aim was to reassure both countries that the US had not forgotten them, but without unduly annoying Moscow or undermining the reset. Biden said that America still supported their bids to join NATO, though in the case of Georgia, he tempered this with criticism of the country's record on democracy and media freedom, signalling a shift away from the uncritical support that the Bush administration had offered Saakashvili. He also warned the Georgian government against military control over Abkhazia and South Ossetia. Whatever Biden said, however, NATO membership for both countries remained a non-starter, given the opposition of the French and Germans. Their veto was no bad thing for the Obama administration, given the ferocious reaction it would provoke from Russia.

That December, Anders Fogh Rasmussen, the new NATO secretary general, found Putin in characteristically pugnacious mood when he went to Moscow for the first time since becoming head of the Alliance in August. He knew Putin from previous meetings when he was Danish prime minister and so was 'prepared for a very direct conversation'. Barely had they sat down than the Russian leader launched into a familiar refrain: an attack on NATO, which he said no longer served any purpose and should be dissolved. Putin's confrontational body language made him seem to Rasmussen like someone spoiling for a fight. 'After the end of the Cold War, we dissolved the Warsaw Pact. Similarly, you should dissolve NATO. That is a relic from the Cold War,' the Russian leader told him.[12] Rasmussen replied that his intention was precisely the opposite: to 'strengthen NATO as the bedrock of Euro-Atlantic security'.

Rasmussen had hoped that Medvedev, younger, more liberal and more Western-orientated, would bring a more positive and dynamic tone to Russia's relations with NATO. But while Medvedev was polite, Putin, who was still pulling all the strings, was brusque and dismissive.

'I realised it would be uphill work to make any progress,' Rasmussen recalled.[13]

Among the issues under discussion were missile defence and arms control in Europe. The most immediate problem was securing the follow-up to the Strategic Arms Reduction Treaty (START). Over months of painstaking negotiations in Geneva, both sides edged towards an agreement that would halve the number of strategic nuclear missile launchers in the two countries. Unusually for such a technical issue, Obama and Medvedev were both personally involved, sharing no fewer than fourteen telephone calls or meetings on the subject – including one at the UN climate change meeting in snowy Copenhagen that December, where shivering delegates met to discuss how to stop global warming. The initial aim had been to get a new arms deal concluded by 5 December, almost two weeks earlier than the date at which the old one expired. The deadline came and went. Then in February the Russians tried to make their agreement conditional on American concessions over missile defence. Obama stood firm, however, claiming he would never be able to get such a deal through the Senate. Russia finally caved in.

The new START was eventually signed by Obama and Medvedev in a grand ceremony in Prague on 8 April 2010. The vision of a nuclear-free world that Obama had laid out in the same city a year earlier still seemed a dream – but this was at least a small step in the right direction.

17

SILICON VALLEY

STEVE JOBS PRESENTED HIM WITH AN iPhone 4 an hour before it hit the shelves. The founders of Twitter taught him how to send his first tweet. The head of Cisco showed him the latest in video conferencing and promised to invest a billion dollars in developing innovation and entrepreneurship in Russia. When President Medvedev set off on a tour of Silicon Valley in June 2010, technology chiefs rolled out the red carpet. Dressed in jeans and an open-collared shirt, he gave a speech at Stanford University while reading the text from an Apple iPad. 'I wanted to see with my own eyes the origin of success,' Medvedev told his audience. 'I'm inspired with what I saw here in Silicon Valley and at Stanford. In a very good way, I am kind of jealous of all you here.'

Medvedev was only the second serving Kremlin leader to have visited California. When Khrushchev had done so half a century earlier during his trip around the United States, he had taken in the IBM plant in San Jose – though he was not much interested in the computers and far more intrigued by the self-service canteen, an innovation that he vowed to introduce on his return to the Soviet Union.[1]* Like his predecessor,

---

* In his book, Khrushchev's son, Sergei, describes his father enthusiastically pushing his tray along the counter, followed by Andrei Gromyko, the foreign minister, and other members of the delegation. All coped well apart from Viacheslav Yelutin, the minister for further education, who dropped his tray through an unexpected opening in the counter, spilling cabbage on his trousers – much to the amusement of Khrushchev, who joked that he would have to train since his arms were not used to work.

Medvedev was impressed by what he witnessed. 'My purpose is not just to see what is going on there. It is not a guided tour,' he declared at a reception hosted by the film star and California Governor Arnold Schwarzenegger. 'I would like to have my visit translated into full-fledged relations and into cooperation with those companies.' As he prepared to leave, Medvedev turned to Schwarzenegger and declared, in a line from *Terminator 2: Judgment Day*, 'I'll be back. Hasta la vista, baby.' One tech star whom Medvedev did not meet during his visit was Russian-born Sergey Brin, a co-founder of Google, who in an interview a few years earlier had scathingly described the corrupt land of his birth as 'Nigeria with snow' and asked why a 'bunch of criminal cowboys' should control the world's energy supply.

Since coming to power, Medvedev had expressed his determination to carry out a wide-ranging reform of the Russian economy, which had become all the more vital due to the economic crisis that followed the collapse of Lehman Brothers in September 2008. The oil price, which hit a record $145 per barrel in July 2008, had slumped to $30 just before Christmas and was only back up to $78 by the time of Medvedev's visit. For the first decade of the millennium, Russia's GDP had grown an average of 7% a year, one of the fastest rates in the world. In the first quarter of 2009, it plunged by 9.5%.

The Russian government's immediate problem was to stave off economic collapse. It did so by dipping into the stabilisation fund that had grown steadily since it was set up in 2004. The fund was a tribute to the sound management of public finances practised by Putin's governments. They had been less good, however, at restructuring the Russian economy away from its overwhelming dependence on oil and other raw materials and encouraging the production of goods and services that could compete with their Western equivalents.

Developing tech industries seemed to offer a solution. One of the aims of the US–Russia Bilateral Presidential Commission, set up during Obama's visit to Moscow in July 2009, was to identify areas where the two countries could cooperate and pursue joint projects. Technology transfer was an important part of this and the commission played a key role in everything from intellectual property sharing and exporting to facilitating American investment in Russia and vice versa.

In November 2009, Medvedev announced plans for the Skolkovo Innovation Center, a complex on a greenfield site south-west of Moscow purpose-built for science and technology companies. Historically, Russia – and the Soviet Union before it – had achieved considerable success in science and technology but had struggled to market its inventions. The aim of the new complex was not just to develop technology start-ups, but, as in Silicon Valley, to bring them to people who could finance and market them. It was nicknamed Silicon Steppe.

Medvedev had mentioned his plans for the complex to Hillary Clinton when they met in Moscow the previous month and she 'suggested that he visit the original in California'. In May 2010, before Medvedev's trip to America, the state department facilitated a trip to Moscow by twenty-two of the biggest names in US venture capital; weeks later the first memorandums of understanding were signed by Skolkovo and American companies.

The US government saw advantages in the partnership, which aimed to match Russia's brainpower in science, engineering, mathematics and computers with US investment and entrepreneurial know-how. The state department also helped Rusnano, the Russian state investment fund, identify American tech companies worthy of Russian investment. Yet there was also a darker side to Skolkovo. Research into the centre by the US Army Foreign Military Studies Program published in 2013 alleged its purpose was to serve as a 'vehicle for world-wide technology transfer to Russia in the areas of information technology, biomedicine, energy, satellite and space technology, and nuclear technology'. In December 2011, it claimed, Skolkovo had approved its first weapons-related project: the development of a hypersonic cruise missile engine. Surveillance equipment and vehicles capable of delivering airborne Russian troops were also developed there. 'Skolkovo is arguably an overt alternative to clandestine industrial espionage – with the additional distinction that it can achieve such a transfer on a much larger scale and more efficiently,' it said.[2]

This should not have come as a surprise: despite the apparent similarities between them, Skolkovo was very different from Silicon Valley. Rather than evolving from the bottom up, it was the creation of the Russian government, which committed $5 billion over three years to provide housing for thirty thousand people, as well as schools, shops and parks. Many of its research projects incorporated 'dual-use' civilian and military applications. It was also claimed that the FSB ran some of its information warfare operations from there.

These allegations would later be brought together in a report published in July 2016 at the height of the US election campaign by the Government Accountability Institute, whose head, Peter Schweizer, is a long-standing critic of Hillary Clinton. The report also revealed another curious twist: Russian government officials and American corporations that took part in the technology transfer linked to Skolkovo between them funnelled tens of millions of dollars to the Clinton Foundation. 'Even if it could be proven that these tens of millions of dollars in Clinton Foundation donations by Skolkovo's key partners played no role in the Clinton state department's missing or ignoring obvious red flags about the Russian enterprise, the perception would still be problematic,' Schweizer wrote.[3]

SUCH CRITICISM LAY IN THE FUTURE as Medvedev met the movers and shakers of Silicon Valley. With his boyish looks and informal manner, the Russian president appeared at ease here in a way that Putin or Yeltsin before him would never have been. Medvedev reinforced the impression of being a new style of Russian leader when he travelled on to a summit with Obama – the pair's seventh meeting – in Washington.

US administration officials spoke of a new phase in the 'reset'. After spending the previous few months focused largely on security issues, both sides wanted to move on to economic issues, of which cooperation on technology was a part. 'Twenty years after the end of the Cold War, the US–Russian relationship has to be about more than just security and arms control,' declared Obama. 'It has to be about our shared prosperity and what we can build together.' Medvedev was pushing for progress on Russia's long-running demand to be admitted to the World Trade Organization, which it saw as the key to attracting foreign investment. 'We are tired of sitting in the waiting room, trying to enter this organisation,' he told a press conference. Obama wanted him first to agree to lift a ban Russia had imposed on imports of American chickens that was hitting his country's poultry industry, hardly an onerous condition compared to past negotiations between the countries.

The personal chemistry between the two men was on display when Obama took his guest out for a meal at Ray's Hell Burger in Arlington, Virginia in one of those staged events without which no summit is complete. Striving for informality, Obama urged Medvedev to take off his jacket after they emerged from the car in the 37°C (100°F) heat. 'Is it safe?' Medvedev could be heard asking before popping his jacket onto the back seat of the limousine. 'It's safe,' assured Obama. 'No one's going to steal it.'

And so, as the cameras whirred, they strode into the burger bar in white shirts and ties, like a couple of office workers out on their lunch break, posing for photographs with a group of surprised American soldiers before making their way to the counter where Obama did the honours: a cheeseburger with sautéed onions, jalapeño peppers and mushrooms for Medvedev, and one with sautéed onions, lettuce and tomato for himself. They shared a large fries. 'We're gonna turn him on to a real American burger,' Obama said.

As Medvedev made a token effort to go for his wallet, Obama insisted on paying the $24.50 himself. 'This one's on me. Big spender. I want to show off,' he joked. At a joint press conference later, Medvedev thanked Obama for lunch, joking: 'It's not quite healthy but it's very tasty and you can feel the spirit of America.'

DESPITE OBAMA'S DETERMINATION TO RESET RELATIONS with Russia, a reminder of the Cold War threatened to overshadow the summit. On the eve of Medvedev's visit, the FBI had uncovered a Russian spy ring of ten sleeper agents it claimed had been planted in the country years earlier. Among them was Anna Chapman, a glamorous young woman working in real estate in Manhattan. The agents, who lived seemingly normal lives in New York, New Jersey and Boston, had been sent to 'search and develop ties in policymaking circles in US and send intels to C [for centre, meaning Moscow]', according to a document purporting to be their mission statement, later released by the FBI.

The ten had been under surveillance for some time, but the FBI decided to pounce after receiving information that some of them were planning to leave America. Five days before Medvedev was due to arrive on his visit, Obama convened a meeting of the National Security Council. No one wanted the latest stage in the reset to be overshadowed by an old-style spy scandal and so the FBI was ordered to hold off. 'The president wanted to handle this in a way that was professional and did not feel like it was the Cold War,' said McFaul.[4] Two days after Medvedev had gone, Chapman met a man in a New York coffee shop she thought was a fellow Russian agent. He was really an undercover FBI man. Arrested along with the others on 27 June, she pleaded guilty to a charge of conspiracy to act as an agent of a foreign government.

The sleepers did not appear to have acquired any secrets and were not even charged with espionage. Their thin pickings were not surprising given that they were living apparently normal lives, with no access to important people or sensitive information. The American press treated the incident as little more than a joke, mocking their use of false names and invisible ink and suggested they could have learnt more by surfing the internet.

They were sent home less than two weeks after their arrest in exchange for four men who had been caught by Russia and accused of passing information to MI6 and the FBI. Chapman went on to acquire a curious celebrity, posing in lingerie as the cover girl for the Russian edition of the magazine *Maxim*, making a surprise appearance at the launch of a Soyuz rocket heading for the International Space Station and hosting her own television show. (She later reappeared at Skolkovo, claiming to be starting a new career in venture capitalism.)

The Russian foreign ministry initially dismissed the American accusations as baseless and tried to downplay the incident. Putin revelled in it, however, claiming to have got together with Chapman and the others after their return and sung 'patriotic' songs with them – including one from *The Shield and the Sword*, the 1968 Soviet-era spy film that had prompted his own KGB career. He also railed against their betrayal, apparently by a double agent. 'It was the result of treason,' Putin said, predicting a grim future for those who blew their cover. 'It always ends badly for traitors: as a rule, their end comes from drink or drugs, lying in the gutter. And for what?'[5]

THE INCIDENT PASSED WITHOUT MANY REPERCUSSIONS. Obama had become comfortable dealing with Medvedev and was proud of the extent to which he had succeeded in his 'reset' of relations with the Kremlin. The strength of the two men's relationship – and also its limits – were to be highlighted by a political tsunami that was about to engulf the world. When Mohamed Bouazizi, a Tunisian street vendor, set himself on fire on 17 December 2010, it triggered a chain of events that toppled the leaders of some countries and plunged others into brutal civil war in a violent echo of the Colour Revolutions. The

Tunisian President Zine El Abidine Ben Ali, who had ruled his country for a quarter of a century, was the first to go, stepping down within a month after a series of street protests. Then, on 11 February, his Egyptian counterpart, Hosni Mubarak, a long-time US ally, resigned after Washington made it clear it would not back him if he used force to quell growing popular unrest.

A crisis was also brewing in Libya, where an uprising against Muammar Gaddafi's rule began a few days later in the eastern city of Benghazi. Gaddafi, however, was not prepared simply to back down, and Libya was soon on the path to a bloody civil war that would split it down geographic and tribal lines. As Gaddafi's forces bore down on Benghazi, pressure grew from France and Britain for the imposition of a no-fly zone on the country. Their call was soon joined by the Arab League. America was initially reluctant to be involved, but Hillary Clinton became persuaded of the need to act and she convinced Obama. He wanted something more than just a no-fly zone, though: under the plan he approved, US missiles would first take out Libya's air defence systems and then NATO warplanes would attack Gaddafi's forces. Obama nevertheless insisted that US intervention should be limited in time and not involve ground troops. He did not want a repeat of Iraq.

Such action still required a UN mandate, which raised the potential problem of a Russian veto. Since NATO's bombing of Yugoslavia in 1999, the Kremlin had opposed such interventions, especially when they were directed against regimes such as Libya's with which it had extensive commercial ties. But in answer to a question at that February's session of the World Economic Forum in Davos, Medvedev appeared to hint at a new line by expressing sympathy for the demands of the Arab Spring protesters. Biden took advantage of a visit to Moscow a few weeks later to lobby the Russian president to support action against Gaddafi. Medvedev's stance put him at odds with both the foreign ministry and security apparatus, which were wary of what they saw as an attempt by America to impose its writ on yet another part of the world.

On 17 March, the Security Council authorised its member nations to take 'all necessary measures' to protect civilians in Libya, which was interpreted as allowing for a wide range of actions including strikes on air defence systems and missile attacks from ships. Ten countries backed the measure; Russia and China abstained. Two days later, military operations began, with a French plane firing the first shots. Medvedev, it was claimed, had contemplated going further and voting in favour of the motion before being persuaded otherwise by his officials. Putin, however, was appalled even by the abstention. In a speech the following week at a missile factory, he likened the assault on Libya to a medieval crusade and compared it with Bush's invasion of Iraq. 'This is becoming a persistent tendency in US policy,' Putin said. 'During the Clinton era they bombed Belgrade. Bush sent forces into Afghanistan, then under an invented, false pretext they sent forces into Iraq . . . Now it is Libya's turn . . . Where is the logic and the conscience?'

Medvedev was livid: foreign policy was meant to be his domain as president. A few hours later he summoned journalists to an outdoor press conference at his dacha where, dressed in a leather bomber jacket, he defended the Security Council's action. 'These are balanced decisions that were very carefully thought through,' he said. 'It would be wrong for us to start flapping about now and say that we didn't know what we were doing.'[6] Medvedev went further that May during the G8 meeting in the French resort of Deauville, where he said the world no longer saw Gaddafi as Libyan leader and suggested a discussion about which country should take him in.[7] Medvedev's stance was significant not just for what it meant for Libya but also for its implications for the relationship between him and Putin. Would the 'tandem' continue to roll on or would Medvedev be pushed aside to allow Putin to return to his old job at the next election?

Libya was not the only issue on which Medvedev had been asserting himself. In December 2010, Putin used his annual press conference to comment on the second trial of Mikhail Khodorkovsky, the oligarch who had fallen foul of him years before, by declaring 'a thief belongs in jail', and Medvedev appeared to slap him down, saying no official should comment on a trial before the verdict. His intervention did not do the former Yukos chief much good, however: the judgement, read a few days later, effectively added another seven years to his jail sentence.

Medvedev appeared to get his way the following March, though, when he issued a decree requiring cabinet ministers, many of whom were Putin allies, to give up their seats at state companies. Those affected included Igor Sechin, the deputy prime minister – one of Putin's closest associates and a rival of Medvedev – who dutifully gave up his position as chairman of the board of Rosneft, the oil company.

That May, Medvedev even appeared to take a dig at Putin, declaring: 'A person who thinks he can stay in power indefinitely is a danger to society. Russian history shows that monopolising power leads to stagnation or civil war.'

For his part, Putin launched an organisation called the All-Russia People's Front, which was intended to be a coalition between the ruling United Russia Party and other people and groups willing to rally round him. As Dmitry Peskov, Putin's spokesman, put it: 'It is a supra-party that is not based on the party. Rather, it is focused on Putin, the creator of this idea.' Medvedev, by contrast, had no role in it.[8] Putin was also honing his image with a series of Action Man stunts: the world had already been treated to the sight of him riding a horse bare-chested in southern Siberia in summer 2009. More recently, he had been photographed driving a snowmobile in Krasnaya Polyana, Sochi, fitting a tracking collar to a polar bear in the Arctic and firing darts at an endangered grey whale in the Sea of Japan. (The coming August would see the most bizarre stunt yet: Putin, clad in a rubber suit, emerging from the Black Sea clutching two ancient Greek urns that he had 'discovered' in the shallows; even the Kremlin had to admit that it was rigged.)

Yet if there really was a power struggle between Putin and Medvedev, it had been a very brief and unequal one: in a report in the *Sunday Times* on 22 May, Mark Franchetti, the paper's veteran Moscow correspondent, claimed that Putin had decided he was going to run again for the presidency – which meant Medvedev had to step out of his way. 'There's rivalry with Putin but they're both too smart to get drawn into a nasty personal conflict,' a source told Franchetti.[9] 'The difference is simple: Putin can ask Medvedev to step aside. No matter how reluctantly, he'll oblige. But Medvedev can't stop Putin coming back. And Putin wants to be president again.'

18

THE RETURN OF THE CHIEF

THE DECISION HAD BEEN TAKEN LONG before, but in the end it was up to Medvedev to confirm the inevitable to the crowd of eleven thousand activists from the United Russia Party gathered in Moscow's Luzhniki Stadium. 'I think it would be correct for the Congress to support the candidacy of the party chairman, Vladimir Putin, to the post of president of the country,' said Medvedev, his face projected onto a giant screen above the stage. He smiled fleetingly as the crowd roared and the cameras turned their attention towards Putin, who was seated in the audience. Putin called it a 'great honour', telling the crowd: 'I am counting on your support.'

The announcement, made on 24 September 2011, ended the uncertainty over which of the two members of Russia's ruling tandem would stand in the presidential election the following March. But although there was jubilation among those in the stadium at the prospect of the return of their chief to the top job, others were not so impressed. 'There is no reason for celebration,' tweeted Arkady Dvorkovich, one of Medvedev's closest aides. 'Now it is time to switch to the sports channel.' The political consultant Gleb Pavlovsky, who had severed ties with the Kremlin earlier in the year, was scathing, describing the move as 'a blow to the prestige of the institution of the presidency in Russia'. Alexei Kudrin, the finance minister, who had won plaudits for his handling of the Russian economy over the previous decade, stepped down, saying he could not serve under Medvedev as prime minister.

The Obama administration put a brave face on the announcement. 'The reset has always been about national interests and not individual personalities,' said Tommy Vietor, the spokesman for the National Security Council. 'We will continue to build on the progress of the reset whoever serves as the next president of Russia.'

Parliamentary elections on 4 December gave voters a chance to give their verdict: despite the usual wall-to-wall television coverage for United Russia, the party won just forty-nine per cent of the vote, down from sixty-four per cent in the previous poll, with the other main parties all gaining at its expense. Claims of vote-rigging abounded and anger quickly exploded onto the streets of Moscow: the day after the poll, as the votes came in, several thousand demonstrators gathered in Chistye Prudy in central Moscow chanting 'Putin's a thief!'. A leading voice was that of Alexei Navalny, a charismatic lawyer, blogger and anti-corruption campaigner who had sprung to prominence earlier that year after labelling United Russia the 'party of swindlers and thieves'.

'We should remember that they are nobody. And we are the power,' Navalny told the crowd. 'We want another president and not a thief and crook!' He was arrested but defiantly tweeted a photograph of himself and fellow detainees from inside the police van to his more than 100,000 Twitter followers. Hillary Clinton was among those who questioned the poll, expressing 'serious concern' about the conduct of the election. 'The Russian people, like people everywhere, deserve the right to have their voices heard and their votes counted,' she said. 'And that means they deserve free, fair, transparent elections and leaders who are accountable to them.'

An angry Putin responded by accusing Clinton of fomenting unrest and claimed that hundreds of millions of dollars in 'foreign money' was being used to influence Russian politics. The secretary of state 'set the tone for some actors in our country and gave them a signal,' he complained. 'They heard the signal and with the support of the US state department began active work.' For a former KGB man, the word 'signal' seemed carefully chosen, almost as if he were accusing Clinton of activating a sleeper cell. Such talk of a deliberate Western plot to undermine Russia was straight out of the Soviet era.

The protests continued, however, and on 10 December, a Saturday, the largest demonstration yet was held on Bolotnaya Square, across the Moscow river from the Kremlin. Nothing of this scale had been seen in the city since the 1990s. Putin poured scorn on the protesters, saying he had mistaken the white ribbons pinned to their clothes for condoms and thought it was an anti-AIDS rally. Russia's internet-savvy protesters responded by mocking up a picture of Putin wearing a condom across his chest, which went viral within minutes.

Navalny, serving fifteen days in jail, missed the protest. But he was freed in time to exhort people to gather again two weeks later. During an impromptu 3:00A.M. news conference on a snowy street after being released from the detention centre, he turned his fire on Putin and the forthcoming election. 'He won't be a legitimate president,' he said. 'What will happen on 4 March, if it happens, will be an illegal succession to the throne.' The crowds were larger than two weeks earlier. Organisers claimed as many as 120,000 people attended the demonstration; police insisted it was just 30,000.

The protest movement, named For Fair Elections, demanded an annulment of the parliamentary vote; the replacement of Vladimir Churov, the head of the electoral commission; and an investigation into fraud, followed by a new poll. Fearful that Russia might be about to undergo its own Colour Revolution, the authorities organised their own counterdemonstrations with the help of Nashi, a pro-Kremlin youth movement created in response to the Orange Revolution that now had more than 100,000 members, and the Young Guard, the youth wing of Putin's United Russia Party.

The Kremlin's attempts to paint the protests as a Western plot were given a boost by the arrival of US Ambassador Michael McFaul in Moscow. During his work for the Obama administration, McFaul had been closely identified with the 'reset'. But his long-standing and very public interest in regime change made him an easy target for the Russian media. On just his second day in post, McFaul accompanied Bill Burns, the deputy secretary of state and himself a former US ambassador to Moscow, to a series of meetings with opposition leaders and activists. That evening, McFaul was denounced by Mikhail Leontyev, one of the attack dogs of Channel One, the main state-controlled television station, in his programme *Odnako* ('However'). The new ambassador, the programme claimed, was by his own admission an expert on 'democracy, movements against dictators and revolution'. Had he come to 'finish the revolution?' in Russia, Leontyev demanded rhetorically, in a reference to the title of one of McFaul's books: *Russia's Unfinished Revolution: Political Change from Gorbachev to Putin.* His commentary, given the title 'Receiving Instructions at the United States Embassy', followed video footage of opposition leaders and activists leaving the building.

Navalny was not among those who visited the embassy, but that did not stop Leontyev from suggesting he was among those being manipulated by America. The 'internet führer', as he called Navalny, had spent time at Yale in 2010 on a course for emerging leaders organised by the National Democratic Institute, a body 'known to be close to American special services' and for which McFaul had previously worked. A columnist for the newspaper *Izvestia* chimed in the next day, saying McFaul's appointment marked a return to the eighteenth century, when 'an ambassador's participation in intrigues and court conspiracies was ordinary business'. 'In the annals of American diplomacy, few honeymoons have been shorter than the one granted to Michael A. McFaul,' wrote Ellen Barry in the *New York Times*, summing up the ambassador's first difficult week in his post.[1]

McFaul was unbowed, insisting he was in Russia to 'execute and deepen and strengthen' the reset policy rather than pursue his interest in democratisation. 'Just because you write about cancer doesn't mean you advocate cancer. I'm a social scientist. I've written about democratisation, but that's my previous life,' he told Barry. But the attacks continued: Russian media portrayed the US government and other Western states as plotting to destabilise and weaken the country through their support for democracy, civil society and the political opposition, and denounced their diplomats as spies. Groups such as the National Democratic Institute, with its links to Madeleine Albright, and the International Republican Institute, with ties to McCain, were singled out for special attention.

The Russian media soon had a more colourful target in the form of Pussy Riot, a feminist punk rock protest group of around a dozen women who had made a name for themselves with high-profile provocative stunts. The group moved to a new level on 21 February, when five of its members entered Moscow's Cathedral of Christ the Saviour and, dressed in colourful balaclavas, began to sing and dance. It was barely a minute before security came and hurried them out, but the recording, coupled with footage they had shot in another church, gave them enough material to put together a raucous music video entitled 'Punk Prayer – Mother of God, Chase Putin Away'.

On 3 March, two of the group's leaders, Nadezhda Tolokonnikova and Maria Alyokhina, were arrested. A third, Yekaterina Samutsevich, was picked up just under two weeks later. They were charged not just with hooliganism, a petty crime usually punishable with a fine, but with the far more serious offence of 'hooliganism motivated by religious hatred'. That August they were jailed for two years. Their stunt had backfired, at least as far as Russian public opinion was concerned. While Western governments, commentators and activists complained at the severity of the sentence given to the women, many ordinary Russians thought them guilty of blasphemy.

The next day Russians went to the polls. Putin secured his expected first-round victory, with 63.6% of the vote. 'We have won!' the past and future president told a throng of tens of thousands of his supporters on Manezh Square, just outside the Kremlin walls, tears streaming down his right cheek and with Medvedev at his side. 'We have gained a clean victory. *Slava Rossiya* [Glory to Russia]!'

SO HAD ANYTHING REALLY CHANGED ON 4 March 2012? If Putin had effectively been running the state for the previous five years, did his return to the presidency make any difference? The popular mood, especially in Moscow, was certainly different, as shown by the street protests, which reached a climax on 6 May, the day before Putin's inauguration, when an estimated twenty thousand people gathered in Bolotnaya Square. More than four hundred were arrested and scores injured when protesters briefly broke through police lines – among them Navalny. There were more protests and yet more arrests the following day.

The authorities did not leave it at that. Describing the events of 6 May as a mass riot or even an attempted coup, they launched a major investigation that reportedly involved more than two hundred investigators and the questioning of thirteen thousand witnesses. More than thirty people, many of them ordinary people rather than activists, were charged and given jail sentences of up to four and a half years. In the months that followed, investigators used the protest as a pretext for opening other cases that had no connection to the events of that day. In subsequent years, those who went to the square on 6 May to mark the anniversary were themselves arrested.

The month after the protest, the Duma passed a law boosting the fines for people violating public order from a maximum of 5,000 roubles (about $150) to 300,000 roubles (more than $9,000). Endorsing the legislation, Putin declared: 'We must shield our people from radical actions.' There was more to come: another new law in July required non-profit organisations that received foreign donations and engaged in 'political activity' to register themselves as 'foreign agents'. Then in September, following a growing campaign against 'foreign interference' in Russian politics, it was announced that the US Agency for International Development (USAID) was being expelled from the country. The organisation had operated freely in Russia in the two decades since the end of the Soviet Union, handing out an estimated $2.6 billion. Spending had fallen dramatically since the heady days of the 1990s to a modest $49.47 million for fiscal 2012, but even this was seen as an affront by the Kremlin. That November Putin signed a law extending the definition of treason to include the provision of consultancy or 'other assistance' to any foreign state or international body 'directed against Russia's security'.

This harsh response was more than just a knee-jerk reversion to the kind of repressive measures used during the Soviet era. There was a more fundamental change afoot. During his first eight years, Putin had governed according to an unwritten pact: citizens stayed out of the state's business, and in return it guaranteed them growing prosperity, underwritten by surging oil revenues. Now, as the economy foundered, he was seeking a new source of legitimacy in what has been described as 'patriotic mobilisation'. This new direction was accompanied by tighter control of television and a tougher line against opposition parties and civil society. The move was given a greater urgency by the Arab Spring, which provided a salutary reminder of the ease with which regimes could be toppled if popular protests were allowed to get out of hand.

In an article entitled 'Putinology',[2] Leon Aron of the American Enterprise Institute identified five elements on which the new ideological framework was based: 'emotive nationalism; intrusive social conservatism; the retrieval of the Soviet legitimising mythology (most of all about the Second World War and Stalin); the Russian Orthodox Church as arbiter and enforcer of national mores; and Russian ethnicity as the backbone of the Russian state'. Underpinning it all was a form of exceptionalism that argues that Russia has a unique vocation. Just as the Soviet Union had once claimed to be the centre of world communism, so Russia was now positioning itself as a beacon of traditional, conservative values in a decadent, liberal world. This marked the beginning of a third path for the country, that was based neither on Soviet nostalgia nor on integration with the West.

The Russian Orthodox Church, oppressed during Soviet times,* had been resurgent since the fall of communism and was now ready to serve its new master, just as it had in Tsarist times when it had been intimately woven into the affairs of state and had wielded extraordinary power. Its head, Patriarch Kirill of Moscow and all Rus', who was appointed in 2009, was close to Putin and declared prior to the 2012 presidential election that the prosperity and stability Russia had enjoyed under Putin's leadership was a 'miracle of God'. There were echoes of the sixteenth-century monk, Philotheus of Pskov, who described Russia as the 'third Rome' with a special role as the only Orthodox country in a world that had given up on true Christianity. 'Two Romes have fallen. The third stands. And there will be no fourth. No one shall replace your Christian Tsardom!' he declared in 1510 to Grand Duke Vasili III.

The ideas of Philotheus were taken on by a collection of modern-day thinkers, among them Aleksandr Dugin, a charismatic Russian political scientist and proponent of a philosophy called 'Euroasianism'. In Dugin's view, the motherland is threatened by a Western conspiracy known as Atlanticism against which it must create a bastion of 'Eurasian' power. To save itself, Russia must develop a unique civilisation and an empire that includes not just the former Soviet states, but also much of the European Union.† He calls it the 'fourth political theory', after communism, fascism and liberalism. With his long beard and penchant for dramatic gestures – he once posed in a video holding a rocket launcher – Dugin was a gift to the Western media in search of a Rasputin-like figure in the Kremlin. Yet descriptions of him as 'Putin's brain' were fanciful. Indeed, it was not clear that the two men had even met.

One thinker whose influence Putin did acknowledge, however, was Ivan Ilyin, a White Russian philosopher who had repeatedly run afoul

---

* Although its leaders also cooperated with the state and its ranks were infiltrated by the KGB.
† But not Britain, which Dugin, writing two decades before the UK's Brexit vote, said should be cut off from Europe.

of the Bolsheviks before being expelled from the country in 1922 together with two hundred fellow intellectuals on what became known as the 'philosophers' steamboat'. In 2005, Putin had supervised the repatriation of Ilyin's body – together with the remains of General Anton Denikin, a Tsarist commander – and their reburial in Moscow's Donskoi Monastery. Ilyin saw the Bolshevik revolution as a product of the spiritual failings of the Russian people and considered the key to the country's revival to be love of God and of Russia, respect for the law and devotion to the state and the common good, rather than personal or party interest. Opposed both to Soviet communism and Western democracy, he believed in a special path for Russia based on promotion of the Orthodox Church and traditional values that would bring about a spiritual renewal of the Russian people. The main principles could be summed up in three words: *gosudarstvennost* ('statehood'), *pravosoznanive* ('legal consciousness') and *natsionalizm* ('nationalism').

Sensitive perhaps to comparisons with the Soviet past, Putin was careful not to accord Ilyin anything like the reverence that the communists had for Marx. Yet Ilyin's *Nashi Zadachi* ('Our Tasks') was one of three books distributed by the Kremlin as recommended reading to regional governors and senior members of the United Russia Party in early 2014. Putin also quoted Ilyin several times in speeches.

To describe such ideas as a ruling ideology would be an exaggeration. Putin is above all a pragmatist and the ideological underpinning for his actions appears often to be thought up after the event. Yet it is not difficult to see echoes of Ilyin's thoughts in the Kremlin – especially the belief in a global conspiracy against Russia. 'Ilyin's views synchronise perfectly with Putin's propaganda narrative,' one analysis of his ideas put it.[3] 'The collapse of the Soviet Union was hardly just, and Russians had been duped to believe in the promises of democracy that resulted in a decade of poverty, humiliation, and political impotency. Democracy did not work for Russia; the nation was corrupted by Western values and is under constant attack from those who would seek to dismantle it.'

By superimposing this narrative, Putin began to pose as the guardian of moral conservatism. One unpleasant side effect of this was an increasingly vocal disdain of homosexuality, often equating it with paedophilia. The Kremlin's hostility to the antics of Pussy Riot exemplified this new moral stewardship; so, on a more trivial level, did Russian outrage over the antics of Conchita Wurst, the bearded Austrian drag queen who won the 2014 Eurovision Song Contest. Such conservative attitudes began to spread through the Russian cultural world. The Oscar-fancied film, *Leviathan*, angered the authorities with its depiction of the brutality of life in a tiny Arctic fishing village, while the acclaimed Novosibirsk Opera and Ballet Theatre, dubbed the 'Siberian Colosseum', was accused of blasphemy in reaction to its innovative production of *Tannhäuser*. As one Russian writer on the arts put it: 'In the 1990s, Russia was a country where traditionalism was marginalised and liberalism was triumphant. Today we have a country where reactionary clerics and the all-approving majority are irritated by anything innovative.'[4]

Hopes that Russia was converging with the West were finally dead and buried. It was no longer a matter of reasserting Russia's rights; the country had radically changed course. And for the first time in nearly a hundred years, the Kremlin was drawing parallels with its imperial past.

WASHINGTON WAS SLOW TO REACT TO the new mood in Russia. This was in part because of the constraints posed by the presidential campaign, with Obama now fighting for his second term. But the president had invested too much in the reset simply to give it up. Indeed, the administration could point to some solid achievements over the previous four years, in terms of arms control, Russian support over sanctions on Iran and cooperation with Moscow over access for US troops to Afghanistan. Russia was also finally poised to join the World Trade Organization after eighteen years of negotiation. In a statement congratulating Putin on his return to the Kremlin, Obama made no mention of democracy or human rights, proposing instead that 'the successful reset in relations should be built upon during the coming years'. He also invited Putin to come to Washington shortly after his inauguration in May to discuss an agenda that Obama said would include a new agreement on reducing nuclear weapons.

During a summit with Medvedev in Seoul later in March, when he thought the cameras were no longer running, Obama was overheard assuring the outgoing Russian president that he would have 'more flexibility' to deal with contentious issues such as missile defence after that November's election and asked for more 'space' in the meantime.

'I understand your message about space,' Medvedev replied. 'I will transmit this information to Vladimir.' The exchange, parts of it inaudible, was monitored by a White House pool of television journalists as well as Russian reporters listening live from their press centre.

Obama's remarks were immediately seized on by Mitt Romney, his Republican rival. He had consistently criticised the reset and promised, if elected, to pursue a tougher line against Moscow. Russia was 'without question our number one geopolitical foe', Romney said in an interview with CNN. 'Of course the greatest threat that the world faces is a nuclear Iran, and a nuclear North Korea is already troubling enough . . . But when these terrible actors pursue their course in the world and we go to the United Nations looking for ways to stop them; when [Syrian] President Bashir al-Assad for instance is murdering his own people . . . who is it that always stands up with the world's worst actors, it's always Russia, typically with China alongside.'

As if to bolster Romney's case, Putin did not reciprocate Obama's conciliatory stance. Claiming he was too busy finalising appointments to his cabinet, he skipped the G8 meeting in Camp David on 18–19 May, eleven days after his inauguration, sending Medvedev instead. There was speculation that the move might have been inspired by Hillary Clinton's criticism of the previous December's parliamentary poll. Or perhaps by Putin's anger that Obama had waited several days before congratulating him on his victory. As Clinton put it in her memoirs, 'A cool wind was blowing from the east.'5

It was not until the G20 in San José del Cabo in Mexico the following month that Obama sat down again with Putin. Before the meeting, Clinton sent Obama a memo. Although not going as far as Romney, she urged the president to take a tougher line with the Russian leader, who was 'deeply resentful of the US and suspicious of our actions' and intent on reclaiming lost influence in the former Soviet space. Putin might call his project 'regional integration' but it was 'code for rebuilding a lost empire', Clinton argued.6 'Bargain hard,' she urged Obama, because Putin would 'give no gifts'.

The meeting in Mexico was uncomfortable. Against the backdrop of Syria's descent into civil war, Obama tried to persuade Putin to work with him to oust President Assad and assuage his concerns that America may be trying to come between Russia and its last ally in the Middle East. But Putin was little inclined to abandon the Syrian leader, expressing concern at the West's lack of a coherent plan for the country after his departure and lecturing Obama on the failure of the transition in Libya and Egypt. The body language said it all: during the time it took for handlers to usher reporters out of the room after their prepared remarks, Obama and Putin sat silently, side by side, without even bothering with the usual pleasantries, in what one reporter described as 'a grim tableau that seemed to bespeak the frustration on both sides'.[7] McFaul insisted, unconvincingly, that there was 'nothing extraordinary' about Putin's demeanour, adding: 'That's the way he looks, that's the way he acts.'

Another potential problem was also looming: in November 2008, Sergei Magnitsky, a Russian lawyer, had been arrested and taken to Moscow's notorious Butyrka jail. An auditor at a Moscow law firm, he blew the whistle on what appeared to be the largest tax fraud in Russian history, which was carried out by officials. Magnitsky's punishment for speaking out was to be arrested and held without trial in appalling conditions, denied visits from his family or even medical treatment. In November 2009, after almost a year of detention, Magnitsky, aged just thirty-seven, was found dead in his cell. Authorities claimed first that he had died of a rupture to the abdominal membrane and then that he had suffered a heart attack. They refused to allow an independent autopsy. Human rights groups claimed he had been beaten to death.

In a country where thousands of people died regularly each year in jail, Magnitsky's case would have gone unnoticed by all but his friends and family if he had not been working for Bill Browder, an American financier, who had himself fallen out of favour with the Kremlin. Browder had made a fortune investing in Russia in the 1990s and began to lobby for an improvement to the country's disastrously poor corporate governance. Perhaps not unsurprisingly, he made powerful enemies and in 2005, when he returned to Moscow after a weekend in London, he was barred from entering the country. He had hired Magnitsky to defend him against spurious charges of tax evasion and Magnitsky had agreed to fight the case, although he knew it would ruffle feathers. Now Browder was determined to have those responsible for Magnitsky's death punished; despairing of obtaining justice in Russia, he turned to America instead.

The administration was reluctant to rock the boat at a time when it was trying to reach agreement with Russia over Syria and a series of other outstanding contentious issues. But Browder proved to be a highly effective lobbyist and, with the help of Ben Cardin, a Democratic senator from Maryland, succeeded in having a bill drafted that would publicly name anyone involved in the false arrest, torture or death of Magnitsky and have them banned from entering America and their US assets frozen.

Browder and his supporters also came up with a clever way of getting the measure passed: the Russian parliament was poised to approve the country's entry into the World Trade Organization, but in order for US businesses to benefit, Congress had to repeal the Jackson-Vanik amendment to the 1974 Trade Act, a Cold War relic that affected trade with countries that restricted emigration and other human rights. In an attempt to force the administration's hand, the congressional coalition that came together around the Magnitsky Act linked the two together. That June the Foreign Affairs Committee of the House of Representatives passed the 'Sergei Magnitsky Rule of Law Accountability Act of 2012', which set out to impose sanctions on those 'responsible for the harassment, abuse, and death' of the Russian lawyer.

Despite increasingly ominous noises both from Congress and from Moscow, Obama stuck to his position on Russia throughout that summer, reluctant to acknowledge that his 'reset' had failed – or worse, that he had been naive. During his acceptance speech at the Democratic convention in Charlotte, North Carolina that September he harked back to Romney's CNN interview, accusing him of wanting 'to take us back to an era of blustering and blundering that cost America so dearly'. To applause and laughter from the audience, Obama added: 'After all, you don't call Russia our number one enemy – not Al Qaeda, Russia – unless you're still stuck in a Cold War mind warp.'[8] The comments even won Obama a rare endorsement from Putin: speaking to the state-run Russia Today television channel, he called his US counterpart 'a genuine person' who 'really wants to change much for the better', and said a second Obama term could help solve disputes over missile defence.

OBAMA SECURED HIS EXPECTED RE-ELECTION THAT November, taking 51.1% of the vote to Romney's 47.2%, but relations with Russia took a further hit the following month when the Senate passed the House version of the Magnitsky Act. Eight days later, Obama signed it. A furious Putin called the move hypocritical, pointing to human rights abuses by America, especially in Iraq and in Afghanistan. He also referred to the detention centre in Guantánamo Bay, Cuba, which Obama had vowed to close but which was still open, and where nine detainees had died in custody. 'Mr Magnitsky died in prison – a tragedy. Of course, we regret this. But what about in their prisons? No one dies?' Putin demanded.

Retaliation took a curious form: responding to what it claimed were frequent cases of abuse suffered by Russian children adopted by American parents, the Russian parliament vowed to put a stop to all such adoptions. The law, passed overwhelmingly by the Duma on 19 December, was named after Dmitri Yakovlev, a Russian toddler who died of heatstroke in a Virginia suburb of Washington in July 2008, after his adoptive American father, Miles Harrison, left him in a parked car for nine hours. Harrison was acquitted of involuntary manslaughter after the judge ruled that he had been negligent but had not shown 'callous disregard for human life', which was required for conviction.

It was not immediately clear whether Putin would back the law. Some, including Lavrov, the foreign minister, were openly opposed. Critics said it would punish Russian orphans more than adoptive parents. The opposition-minded newspaper, *Novaya Gazeta*, quickly accumulated tens of thousands of signatures for its petition to 'protect Russian children from the meanness of Russian lawmakers!'. But after the Federation Council, the upper house, also passed the law, Putin signed it off. Thousands of people took to the streets of Moscow to protest, but the government was not about to back down.

Despite this latest obstacle to relations, Obama seemed determined to try to keep relations with Russia on track. According to Landler's study of foreign policy under Obama and Clinton, 'resetting the reset became a running joke', with the National Security Council forever discussing what new initiatives to propose to Russia and whom to send as an emissary to Moscow. Tellingly, Russia received only one glancing mention in Obama's State of the Union speech. A voice of dissent was sounded by Hillary Clinton in the 'exit memo' she wrote Obama in January 2013 before leaving the state department. 'Don't appear too eager to work together. Don't flatter Putin with high-level attention . . . Strength and resolve were the only language Putin would understand,' she wrote. The Russian leader, she concluded, remained fixated on 'reclaiming the Soviet Empire and crushing domestic dissent' and represented a danger 'to his neighbours and the global order'. Difficult days lay ahead and America's relationship with Russia 'would likely get worse before it got better'.

Clinton's comments, in retrospect, turned out to be remarkably prescient, though the next blow to US–Russia relations came from an unexpected quarter: Edward Snowden was a twenty-nine-year-old former National Security Agency contractor, who in June 2013 outed himself – in an interview with the *Guardian* conducted in a hotel room in Hong Kong – as the source of a series of embarrassing disclosures about America's surveillance programmes that had been running in the media for the previous few days.

While America was trying to get him extradited from Hong Kong, matters suddenly became more complicated: on 23 June Snowden boarded an Aeroflot flight for Moscow, apparently hoping to travel on to Cuba and then Ecuador. But the Cubans declined to let him in, apparently under pressure from America, and so Snowden remained in the transit area at Sheremetyevo airport. America demanded his extradition and Russia refused. Later that summer, Russian authorities granted him asylum. Putin described Snowden's arrival in Moscow as 'a surprise' and 'like an unwanted Christmas gift'. Some in America speculated that he had been working for the Russians all along – but offered no proof.

The White House was furious at Russia's refusal to hand Snowden over. On 7 August, in a rare calculated snub to Putin, it announced that Obama was skipping a planned stopover in Moscow for a one-to-one meeting with the Russian leader ahead of the G20 in St Petersburg because it was unlikely to be productive. In a statement the administration cited lack of progress on arms control, trade, missile defence and human rights, adding: 'Russia's disappointing decision to grant Edward Snowden temporary asylum was also a factor that we considered in assessing the current state of our bilateral relationship. Our cooperation on these issues remains a priority for the United States.'

During a press conference two days later, Obama painted a gloomy picture. Under Medvedev, there had been progress, he said, but Putin's return had led to a change of mood. 'I think we saw more rhetoric on the Russian side that was anti-American, that played into some of the old stereotypes about the Cold War contests between the United States and Russia,' Obama said. 'And I've encouraged Mr Putin to think forward as opposed to backwards on those issues – with mixed success.'

Russia's decision to shelter Snowden was merely the latest in a series of disputes that included the worsening crisis in Syria, the deteriorating human rights situation and the Kremlin's increasingly strident anti-gay and lesbian stance, which threatened to overshadow the Winter Olympics in Sochi scheduled for the following February. 'It is probably appropriate for us to take a pause, reassess where it is that Russia is going, what our core interests are, and calibrate the relationship so that we're doing things that are good for the United States and hopefully good for Russia as well, but recognising that there just are going to be some differences and we're not going to be able to completely disguise them,' Obama said.

He made it very clear that it was up to Putin to change his attitude and stop seeing their relations as a zero-sum game. 'If issues are framed as "if the US is for it then Russia should be against it", or we're going to be finding ways where we can poke each other at every opportunity, then probably we don't get as much stuff done.' Yet Obama also had faint praise for the Russian leader. 'I don't have a bad personal relationship with Putin,' he said. 'When we have conversations, they're candid, they're blunt; oftentimes, they're constructive. I know the press likes to focus on body language and he's got that kind of slouch, looking like the bored kid in the back of the classroom. But the truth is, is that when we're in conversations together, oftentimes it's very productive.'

NOTWITHSTANDING THE DAMAGE DONE BY SNOWDEN, it was Syria that was emerging as the most intractable on the growing list of disputes between Russia and America. Tensions came to a head after a barrage of rockets filled with the nerve agent sarin rained down on Ghoutta, a suburb of Damascus, on 21 August 2013, killing at least fourteen hundred people. Suspicion pointed at Assad's forces, which over the previous thirty-five years had amassed a huge arsenal of mustard gas, sarin and other chemical agents. The regime denied responsibility and blamed the rebels, who it claimed had seized a stockpile of weapons.

While America had taken part in air strikes on Gaddafi's forces in Libya, Obama had refrained from direct military involvement in Syria. He had argued in late summer 2011 for Assad to step aside, but initially assumed that, like Egypt's Mubarak, the Syrian leader would fall of his own accord. Assad instead dug in. Obama believed it would not be possible to change the situation on the ground without committing the US and was not about to follow Bush's involvement in Iraq, opposition to which had been one of the centrepieces of his campaign in 2008. In August 2012, however, to the surprise of his aides, Obama signalled a subtle change of course: in response to a question, he said that if Assad were to use chemical weapons, he would be crossing a 'red line' that would provoke a US military response. A year later, with the attack on Ghoutta, that line appeared to have been crossed.

Obama ordered the Pentagon to draw up target lists. There was support from Europe, too. François Hollande, the French socialist president, was ready to strike. David Cameron also wanted to intervene, but had to obtain approval from the British parliament: the vote was set for 29 August. Angela Merkel, by contrast, was opposed.

Yet Obama was beginning to get cold feet over carrying out an attack that was not sanctioned either by international law or by Congress. James Clapper, his director of national intelligence, told him the intelligence on Syria's use of sarin, though robust, was not a 'slam dunk'.* There were other concerns, too: they could not destroy the chemical weapons themselves, for fear of releasing them into the air. Nor was it clear what implications an attack would have for America's talks with Iran, a key ally of Assad. Then, in a humiliation for David Cameron, the British parliament voted 285 to 272 against authorising a strike.

It was late the following afternoon, during a walk with Denis McDonough, his chief of staff, on the South Lawn of the White House, that Obama decided he was not prepared to authorise a strike.† When he returned to the Oval Office, Obama told shocked aides that he was putting off the attack, expected to take place the next day. He would go ahead only after gaining the approval of Congress, which was not due to return from its summer recess until 9 September. The next day Obama went public with his decision.

The world waited for what America would do next. The following week, the Senate's Foreign Relations Committee voted ten to seven in

---

* The phrase was carefully chosen: George Tenet, the former CIA director, had promised George W. Bush a 'slam dunk' in Iraq.

† According to a detailed account by Jeffrey Goldberg that appeared in the April 2016 edition of *The Atlantic*.

favour of military action, but it looked unlikely to win the support of a majority in the broader Congress. Solution to the impasse came in an unexpected form. When Obama and Putin sat down for a private meeting at the G20 summit, held on 5–6 September in St Petersburg, they agreed a plan: Russia would persuade Assad to surrender his chemical weapons to international control. The Syrian leader readily agreed. Obama insisted that, despite the deal, the US military would remain ready to stage a strike to protect America's security, but the likelihood of it happening looked slim.

Obama and his aides hailed the agreement as the best possible outcome. Yet the president's drawing of a red line that he did not then enforce seemed to his supporters and critics alike to set a damaging precedent. The real winner, it seemed, was Putin: his ally, Assad, had been spared air strikes on his country and his own role as a player in the Middle East had been boosted.

Lest anyone had missed the message, Putin trumpeted his success in an editorial in the *New York Times* placed by Ketchum, a PR agency that, according to American media reports, had earned millions of dollars from the Kremlin since 2006 largely for promoting 'Russia as a place favourable for foreign investments'.*

In the piece, headlined 'A Plea for Caution from Russia', which appeared in the paper on 12 September, Putin warned against an attack on Syria, saying it would 'result in more innocent victims and escalation, potentially spreading the conflict far beyond Syria's borders . . . and unleash a new wave of terrorism'. Instead he urged America and the rest of the international community to throw their weight behind the plan to secure Assad's arsenal.

Putin also launched into a broader critique of US policy and the country's interventions in Afghanistan, Iraq and Libya. 'Millions around the world increasingly see America not as a model of democracy but as relying solely on brute force, cobbling coalitions together under the slogan "you're either with us or against us", Putin said. He concluded

---

* Ketchum ceased work for the Kremlin in 2015, after reportedly having been paid $30 million over the previous nine years, according to company filings with the US department of justice quoted in the US media. Dmitry Peskov, the Kremlin spokesman, said that the contract was not renewed because of 'the anti-Russian hysteria, the information war that is going on'. http://money.cnn.com/2015/03/12/media/russia-putin-pr-ketchum/

with a sideswipe at a line in Obama's address in which he had spoken of America's 'exceptional' nature.

'It is extremely dangerous to encourage people to see themselves as exceptional, whatever the motivation,' Putin wrote. 'There are big countries and small countries, rich and poor, those with long democratic traditions and those still finding their way to democracy. Their policies differ, too. We are all different, but when we ask for the Lord's blessings, we must not forget that God created us equal.'

Putin's words – and the *New York Times*' decision to run them – provoked a massive reaction: while some on social media expressed support for his ideas, politicians were outraged. John Boehner, the speaker of the House, said he was 'insulted'; Senator Robert Menendez, a Democrat from New Jersey, claimed the article made him almost want to throw up. Nancy Pelosi, the House minority leader, wondered whether Putin's words on equality applied 'to gays and lesbians in Russia as well'. The White House shrugged off the fuss around Putin's jabs at Obama, describing them as 'irrelevant'.

Putin had begun his commentary by expressing a desire to talk directly to 'American people and their political leaders'. If he thought he would endear himself to them by questioning their claim to be 'exceptional', he was mistaken.

19

UKRAINE

O<small>N</small> S<small>ATURDAY</small> 22 F<small>EBRUARY</small> 2014, K<small>IEV</small> woke to a wet, grey dawn. After several days of bloody clashes that had turned the Ukrainian capital into a killing field, the police had vanished. The presidential buildings were empty and unguarded. The dreaded Berkut special police, whose name had become synonymous with brutality, had disappeared without a trace. The centre of the city was now in the hands of the protesters. But was this victory, or just a lull while the security forces regrouped? And most importantly, where was President Viktor Yanukovych? Disgraced after the rigged election of 2004, the villain of the Orange Revolution had bounced back to secure re-election in 2010. But now he had again fallen victim to the popular will and fled his capital.

The mood on the Maidan Nezalezhnosti, the symbolic headquarters of the protesters, was jubilant. Three months of street protests against Yanukovych's attempts to orientate his country towards Russia rather than Europe had ended in victory for what became known as the *Euromaidan*. Yet joy was merged with sorrow at the death of protesters, who were venerated as the 'Heavenly Hundred'. The Ukrainian parliament, which had turned against Yanukovych earlier in the week, declared the absent president unable to fulfil his duties and set elections for 25 May to choose a successor.

The same day, twelve miles north of Kiev, on the banks of the Dnieper, the gates of Yanukovych's Mezhyhirya palace were flung open to reveal a classic example of dictator chic, with a mock-Spanish galleon, golf course, museum for classic cars and a petting zoo complete with ostriches. Ordinary Ukrainians who came for a glimpse of their former leader's home were amazed, as one reporter put it, to find 'a display of wealth and vulgarity that was part presidential palace in the style of the former Romanian dictator Nicolae Ceauşescu, part the crazed whimsy of Michael Jackson's Neverland ranch'.[1] Even more intriguing were the documents found floating in the water in a reservoir in the grounds of the estate, some of which were partially charred after a last failed attempt to burn them. They provided an insight into the workings of the regime – ranging from details about how the president's estate was funded to detailed plans, never implemented, to deploy the army to clear the Maidan of protesters. Their presence was a sign of quite how frantic the final moments of the regime had been.

That afternoon, Yanukovych, who had slipped away quietly in the night, appeared on Ukrainian television, apparently from the eastern city of Kharkiv, near the Russian border. Insisting that he remained the legitimately elected president, he claimed that he had been forced to leave Kiev by a coup and was not planning to resign. 'What is happening today, mostly, is vandalism, banditism and a coup d'état,' he said. 'I will remain on the territory of Ukraine.' It later transpired that his message had been recorded several hours earlier.

Events were moving fast, however. That evening, Yulia Tymoshenko, the braided-haired heroine of the Orange Revolution, who had been jailed in October 2011 for embezzlement and abuse of power, was released from the hospital in eastern Ukraine where she had been held under police guard. Confined to a wheelchair by a back injury, she appeared on the stage in the Maidan calling her audience 'heroes' and added: 'I was dreaming to see your eyes. I was dreaming to feel the power that changed everything.' Despite the cheers and cries of 'Yulia' from the crowd, others seemed suspicious of a woman closely identified with Ukraine's bad old ways. It was time for a new leader. Meanwhile, in an ominous foretaste of what was to come, a rally was held in the Crimean port city of Sevastopol, home of the Russian navy's Black Sea Fleet. The protesters there demanded 'reunification with Russia'.

The events that culminated in Yanukovych's flight from Kiev were among the most dramatic to have taken place on the territory of the former Soviet Union. They were also the most divisive. According to the Western narrative, this was an uprising by freedom-loving people against a corrupt and increasingly authoritarian leader who was systematically looting the country and selling out to Moscow. Russia saw things differently: a group of neo-fascists had overthrown Ukraine's legitimate government and seized power, egged on by the CIA and other Western intelligence agencies determined to remove the country from the Kremlin's sphere of influence.

THE ROOTS OF THE CRISIS LAY a decade earlier in the Orange Revolution and the failure of those it brought to power to satisfy the hopes that had been raised. The revolution's hero, Viktor Yushchenko, had become president, determined to turn Ukraine towards the West and root out the corruption that had long plagued Ukraine, but he had proved an ineffective leader and was locked in an almost permanent power struggle with Tymoshenko. The situation was worsened by the global economic crisis, which sent the Ukrainian GDP tumbling by fifteen per cent in 2009.

In the meantime, the other Viktor, Yanukovych, the man whom Yushchenko had beaten in 2004, was climbing in the polls, thanks in part to help from a group of American political consultants. Among them was Paul Manafort, a long-time American Republican strategist, who had worked for various dubious foreign figures such as Ferdinand Marcos of the Philippines, and who in 2016 would briefly head Donald Trump's US presidential campaign. With Manafort's help, Yanukovych's Party of the Regions was 'working to change its image from that of a haven for mobsters into that of a legitimate political party', John Herbst, the US ambassador, observed in a cable later published by WikiLeaks.

What Herbst described as an 'extreme makeover' worked. Under Manafort's tutelage, Yanukovych's rambling communist-style speeches became snappier and his bouffant hairdo, a favourite of Soviet apparatchiks, was replaced with a sleeker style. In the presidential election of January 2010, he topped the first round with 35.32% in a crowded field of eighteen, way ahead of Tymoshenko, who was in second place with 25.5%. Yushchenko scored just 5.45% – the worst result of any sitting president in history. Yanukovych then went on to beat Tymoshenko by 48.95% to 45.47% in the run-off. The result showed a country as divided as ever: Tymoshenko prevailed in the predominantly

Ukrainian-speaking north and west, but Yanukovych dominated the largely Russian-speaking south and east. With Ukrainians yearning for stability, Yanukovych had managed to portray himself as a moderate professional able to unify the country. It was a remarkable comeback from the days when eggs were being thrown at his head.

Yanukovych's first trip abroad was to Brussels. But he was also keen to repair relations with Moscow, which had soured under his pro-Western predecessor: in April he signed a deal with Medvedev to extend from 2017 to 2042 the Russian Black Sea Fleet's lease on its base in Crimea, in return for a discount on Russian gas supplies. Two months later, the Ukrainian parliament approved a law proposed by Yanukovych that abandoned the previous administration's goal of 'integration into Euro-Atlantic security and NATO membership'. Ukraine might coop-erate with the Western Alliance, but not join it or any other military bloc. Yet hopes of a fresh start soon proved illusory. Rather than fill his government with professionals and technocrats, Yanukovych appointed associates from his home region of Donbass, Ukraine's rust belt, who had little experience of democracy and lacked the know-how to run a market economy. Proposed economic reforms did not mat-erialise. Nor did he succeed in re-establishing the delicate balance in Ukraine between East and West.

During his time in office, Yushchenko had alienated Russian speakers by pushing Ukrainian language, culture and identity: he highlighted the *Holodomor,* the man-made famine of 1932–3 blamed on Stalin, and bestowed the title 'Hero of Ukraine' on Stepan Bandera, the Second World War nationalist leader denounced in official Soviet history as a Nazi puppet. Under Yanukovych, the pendulum swung back too far in the opposite direction: one of his first actions was to sign a law allowing Russian to be used alongside Ukrainian in courts, schools and other government institutions in parts of the country that wanted it. This led to fist fights in parliament and violent protests on the streets, but thirteen of Ukraine's twenty-seven regions, mostly in the industrial eastern parts of the country, quickly adopted Russian as their second official language. Yanukovych also turned on Tymoshenko, who was jailed for abuse of power during her time as prime minister under Yushchenko, after a trial roundly condemned as politically motivated.

Curiously, as Yanukovych's problems mounted and his popularity slumped, he initially looked to Europe for a way out, reviving talks begun by his predecessor with the European Union, which had stalled after he came to power over concerns in Brussels about Ukraine's flawed legal and electoral system. Agreement was complicated by the close interest taken by the EU in the fate of Tymoshenko, whose jailing was seen as highlighting such flaws and whose release it demanded. The two sides gradually ironed out their differences, though, and on 30 March 2012 the EU Association Agreement was initialled in Brussels.

Yet Yanukovych was also being pulled towards the East. Since the collapse of the Soviet Union, Russia had been trying to find a way of maintaining ties with the other former Soviet republics – a process that began with the agreement at Belavezha in December 1991, which was not only about breaking up the USSR but also replacing it with the Commonwealth of Independent States. Such attempts had foundered in large part due to a suspicion by other member states of anything that smacked of attempts by Russia to reassert its control over its neighbours. After Yeltsin's failures, Putin had stepped up its efforts: his latest attempt, the Eurasian Customs Union, created in 2010, appeared modelled on the European Union, with Russia, Kazakhstan and Belarus as its founding members.

In launching the project, Putin denied it was an attempt to re-create the Soviet Union. 'There is no talk of re-forming the USSR in some form,' Putin wrote in a newspaper article in October 2012. 'It would be naive to restore or copy what has been abandoned in the past but close integration – on the basis of new values, politics, and economy – is the order of the day.' But America was not convinced: in a speech two months later in December 2012, Hillary Clinton denounced the union as 'a move to re-Sovietise the region', adding: 'We know what the goal is and we are trying to figure out effective ways to slow down or prevent it.' The Kremlin accused Clinton of 'a completely wrong understanding of the situation', stressing that the union was purely about a new type of voluntary economic integration.

Ukraine's size, location and industrial potential made its membership vital for the success of the Eurasian Customs Union, as had been the case with all previous efforts at reintegrating the former Soviet states. Yanukovych was happy to play along with Moscow on this. Despite pursuing ties with the EU, he was also talking to Russia about 'finding the right model' for Ukraine's relationship with its union. Yet he could not have it both ways. 'One country cannot at the same time be a member of a customs union and be in a deep common free-trade area with the European Union,' José Manuel Barroso, the European Commission president, told Yanukovych at their summit in February 2013. The EU was also upping pressure on Kiev over Tymoshenko and over the slow pace of reform.

Russia was not willing to let Ukraine turn towards the West, and as the country's largest trading partner, it had considerable leverage. Medvedev, by then back as prime minister, dismissed Ukraine's attempts to establish a semi-detached relationship with the Eurasian Customs Union, saying it had to choose between 'all and nothing'. Russia made clear to Yanukovych that closer ties with the EU would be followed by restrictions on the import of Ukrainian goods. Companies in eastern Ukraine – Yanukovych's power base and the site of most of the country's heavy industry – would have been hit hardest by Russia's escalation. Ukraine was also heavily dependent on Russian energy supplies. The EU, which had badly underestimated the ferocity of the Kremlin's reaction, offered little by way of a sweetener – nothing like the $20 billion a year Yanukovych said he needed to adapt his country to European standards.

Yanukovych finally buckled to Kremlin pressure: on 21 November his government announced it would not go ahead with the agreement with the EU, which had been due to be signed at a summit in Vilnius beginning a week later. The Ukrainian government said it would instead 'renew dialogue' with the Eurasian Customs Union. The same day, the Verkhovna Rada, the parliament, voted down six resolutions that would have been required to free Tymoshenko.

Among those watching proceedings in the Ukrainian parliament was Mustafa Nayyem, a young Afghan-born journalist. At first he thought this was nothing more than a manoeuvre by Yanukovych to try to extract more money or concessions from the European Union. It soon became clear, however, that the government had radically changed course. As outrage spread on social media, Nayyem sent out a tweet: 'Let's meet at 22.30 next to the Independence Monument. Dress warmly, bring umbrellas, tea, coffee and friends.'

When Nayyem arrived in the Maidan there were just fifty people there. Before long there were more than a thousand. In the days leading up to the EU summit, growing numbers of people began to gather each day in the square. Yanukovych went to Vilnius to meet European leaders as planned, but rather than sign the agreement, he proposed three-way talks between Russia, Ukraine and the EU. Barroso rejected the idea of giving Moscow a say in its neighbour's future, however, and Yanukovych returned home empty-handed.

Ukraine's fate was sealed. Forced to choose between Russia and the EU, Yanukovych felt he had no alternative but to go with Moscow. Back in Kiev, the organisers of the protests had considered calling off their action now that the summit had ended and the door to Europe was closed. But everything changed in the early hours of the next morning, when hundreds of members of the Berkut riot police moved in, ordering the few hundred protesters still gathered there to disperse. They refused. At least three dozen were beaten and thirty-five were arrested. Far from dissuading the protesters, it only encouraged them; later that day they returned.

Yanukovych tried various tactics to calm the protesters and keep his grip on power, but he faced a losing battle. As the protests continued, fuelled by anger at the brutality of the police, hundreds of thousands of people poured into the Maidan. On 8 December, during their largest protest to date, they toppled a giant statue of Lenin and smashed it to pieces. A permanent tent city began to appear in the square. The protesters, who ranged from pro-EU liberals to thuggish far-right nationalists, lacked a single leader. But what had begun as a protest over a trade agreement was turning into a full-blown uprising aimed at ousting Yanukovych and reorientating Ukraine's alliances.

For the West, the protesters, with their fresh faces and determination that their country should 'join Europe', were redolent of those involved in the Colour Revolutions of a decade earlier and in the Arab Spring. Western leaders were quick to demonstrate solidarity – prompting Russia to denounce them for 'crude' meddling in Ukraine's affairs. First to make the pilgrimage to Kiev was Guido Westerwelle, the German foreign minister, who toured the protest camp on 4 December. A few days later he was followed by Catherine Ashton, the EU foreign policy chief, and Victoria Nuland, the US state department's hawkish assistant secretary of state for European and Eurasian affairs. In one of the more surreal moments of the crisis, she walked around the Maidan carrying a plastic bag stuffed with loaves of bread. 'Good to see you!' Nuland said, approaching a bemused elderly woman in a blue parka. 'We're here from America. Would you like some bread?' The smiling woman politely declined, waving away the gift.

A few days later, Senator John McCain, a veteran of the Colour Revolutions, arrived. 'The free world is with you, America is with you, I am with you,' he told the cheering crowd. 'Ukraine will make Europe better and Europe will make Ukraine better.' In an interview with CNN the next day, he set out the issues in characteristically black-and-white terms: 'What we're trying to do is try to bring about a peaceful transition here,' he said. 'These people love the United States of America, they love freedom – and I don't think you could view this as anything other than our traditional support for people who want free and democratic society.' The US administration was more cautious. Although it wanted to stand up for democratic values, the Maidan was a distraction from the more pressing issues dividing Washington and Moscow, such as the civil war in Syria and Iran's nuclear programme.

The situation on the ground, meanwhile, was deteriorating: on 16 January, Yanukovych's backers in parliament pushed through sweeping legislation outlawing the tents that had covered the Maidan, coupled with other measures to suppress political dissent and restrict freedom of speech. More protests followed, which turned increasingly violent. Demonstrators donned ski masks and bicycle helmets, set fire to tyres and even deployed a 10ft-high catapult capable of firing bags of cobblestones at police. The police responded with stun grenades and plastic bullets. On 22 January, the conflict claimed its first three fatalities: two demonstrators were shot by police and a third fell to his death from a 43ft (13m) colonnade in front of Dynamo Stadium. Yanukovych tried to defuse the crisis by offering places in his government to the opposition leaders, but they declined.

America was also becoming involved, behind the scenes. The day before the lavish opening ceremony at the Sochi Winter Olympics, a recording of a phone call between Assistant Secretary of State Victoria Nuland and Geoffrey Pyatt, the US ambassador to Ukraine, found its way onto YouTube – apparently courtesy of the Russian intelligence services. During the conversation, believed to have taken place a few weeks earlier, the two American officials discussed which opposition figures should go into the government, perhaps as prime minister, if it were possible to do a deal with Yanukovych. 'I don't think "Klitsch" should go into the government,' Nuland said of Vitali

Klitschko, the former world heavyweight boxing champion turned politician. 'I don't think it's necessary, I don't think it's a good idea.' After a long pause, Pyatt agreed: 'Just let him stay out and do his political homework and stuff.'

They agreed instead that the former economics minister, Arseniy Yatsenyuk – or 'Yats' to the Americans – should be the one to go in, on the grounds that he was 'the guy who's got the economic experience, the governing experience'. They also noted that Oleh Tyahnybok, who represented an outright fascist-nationalist party, might be a 'problem', but appeared to treat him as someone with whom they could work. The conversation then turned to the European Union and their frustration that it was not doing more to undercut Russia. 'Fuck the EU!' exclaimed Nuland.

These comments did not go down well with Angela Merkel, who was already smarting over revelations by Snowden that America's National Security Agency had been bugging her phone. She called Nuland's words 'totally unacceptable'. The state department made no attempt to deny the authenticity of the recording, turning their fire instead on those who had leaked it. Nuland laughed off the incident, praising the quality of the audio and describing the episode as 'pretty impressive tradecraft' – implying the leak was the work of the intelligence agencies.

There was speculation that the crisis would take a turn for the worse after the Sochi Olympics ended on 23 February and Putin could stop playing the congenial host. Would Russia cut off supplies of gas to Ukraine, perhaps, or even intervene militarily? In the event, the denouement, which occurred three days earlier, proved very different: after two days of mounting casualties, radical street fighters forced their way through police lines, ushering in a day of violence that turned the centre of Kiev into a war zone and ending with a death toll of at least seventy. Many of the victims fell to snipers, thought to be working for the police. Undaunted, the demonstrators counter-attacked, reoccupying buildings they had evacuated earlier in the week.

Yanukovych was rumoured to be considering introducing a state of emergency, which would have allowed him to deploy the military. But he was swiftly losing his authority; at a joint session of parliament later that day, opposition leaders joined defectors from his own party to pass a resolution obliging interior ministry troops to return to barracks and barring the use of firearms. Parliament ruled that only it, rather than the president, could call a state of emergency.

The situation was spiralling towards crisis. The previous day, the German, French and Polish foreign ministers had arrived in Kiev in an attempt to broker a political solution. Russia was also becoming involved. That afternoon Vladimir Lukin, the former Russian ambassador to Washington and outgoing human rights commissioner, received a call from Putin. 'He said he wanted me to go down to Kiev as soon as possible,' Lukin recalls. 'Negotiations were going on and the situation was very tense.'[2]

Lukin hurried to the Kremlin for a meeting with officials from the foreign ministry and the FSB. Arriving at Putin's office, he found the Russian leader on the phone to Angela Merkel. He was turning to leave, but Putin gestured to him to stay.

That evening they flew down to Kiev on a private Falcon jet. By the time Lukin arrived, details were beginning to emerge of a deal between Yanukovych and the opposition, brokered by the three EU foreign ministers. Its terms included a return within forty-eight hours to the constitution of 2004, which reduced the powers of the president in favour of the prime minister; formation of a government of national unity within ten days after that; a new constitution by September and new presidential elections by December. It was also agreed there should be an investigation into the recent violence and no declaration of a state of emergency.

While copies of the documents were being printed, Lukin and Yanukovych slipped away into a side room. As they began to talk, Yanukovych, a tall man, inclined his head towards his guest. 'Speak more quietly, Vladimir Petrovich,' he told him. 'They're listening to us.'[3]

Lukin was struck by the Ukrainian leader's apparent inability, even then, to grasp that his country was in the midst of a revolution. 'He was happy with the agreement, because he thought he would benefit whatever happened,' says Lukin of Yanukovych. 'If he won the next election, then he would remain president. And even if he lost, his party would still have a majority in parliament, which would mean that, once the country had reverted to the 2004 constitution, he would be prime minister and in charge.

'He did not understand that it was a revolution, which meant that the question of power would be resolved very simply. It was a situation like in China during Tiananmen Square. The difference was that Yanukovych either could not – or did not want to – do what Deng Xiaoping did. He didn't want to because he feared it was no longer possible.'

It was agreed that they would all reconvene at midday the next day. In the meantime, Lukin went back to the embassy to telephone Lavrov, the Russian foreign minister. A few hours later, Lukin received a call back from Moscow with his instructions: he was not to sign the agreement. The situation was spinning out of control so fast that Russia did not want to commit to anything.

The next day they reassembled as planned in the ornate Blue Hall of the presidential headquarters. As they went into the room, Radek Sikorski, the Polish foreign minister, was overheard telling one of the opposition leaders: 'If you don't support this deal, you will have martial law, the army, you'll be dead.' Klitschko switched seats so he did not have to sit next to the president. An unsmiling Yanukovych signed the agreement, as did Klitschko, Yatsenyuk and Tyahnybok, the three key opposition figures. It was witnessed by Sikorski and the two other EU foreign ministers – but not by Lukin. After the ceremony was over, Mikhail Zurabov, the Russian ambassador, urged him to leave for the airport, where the Falcon was waiting to fly him back to Moscow.

The deal was hailed by Western leaders, among them David Cameron, the British prime minister, who said he thought it would 'foster a lasting political solution' that would offer a 'real chance' to end the bloodshed. 'Ukraine has pulled back from the brink,' said Tony Blinken, the White House deputy national security adviser, though he admitted that 'we're not out of the woods yet'. In a further sign of goodwill, the parliament voted overwhelmingly to decriminalise the count under which Tymoshenko had been imprisoned, paving the way for her release – to cheers from those who had been watching the extraordinary parliamentary session on giant screens in the Maidan.

Selling the deal to the crowd proved more difficult. Emotions in the square were running high. Funeral services had been held during the day for some of the seventy-seven people who had died there; the idea that Yanukovych, the man they blamed for the slaughter, would remain president for the rest of the year seemed intolerable. When Klitschko went to the Maidan that evening, he was met with catcalls and derisive whistling. A coffin was hauled onto the stage in memory of the dead. A protester dressed in battle fatigues won roars of approval when he jumped onto the stage, grabbed the microphone and said: 'If it is not announced by ten tomorrow that Yanukovych is gone, we're going to attack with weapons.'

In the parliament building, Yanukovych turned to Colonel General Sergei Beseda, head of a seven-member delegation from the Russian FSB, who had been advising him on the crisis. Beseda told him there was only one solution: unleash the army on the protesters camped in the square and 'crush them once and for all', according to an account in the *Sunday Times*, based on information from Ukrainian intelligence sources.[4] If not, Yanukovych was warned, he risked suffering the fate of Nicolae Ceaușescu, the hated Romanian leader who was shot after his own people rose up against him twenty-five years earlier.

Yanukovych did not have the stomach to tough it out. He appears never to have returned to his official residence: instead, with his girl-friend, Lyubov Polezhay, twenty-four years his junior, and a little fluffy white dog at his side, he took a helicopter to eastern Ukraine, landing first in Kharkiv and then again in Donetsk. It was there he boarded a Falcon with the aim of flying to Russia. Border guards prevented the plane from taking off, however, because it lacked the proper documentation, and Yanukovych disembarked and was whisked off the tarmac in an armoured car.*

On 24 February Ukraine's acting government declared Yanukovych a fugitive sought for mass murder. The government made an appeal through the Facebook account of Arsen Avakov, the interim interior minister, in the apparent hope that a border guard would stop him. It was too late: Yanukovych had already continued his journey by car, boat and helicopter, making it to Rostov-on-Don on the Russian side of the border.

ATTEMPTS BY RUSSIA TO PORTRAY THE events of that weekend in Kiev as the result of a coup carefully organised and stage-managed by the CIA fit uneasily with the scale and spontaneity of the protests and determination of those who took part. For the massive crowds who braved the bitter winter weather to camp out in the Maidan there was

---

* When border guards arrived to check the plane's papers they were confronted by a group of armed men who offered money in return for allowing it to take off without the necessary documentation. The border guards refused. They apparently did not realise the president was on board.

more at stake than Ukraine's relationship with Europe; there was wide-spread anger with a regime perceived as inept and kleptocratic and drifting away from democracy. Such anger may have been spontaneous; it may also have been stirred up by those with an axe to grind against the government. Lukin, for one, saw the origins of the uprising in a battle for influence between Yanukovych and his allies on one side, and a rival group of oligarchs on the other.

There was no doubt, though, about the role played by Western politicians in encouraging the protesters. Or – thanks to the leaked tape of the telephone conversation between Nuland and Pyatt – of the extent of attempts by Washington to influence the political transition. As was the case with the Colour Revolutions, the pro-democracy groups also received considerable financial help from the West. One of the most generous donors was George Soros, the billionaire investor who combined support for democracy in Ukraine with considerable commercial interests in the country. Russia, too, had been heavily involved, supporting Russian-language groups and using its propa-ganda machine to taint the pro-European demonstrators as neo-fascists and *Banderovtsi*, the derogatory term given to followers of Stepan Bandera.

For all his faults, Yanukovych was the legitimately elected president of Ukraine and attempts to unseat him were undemocratic. Yet it was his own decision to abandon his capital that cost him his job. He could have stayed and insisted on implementation of the compromise brokered by the EU foreign ministers. Claims by supporters that he abandoned the capital because he was in fear of his life do not appear to be borne out by the evidence and only add to the view, taken even by his backers in Moscow, that he was a coward.

Underlying the dramatic events of those few days was a more funda-mental problem faced by Ukraine. Even after more than two decades of independence, the country remained almost equally divided between those who looked to Europe and those who looked to Russia. Yet its leaders had still not learnt the art of compromise. Since 1991, power had swung backward and forward between the West and the East, and once in office, each faction sought to impose its will on the other rather than find a way of smoothing over the crack running through the centre of the country. The same thing was happening again.

The EU must bear its share of the blame for pushing Ukraine into a position where it had to choose between Europe and Russia, without taking into account that different parts of the country wanted different things. There was also a failure to appreciate the Kremlin's sensitivities. Yanukovych was being offered few incentives, let alone the prospect of full membership of the EU. All that was on the table was a trade deal and even that had strings attached: namely the need for Ukraine to agree to painful reforms of its economy. It was no surprise that he ultimately plumped for Russia.

Some of the most withering criticism came from Henry Kissinger. In a commentary for the *Washington Post*, published just over a week after Yanukovych's fall, he accused the EU of turning a 'negotiation into a crisis' by failing to appreciate that in Russia's eyes Ukraine 'could never be just a foreign country'. But at the same time, he argued, the Kremlin needed to understand that it had to give up trying to force Ukraine into accepting satellite status or risk plunging the world back into another Cold War. 'Far too often the Ukrainian issue is posed as a showdown: whether Ukraine joins the East or the West,' Kissinger wrote.[5] 'But if Ukraine is to survive and thrive, it must not be either side's outpost against the other – it should function as a bridge between them.'

It was difficult to disagree with Kissinger's words. But by the time they appeared, it was already too late. The crisis over Ukraine was about to become more acute – and bloodier.

20

A PIECE OF PARADISE

In November 1782, when Catherine the Great was hesitating over whether to press ahead with the annexation of the Crimean peninsula, Prince Grigory Potemkin urged her on. 'There is no power in Europe that has not participated in the carving up of Asia, Africa, America,' her lover and favourite general wrote to her. 'Believe me that doing this will give you immortal glory greater than any other Russian sovereign ever . . . With the Crimea, dominance over the Black Sea will be achieved. Russia needs paradise.'

Catherine heeded Potemkin's words. The following year she declared Crimea to be Russia's forever, adding eighteen thousand square miles to her empire, extending its borders to the Black Sea and paving the way for her country's rise as a naval power. In order to secure the peninsula's borders, she ordered the building of the fortress of Sevastopol and the creation of the Black Sea Fleet. Russia had claimed its piece of paradise.

On 19 February 1954, at the stroke of a pen, Crimea was part of Russia no longer. At a meeting of the Presidium of the USSR Supreme Soviet, the Soviet Union's supreme lawmaking body, it was agreed that the peninsula should be transferred from Russia to Ukraine: Nikita Khrushchev needed the support of the leadership of the powerful Ukrainian Communist Party to confirm him as Stalin's successor and saw the gift as a way of ensuring they backed him. The people of Crimea were overwhelmingly Russian rather than Ukrainian. But from that moment on they found themselves ruled from Kiev.

The impact of the change was limited as long as the Soviet Union existed and the borders between Russia and Ukraine were internal and administrative. This changed after 1991, when Crimea became part of a newly independent Ukraine. The people of Crimea had voted narrowly in favour of independence in that December's referendum, but their vote was inspired more by dissatisfaction with the Soviet Union than with a desire for a future with Ukraine. In the years that followed, relations between Crimean authorities and the rulers of the new Ukrainian state were tense; attempts by the peninsula to achieve more autonomy were resisted by Kiev. Many of the ethnic Russians who lived in Crimea dreamt of becoming part of Russia, a sentiment that was reinforced over the years by the latter's growing affluence relative to Ukraine.

Matters were complicated by the continued presence of the Black Sea Fleet in Sevastopol. Ukraine tried to claim the fleet as its own, but with the majority of officers loyal to Russia, the government knew it faced a potential mutiny if it pressed ahead. As a compromise, the two countries initially agreed to run the fleet jointly, but then in 1997 it was divided into two parts. Russia was allowed to continue to use the port for another twenty years and to keep up to twenty-five thousand troops there, as well as artillery, armoured vehicles and planes. The military foothold on the peninsula that this gave Russia was crucial in the days that followed the fall of Yanukovych.

Many in Crimea had watched the events unfolding in faraway Kiev with concern and were ready to believe a propaganda offensive by Russian media – widely watched in Ukraine – that portrayed those now in charge of Ukraine as dreaded modern-day neo-fascist *Banderovtsi*. Putin, meanwhile, was ready to pounce. On 18 February 2014, after violence flared in Kiev, Moscow had put Russian special forces on alert in Sevastopol and in the nearby southern Russian port city of Novorossiysk. Two days later, Russian troops were ordered to blockade Ukrainian military installations in Crimea, ostensibly to prevent bloodshed between the pro- and anti-Kiev groups. Early on 23 February, at the end of an all-night meeting with his security chiefs, Putin reportedly took the most momentous decision of his presidency: to annexe Crimea.

'I told my colleagues that the situation in Ukraine was developing in such a way that we had to start working on returning Crimea to

Russia,' Putin told an officially sanctioned documentary, broadcast a year later on Russian television. 'We could not abandon this territory and the people who lived there to the mercy of fate, under the steam-roller of nationalism.'

Events moved fast: on 26 February, thousands of ethnic Russians chanting 'Crimea is Russian' and waving Russian flags gathered outside the regional parliament in Simferopol, the capital, to demand autonomy and independence. They clashed with several thousand Crimean Tatars, the indigenous Muslim population, who were holding a counterdemon-stration. A decision by the Ukrainian parliament to repeal the 2012 language law in one of its first acts after Yanukovych's departure added to tensions. Roadblocks flying the Russian tricolour appeared on the main roads running to Sevastopol. Putin, meanwhile, ordered an unplanned military exercise involving tens of thousands of members of Russian ground and air forces on the border with Ukraine.

At 4:20A.M. the next day, heavily armed pro-Russian gunmen seized Crimea's parliament and government building. During an emergency session, the parliament dismissed the government and appointed a new prime minister, Sergey Aksyonov, a local pro-Russian businessman and former boxer known locally by his underworld nickname of 'Goblin'. They also agreed to hold a referendum on 25 May on greater autonomy. The votes that led to both decisions were said to be over-whelming, but it was impossible to be sure: the mysterious gunmen cut off all the building's communications and took away MPs' phones as they went in.

'Provocateurs are on the march,' declared Arsen Avakov, Ukraine's acting interior minister. 'It's a time for cool heads, the healthy consol-idation of forces and careful action.' But police and other local officials in Crimea were reluctant to obey orders from the new government in Kiev, which they considered illegitimate, and there was little the latter could do to enforce its will. Meanwhile, crowds chanting 'Rossiya, Rossiya [Russia, Russia]' began to build up outside the parliament building in Simferopol and barricaded its entrance with wooden boxes and metal bins.

Men wearing what looked suspiciously like green Russian military camouflage uniforms began to appear: they popped up first at Simferopol airport in the early hours of 28 February and took control. Later that day, they seized Sevastopol airport too. By the following

evening they were guarding key government buildings, had blockaded
Ukrainian border troops at Balaklava Bay and set up checkpoints on
roads across Crimea. The next day they surrounded a Ukrainian marine
infantry detachment stationed around Feodosia in the south-east of
the peninsula and ordered it to surrender. Many similar takeovers
followed. Russia kept up its relentless propaganda campaign, citing
undefined threats to its citizens and proclaimed 'massive defections'
of Ukrainian forces in Crimea. The mysterious uniformed men had
no insignia, but were thought to be from the 810th Marine Infantry
Brigade, which had guarded the base in Sevastopol for decades. Unlike
the mobs occupying parliament, they were calm and in control. On
their Twitter feed they called themselves *Vezhliviye Lyudi* ('polite
people'). They were immediately dubbed 'little green men', and they
were rapidly taking over Crimea.

America watched developments with alarm, warning Russia that
there would be unspecified 'costs' if it violated Ukraine's sovereignty.
In a ninety-minute phone call with Putin, Obama urged him to withdraw his forces to their bases in Crimea and stop 'any interference' in
other parts of Ukraine. In a statement afterwards, the White House
said the United States would suspend participation in preparatory
meetings for the G8 economic conference to be held in Sochi in June,
and warned of 'greater political and economic isolation' for Russia. The
Kremlin, in a somewhat different account of the same call, said Putin
had spoken of 'a real threat to the lives and health of Russian citizens
in Ukraine', and warned that it retained the right to protect them and
its own interests if the violence spread to the east of the country or to
Crimea. Putin knew he could call Obama's bluff: it was clear that Russia
had more at stake than America.

Putin had until now made no public comment on the events in
Ukraine. On 4 March he finally broke his silence to denounce the
takeover in Kiev as an unconstitutional coup d'état. The soldiers occupying military bases were not Russian soldiers, but local self-defence
forces, he insisted. Although there was no need to send forces into
Ukraine for the time being, Russia reserved the right to use 'all means'
as a last resort to prevent anarchy.

Two days later, the Crimean parliament voted to join Russia; on 16
March the decision was put to a referendum. According to official results,
the independence vote was backed by 96.77% on a turnout of 83.1%.

Allegations of abuse were rife, and although Russian media claimed that as many as 135 international observers had monitored the election, they were drawn from far-right, anti-American and pro-Russian parties in Europe and beyond. Yet there seemed little doubt that a majority of Crimea's residents was in favour of the break with Ukraine.

On 18 March 2014, more than two hundred years after Catherine had first acquired her slice of paradise – and sixty years after it was signed away by Khrushchev – the peninsula was formally brought back under Russian control. Ukraine was neither able nor willing to fight to keep Crimea. Outgunned and with morale low, its forces had little choice but to give up. Some returned to Ukraine proper; others crossed to the other side. An international border had been redrawn at the point of a gun.

PUTIN'S ACTIONS PLUNGED RUSSIA'S RELATIONS WITH the West into their most serious crisis since the Cold War. Yet Putin seemed undaunted by the opprobrium that rained down on him, not least because of the enormous propaganda benefits at home: bringing Crimea back under Russian control was sold to the Russian public as the long-overdue righting of a historical wrong. The addition of the peninsula's 1.5 million ethnic Russians to the motherland also fitted well with Putin's attempt to portray himself as the leader of the *Russkiy Mir* – a Russian world that included compatriots left outside the borders of the Russian Federation after the collapse of the Soviet Union.

Nor should the West have been surprised by Putin's action: the prospect of annexing Crimea had been raised as far back as the 2008 Bucharest summit, when Ukrainian membership of NATO was being discussed, according to Mikhail Zygar, founder of the independent Dozhd television channel. At the time, Putin had warned that if Ukraine joined the Alliance, it risked doing so without Crimea and its eastern provinces. A number of Western analysts also pointed to Crimea as the next possible target for assertive Russian action – among them Roderic Lyne, British ambassador to Moscow from 2000 to 2004. 'The generals have the bit between their teeth, and the "Crimea next" party will be in full cry,' Lyne warned in an article published in October 2008 in which he drew on the lessons of the crisis that summer over Georgia.[1] Chief among those lessons was the hostile reaction expected from Russia to any attempt to turn Ukraine towards the West, especially if it involved the prospect of NATO membership. 'We must assume that Russia would exert itself mightily, risk a great deal and pay a high price to prevent Ukraine from becoming, as Russians would see it, a platform for American power,' Lyne added presciently.

Crimea as an issue faded in importance after Yanukovych did a deal with Russia after coming to power in 2010 – to extend the lease for the Black Sea Fleet. But when the protests began on the Maidan, senior members of Russia's military and security services, as well as 'patriotic businessmen', began to start talking again about the idea of taking back '*Krym Nash* [Our Crimea]'. Furthermore, such an operation looked achievable at minimal cost: Nikolai Patrushev, secretary of the Security Council, and Alexander Bortnikov, head of the FSB, assured Putin that their private polling showed that the majority of Crimeans would look positively towards the idea of joining Russia, while the Ukrainian military was so underfunded and badly disorganised it looked unlikely to mount any resistance – especially since many of its officers stationed on the peninsula were loyal to Moscow rather than Kiev.

It was the ousting of Yanukovych that provided a catalyst for action. Putin may have been motivated in part by the desire to get his hands on the vast unexploited oil and gas reserves that lie off the Crimean coast. Possession of the peninsula would also allow a more direct route for the planned South Stream pipeline running under the Black Sea from Russia to Bulgaria and then on to Southern Europe. But while this was undoubtedly a bonus, the improvised nature of the operation suggests that the main reason Putin acted was fear that Ukraine's new pro-Western leaders might attempt to evict Russia's Black Sea Fleet from its Sevastopol base, which was strategically crucial. Worse, they might then invite in NATO forces in its place. 'Putin's seizure of Crimea appears to have been an improvised gambit, developed under pressure, that was triggered by the fear of losing Russia's strategically important naval base in Sevastopol,' concluded Daniel Treisman, who pieced together details of the operation in an account for *Foreign Affairs*.[2]

This version was confirmed to me by Dmitry Peskov, Putin's spokesman, who claimed that the Kremlin leader ordered the seizure of Crimea after being shown what he believed to be American plans to establish a naval base on the peninsula. 'Strategically Crimea is very important,' Peskov said.[3] 'If NATO anti-missile systems or offensive missiles had been deployed there, it would have been very dangerous for Russia and could have changed the balance of power in the region. It was one of the reasons Putin acted. But this question would never have been on the agenda if it had not been for the take-over in Kiev.'

Regardless of when and why the decision to annexe Crimea was taken, there is no doubt that it reflected Putin's growing assertiveness at home and abroad since his return to the presidency in 2012. Since the collapse of the Soviet Union, Russia had considered the former Soviet space as part of its legitimate sphere of influence, even though in the early years it could do little more than meddle. Putin did not try to stop the Baltic states joining NATO in March 2004, nor did he interfere when Ukraine turned towards the West after the Orange Revolution a few months later; his patience was rewarded when Yushchenko's government fell apart and the more pro-Russian Yanukovych eventually took his place.

Yet Russia – and Putin – had changed, and in his Munich speech of 2007 the Kremlin leader had signalled a new determination to pursue Russia's national interests. This determination was helped by buoyant oil prices, which remained at well over $90 a barrel, keeping the Russian state's finances strong and living standards high. Experience had also taught Putin that the West would do nothing to stop him. For all Bush's determined pursuit of his 'freedom agenda', he had let Russia get away with its intervention in Georgia with little more than a mild reprimand. Obama had followed up after coming to office by offering Moscow a 'reset'. Obama's performance since – in particular his reluctance to enforce his 'red line' on Syria – would have further emboldened Putin as he contemplated action.

But was the seizure of Crimea a one-off event, or the beginning of a broader push by Putin to redraw Russia's borders? The events of the next few weeks were to provide an alarming foretaste of what was to come.

THE ANNEXATION OF CRIMEA PROMPTED PREDICTABLE outrage from the West: the same day that the peninsula's parliament voted to join Russia, Obama ordered sanctions, including travel bans and asset freezes, against individuals who had 'asserted governmental authority in the Crimean region without the authorisation of the Government of Ukraine'. On 17 March, the day after the referendum, Obama extended the sanctions, taking in, among others, three members of Putin's inner circle. The EU responded with slightly more limited sanctions of its own, despite the reluctance of some member states, such as Italy, Spain and Cyprus, which were worried about the impact on their own financial and trade links with Russia. Other countries followed. Merkel said Europe was looking for Russia to provide concrete evidence 'in the next few days' that it was trying to calm the situation.

Yet that was as far as it went. The new government in Kiev had neither the will nor the military forces to attempt to take back Crimea. Nor was the West going to do so on its behalf. Ukraine was not a member of NATO, and the Alliance was under no obligation to defend it. The Budapest Declaration of 1994 in which America, Russia and Britain had agreed to respect Ukraine's borders appeared forgotten. Far from backing down, on 20 March Russia announced sanctions of its own against certain American citizens, among them Senator McCain. Putin justified the annexation of Crimea as an act of self-determination in favour of its Russian majority, drawing on the precedent set by Kosovo's declaration of independence in 2008. Merkel dismissed the comparison as 'shameful'.

In the meantime, trouble was also brewing elsewhere in Ukraine. The Maidan had been dominated by people from the capital and the west of the country. What they – and the West – a popular uprising against a corrupt ruler looked very different to many in the south and east of Ukraine who, like the people of Crimea, had consistently voted for Yanukovych's Party of the Regions. They, too, were ready to believe the worst of the country's new rulers – an impression that had been strengthened by the speed with which the new Ukrainian parliament repealed the 2012 language law. Oleksandr Turchynov, the interim president, vetoed the move, but it was seen by Russian speakers as an attack on their rights and a harbinger of trouble to come.

Within a few days, 'self-defence' groups sprang up in a dozen or so cities in the east, inflamed by an intensification of the Russia-language media's propaganda campaign against Ukraine's new 'fascist' leaders. The degree of organisation exhibited by these groups, coupled with the arrival of 'activists' from across the border, suggested this was a far from spontaneous uprising: the protests were clearly being inspired and to some extent directed from Russia. On 7 April, separatists proclaimed the Donetsk People's Republic; on 27 April, their counterparts in Luhansk, 150 kilometres to the north-east, proclaimed their own republic. Defiance of Kiev soon turned to violence.

So where would the separatists – and their backers in the Kremlin

– go next? Putin offered a clue during a televised question-and-answer session on 17 April when he repeatedly spoke of '*Novorossiya*'. The term was coined in the eighteenth century to refer to a swathe of territory north of the Black Sea, from the Russian border all the way across to the frontier with modern-day Moldova, west of Ukraine, which was conquered by Catherine the Great and given to Potemkin to administer. It included not just Donetsk and Luhansk, but also the port city of Odessa in the south-west and the industrial centre of Dnipropetrovsk in the north. Such lands were 'not part of Ukraine in Tsarist times; they were transferred [from Russia] in 1920', Putin noted. 'Why? God knows.'

At first the rebels faced little resistance: the Ukrainian army was in a parlous state after more than two decades of independence during which time it had been starved of funding – with much of its meagre budget lost to corruption. But amid the chaos, dozens of militias began to spring up, drawing in those who had manned the barricades in the Maidan. Ihor Kolomoisky, one of Ukraine's richest oligarchs, was among those who helped finance them.

The process of creating a military force loyal to the new government was stepped up after the presidential election on 25 May, which was won by another oligarch, Petro Poroshenko, with an impressive fifty-four per cent of the vote. Poroshenko was best known as the owner of Roshen, a confectionery maker, which earned him the nickname 'the Chocolate King'. He also owned Channel 5, an all-news television channel that had been sympathetic to the Maidan uprising. Typically for Ukraine, where business and politics are closely intertwined, he had also had several stints in government, including a spell as foreign minister. Poroshenko vowed to make stopping the war his priority. But attempts to start a peace process failed and he resorted to military means instead. A summer offensive began well: the Ukrainian army and militias made considerable gains, recapturing dozens of towns and villages held by the rebels. On 5 July the triumphant president ordered his military to raise the Ukrainian flag over Sloviansk, an impoverished industrial town of 100,000 that his forces had been shelling for weeks. When Ukrainian forces moved in, they found 250 prisoners who had been held in a basement under the town hall.

Then on 17 July came a dramatic and tragic twist: a Malaysian Airlines Boeing 777-200ER with 298 passengers and crew on board crashed near Torez in Donetsk oblast, an area twenty-five miles from the Russian border controlled by the Donbass People's Militia. The cause of the disaster quickly became clear: Flight MH17, en route from Amsterdam to Kuala Lumpur, had been shot down by a Buk 9M38 surface-to-air missile fired by pro-Russian insurgents who had apparently mistaken it for a Ukrainian military aircraft. As was to be confirmed by an exhaustive Dutch-led international investigation that reported in September 2016, the missile had been brought across the border from Russia in the early hours of that morning aboard a flatbed trailer and fired from a field four miles south of the town of Snizhne, an area under the control of the rebels. It exploded close to the cockpit of the plane. After those responsible realised to their horror what they had done, the system was reloaded onto the trailer and towed back to Russia.

The rebels – and their backers in the Kremlin – tried to ride out the crisis with their usual mixture of evasion, bluster and conspiracy theories: Russian media initially reported that the airliner had been shot down by Ukraine in a failed attempt to assassinate Putin; it was also variously claimed that Ukrainian air traffic controllers had deliberately redirected it to fly over a war zone and that it had been brought down by Kiev's forces to discredit the rebels, using a Ukrainian rather than a Russian missile. A few months later, Russia's Channel One television produced what it claimed was a leaked spy satellite photograph showing the plane being hit from behind by a Ukrainian fighter jet. Even more bizarre was the claim circulating on the internet that MH17 had been loaded with corpses – perhaps from MH370, another Malaysian Airlines Boeing 777-200ER that disappeared without trace while flying from Kuala Lumpur to Beijing four months earlier – and then flown by remote control.*

---

* The Kremlin was to continue to try to deny any responsibility for the disaster even after publication of the September 2016 report, for which the Dutch-led investigation examined thousands of pieces of debris from the crash scene, listened to 150,000 intercepted telephone calls and studied half a million photographs. Key testimony came from an unnamed rebel soldier who had guarded the missile convoy on its return to Russia after the launch. One of the most convincing pieces of evidence found by the investigators was traces of shrapnel in the bodies of the pilots that came from a warhead from a Buk missile of a type in Russia's arsenal but not Ukraine's. Plastered onto the shard were microscopic traces of the glass used by Boeing in the cockpit of the 777. Russia anticipated the investigation's conclusion by releasing new radar images two days earlier that it claimed disproved the theory. They were not convincing and contradicted the earlier Russian explanations of the disaster.

The tragedy might have been expected to have shamed the Kremlin into a change of policy. Far from it: given the fervour with which the Russian media continued to denounce the illegitimacy of the Ukrainian government, and to highlight atrocities carried out by its forces, Putin could not allow the separatists to be defeated. Help was sent across the border: just as had been the case in Crimea, heavily armed outsiders with Russian accents began to appear in villages in eastern Ukraine and set up roadblocks. They did not have any insignia on their uniforms and the identifying marks on their vehicles had been painted over in white. Yet there were other more subtle indications of their origins: the writing on the ration packs they traded with locals for fruit and vegetables was in Russian rather than Ukrainian. Their lack of knowledge of local geography made it clear that they were from elsewhere. The little green men were back.

In the meantime, Western countries were stepping up their sanctions against Russia. Putin responded on 6 August by imposing a one-year ban on the import of food products from countries that had imposed sanctions. With EU food exports to Russia worth almost €12 billion a year, Putin's move was a major blow to Europe's farmers. It also hit Russian middle-class shoppers, who had become used to picking up French wine and Italian Parmesan and prosciutto at their local supermarkets.

To Russia's dismay, a leading role in building the coalition against Putin was played by Germany. This was all the more surprising since Germany had hitherto been one of Russia's leading champions in Europe, in part because of the estimated $84 billion a year in trade between the two countries and in part out of a sense of gratitude to the Kremlin for having allowed unification with the former communist east. Merkel had three face-to-face meetings and forty telephone conversations with Putin over the course of 2014 – more than David Cameron, François Hollande and Barack Obama put together – in the search for a solution. Having grown up in the former East Germany and travelled widely in the Soviet Union, Merkel understood Putin and his mentality. Yet according to aides, she was outraged by the 'blatant untruths' he told her and became convinced that the only language he understood was force. Asserting the primacy of politics over economics, she then proceeded to take on the *Putinversteher* (Putin apologists) in her own coalition and in industry before turning her attentions to the rest of the EU, which gradually swung behind her – in some cases reluctantly.

The moment Merkel finally became convinced that there could be no reconciliation with the Russian leader was when he began to rail against the decadence of the West and the 'decay of values' exemplified by its promotion of gay rights, one source close to Putin told the *Sunday Times*.[4] 'The chancellor has come to believe that Putin is driven by an ultra-conservative mindset that is shared by his inner circle and is based on a belief that Russia's values are superior and irreconcilable to those of the West,' the source said; Merkel understood 'there will be no deals with Putin, unless they are on his own terms, and that is neither acceptable nor possible'.

In the meantime, Russian reinforcements sent to Ukraine were quickly making their mark. On 25 August the separatists mounted a counteroffensive that stalled the Ukrainian government's advance against Donetsk and Luhansk. After a three-week battle, they had thwarted an attempt by Kiev's forces to take Ilovaysk, massacring them as they retreated. Up to one thousand soldiers died. The battle produced one of the most horrible images of the war: the body of a soldier hanging from a power cable onto which he had been flung when his armoured personnel carrier was hit. Russia, predictably, denied it had sent forces to help the separatists, but satellite images suggested that vast amounts of troops and military equipment had crossed the border from Russia. NATO commander Brigadier General Nico Tak claimed on 28 August that 'well over' one thousand Russian soldiers were operating in the Donbass conflict zone. The real figure was probably several times higher.

With the war now going against it, Kiev had little alternative but to negotiate. 'We cannot win the war in Donbass with military means; Russia won't allow us to do that,' Poroshenko admitted. The more Ukrainian soldiers deployed, 'the more Russian soldiers will show up'.[5] On 5 September a ceasefire was signed in Minsk and two weeks later a deal was agreed between Ukraine, Russia, the rebels and the Organization for Security and Cooperation in Europe: military formations would be frozen and heavy weapons pulled back fifteen kilometres. As part of the deal, a law was passed that granted significant autonomy to the separatist regions for three years and provided for the election of local councils there on 7 December.

The deal quickly started to unravel, however. Fighting began to break out again. Then on 2 November, authorities in the two self-proclaimed republics of Luhansk and Donetsk held elections – one month earlier than they should have done under the Minsk agreement. Poroshenko replied by demanding that parliament revoke the 'special status' that the pair had been given. Russian forces, meanwhile, continued to pour across the border. On 13 January, the separatists started a winter offensive with a fresh assault on Donetsk airport. They took it eight days later. The gleaming new terminal built for the Euro 2012 football championship had already been largely destroyed, but it was the last part of the city held by government forces, and its capture was an important symbolic victory for the separatists. It was their aim to seize enough territory to create a viable state and to force the authorities in Kiev to sign a new settlement more favourable to them than the Minsk agreement.

The Ukrainians again faced a dilemma. They could either continue to fight, risk losing more land and divert attention away from the much-needed rebuilding of their country or else go back to the negotiating table and accept less favourable terms. They chose the latter option. Minsk II was signed on 12 February 2015; a ceasefire came into force three days later. Although the deal largely held elsewhere, this was not the case in Debaltseve, an important road and rail junction sandwiched between the two rebel republics, which Ukrainian government forces had seized from the separatists the previous July. The rebels needed Debaltseve to create their state and encircled it. On 18 February, a column of about two thousand Ukrainian men retreated, but they were ambushed by the rebels and suffered serious casualties. In a major humiliation for Poroshenko, the flag of Novorossiya was raised over Debaltseve later that day.

Fighting continued in the months that followed, albeit at a lower level. There was also an apparent change of tactics by Moscow. On 20 May, a few weeks ahead of a decision by the European Union on whether to renew sanctions against Ukraine, supporters of the two rebel republics announced the freezing of the 'Novorossiya' project on the grounds that it did not comply with Minsk II. Western sanctions were renewed nonetheless; Putin reciprocated. Following months of ceasefire violations, the Ukrainian government and the leaders of Donetsk and Luhansk jointly agreed to halt all fighting, starting on

1 September. Despite some breaches, the ceasefire largely held. Stepan Poltorak, the Ukrainian defence minister, reported shortly afterwards that violence in the Donbass had reached its lowest level since the start of the war.

Yet Ukraine was now a divided country. The three million people who lived in the east had been 'plunged into the strange vortex of former Soviet politics known as a frozen zone', similar to South Ossetia and Abkhazia in Georgia or Transnistria in Moldova, wrote Andrew Kramer of the *New York Times* in a poignant report from Donetsk that November.[6] 'In each case, the Kremlin intervened or provided arms on the pretext of protecting ethnic Russians or local allies, then it installed pro-Russian governments that it has used to manipulate events in the host countries.' In eastern Ukraine, as in the other areas, the atmosphere was reminiscent of the distant Soviet past. In government offices, portraits of Stalin 'looking avuncular and kind' gazed down on visitors. The secret police in Donetsk was called the MGB, the same name that was used in the Soviet dictator's last years. No opportunity was lost to celebrate the Second World War victory over the Nazis. The authorities in Kiev were denounced in the local media as neo-fascists. This state of affairs continued into 2016, with minor outbreaks of fighting along the line of contact, but without any territorial changes. Eastern Ukraine had become Europe's forgotten war.

THE HUMAN COST OF THE CONFLICT in eastern Ukraine was enormous: an estimate published in June 2016 put the death toll at ten thousand; many more people had been injured and at least 2.5 million civilians displaced. The dead were thought to include at least two thousand Russian soldiers, though this was never confirmed by the Kremlin.[7] From Putin's point of view, however, his intervention, like that in Georgia six years earlier, had achieved the desired effect. Not only had he secured control of the peninsula, righting what he depicted as a historical wrong, he had also scuppered any chance of NATO membership for Ukraine, since the Alliance's rules preclude granting admission to a country that is not in full control of its territory. He had also dramatically illustrated the limits of Western power by showing his ability to redraw borders within the former Soviet space.

Regardless of its strategic benefits, though, Crimea was to prove a severe economic drain on the Russian economy. The cost to the state budget of keeping it afloat was estimated at about $4.5 billion a year; a planned bridge linking the peninsula to the Russian mainland was expected to cost $4 billion. Russia would eventually reap the benefits of the oil and gas off the coast, but the revenue would take years to come through.

Yet all this was ignored amid the outburst of patriotic fervour. The Kremlin's control of the media ensured that Putin's popularity grew rather than declined: Russia's economic woes, caused by a combination of fundamental structural problems and falling oil prices, could now be blamed on Western sanctions. Imaginative businesspeople found ways around the ban on food imports: mussels purportedly from Belarus, which has a customs-free zone with Russia, began to appear on restaurant menus – particularly surprising given that the country is landlocked. Domestic producers learnt to make their own versions of mozzarella and Parma ham. Russians found themselves cast in a familiar role: encircled by enemies bent on the destruction of their country.

As Leonid Gozman, a liberal Russian political commentator, put it in April 2015: 'It may astonish my friends in the West, but the attitude of Russians today towards the United States and Americans is worse than it was for most of the Cold War, when Americans were viewed as "good guys" living in a bad, imperialist state. Now, many Russians view not only US leaders but US citizens as "bad guys". One poll showed that the proportion of Russians who described relations with the US as 'hostile' surged from four per cent in January 2014 to forty-two per cent a year later.

Obama, by contrast, faced criticism over his apparent inability – or unwillingness – to deter Russian aggression. In its National Security Strategy published in February 2015, the White House stated that Russian aggression should be resisted and that the Ukrainian people should be supported 'as they choose their own future and develop their democracy and economy'. Yet such support did not extend to providing Ukraine with anything beyond 'non-lethal aid'. The administration argued that if America armed the Ukrainians, then, as Poroshenko had publicly acknowledged at the time of the first Minsk agreement, the Russians would respond by stepping up assistance for the rebels. The result would be a continuation of the stalemate – but with more casualties. Given how much more was at stake for Russia than for

America, this was an arms race that Washington could never realistically expect to win.

The French and German governments agreed with Obama, but there was dissent at home – most notably from Senator McCain. Although not going so far as to advocate putting American boots on the ground, he argued that Washington should at least supply Ukraine with the advanced weaponry it needed to defeat the rebels. 'It is shameful that we will not provide [the Ukrainians] with weapons to defend themselves,' the hawkish senator declared during a visit to Kiev that June. 'They are fighting with twentieth-century weapons against Russia's twenty-first-century weapons. That's not a fair fight.'

It was nevertheless clear that, unlike the aftermath of the Georgian crisis, there could be no return to business as usual. The annexation of Crimea had fundamentally transformed Russia's relations with the West for the worse. Despite the souring of the mood that followed Putin's re-election in 2012, there had still seemed a chance that the two countries could cooperate on certain issues. Now Obama's reset seemed well and truly over; indeed, in retrospect it looked dangerously naive.

Nor was it easy to foresee a way out of the dead end. Western policymakers continued to insist that the only solution was to revert to the status quo ante-bellum: the return of the contested peninsula to Ukraine and a total withdrawal of Russian forces. Anything else would smack of appeasement. But the Kremlin showed no signs of buckling under the pressure. Returning Crimea to Ukraine would have meant an enormous loss of face for Putin who, despite his control of Russia's state media, would have found it difficult to portray it as anything other than a bitter defeat. And what of Crimea's predominantly ethnic Russian population? Would they happily return to being ruled from Kiev?

An end to the meddling in eastern Ukraine should have been easier to bring about, given the Kremlin's repeated, if unconvincing, denial of involvement. Russia seemed to hope for an eventual 'compromise' under which it would be allowed to keep Crimea in return for pulling the plug on the rebels and withdrawal from eastern Ukraine. Yet this would not necessarily bring peace. The separatist uprising had undoubtedly been incited by Moscow, but it had gone on to acquire a momentum of its own. Months of military bombardment had divided communities and created such bitterness towards Kiev that it was difficult to imagine the self-styled leaders of the breakaway eastern republics putting down their weapons. Indeed, thanks to their links with organised crime, many were doing well financially from the continuing crisis.

In a wide-ranging interview with Jeffrey Goldberg, published in *The Atlantic* magazine in April 2016, Obama gave a characteristically frank admission of the limitations of US policy towards Ukraine. 'The fact is that Ukraine, which is a non-NATO country, is going to be vulnerable to military domination by Russia no matter what we do,' he said. 'Putin acted in Ukraine in response to a client state that was about to slip out of his grasp. And he improvised in a way to hang on to his control there.' But just because Russia would always dominate Ukraine, this did not mean that Putin had won. 'Russia was much more powerful when Ukraine looked like an independent country but was a kleptocracy that he could pull the strings on,' Obama added. 'Real power means you can get what you want without having to exert violence.'

21

'YOU DO IT TOO'

Situated in the Primorsky district in the north-west of St Petersburg, the office building at 55 Savushkina Street is a modern four-storey edifice of glass and concrete typical of those that have sprung up across Russia's second city since the end of communism. Behind the front doors a short flight of stairs leads up to a lobby and a pair of metal turnstiles. The bland exterior belies the curious nature of what until recently went on inside. Here, in a suite of offices belonging to an organisation known as the Internet Research Agency, an army of young people used social media to wage war against the West.

Their task was to write posts denigrating America and its allies and to talk up the Putin regime. Hiding their true identities and location behind internet proxy servers, they did their work on Twitter, Instagram, Facebook and its Russian equivalent VKontakte, as well as the comment sections of Russian and foreign newspapers and websites. Up to four hundred of them were reportedly employed at any one time.

Every morning they would be given a list of targets to attack and an outline of the themes to be tackled. The Russian economy? It was recovering far better than predicted after the financial crisis. The murder of Boris Nemtsov, the opposition leader and former deputy prime minister gunned down in February 2015 as he walked near the Kremlin? Probably carried out by the opposition in order to pin the blame on Putin. Oh, and Nemtsov's girlfriend, although describing herself as a model, was actually a prostitute. The most popular of the themes was the situation in Ukraine: workers were encouraged to disparage President Petro Poroshenko and the 'fascists' that had taken power in Kiev and to highlight atrocities carried out by the Ukrainian army.

It was here that Lyudmila Savchuk, a single mother of one in her mid-thirties, went to work in January 2015. She was assigned to the special projects department. For a salary of 50,000 roubles a month (£600) – high by Russian standards – she would work three twelve-hour shifts a week. During each shift she would be expected to write five political posts, ten non-political ones and at least 150 comments on fellow trolls' posts. She did so through the prism of three fake personas whose blogs she wrote on LiveJournal, a hugely popular social media site in Russia, weaving pro-Putin propaganda and attacks on opponents of the regime into invented stories of everyday life.

'One time we were supposed to write about how terrible things are in the European Union,' Savchuk recalled.[1] 'Another time we were supposed to praise Russian Defence Minister Sergey Shoygu. You sit there and write things like: "Yesterday I went for a walk and the idea came to me about how bad the situation is in Europe".' In one post, entitled 'Bad premonitions: Why I'm worried about my sister living in Europe', one of Savchuk's imaginary personas, a fortune-teller called Cantadora, wrote how sanctions had made life grim for her sister in Germany.

In her job interview, Savchuk had claimed to be a 'housewife with no real views'. In reality, she was a long-time environmentalist and critic of Putin who had joined the Internet Research Agency to expose its activities. Before making her application she went carefully through her own social media postings, removing politically contentious posts and replacing them with recipes.

During her time at 55 Savushkina Street, Savchuk copied dozens of documents and pumped her fellow workers for information. She also made a clandestine video of the office. The following month she handed over her findings to *Moi Raion*, an independent St Petersburg newspaper. Its report, when published, provided the most detailed inside account to date of the workings of Russia's troll army. Savchuk quit the next day, launching a campaign to shut down the Internet Research Agency, which she believed was run by a wealthy businessman with links to the Kremlin. To maximise exposure she also took the company to court, suing it for alleged non-payment of wages and for failing to give its workers proper contracts. That August a court found in her favour, paying her symbolic damages of one rouble (one pence).

The operation was one of scores around Russia aimed at both domestic and international audiences, the funding of which was opaque. Their origins lay in the protests prompted by the December 2011 parliamentary elections, which were largely organised via social media. During Putin's first term, he had concentrated on taking control of television, leaving the Russian-language internet, known as the 'Runet', which was largely used by the educated urban middle class, to flourish in a world free of censorship. Medvedev, meanwhile, had embraced social media as part of his image.

Everything changed once Putin came to appreciate how the opposition could use the internet as a weapon against him. New laws were introduced to regulate the medium: one, passed in April 2014, ordered social media sites to keep their servers in Russia and save all information about their users for at least six months. At the same time, investors linked to the Russian leader gained control of VKontakte. That August another law came into force obliging bloggers with more than three thousand followers to register with the government.

In a speech at a media forum in St Petersburg, Putin described the internet as originally having been a 'CIA project' that was 'still developing as such'. To resist Western influence, Russia needed to 'fight for its interests' online, he proclaimed. At the same time, an army of trolls such as Savchuk were put to work to spread a positive message – not just among fellow Russians, but, equally importantly, to people abroad.

LIKE ANY NATION, THE RUSSIAN STATE has long understood the importance of working on its image. After the abortive 1905 revolution which shook the monarchy, advisers to Nicholas II attempted to promote him through pamphlets, portraits, photographs and events marking the 1913 tercentenary of the Romanov dynasty. The Bolsheviks made propaganda a central pillar of their regime. Rigorous censorship at home was combined with a determined effort to showcase the Soviet Union and its unique political and economic system to the world. Launched in 1929, Radio Moscow broadcast at its peak in more than seventy languages using transmitters in the Soviet Union, Eastern Europe and Cuba. The Sovinform agency, later renamed Novosti, published sixty illustrated newspapers and magazines with the aim of painting a rosy picture of the Soviet Union abroad and giving Soviet citizens an ideologically appropriate view of the rest of the world.

As part of this, the KGB became expert in planting anti-Western stories that would typically appear first in publications in developing countries and then, after being picked up by other media organisations, gradually make their way to the West. Most notorious of these was 'Operation Infektion', a disinformation campaign begun in the early 1980s that set out to demonstrate that the HIV virus had been created by the Pentagon as part of a biological weapons research project at Fort Detrick in Maryland. After the collapse of communism, it also became clear the extent to which the Soviet Communist Party had been bankrolling various organisations in the West. Until 1974, for example, Britain's *Morning Star* received direct contributions from the Kremlin, and when this stopped it was indirectly supported by bulk orders that boosted its anaemic circulation by as many as six thousand copies a day; they were abruptly halted in 1989 with a week's notice, causing what was described as 'huge financial disruption'.

Such tactics largely fell out of favour during the 1990s when relations with the West improved, but have since returned with a vengeance – although the nature of the message has changed. Soviet-era propagandists attempted to 'sell' their own political and social system to the world in the hope of spreading revolution or, at least, winning converts to their cause. Their modern-day counterparts have a different task. They do not claim to have a unique model to export but instead present Putin's Russia as home to the kind of values prevalent in the Europe of the 1940s or 1950s: social conservatism, orthodoxy and hostility towards 'propaganda of non-traditional sexual relations to minors' (eliding homosexuality with a threat to child safety). This is coupled with the hostility to US hegemony in world affairs that they inherited from the Soviet era. The approach is therefore less about self-promotion and more about undermining Western society and institutions. It thrives on conspiracy theories: the 9/11 attacks were an inside job, while Zika (like AIDS before it) was created by the Americans. The aim is to highlight contradictions and sow discord and to deflect criticism of Russia by accusing its critics in the West of double standards.

Vladimir Pozner, a veteran broadcaster now in his early eighties who for decades was the voice and face of the Soviet Union in America, brings a personal perspective to the issue. His Soviet broadcasts to the English-speaking world were 'more about the Soviet Union and less about the rest of the world', he recalled over brunch in Moscow's Café Pushkin. 'As a propagandist I talked about what was going on in the Soviet Union: I talked about my mother-in-law, who was on a pension, I talked about public health, and so on. I didn't talk about what Americans were doing somewhere in Vietnam.

'It was not anti-Western, it was pro-Soviet. There used to be a great pride in what we had done. Gagarin, Sputnik. It was like, "wow – look at us" . . . It was all about ideology: presenting a certain set of ideas as something really attractive and, in a way, presenting the future.'[2]

'Now it's very different,' Pozner added. 'This is propaganda in the direct sense of the word. It's half-lies, lies attempting to change people's view about their own country rather than about Russia . . . This is anti-Western, it's not pro-Russian. That's a very important difference.'

In Europe, the most receptive audience for the Kremlin's message is among supporters of the far right, who not only tend to identify with this kind of nostalgic social conservatism but are also wary of migrants and deeply suspicious of the European Union – a convenient bonus for Putin, who sees the weakening or even break-up of the EU as a chance to undermine the united front against Russia. Some of this propaganda also enjoys sympathy from those on the anti-globalist left for whom hostility to America is everything – even though it means they are effectively supporting a regime whose stance on civil liberties and on homosexuality would normally be anathema to them.

Underlying this is a philosophy that has been dubbed 'what aboutism', a form of moral relativism that responds to criticism with the simple response: 'But you do it too.' 'What aboutism' has its origins during the Cold War, when Western criticism of Soviet actions such as the invasion of Afghanistan, the imprisonment of dissidents or imposition of martial law was frequently met not with an attempt at justification but instead with a riposte about US involvement in Latin America, apartheid in South Africa or British policy in Northern Ireland. The approach was summed up by the phrase: '*U nych negrov linchuyut* [Over there they lynch Negroes]'. The appeal of the policy is obvious: you cannot be blamed for the bad things you do because there is another country that has done things that are just as bad – or worse.

The modern incarnation of this tactic has been neatly summarised by Roman Skaskiw, a Ukrainian-American journalist who has lived in Ukraine since 2012: 'The truth is immaterial and only Russia's interests matter,' he wrote in an article that appeared in March 2016.[3] 'For Russia, read Putin.' Skaskiw broke down the policy into nine elements:

1. Rely on dissenting political groups to deliver your message abroad; far right is as good as far left in Europe.
2. Domestic propaganda is most important to control the Russian population, whose living standards are plummeting.
3. Destroy and ridicule the idea of truth.
4. Putin is strong. Russia is strong.
5. Headlines are more important than reality.
6. Demoralise.
7. Move the conversation.
8. Pollute the information space.
9. Accuse the enemy of doing what you are doing to confuse the conversation.

ONE OF THE MOST POWERFUL WEAPONS in Russia's propaganda portfolio is Russia Today, a television station that was set up initially as an English-language service in 2005, with Arabic- and Spanish-language versions following soon afterwards. The station, which also has a strong internet presence, was the product of a growing realisation by the Kremlin that it had an image problem abroad. A survey commissioned by Putin's government two years earlier had asked Americans to name the top ten things they associated with Russia. The top four were communism, the KGB, snow and the mafia. The only brands that came to the minds of those questioned were Kalashnikov rifles and Molotov cocktails. Something clearly had to be done to burnish Russia's image, especially since it was due to host the G8 summit for the first time in St Petersburg in July 2006.

To counter suggestions that the station would deliver a stodgy, Soviet-style propaganda effort, its director general was a lively twenty-six-year-old named Margarita Simonyan, a Russian of Armenian origin who had once worked as a Kremlin pool reporter for state television, where she was reputed to be one of Putin's favourite journalists. Some five hundred staff – including two hundred journalists – were hired and bureaux opened in London, Washington, Jerusalem and Brussels, with operations controlled from Moscow. The initial budget was report-edly $60 million a year, with more coming from advertising. The on-screen reporters were not Russians but fresh-faced young Britons and Americans lured to the station by far bigger salaries and higher-profile jobs than they could expect at home.

To switch from a Western channel to RT, as the station was renamed in 2009, is like stepping into a looking-glass world in which conspiracy theory is presented as fact, fringe opinions are treated as part of the mainstream and black is described as white. The channel's coverage of the Ukraine crisis demonstrated such an approach to dramatic effect. Peter Pomerantsev, a Russian-born British expert on Russia's informa-tion policy, was one of the first to talk of a 'post-fact' or 'post-truth' world, in which 'there are no facts, only interpretations, to mean that every version of events is just another narrative, where lies can be excused as "an alternative point of view" or "an opinion", because "it's all relative" and "everyone has their own truth"'.[4] According to this logic, Pomerantsev argues, when Putin went on television during the annex-ation of Crimea and insisted there were no Russian soldiers in Ukraine, 'he wasn't lying so much as saying the truth doesn't matter'. 'Putin doesn't need to have a more convincing story, he just has to make it clear that everybody lies, undermine the moral superiority of his enemies and convince his people there is no alternative to him,' he adds.

The approach seems to work, with the channel establishing itself in the media landscape alongside the likes of the BBC World Service, CNN, Al-Jazeera and the rest. In February 2010, RT started a service aimed at America alongside its global English-language service. It followed this in October 2014 with a dedicated British channel, RT UK, which promised to 'challenge dominant power structures in Britain by broadcasting live and original programming with a progressive UK focus'. The Kremlin has also been stepping up consid-erably the budget of Rossiya Segodnya, a news agency created by executive order of the Russian president in December 2013 that runs Sputnik, an online news and radio broadcast service aimed at an international audience. It has not been all smooth running, however; hiccups included a couple of embarrassing on-screen resignations during Russia's annexation of Crimea: Liz Wahl, a US-based anchor for RT, declared during a live broadcast that she could no longer 'be part of a network funded by the Russian government that whitewashes the actions of Putin'. Ofcom, the British media regulator, took the station to task fourteen times in its first ten years for misleading or biased reporting.

When Russia Today was launched, it was intended to 'provide an international audience with an understanding of what is going on in Russia from Russia's point of view'. Yet for a station controlled from Moscow, the station talks relatively little about its home country. The shortening of its name seemed intended to downplay the Russian connection. The station's slogan 'Question More' epitomises its approach.

One of the motivations for creating the station was a desire to bypass the Moscow correspondents of foreign media organisations, who were felt to be painting an image of Russia that was not positive enough – supposedly because they were coming too much under the influence of the capital's liberal intelligentsia, who were suspicious of Putin. This feeling also inspired the creation in 2004 of the Valdai Discussion Club, an annual meeting of foreign experts and journalists with top Russian officials – including Putin – to which Moscow-based journalists were not invited.

At the same time, the Kremlin was also investing heavily in hiring high-profile lobbyists: in December 2005, just weeks after he left office, the former German chancellor, Gerhard Schröder, took a job as chairman of the board of a Russian–German gas pipeline that was majority owned by Gazprom, raising eyebrows in his homeland. In parallel with this, the Kremlin spent millions of dollars on public relations, hiring Ketchum, a leading US PR firm, and its European partner, Brussels-based g+.

Getting the Kremlin 'on message' was not always easy, according to Angus Roxburgh, a former BBC Moscow correspondent who has described his work for g+ in his book, *The Strongman: Vladimir Putin and the Struggle for Russia*. Despite Roxburgh's best efforts, the Russians found it difficult to grasp how Western media worked: they did not understand that it was not possible to pay to place favourable stories in the media, were convinced that journalists wrote only what the owners of their newspapers (or governments) wanted and that governments punished those who wrote critically about them by harassing them and denying them entry to future events. 'The Kremlin wanted us to help distribute the message, not change it,' Roxburgh complained.[5]

Think-tanks have become another weapon in the Russian armoury.

The Paris-based Institute of Democracy and Cooperation, headed by Natalia Narochnitskaya, a former member of the Duma with hard-line nationalist views, was set up in 2008 with the apparent aim of creating another source of pro-Russian attitudes. In July 2016, a far larger and higher-profile think-tank, the Dialogue of Civilizations Research Institute, was set up in Berlin by Vladimir Yakunin, a Russian businessman and a member of Putin's close circle. The institute's co-founder, Peter Schulze, a German political scientist, insisted that the institute, which grew out of an annual get-together on the Greek island of Rhodes, would not 'represent any Russian interests' and would not receive any government funding. German media reports claimed Yakunin himself was planning to invest €25 million over the following five years. The institute claimed on its website that 'mutual understanding is the fundamental prerequisite for humankind's inclusive development', but Yakunin's own views were anything but inclusive: he supported the Kremlin's 'gay propaganda law' and claimed that the Ukrainian protest movement had been hijacked by neo-Nazis. He was also placed on the US state department's sanctioned list in the wake of Russia's annexation of Crimea.

There were also links between Russian-funded organisations and NGOs and pressure groups in Britain and other European countries. An investigation by the *Sunday Times*, for example, published in October 2016, revealed ties between Stop the War and two Moscow-based groups: the Anti-Globalisation Movement of Russia (AGMR), which aims to 'fight global dominance of transnational corporations' and has been described by Chatham House, the foreign affairs think-tank, as a 'key actor' in Russia's apparatus of international 'soft power'; and the Institute of Globalisation and Social Movements (IGSO), a Kremlin-funded think-tank.[6]

Anne Applebaum, an American author, commentator and fierce critic of Putin, has pointed to parallels between such bodies and the Cold War 'front organisations' that were allegedly independent but secretly supported with Soviet money. 'Such groups were run by "agents of influence" – people who knowingly promoted the interests of the Soviet Union inside the West – or "useful idiots", people who did the same thing, unconsciously, usually out of ideological naiveté,' she wrote.[7] Yet the people behind these modern-day organisations are not idiots; nor, in contrast to their pro-Soviet predecessors, do they try to hide their links with Russia. 'So what do we call them?' Applebaum asked. 'We need a new vocabulary for a new era.'

Such policies, taken together, could be mistaken for 'soft power' of the sort Western countries openly exercise. Yet Russian understanding of the term is different: the phrase used in Russian, *myakaya sila*, translates better as soft 'force' rather than 'power'. While the West sees soft power as being about creating a positive image of, say, America or Britain, Putin's Russia treats it as part of a toolkit for waging an information war that also includes deliberate misinformation, manipulation of public opinion and cyberwarfare. As Putin himself put it: 'Soft power is a set of tools and methods to achieve foreign policy goals without the use of weapons, through the use of information and other levers of influence.'

Such an approach appeared to be reflected in a much-quoted article by General Valery Gerasimov, chief of the general staff of the Russian Federation armed forces, which was published in a Russian military journal in February 2013. 'The very "rules of war" have changed,' Gerasimov wrote. 'The role of non-military means of achieving political and strategic goals has grown, and, in many cases, they have exceeded the power of force of weapons in their effectiveness.'[8] The article, which spoke of 'non-linear warfare' was seized on by Western analysts, some of whom spoke of a 'Gerasimov doctrine'. Others downplayed its significance, however, while Gerasimov himself, in more recent writings, has indicated his views were misinterpreted in the West.

Regardless of the significance of Gerasimov's ideas, the Kremlin has certainly made considerable efforts within the former Soviet states to play up historic ties with Russia and to denigrate the countries' own leaders if they are not seen as sufficiently sympathetic to Russia. In Ukraine, Georgia and Moldova in particular, which have declared their intention to integrate with the West, a network of pro-Kremlin groups promotes *Russkiy Mir* ('Russian World'), a flexible tool that justifies increasing Russian actions in the post-Soviet space and beyond. As Orysia Lutsevych argued in a research paper for Chatham House, Russian pseudo-NGOs undermine the social cohesion of neighbouring states through the consolidation of pro-Russian forces and ethno-geopolitics, denigration of national identities and the promotion of anti-US, conservative Orthodox and Eurasianist values. In doing so, they often work hand in hand with the Russian Orthodox Church.[9]

Such soft power is complemented by the activities of paramilitary groups such as the Cossacks and the Night Wolves, a bikers' club with more than five thousand members that set out to 'gather Russian lands' in the post-Soviet states and held annual rallies in Crimea in the years before it was seized by Russia. Putin gave the group his blessing, riding with them and posing for photographs with their leader, Alexander Zaldostanov, nicknamed 'The Surgeon'.

Further west, the Kremlin has been accused of trying to 'buy' political influence with anti-establishment political parties in Europe, although such assertions are difficult to prove. In December 2014, Médiapart, a French investigative website, revealed that Marine Le Pen's National Front had taken out a €9 million loan from the First Czech-Russian Bank, a financial institution based in Moscow, to fund its campaign. The National Front claimed that it had been obliged to look abroad because no French bank would lend to it, but the move inevitably prompted critics to accuse the party of being in the Kremlin's pocket. Le Pen, it was noted, was an admirer of Putin, whom she praised for 'restoring pride to a nation that had suffered seventy years of humiliation and persecution'. She was also critical of the EU for its recognition of the 'totally illegitimate government in Ukraine'. Le Pen rode out the storm, and, tellingly, it was the National Front itself that announced in February 2016 that it was hoping Russian banks would lend it the €25 million it needed to finance its campaign for the 2017 presidential election.

Other parties, largely on the right of European politics, are also being cultivated by Russia, among them the Alternative für Deutschland (AfD), a right-wing party hostile to the EU and to immigrants. In an investigation entitled 'Moscow's Fifth Column: German Populists Forge Ties with Russia' published in April 2016, *Der Spiegel* reported on the AfD's extensive links with Russia – including the participation by Marcus Pretzell, one of the party's most senior figures, as guest of honour at a conference in Yalta, in Russian-occupied Crimea, alongside several people on the European and American sanctioned lists – and on its attempts to forge an alliance between the AfD's youth wing and that of Putin's United Russia. Unlike Le Pen's National Front, the party denies any financial links with Russia.

'The right-wing populists [of the AfD] are undeterred by the Kremlin's anti-liberal, anti-American and homophobic ideology,' the magazine noted.[10] 'On the contrary: for large parts of the AfD party base, those factors appear to make Russia an attractive partner. At the same time, the AfD, with its critical stance toward the EU and NATO, also appears to be a natural partner for Putin.' There is similar sympathy towards Russia within the Freedom Party of Austria and its Dutch namesake, and within other parties in Eastern Europe, especially in Hungary, Slovakia and the Czech Republic.

FOR SEVERAL YEARS, WESTERN COUNTRIES WATCHED this growing Russian propaganda initiative without much concern, confident that their own societies and established media brands were strong enough to see off any assault on their values. Indeed, Western media – especially broadcasters – are to a great extent the victims of their own editorial guidelines, which require them to provide balanced reporting. This means the Kremlin's version of events, even if far-fetched, is still reported in order to give the view from the other side.

The conflict in Ukraine has shown the need for a more robust approach, given Russia's use of disinformation as a weapon in its efforts to destabilise the country. In March 2014, the month that Putin annexed Crimea, a group of Ukrainian journalists set up an organisation called StopFake to check facts, verify information and challenge disinformation about their country in the Russian media and elsewhere. The site, which appears in several languages including English, Ukrainian and Russian, even has a regular video round-up in which it debunks some of the most egregious examples.

Some of the stories highlighted were shocking: Russian state television's Channel One, for example, ran a report claiming that a three-year-old boy had been publicly crucified by Ukrainian government forces in Slavyansk, in the east of the country. A woman claiming to be an eyewitness described in detail how the child was nailed 'like Jesus' to a bulletin board in the town, but strangely no one else from the town corroborated her story. Other reports bordered on the absurd, such as those involving Maria Tsypko, a woman apparently in her late thirties, who became an unlikely media star after popping up in a variety of different guises in pro-Kremlin television reports on the war in eastern Ukraine. Once she appeared as a pro-Russian protester in the eastern Ukrainian city of Kharkov; another time as the mother of a soldier sent by the Ukrainian army to the front; a third time as a lawyer who was coordinating an independence referendum in Luhansk; and a fourth as a 'humanitarian worker' in Debaltseve, soon after it was taken by separatist militias. For some of her appearances she seemed to have dyed her hair red, but she invariably wore the same thick golden necklace and heavy gold earrings. The underlying message was always the same: as a Ukrainian resident affected by the conflict, she was expressing her discontent with the government in Kiev.

Such tactics have caused concern in the Baltic states, whose leaders are worried that their substantial ethnic Russian populations could be manipulated by the Kremlin into becoming a fifth column that could act against them. Estonia, which prides itself on being the most digitally progressive country in Europe, has become more sensitive than most to cyberwarfare since 2007 when it suffered a crippling denial-of-service attack. The attack was believed to have originated in Russia, since it was carried out the day after Estonian authorities removed a large statue celebrating the Second World War achievements of the Red Army from the centre of Tallinn, the capital.

In Germany, the tipping point came in January 2016 after a report for Channel One, the state television station, claimed that a thirteen-year-old girl from a Russian immigrant family in Berlin, named only as Lisa F., had been abducted on her way to school and held for thirty hours by a group of 'southern-looking' asylum seekers who gang-raped her. The report, by Ivan Blagoy, its German correspondent, was spread on social media and quickly watched more than a million times on Facebook. It prompted demonstrations in Berlin and other German cities by thousands of the country's Russian speakers, many of them relatively recent arrivals. The report's impact was all the greater since it coincided with a bout of national soul-searching prompted by claims from more than six hundred women in Cologne that they had suffered sexual attacks on New Year's Eve by groups of male immigrants, which had been largely downplayed by the German media.

Lisa F. subsequently admitted to prosecutors that she had made up the story. But this did not prevent Sergey Lavrov, the Russian foreign minister, from using his annual press conference to attack Germany for 'covering up reality in a politically correct manner for the sake of domestic policies'. For Merkel's government this was the last straw, since Lavrov had made his comments despite the summoning of Vladimir Grinin, the Russian ambassador to Berlin, to the German foreign office with a request to tone down Russian media's coverage of the case. Concerned at what appeared to be a deliberate attempt to use the migrant crisis to destabilise her government, Angela Merkel ordered the country's secret services to mount an investigation.

Other bodies were also studying methods of combating Russian propaganda. In March 2015, EU leaders agreed to look into ways to 'challenge Russia's ongoing disinformation campaign'. The result was the creation of a unit known as 'EastStratCom Task Force'. Established that April, it was given the remit of monitoring and analysing Russian-language media reports, particularly those broadcast in the EU's six 'Eastern Partnership' countries – former Soviet satellites with large Russian-speaking populations, including Ukraine and the three states in the Caucasus. The unit puts out two weekly publications – a *Disinformation Review*, that collects examples of disinformation, and *The Disinformation Digest*, that analyses how pro-Kremlin media see the world and follows trends on Russian social media to put them into their wider context.

NATO has also been looking at how to combat what it has described as Russia's 'weaponisation of information' by creating a new, more powerful communications section. This could include moving more quickly to declassify images – such as those of Russian troop movements – to reveal what is going on. This would be a departure from the Crimean crisis, when it failed to release real-time spy satellite images showing Russian troop deployments and instead waited several months, even then only showing images from commercial satellites.

Although Britain and other countries are enthusiastic proponents of such a strategy, the United States has long been wary of anything that could be construed as propaganda. In a column published in the *Washington Post* in May 2016, Anne Applebaum and Edward Lucas, a fellow conservative commentator on Russian affairs, berated America for failing to do enough to combat the problem. There is no public analytical database of 'what Russia says, when and where', they argued.[11] Nor do we know 'which elements of the Russian message are effective, who believed them and why'. The authors' conclusion: 'It's high time we learned.'

Pressure for a change of stance was intensified two months later by the leaking of emails from the Democratic National Committee (DNC) in an operation blamed by US officials on hackers linked to Russia.

On 22 July, three days before the start of the Democratic convention, WikiLeaks released a collection of 19,252 emails and 8,034 attachments from the DNC, laying bare Democratic scheming against Senator Bernie Sanders, who had only recently admitted defeat by Hillary Clinton in the primaries. Sanders loyalists were outraged by the revelations, which cast a shadow over the first days of the convention and led to the resignation of the committee's chairwoman, Debbie Wasserman Schultz. WikiLeaks' founder, Julian Assange, a fierce critic of Clinton, refused to say where he had obtained the documents. But the attack was thought to have come from an entity known as 'Fancy Bear' which is connected to the GRU, Russia's military intelligence service, an official involved in the investigation told the *New York Times*. The same arm of Russia's intelligence operation was also implicated in the attack on computer systems used by Clinton's presidential campaign workers. Russia, it was claimed, was trying to undermine Clinton and help her Republican rival, Donald Trump.

Then, several weeks later, during the final weeks of the presidential election campaign, WikiLeaks released thousands of emails, many of them sensitive, written by John Podesta, Clinton's campaign chairman. Podesta blamed Russia. 'I've been involved in politics for nearly five decades,' he said. 'This definitely is the first campaign that I've been involved with in which I've had to tangle with Russian intelligence agencies who seem to be doing everything that they can on behalf of our opponent.' The Obama administration publicly acknowledged for the first time that it believed the Kremlin was responsible. 'Only Russia's senior-most officials could have authorised these activities,' said James Clapper, the director of national intelligence, in an apparent swipe at Putin.

The leaks were greeted with a mixture of shock and anger in America. It was one thing for Russian hackers to leak a recording of a phone call between Assistant Secretary of State Victoria Nuland and the US ambassador to Ukraine, as they had done two years earlier; interfering in America's presidential election process was a step too far. Intelligence officials quoted by American media claimed the administration was planning a retaliatory cyber covert action, which would perhaps involve releasing documents that would shed light on the unsavoury actions of Putin or the murky financial transactions of some of his allies. Joe Biden said 'we're sending a message' to Putin that 'will be at the time of our choosing, and under the circumstances that will have the greatest impact'.

Michael McFaul, whose own private phone calls were hacked and published while he was US ambassador to Moscow, argued that the attack should serve as a wake-up call for America to combat increasing efforts by Russia and other autocracies to weaken democracy abroad by giving rhetorical and financial support to political parties and organisations with illiberal, nationalist agendas. This should come not directly from the US government, for fear recipients could be tainted by being accused of being in its pocket, but from independent foundations, whose establishment should be encouraged, he argued.

'We should think of advancing democratic ideas abroad primarily as an educational project, almost never as a military campaign,' McFaul wrote.[12] 'Universities, books and websites are the best tools, not the 82nd Airborne. The United States can expand resources for learning about democracy.'

22

TOWARDS EURASIA

Moscow had not seen anything like it since the end of the Soviet Union. On 9 May 2015, the seventieth anniversary of the Soviet defeat of Nazi Germany, a dizzying array of Russian weaponry rolled through the centre of the capital in a perfectly choreographed display of military might. Some 16,000 soldiers and 200 armoured vehicles passed through Red Square, among them the much-awaited new T-14 Armata tank. The sky overhead was full of 150 airplanes and helicopters. Later, an 'immortal regiment' of 250,000 people marched through the city carrying portraits of relatives who had fought in the Second World War, still known in Russia as the Great Patriotic War. They were led by Putin, who carried a picture of his father, also called Vladimir, who was injured by a German grenade. This was not just a commemoration of the proudest day in Russian history. With Putin still riding a wave of patriotism following his annexing of Crimea, it was also an expression of the country's military might and a warning to those who did not give it the respect it deserved.

The contrast with the sixtieth anniversary could not have been greater. In 2005, Putin had stood proudly alongside the presidents of the United States and France. Ten years on, in a reflection of the strain that the Ukraine crisis had put on relations with the West, pride of place on the reviewing platform was given instead to Xi Jinping, the Chinese president. Nursultan Nazarbayev, his Kazakh counterpart, was the most prominent of several leaders of the former Soviet republics.

Alongside them was a veritable rogues' gallery, whose members included Robert Mugabe of Zimbabwe, Nicolás Maduro of Venezuela and Raúl Castro of Cuba. No leader of any major Western country was in attendance.

The roll call of those prepared to stand alongside Putin showed how his place in the world – and in particular his relations with America and Europe – had been transformed over the fifteen years since he had first come to office. The cooperation of the first few years of the new century had been forgotten; the annexation of Crimea had proved to be the final blow to Obama's reset. The stalemate caused by Russia's continued involvement in eastern Ukraine had put a definitive end to any further expansion of NATO and had allowed Putin to reassert his right of veto over any change in the 'near abroad'. Despite the damage done to the Russian economy by sanctions, his position at home seemed secure and his approval ratings were high, thanks in large part to his continued control of the media. Yet Putin's role on the world stage remained that of a wrecker of the established order rather than as a positive force. The lands controlled by the Kremlin were considerably smaller than those ruled by the Soviet Union. The attempt to position Russia as a socially conservative rival to the liberal democracies of the West had attracted few takers in Europe beyond backers of the fringe parties on the right.

Nor could Putin hope to compensate for his isolation with a pivot to the east. China was ready to be a partner, but not an equal one: while China's economy continued to grow, Russia's was stagnating. While China emerged as a global power, Russia found itself reduced to a regional one. Despite public expressions of camaraderie, Xi was very clearly the senior partner in the emerging relationship – a demonstration of quite how far the balance of power had shifted since the days of the Soviet Union. Out of economic necessity, Putin turned to China, offering to sell Beijing the military hardware Russia had once so jealously guarded, and giving China access to its strategic oilfields.

DESPITE THE CONTINUING COOLNESS OF RELATIONS between America and Russia, cooperation was still possible, as was demonstrated in April 2015 when the two countries, together with Britain, China, France and Germany, reached a framework agreement on curbing Iran's nuclear programme. Moscow had a variety of reasons for going along with the accord: it did not want Tehran to have nuclear weapons any more than America did, and feared that Washington and some of its allies would take military action against Iran if talks failed. There were also potential diplomatic benefits to Russia in stressing to Iran the role it played in getting the sanctions lifted, while making clear to the West that it had supported the drive to prevent the country from becoming a nuclear power. There was the matter, too, of America's long-running plan to develop a missile defence system in Europe. Washington had always claimed, somewhat improbably, that the system was aimed at 'rogue states' (such as Iran) rather than at Russia. By that logic, Lavrov argued, any removal of the Iranian threat would make it more difficult for America to press on with the contested system.

While the Iran deal was the product of long, careful negotiations, Putin also demonstrated that he had not lost his ability to surprise. On 30 September 2015, Russian warplanes laden with bombs took off from the country's airbase in Latakia, Syria. They began targeting rebel groups opposed to Moscow's ally, President Bashar al-Assad; among those hit was at least one group that had been trained by the CIA. The significance of the move soon became clear: although still on the back foot over Ukraine, Putin had opened a dramatic new front in his battle with Washington.

Russia's intervention added a further complication to an already complicated conflict, and in the process exposed America's failures in the region. Obama had stepped back at the last moment from taking military action against Assad in August 2013 and had made no attempt to change that policy in the two years since, despite continuing evidence of atrocities by Assad's forces. Instead, America had turned its fire on Isis, which had proclaimed itself a 'worldwide caliphate' in June 2014 after seizing territory in both Syria and Iraq. Three months later, announcing a broadening of his campaign against the group, Obama ordered air strikes against the Islamists in Syria in addition to its military operations already under way in Iraq. Yet the West's preferred outcome, a victory for the 'moderate' opposition to Assad, seemed no closer to realisation – not least because of the difficulty of identifying anyone that fitted such a description among the shifting mass of opposition groups, many of them with links to the Islamists, let alone then turning them into an organised force with any chance of overthrowing the Syrian leader.

Putin justified Russia's entry into the conflict by saying it was acting 'preventatively, to fight and destroy militants and terrorists on the territories that they already occupied, not wait for them to come to our house'. The Americans countered that the Russians' main target was not the so-called Islamic State, but rather the other opposition groups challenging Assad – including the moderate, pro-Western ones. This, Washington claimed, was demonstrated by the fact that Russia had dropped bombs north of the central city of Homs where there were actually few, if any, Isis militants. 'By supporting Assad and seemingly taking on everyone who is fighting Assad, you're taking on the whole rest of the country of Syria,' said Ashton Carter, the US defence secretary. Russia's action, he argued, was tantamount to 'pouring gasoline on the fire'.

The Russian action had been foreshadowed by a rapid build-up at the base over the previous three weeks. Yet it still seemed to have come as a surprise to America. The US state department said it had been given just one hour's notice of the air strikes, by a Russian diplomat in Baghdad. Russia's military involvement also added a new, powerful but unpredictable combatant to an already crowded field of operations, raising the prospect of possible accidental clashes between US and Russian aircraft. More bombing also looked certain to increase the flow of refugees within Syria and towards Europe, escalating what was already becoming a serious crisis for the EU, whose members were divided over how to cope with the unprecedented influx of more than a million people in the matter of a few months. Was that part of Putin's plan? It would be difficult to prove, but by this point, anything that weakened European unity served Russia's geopolitical interest.

Russian media responded swiftly to the new reality, switching their focus away from chronicling the evils of the Ukrainian 'fascists' to targeting the Islamists. This time they were also free to highlight the heroism of Russian forces, who in Syria, unlike in Ukraine, were fighting an open war. The conflict provided the Kremlin with an opportunity as well to show off its military capabilities, most dramatically on 7 October when two dozen cruise missiles fired from four Russian warships in the Caspian Sea flew more than a thousand miles over Iran and Iraq before striking targets in Syria. This demonstration of shock and awe, Russian-style, seemed dictated less by military considerations than by a desire to impress the world – and the audience back home. Russian television viewers were treated to movie-like images of jets bombing targets, palls of smoke rising in their wake. The propaganda push extended even to the weather forecast on Russian television, with one forecaster telling viewers about the suitability of the climatic conditions in Syria for air strikes. Domestic support for the offensive surged from 14% to 72% within a few weeks, according to polling by the respected Levada Center.

Western leaders and commentators were quick to predict disaster for Russia, drawing comparisons with the Soviet Union's involvement in Afghanistan three decades earlier. The doom-mongers' claims appeared to gain credence from the downing on 31 October of a Metrojet Airbus 320 carrying Russian holidaymakers home from the Egyptian resort of Sharm el-Sheikh, with the loss of 224 lives, in what Isis claimed was payback for Russia's involvement in Syria. Yet such criticisms proved misplaced: Putin's main aim – preventing the collapse of the Syrian regime – was relatively easy to bring about through judicious application of Russian air power. It also seemed more achievable than the West's rather nebulous policy, which was based on trying to identify and support 'good' rebels while keeping arms away from 'bad' ones.

On 14 March 2016 Putin announced that he was withdrawing the main part of Russia's forces, claiming the twenty-two-week intervention had achieved nearly all of his objectives. Shortly afterwards, a number of Russia's fixed-wing aircraft and helicopters pulled out – as abruptly as they had arrived. The tide had been turned: Assad, whose future just a few months earlier had looked uncertain, was now back in control of a substantial part of Syria.

Putin marked the withdrawal with a flourish: in May, a month after Isis forces were driven from the ancient city of Palmyra, musicians from St Petersburg's Mariinsky Theatre staged a surprise concert in the amphitheatre. The orchestra was conducted by Valery Gergiev, a close associate of Putin, who described the concert as a protest against the barbarism and violence of the Isis militants who had used the amphitheatre for executions. Among the performers was another of the president's friends, the cellist Sergei Roldugin, who had just been linked by documents from the Panama Papers leak to a number of offshore companies with cash flows of up to $2 billion.* Putin himself did not make the trip to Syria, but instead addressed the audience by video link from his dacha in Sochi.

Few members of the audience, a mixture of military personnel and locals, looked much like classical music fans. Yet the event was not so much for them as for the world. It was reminiscent of a previous Mariinsky performance, also conducted by Gergiev, in August 2008 in front of the bombed-out parliament of the self-proclaimed Republic of South Ossetia after Russia's defeat of the Georgian army. The reminder to the world of Russian military prowess was timed to coincide with the annual 9 May Victory Day celebrations due to take place a few days later.

As ever with Putin, though, all was not quite as it seemed: despite the announced pull-out, a steady flow of Russian supply vessels continued to visit the naval facility in the Syrian port of Tartous. An investigation by the Reuters news agency published just over two weeks later found that Russia had shipped more equipment and supplies to Syria since announcing its intention to leave than it had brought back.[1] It also appeared to have reinforced its fleet in the Mediterranean and now had more warships near the Syrian coast than at the time of Putin's declaration.

Then, in September 2016, Russian forces joined their Syrian allies in a ferocious aerial bombardment of the rebel-held eastern part of Aleppo, a city of 2.5 million before the outbreak of the civil war. The sheer scale of the suffering inflicted on the people of Aleppo, all too visible in video footage, provoked revulsion across the world. Samantha Power, the American ambassador to the UN, accused Russia of 'barbarism'. Boris Johnson, the newly appointed British foreign secretary, demanded it be investigated for war crimes – a call dismissed by the Russian defence ministry as 'Russophobic hysteria'. Johnson also took the unusual move of urging people to demonstrate outside the Russian embassy in London. The Russian embassy responded by tweeting a photograph of a single demonstrator.

But Britain was not proposing intervention to stop the assault on Aleppo. Nor was anyone else – America included, despite official leaks that the White House was considering retaliatory cruise missile strikes

---

* Roldugin insisted the money was a series of donations from rich businesspeople in order to purchase expensive musical instruments for young Russians.

on Syrian military airstrips. Western attention was focused on Iraq and the battle to drive Isis from its stronghold in Mosul, which began in October, while America itself was in the final throes of an election campaign. By helping Assad to regain Aleppo, Putin was hoping to present Obama's successor with facts on the ground. Yet there were signs that Putin, emboldened by a string of military successes, might be preparing to go further: what began as a mission to save Assad could be turning into a campaign to help him win back his entire country.

Putin also had a broader lesson for the world. By showing his ability to turn the tide of the war in Syria, he had made it clear that there could be no solution to the Syrian crisis – or, indeed, other crises, current and future, in the Middle East – without the Kremlin's approval. Putin had demonstrated to the world that Russia was too important to be ostracised.

WHILE ALL EYES WERE TURNED TO Putin's intervention in Syria, the situation in Ukraine, which had done most to bring relations between Russia and the West towards breaking point, remained grim. In the east of the country, low-level fighting continued. The unfortunate residents of the self-proclaimed republics of Donetsk and Luhansk remained trapped in a frozen conflict. In Crimea, meanwhile, authorities were accused by human rights groups of curbing free speech, freedom of association and the media, and of failing properly to investigate beatings, disappearances and extrajudicial killings of Crimean Tatar and pro-Ukrainian activists.

The summer of 2016 brought an increase in violence in eastern Ukraine and reports of clashes on Crimea's border with Ukraine, blamed by the Kremlin on incursions by Ukrainian special forces intent on sabotage – one of whom confessed to his crimes in an interrogation shown on television, looking bruised and battered. Ukraine said he was an innocent truck driver who was kidnapped by Russian forces. As tensions rose, the Kremlin announced that it had begun to deploy its advanced S-400 air defence missile system to the peninsula.

Ukraine was not developing in the way hoped for by those in the Maidan or their backers in the West. The Kremlin's concern about the uprising that had swept away Yanukovych had been driven in part by fears about the example it might set for Russia. If Ukraine developed into a Western-style democracy with a successful economy, it would represent a dangerous model of the bright new future that might await Russians if they toppled their own leader.

Fortunately for Putin there seemed little chance of that happening. After their first two years in power, Ukraine's new leaders were still struggling to get to grips with the most damaging problem that had bedevilled the country since independence: corruption. Despite repeated entreaties from the United States and the International Monetary Fund, President Poroshenko seemed unable – or unwilling – to clean up. 'They are like bad students, always saying, "Professor, just wait until Monday; I will do better",' was how Tymofiy Mylovanov, president of the Kiev School of Economics, described Ukraine's leadership to the *New York Times*.[2] 'Nothing changed. The same elites are there. The same oligarchs.'

Aivaras Abromavičius, who stepped down as Ukraine's minister of economy and trade that February after just fourteen months, paints a depressing picture of the country. For Abromavičius, the main problem is the failure of Ukraine's new leadership to ensure the rule of law. 'It is very clear that both the past prime minister [Arseniy Yatsenyuk] and current president [Poroshenko] have some people in the inner circle that have a very questionable past and present,' he says.[3] 'Their practices raise eyebrows and this is a disappointment, of course. Reforms can only be as progressive as the people carrying them out. You can't surround yourself with the wrong type of personnel or this is the type of result you are going to get.'

In the view of Abromavičius, continued corruption has made it impossible to revive the economy, which is the ultimate key to ending the country's enforced division. 'The grand plan was that the economic situation in Ukraine would recover beyond recognition so that those people in the temporarily occupied territories say "we want to live in Ukraine" and we get them back not by military means but by economic and diplomatic means,' he said. At the time of writing, this plan does not look close to being realised.

Abromavičius's concerns were highlighted by Mikheil Saakashvili, the former Georgian leader, who after a spell of self-imposed exile in New York had moved to Ukraine in May 2015 when Poroshenko, an old friend from Kiev University, made him governor of the Odessa region. Saakashvili set himself the task of rooting out the city's legendary corruption, but in November 2016 he resigned, accusing the central government of obstructing his efforts and launching a blistering attack on Poroshenko.

Following Russia's intervention in Ukraine, attention turned naturally to NATO's north-eastern flank. The United States repeatedly vowed to defend Estonia, Latvia and Lithuania, which, as members of the Alliance, came under its security umbrella in a way that Ukraine did not. Obama underlined this in a speech in September 2014 in Tallinn. 'We'll be here for Estonia,' he declared. 'We will be here for Latvia. We will be here for Lithuania. You lost your independence once before. With NATO, you will never lose it again.'

This was easier said than done: the Baltic states, along with NATO's other new Eastern members, were in a potentially vulnerable position. The Alliance had hitherto refrained from making serious permanent force deployments on their territory, to avoid accusations that it was breaking the spirit of the 1997 NATO–Russia Founding Act, under which it had pledged to rely on reinforcements rather than the 'additional permanent stationing of substantial combat forces' – taken by Moscow as a pledge not to establish bases there. Yet this risked putting the Alliance in an impossible position: obliged under Article 5 of its founding treaty to regard an attack on any one of its members as an attack on all of them, but without the forces in place to deter or repel such an attack. This, in turn, could undermine the fundamental principles according to which NATO operates.

The three Baltic states look especially exposed. The extent of their vulnerability was underlined by an analysis from the army research division of America's RAND Corporation, published in February 2016. Using war-game scenarios played out by serving and former military officers, it estimated that if the Russians invaded, it would take them a maximum of just sixty hours to reach the capitals of Estonia or Latvia. 'The games' findings are unambiguous,' it concluded. 'As currently postured, NATO cannot successfully defend the territory of its most exposed members.'

The Alliance, the report argued, would be left with 'a limited number of options, all bad': faced with superior Russian forces, NATO commanders would either have to launch a belated and costly counter-attack, which could lead to nuclear escalation, or accept defeat with 'predictably disastrous consequences for the alliance and, not incidentally, the people of the Baltics'. Tensions were further raised by a series of Russian exercises near the border, held at short notice, and by the irresponsible behaviour of Russian aircraft, which routinely flew in busy airspace above the Baltic states with their transponders (identification beacons) turned off. During a short visit to Finland that July, Putin told reporters he had accepted a proposal by his Finnish counterpart, Sauli Niinistö, to make sure his planes started to use their transponders. Although ostensibly a gesture of reconciliation, it also implied that Russia expected the stand-offs to continue and, as had been the case back in the Cold War, was looking to establish the rules of the game to increase predictability.

Against the backdrop of such concerns, NATO was drawing up plans for four thousand troops to be based in Estonia, Latvia and Lithuania in what was described as 'enhanced forward presence'. Although far too small to hold back a concerted attack from Russia, they would act as a tripwire or, as one senior military official memorably put it, a 'tethered goat'. Attack them and the full force of NATO would come crashing down on Russia. NATO denied this contravened either the letter or the spirit of the 1997 NATO–Russia Founding agreement, which explicitly spoke of actions the Alliance would take 'in the current and foreseeable security environment'. The environment had changed dramatically in the intervening two decades, largely as a result of Russian aggression, it was argued, making such commitments no longer binding.

Yet there was also the danger that any increase in NATO forces would exacerbate the very threat it was intended to combat. No explanation was offered as to why Russia would want to invade one or more of the Baltic states, beyond claims that Putin desired to provoke the West for the sake of it, or that Russia's intervention in Ukraine had revealed it as an aggressive power intent on reclaiming its lost lands. Yet that would be to misunderstand the reason for Putin's seizure of Crimea and subsequent intervention in eastern Ukraine. Rather than the first staging post in a carefully thought-out plan to reconstitute the Soviet Union, his action appears instead to have been instigated by the fear that a country he and many other Russians still considered part of their homeland was in danger of drifting into the Western camp. He was also counting on a warm reception from the locals and gambled, rightly, that the West would do nothing to stop him.

The Baltic states, small and considered even during Soviet times as somewhat separate, were a different matter. While Putin would undoubtedly enjoy the spectacle of Western disarray that an attack would cause, the prize was considerably smaller and the stakes much higher in the case of an attack on a NATO country. Furthermore, in all three countries he would face hostility not just from the indigenous population but also from a substantial slice of the Russian speakers. If Russia were really set on taking more territory, why had it not simply continued its westward expansion in Ukraine?

Little attempt was made to address such considerations, with politicians and senior military figures on both sides of the Atlantic vying ahead of the NATO summit to talk up the Russian threat. One of the more dramatic interventions came from General Sir Richard Shirreff, the former deputy supreme allied commander in Europe, who in May 2016 published a book entitled *2017 War With Russia: An Urgent Warning from Senior Military Command*. The book – written in the form of a thriller featuring, as one critic put it, a 'Blofeld-like Vladimir Putin character' – takes as its starting point a Russian attack on the Baltic states, and a limp NATO response. Shirreff's decision to write it was significant insofar as it appeared to reflect concern within the top echelons of the British military over the effects of spending cuts on its capability. 'The political and military decisions we are currently making, and have already made, are now propelling us into a future war with Russia,' he argued.

The European Union, meanwhile, was grappling with more pressing problems of its own following the referendum on 23 June in which Britons narrowly voted to leave the bloc – plunging both Britain and the EU into turmoil. During the referendum campaign, the majority of world leaders had made clear their preference for a 'yes' vote; chief among them was Obama, who warned that if Britain went it alone, it would be obliged to 'go to the back of the queue' when it came to concluding a future trade deal with America. As part of what was derided by critics as 'Project Fear', Remain campaigners also argued that leaving the EU would risk playing into Putin's hands by weakening the union and depriving it of one of the toughest voices against Russian aggression. Michael Fallon, the defence secretary, told MPs a Brexit vote would be 'absolutely applauded in Moscow'.

Putin dismissed such claims as 'an inappropriate attempt to influence public opinion' and continued to refuse to comment after the 'No' side won the vote. Others in Russia were less cautious: Moscow's mayor, Sergei Sobyanin, said he expected that the departure of Britain, traditionally one of the most hawkish EU members when it came to Russia, would lead to a more conciliatory line over sanctions. McFaul, the former US ambassador, described the result in a tweet as 'a giant victory for Putin's foreign policy objectives'.

Brexit also looked set to embolden Eurosceptic parties such as France's National Front, Germany's Alternative für Deutschland and the Freedom Parties of the Netherlands and Finland, which combined antipathy towards the European Union with varying degrees of sympathy towards Russia. Elections due in the Netherlands, France and Germany during 2017 looked set to hand these parties substantial gains.

In the longer term, some in Russia argued that the vote would lead to a broader geopolitical realignment, with Britain moving closer to America, leaving the remaining twenty-seven EU members to seek a new, warmer relationship with Russia. 'The most important long-term consequence of all this is that the exit will take Europe away from the Anglo-Saxons, that is, from the US,' wrote Boris Titov, Russia's business ombudsman, on Facebook.[4] 'This is not the independence of Britain from Europe, but the independence of Europe from the USA.' Such thinking seemed all too reminiscent of Orwell's division of the world, in his novel *1984*, into Eastasia, Eurasia and Oceania, with Britain reduced to the latter's Airstrip One.

In the meantime, there was the more immediate problem of what to do about European sanctions against Russia, which were due to expire at the end of July. The bloc's twenty-eight leaders unanimously agreed to extend them for another six months, yet this looked like it could be for the last time: although the Baltic nations, Poland and Britain stood firm, the policy was criticised by the leaders of Italy, Slovakia, Greece and Hungary, while the French parliament was one of several to call for a change in tack. There were signs of disquiet, too, in Germany: while Merkel remained a resolute backer of sanctions, the Social Democratic Party, the junior member of her ruling coalition, wanted a change of course, with one of its leading members, Frank-Walter Steinmeier, the foreign minister, calling for the sanctions to be restructured to push Russia and Ukraine towards reconciliation. He also denounced what he called NATO's 'sabre-rattling and warmongering', saying it would only fuel tensions with Moscow. 'Whoever believes that a symbolic tank parade on the Alliance's eastern border will bring security is mistaken,' Steinmeier said in a newspaper interview.

It was against this backdrop that the leaders of the NATO countries gathered on 8 July for their summit in Warsaw. The meeting was held in the green Column Room of the Presidential Palace – the place where, in 1955, the Soviet Union and its seven satellite nations signed the Warsaw Pact. The choice of location underlined the massive asymmetry that now existed between Russia and the West. All seven of Moscow's former satellites, along with the three formerly Soviet Baltic republics, had since become members of NATO. The economic and military balance was tilted to a far greater extent than before against a diminished Russia and in favour of an enlarged West that now stretched to Russia's border.

The summit's most important decision, the dispatching of four thousand Alliance troops to Poland and the three Baltic states, had been widely trailed. An American-backed missile defence system for Europe was declared operational, and NATO members vowed to increase air and sea patrols to strengthen commitments to defend the Alliance's frontiers. Leaders also agreed to increase cyberwarfare capabilities after Russian attacks against Estonia and elsewhere.

They stood firm on Ukraine, reiterating their refusal to recognise Russia's annexation of Crimea and insisting that Russia must withdraw its troops and return the Ukrainian–Russian border to Kiev's control. They also approved a comprehensive assistance package aimed at making Ukraine's defence and security institutions more effective, efficient and accountable. But, unlike in 2008, there was no talk of a Membership Action Plan that would have put Ukraine on a clear path towards joining NATO. It was instead offering a vaguer-sounding 'comprehensive action plan' that President Poroshenko said would lead to his country becoming an 'enhanced opportunity partner'.

Such reticence on NATO's part was understandable given the division among member states – a point highlighted in somewhat undiplomatic terms during the summit by Gérard Araud, the French ambassador to Washington, in a series of tweets. 'The role of NATO is to provide security to its members. Any enlargement should improve it, not weaken it,' he tweeted. 'NATO insists that candidates should solve their territorial conflicts before joining. No interest to "import" conflicts.' Lest his point was still not clear, Araud added: 'By admitting a new member already involved in a conflict, NATO would be obliged to assist this country against its adversary.'

Russia reacted with predictable hostility to the decisions taken at the summit, underlying the extent to which the two sides were now openly treating each other as 'adversaries' after years of growing tension. NATO was 'focusing its efforts on the containment of a non-existent threat from the east', argued Maria Zakharova, the Russian foreign ministry's feisty spokeswoman, who said that implementation of the anti-missile plans were designed to 'change the existing balance of power' and would cause long-term negative damage to the entire Euro-Atlantic security system.

Mikhail Gorbachev, now in his eighties, also intervened, accusing the Alliance of planning 'offensive operations' against Russia. 'NATO has begun preparations for escalating from the Cold War into a hot one,' he said. 'All the rhetoric in Warsaw just yells of a desire almost to declare war on Russia. They only talk about defence, but actually they are preparing for offensive operations.'

23

THE SIBERIAN CANDIDATE

O N THE EVENING OF SATURDAY 20 August 2016, several dozen people, most of them middle-aged or elderly, stood together in the rain in front of Moscow's White House, as they had done on this day every year for the previous quarter of a century. Some carried Russian flags and photographs of the dramatic events of August 1991. They were there to commemorate Dmitry Komar, Ilya Krichevsky and Vladimir Usov, three young men who died in the uprising against the abortive coup. 'We are gathered here today to remember those who died defending democracy twenty-five years ago,' said Lev Ponomaryov, a Soviet-era dissident and human rights activist, as riot police looked on warily. 'These young men died for our hopes.'

Moscow city authorities had initially denied permission for the meeting, ostensibly because of roadworks. They then backtracked and allowed activists to meet after all. Given the significance of the anniversary, a large turnout might have been expected. Instead, the crowds were smaller than in previous years and dwarfed by those at a rival demonstration voicing nostalgia for the Soviet Union, which was organised by communists and shown on television. During the Yeltsin years, there was always a government presence at the rally and wreaths at the cemetery in honour of the three dead men. This year, the officials all stayed away. Putin and Medvedev were visiting Crimea.

Moscow – and Russia – had moved on. An event once hailed as the beginning of a process that culminated in the collapse of the Soviet

Union and the creation of a new democratic Russia no longer fitted the official narrative. The usually Kremlin-friendly *Moskovsky Komsomolets* published an opinion piece entitled, 'Twenty-five years of imprisonment',[1] illustrated by a cartoon showing a hand with a KGB emblem wrestling a Russian flag away from a group of people. 'August 1991 brought about a stunning wave of enthusiasm. You felt there was no mountain high enough,' wrote commentator Alexander Minkin. 'Those who had power and a unique historical opportunity drop in their lap turned out to be unworthy: they stole and drank the country away, the country and its future. And this still goes on.' Minkin's words were echoed by Pavel Aptekar in an opinion piece in the respected *Vedomosti* daily. 'August 19–21 could have become a symbol of a new Russian state,' he wrote. 'The three August days of 1991 remind the establishment that people could disobey their orders and hold the government accountable. In the past twenty-five years the government has transformed into one that is appalled by the very possibility.'

A poll published on the eve of the anniversary revealed that half of all Russians could not remember what had happened during that summer long ago. A mere eight per cent of Russians described the coup as a victory for democracy; fifteen per cent of people approved of the actions of the coup plotters; thirteen per cent disapproved. Some thirty per cent of all Russians over eighteen years of age considered the outcome as a tragic event with perilous results for the country and the people. Just sixteen per cent said they would take to the streets to prevent a new communist takeover.

The low-key nature of the commemoration – and the contrast with the massive displays that marked the 9 May anniversary of victory over Nazi Germany – reflected the ambivalence of the authorities to the events of August 1991. Putin, a young KGB officer at the time, had not been involved in the coup. Indeed, his mentor, Anatoly Sobchak, the mayor of St Petersburg, where he was serving by then, was one of the most prominent opponents of the plotters. Yet in the intervening years, during which time he had bemoaned the human, economic and strategic consequences of the break-up of the Soviet Union, Putin had had ample time to reconsider his position.

'The current authorities are not communists, but they share the same nationalist ideology as those who plotted the coup,' said Lev Gudkov, head of the Levada Center.[2] 'This means that they prefer to draw a curtain over the events of 1991. Young people know basically nothing about these events. There are no institutions in Russia that encourage a historical memory of this period beyond the myth that we lost a great empire when the Soviet Union collapsed.'

In a commentary published by RT, Dmitry Babich, a Russian journalist who covered the coup, took issue with Western depictions of it as a failed attempt by 'a group of evil old communists' to 'turn back the wheel of history'. Reality, he claimed, was very different: 'In the vast majority of families, the collapse of the historic unified state on the territory of the former Russian empire and the Russo–Ukrainian conflict are seen as senseless tragedies,' he wrote.

As the anniversary came and went, Putin had another priority: the parliamentary election, set for 18 September. Given the extent to which political power was now concentrated in the Kremlin, the result looked unlikely to alter Russia's political direction. The Duma, which had been a lively arena for rival opinions during the Yeltsin era, had been progressively reduced to little more than a rubber stamp under Putin. Yet the election was important as a dry run for the 2018 presidential election in which he looked certain to stand. The authorities were also determined to avoid a repetition of the previous parliamentary poll in December 2011, when anger at vote-rigging and at Putin's decision to return to the presidency spilled over into protests on the street. Ella Pamfilova, a former human rights ombudsman and sometime Kremlin critic, was put in charge of the central election committee with a mandate to make the vote more transparent and 'cleaner'. The election, which was initially scheduled for December, had also been brought forward three months to give the opposition less time to organise and campaign. Potential troublemakers, it was argued, would be too busy bringing in the harvest at their dachas to be bothered with politics.

The backdrop for the poll was not promising. The government – and by extension, United Russia – was blamed for the poor performance of the economy, which was exacerbated by an oil price stuck stubbornly below $50 a barrel and continued European and American sanctions. On the eve of the election, the finance ministry revealed that the government's reserve fund, intended to cover shortfalls in the national budget, had shrunk from £67 billion in 2014 to £23 billion, at which rate it would be exhausted completely by 2017. The obvious solution was to cut spending, yet this would be unpopular and politically risky.

Economic growth, an average of 8% a year during Putin's first two terms, had gone into reverse: the economy shrank by 3.7% in 2015 and was expected to contract a further 1.5% in 2016.

Medvedev, who, as prime minister, topped United Russia's list, got much of the blame. That May, he had been widely mocked on social media when he responded to a complaint from angry pensioners in Crimea about the government's decision not to index pensions with the advice: 'There's no money. But you hang in there!' The move cost United Russia support among pensioners, who had long been among its most loyal voters. Medvedev attracted more criticism when he advised teachers unhappy at their poor wages to get a second job. To add to the teachers' woes, their salaries and those of other workers were often paid late, in an echo of the economic misery of the Yeltsin years, prompting a wave of strikes.

In early September, a few weeks before the election, the Levada Center, Russia's leading independent polling company, published a survey showing that support for United Russia had declined from 39% the previous month to 31%. The authorities reacted in traditional fashion, declaring the organisation a 'foreign agent'. Commentators expressed doubts that the party would reach the 49.3% of the vote it won the last time, let alone the 64.3% it had achieved in 2007.

Yet United Russia would not be allowed to lose. Despite the apparent trappings of democracy, this was not an election in the Western sense. The Kremlin had made use of the electoral rules to disqualify the most dangerous opposition candidates, among them Alexei Navalny's Progress Party, while it used its control of the media to deny airtime to those that it did allow to stand. Those critical of the government were not allowed meeting spaces, billboards were torn down and factory workers were told for whom to vote, or risk losing their jobs. The opposition, too, did not make it easy for itself, with the two main parties, Parnas and Yabloko, refusing to work together. There were also some dirty tricks – chief among them the release of a secret video of the Parnas leader, Mikhail Kasyanov, having sex with his assistant, which was broadcast by a pro-Kremlin TV channel. The portly former prime minister made an unlikely porn star. In July, Putin signed into law the so-called Yarovaya Amendment to Russia's anti-extremism laws, which gave the security forces sweeping new powers, increased controls on social media and telephone calls, and widened the definition of extremist crimes. The move was presented as an antiterrorism measure, but its real purpose was to protect the regime from dissent.

When the results came in, United Russia had won 203 of the 225 seats that were decided on the basis of individual districts and 54.7% of the popular vote in the contest for the other 225 seats fought on party lists. This gave it a total of 343 seats – a 'supermajority' that would give it the power to change the constitution if it wanted. The communists, Liberal Democratic Party and A Just Russia, which largely do the Kremlin's bidding, also made it into parliament, but with just 104 seats between them. Yabloko and Parnas both fell well short of the 5% minimum needed to win seats. Dmitry Gudkov, the sole real opposition deputy in the outgoing Duma, failed to win re-election. One of the leaders of the 2011 protests and a forthright critic of Putin, he won 20% of the vote in his Moscow constituency, compared with 26% for his rival from United Russia.

Despite Pamfilova's efforts, the poll was marred by some instances of blatant vote-rigging, especially in Chechnya and elsewhere in the North Caucasus, which was likely to have given United Russia a few extra percentage points. A particularly egregious case of ballot-stuffing in Rostov-on-Don, captured on video, led to the result there being annulled. Yet there were suggestions that the manipulation went much further: Sergey Shpilkin, a physicist who had published statistical evidence of widespread voter fraud in the 2011 State Duma elections, applied the same basic statistical techniques to the relationship between turnout and the distribution of votes this time round and concluded that United Russia's true share of the vote was actually closer to 40%.

The real victor, though, was indifference. Years of manipulated elections and overwhelming government control over politics and media had convinced many Russians that voting was pointless. This was reflected in the turnout, which, at just under 48%, was the lowest since Russia's return to democracy. The average masked considerable variations: voters in the provinces duly turned out to vote in large numbers for the ruling party, much as they had done for the show elections of the Soviet era, but those in Moscow and St Petersburg, traditionally the two most politically active parts of the country, stayed away. Turnout in the capital was just 35% and in the second city a mere 33%.

'The Kremlin has won, for now,' observed Vladimir Kara-Murza, a journalist and fervent Putin critic.[3] 'But the fact that most Russians now believe that change cannot be achieved through the ballot box is not a promising sign for those in power. Sooner or later, change will come – because of mounting economic troubles, the regime's new foreign policy adventures, or sheer fatigue with a leader who has been in power for a generation.' There were, Kara-Murza argued, two ways for the population to interact with the government: in an election or on the barricades. 'When the first option stops working, people inevitably start to think about the second.'

This did not bode well for the 2018 presidential election. Putin's popularity during his first two terms had been based on a simple deal with the electorate: he guaranteed rising prosperity in return for obedience. After his return in 2012 he continued to enjoy extraordinarily high ratings as a strong leader who had restored his country's greatness by winning back Crimea and making Russia a player in the Middle East. Yet patriotism alone would not necessarily be enough, and he looked unlikely to continue to dodge blame for Russia's worsening economic woes. Given the spending cuts and other unpleasant medicine that had to be administered, there was speculation Putin might bring forward the presidential election so it could be held before austerity began to bite. United Russia's Duma 'supermajority' made achieving this little more than a formality. Alternatively, if the economy failed to deliver, then he might be tempted to play the nationalist card again and embark on another foreign venture in the run-up to the vote.

In the days after the poll, there were indications that Putin was planning a third way of maintaining his grip on power: further repression. A report in *Kommersant* newspaper claimed he was planning a major overhaul of the security forces that would include reuniting the domestic and foreign branches, which had been separated from one another after 1991. Such an all-powerful body would be reminiscent of the old KGB; chillingly, the newspaper suggested it would be called the MGB   Ministry of State Security – as the organisation had been known during the last years of Stalin.

AMERICA, MEANWHILE, WAS IN THE FINAL stages of its own presidential election, which had become a contest between Hillary Clinton and Donald Trump, the billionaire property mogul turned reality-television star who had stunned the political establishment by securing the Republican nomination. The two rivals could not have been more different in their leadership style – and also in their approach to the world. This was particularly the case with their policy towards Russia, which assumed an unexpectedly prominent role during the last months of the contest.

As Obama's first secretary of state, Clinton was necessarily identified with the outgoing president's approach to many issues. It was Clinton who had presented Lavrov with the ill-fated 'reset' button during their encounter in a Geneva hotel; and she, too, had pinned her hopes on a new, more positive relationship with Medvedev after he became president. Yet in the run-up to the announcement in April 2015 of her bid for the White House, she was determined to differentiate her approach from that of Obama, much of which lay in tatters around him. Aides let it be known that despite the time she had spent doing the president's bidding, she had always seen the world differently and had consistently argued for a tougher line against Putin.

Clinton set out her stall in her book, *Hard Choices*, published in 2014, and in subsequent interviews. Obama had reportedly said privately that the first task of a US president in the post-Bush international arena was, 'Don't do stupid shit.' Clinton took issue with this. 'Great nations need organizing principles, and "Don't do stupid stuff" is not an organizing principle,' she said in an interview with *The Atlantic*.[4] The assumption, according to one analyst, was that Clinton as president would 'return the Democratic Party to a more activist, interventionist foreign policy after eight years of a president who has had an easier time articulating his foreign policy in terms of what he would not do ("stupid" stuff) than in explaining what he would'.

In a foreign policy speech to the Brookings Institution in September 2015, Clinton joined Republican criticism of the Obama administration's limited efforts to contain Russia's involvement in Ukraine, putting herself 'in the category of people who wanted to do more in reaction to the annexation of Crimea'. The objective of the Russian government, she claimed, was 'to stymie, to confront, to undermine American power whenever and wherever they can'. This was interpreted as indicating that a Clinton presidency would be more receptive to the idea of supplying arms to the Ukrainian government to fight the Moscow-backed separatists – something Obama was still refusing to do.

The following month, during the first presidential debate of the Democratic primary contest, Clinton denounced Russia's intervention on behalf of President Bashar al-Assad, calling for the imposition of a no-fly zone in Syria – a position that was later to be adopted by many of the Republican contenders. It was important that 'the United States make it very clear to Putin that it's not acceptable for him to be in Syria creating more chaos, bombing people on behalf of Assad', she said. 'And we can't do that if we don't take more of a leadership position.' A year later, as America continued efforts with Russia to try to find a peace deal, Clinton expressed cynicism about Putin's true intentions and questioned his commitment to reaching a settlement.

Yet although Clinton signalled a more interventionist foreign policy than Obama's, this would not simply be a replay of her husband Bill's presidency. These were very different times from the 1990s. The years immediately after the end of communism had been marked by optimism – bordering on arrogance – about America's ability to remake other societies in its own image, prompted by the successful transition of Poland and the other Soviet satellites into liberal democracies, much as Germany and Japan had been reborn half a century earlier. The 2000s showed it was dangerous to believe the trick could be repeated elsewhere: Iraq and Afghanistan demonstrated the limitations of that policy – as did the chaos left after Western intervention in Libya and Russia's retreat from democracy under Putin. The United States no longer dominated the world as it had in the days when Russia was weak, China yet to rise and Francis Fukuyama was talking about the end of history. The American public, too, had become wary of intervention. Isolationism and protectionism were back in fashion.

If Clinton offered a more muscular form of Obama's foreign policy, then Trump proposed an upending of traditional diplomacy and a new business-style approach that had little in common with the interventionism of George W. Bush. According to Trump's view of the world, as it emerged in a number of speeches and comments – many of them off the cuff and some of them contradictory – he would restore 'global peace', rebuild the US military, 'crush and destroy Isis' and contain 'radical Islam'. Yet at the same time, NATO allies would have to start paying their fair share for the privilege of sheltering under the American nuclear umbrella or risk having it withdrawn. The United States should also scale down its tendency to act as a global police force and instead intervene in countries only when American interests were at stake. Trump had little inclination to step up aid for Ukraine; he seemed keener to reduce it, dismissing it as a 'European problem'.

Trump coupled this with apparent admiration for Putin. While the two previous Republican presidential nominees – Mitt Romney and John McCain before him – had retained a Cold War-style suspicion of the Russian leader, Trump repeatedly praised him. 'I think I'd get along very well with Vladimir Putin. I just think so,' Trump said in July 2015 in one of his first comments since launching his presidential bid the previous month. Speaking a year later, he said: 'I would treat Vladimir Putin firmly, but there's nothing I can think of that I'd rather do than have Russia friendly, as opposed to the way they are right now, so that we can go and knock out Isis with other people.' He added: 'I don't think he has any respect for Clinton. I think he respects me. I think it would be great to get along with him.' He courted further controversy in September 2016, claiming that Putin 'has been a leader far more than our president has been a leader'.

Putin, Trump claimed, had been equally supportive of him, calling him 'brilliant'. This turned out to be wishful thinking: *yarki*, the Russian word used by Putin, better translates as 'bright', as in colourful or flamboyant rather than intellectual – a point made by the Kremlin leader himself in a television interview in which he complained about his remarks being mistranslated. Putin nevertheless spoke approvingly of Trump's willingness to improve relations: 'One thing I paid attention to and will definitely welcome is that Mr Trump says he's ready to restore full-fledged Russian–American relations,' Putin said. 'What can be bad about it? Don't you welcome it?'

Doubts about Trump were fuelled by a curious television interview in July 2016 in which Trump declared of Putin: 'He's not going into Ukraine, OK, just so you understand. He's not going to go into Ukraine, all right?' Asked by ABC's George Stephanopoulos if he realised Putin was 'there already', Trump retorted, 'OK – well, he's there in a certain way.' More significant was Trump's vow to 'take a look' at recognising Russia's seizure of Crimea. 'You know, the people of Crimea, from what I've heard, would rather be with Russia than where they were,' he said. Trump attempted to clarify his position on the conflict between Ukraine and Russia in a series of tweets the following morning, after he was criticised for his muddled response, but did not retract his thoughts about Crimea.

Putin also featured in the third and final televised presidential debate on 19 October: after Trump claimed the Russian leader had 'no respect' for Clinton – or indeed for Obama – she shot back: 'Well, that's because he'd rather have a puppet as president of the United States', prompting splutters of outrage from her rival.

Trump's curious enthusiasm for Putin was also reflected in Republican policy towards Russia. At the party's convention in July 2016, an early draft from the platform called on the United States to provide Ukraine with weapons in addition to the substantial non-lethal aid that was already being supplied. The final version, issued apparently after a reported intervention by members of the Trump team, spoke merely of 'providing appropriate assistance'. Such developments were a godsend for Trump's critics, who labelled him the 'Siberian Candidate' – a play on *The Manchurian Candidate*, the political thriller about the son of a prominent American political family who acts as a sleeper cell for a communist conspiracy. Nevertheless, there did not appear to be any evidence that Trump's campaign had received any Russian money. Nor, despite multiple attempts to do deals in the country dating back to the late 1980s, did Trump appear to have much in the way of business interests there. When Trump staged his Miss Universe pageant in Moscow in 2013, he hoped Putin would attend, tweeting: 'Will he become my new best friend?' The Russian leader was otherwise engaged.

Such comments, coupled with Trump's apparent lack of experienced foreign policy advisers, added to anxiety among America's allies as to how his victory would affect US trade, military and diplomatic policy. Never before had a leading presidential candidate left so many people guessing about his likely intentions. 'Scary. That's how we view Trump', one unnamed ambassador from a country with a close relationship to America told the *Washington Post*.[5] 'Could we depend on the United States? We don't know. I can't tell you how the unpredictability we are seeing scares us.'

Trump's political associates also came under scrutiny over their foreign ties. Especially intriguing was the role of Paul Manafort, the Republican political operator who was brought in to chair Trump's campaign in June 2016 when it began to flounder. A steady flow of revelations during the summer about the extent of Manafort's work for Viktor Yanukovych, the discredited Ukrainian president, proved an added embarrassment for the campaign. The final blow was the revelation in August by the *New York Times* that Yanukovych's party had set aside $12.7 million in undisclosed payments for him. Manafort rejected the allegations as 'unfounded, silly, and nonsensical', but a few days later he stepped down – not entirely voluntarily. Trump's son, Eric, spoke of a 'distraction looming over the campaign'.

The campaign was also forced to dissociate itself from Carter Page, a former Merrill Lynch investment banker specialising in oil and gas deals with Russia and the former Soviet states, who was named as an adviser to Trump in March 2016. In a speech in Moscow that July, Page criticised America and other Western powers for a 'hypocritical focus on ideas such as democratisation, inequality, corruption and regime change'. During his visit, it was later claimed, he had met several senior Russian officials and discussed the lifting of sanctions. Among his alleged interlocutors was Igor Sechin, the executive chairman of Rosneft and a key Putin loyalist, who was himself on the sanctions list. Page's activities were reportedly discussed by US intelligence officials with senior members of Congress during briefings about suspected efforts by Moscow to influence the presidential election. Harry Reid, the Democratic Senate minority leader, wrote to the FBI Director James Comey, citing reports of the alleged meetings as evidence of 'significant and disturbing ties' between the Trump campaign and the Kremlin that needed to be investigated by the bureau. Page declined to comment.[6] In December 2015, another Trump adviser, General Michael Flynn, a former head of the US Defense Intelligence Agency, had appeared in Moscow at an anniversary dinner for RT, the Kremlin-backed broadcaster, and spent part of the evening seated next to Putin.

Claims that the Russians had been behind the hacking of the Democratic National Committee's emails and of those of John Podesta, Clinton's campaign chairman, gave the Democrats a further chance to portray Trump as Putin's choice and their candidate as the woman to stand up to him. The Kremlin leader, it was argued, bore a grudge against Clinton for 'encouraging' protests in Russia after the December 2011 parliamentary election and for her harsh words about his attempt to 're-Sovietise' Russia's neighbours. The theme was taken up with enthusiasm by the American media. 'Is Vladimir Putin taking sides in the presidential election?' asked *Time*. The *Washington Post* reported that the FBI was investigating 'a broad covert Russian operation' to sow distrust in the elections. Michael Morell, a former acting director of the CIA, claimed Putin 'had recruited Mr Trump as an unwitting agent of the Russian Federation'. Trump courted further controversy by reacting to the hack of the Democratic National Committee with remarks interpreted as encouraging the Russians to go after Clinton's email too. And, during his first presidential debate with Clinton in September 2016, he raised eyebrows by suggesting it may have been the work of a domestic hacker rather than Russia. 'I don't think anyone knows it was Russia,' Trump said. 'It could be Russia, it could be China and it could also be someone sitting on their bed that weighs 400lbs.' The comment was seized on by Russian media – as was Trump's assertion that America 'cannot be the policeman of the world'.

The full extent of Russia's involvement would become clear only after the election. There seemed little doubt that it went beyond merely undermining the electoral process. John Brennan, the CIA director, told employees that a 'strong consensus' existed among the US intelligence services that Russia had orchestrated hacks and that the online leaks were designed at least in part to help Trump win the White House. Obama, although reluctant to touch on the issue in public before the vote for fear of further inflaming an already bitterly partisan campaign, was more candid when he met Putin on the margins of the G20 summit in Hangzhou, China in September, where he claimed to have told the Russian leader to 'cut it out' and warned of 'serious consequences if he didn't'. 'Not much happens in Russia without Vladimir Putin,' he said. Obama subsequently claimed that the leaks ceased following his intervention – an assertion that was challenged by the Democratic National Committee Chair Donna Brazile, who claimed Russian hackers tried to break into her organisation's computers 'daily, hourly' right up until the election. Either way, the damage had already been done. It was difficult to avoid the impression the Kremlin was rooting for Trump – inspired, according to Clinton, by the 'personal beef' Putin had against her.

In a commentary in the *New York Times*, Ross Douthat reflected on how the traditional attitudes of America's political parties towards

Moscow had been turned on their head. 'Russia's place in American politics used to be (relatively) simple,' he wrote.[7] 'The further right you stood, the more you feared Ivan and his Slavic wiles. The further left, the more you likely thought the Red Menace was mostly just a scare story.' In 2016, by contrast, the Republicans had a candidate 'who has a palpable man-crush on Putin and promises closer ties with his regime', while the Democrats had gone from 'mocking Mitt Romney for describing Russia as America's main geopolitical foe . . . to spinning theories about Trump being an agent of Russian influence that seem ripped from a right-wing periodical circa 1955'.

Underlying this reversal of roles was a fundamental problem that remained unresolved as Obama's second and final term drew to a close. What kind of relationship should America – and the West more broadly – have with its erstwhile Cold War foe? Successive US presidents from Clinton through to George W. Bush to Obama had made a point of trying to integrate Russia into the Western world. The tone and terminology had differed – Clinton's promise of a 'strategic alliance with Russian reform' had given way to Bush's 'strategic partnership' and Obama's 'reset' – but the aim had been broadly similar. Yet despite their best efforts, when each president left office eight years later, relations with Moscow were in an even worse state than when they had arrived. By the time of Obama's departure, they had sunk to a new low.

The assumptions that had guided American policy towards Russia since 1991 were finally shattered by Putin's annexation of Crimea and his military intervention in eastern Ukraine. The process of integrating Russia into the West had come to an end – or rather it had been suspended until Moscow modified its behaviour. But Russia was not prepared to modify its behaviour; nor did it seem interested in integration with the West, at least not on the terms that had hitherto been on offer. Since the time of Putin's Munich speech in 2007, the Kremlin had been working instead towards re-establishing its role as an independent centre of power and an alternative to the United States, much as it had been during the Cold War. With its intervention in Syria it had reasserted itself as a global player and, despite continued sanctions, had left Washington with no alternative but to sit at the table with it. In Europe, meanwhile, it was enjoying some success in cultivating individual governments, especially some of its former satellites, and establishing links with the nationalist right across the continent. Putin was also pressing ahead with his plans to rebuild links with the former Soviet republics through the Eurasian Customs Union. Since May 2014, the treaty was given the more ambitious title of Eurasian Economic Union, even though Putin's chances of building a rival to the European Union were hampered by Ukraine's refusal to join and the sensitivity of the non-Russian members to anything that smacked of encroachment by the Kremlin on their sovereignty.

Looking back on the past quarter of a century, it is difficult to pinpoint the precise moment at which relations between Russia and the West went wrong. In fact, it may be that there was never a moment at which they were going right. Despite the surge of pro-Western sentiment in the early 1990s, the period was marked by fundamental misunderstandings – beginning with the failure on both sides to make explicit how the newly independent Russia should be treated: as a defeated power or an equal partner. Both America and Russia can also rightly accuse many in each other's countries of having continued to behave as if the Cold War had never ended, thereby helping bring about its return. Other misunderstandings followed, most notably over NATO. What the West chose to interpret as assent by Russia to the Alliance's eastward expansion was, in reality, weakness and an inability to resist. Policymakers in Europe and America also failed to appreciate the extent to which an increasingly paranoid Putin saw the Colour Revolutions of the first decade of this century as directed by the CIA and ultimately aimed at toppling his own regime. Such misunderstandings worked both ways, most dramatically over Russia's partial invasion of Georgia in 2008. The West's relatively mild response was interpreted by the Kremlin as acceptance of its assertion of special rights in the 'near abroad'. This wrong impression was reinforced by the reset: for Obama it was intended as a relatively limited policy to work together on areas of common interest, but, coming so soon after Georgia, it was seen by Russia as a vindication of its actions and acceptance by the West of its great power status. In that context, the biggest of the misunderstandings – over Ukraine in 2014 – came to seem inevitable.

Rodric Braithwaite, the last British ambassador to the Soviet Union, recalls a conversation he had with a liberal adviser to Mikhail Gorbachev in November 1991 as the country was about to break up. 'Russia may now be going through a bad time,' he told Braithwaite. 'But the reality is that in a decade or two decades, Russia will reassert itself as the dominant force in this huge geographical area.' Indeed, anyone who understood Russia realised that it would inevitably bounce back from the chaos that accompanied the collapse of the Soviet Union, while its sheer size and history made it unlikely that it would meekly join the ranks of the regional powers. So what role did the West expect Russia to play? Sometimes it must have seemed to policymakers in Moscow that anything they did was condemned: their attempts to continue to do business with traditional allies such as Iran or Syria were greeted with suspicion, while any moves to re-establish ties with neighbouring countries were immediately denounced as part of a sinister master plan to rebuild the Soviet Union.

The course that Russia has taken has also been greatly determined by Yeltsin's choice of successor. It is debatable the extent to which Putin has merely satisfied the traditional Russian yearning for strong leadership and the extent to which he has fuelled it. It is nevertheless intriguing to speculate what kind of Russia would have developed if Yeltsin had handed the keys to the Kremlin to Yevgeny Primakov, the former prime minister, or even more radically, the late reformer Boris Nemtsov, who for a short period was considered to be his successor. Or indeed, if Yeltsin had played the true democrat and not nominated anyone at all, instead creating a level playing field on which rival candidates could compete for votes. But Yeltsin was obsessed with securing a guarantee of immunity for himself and the 'family' from prosecution for their past misdemeanours, and so he picked a former KGB officer, who, in his desire to restore order, pursued policies both at home and abroad that would inevitably challenge the West.

By summer 2016, with just a few months left in the White House, Obama had given up on attempts to forge a new relationship with Putin. When the two men met that September on the margins of the G20 summit in Hangzhou, China – their first encounter in ten months – the body language said it all. Obama described their encounter as 'candid, blunt and businesslike'. The contrast with Bush's starry-eyed first encounter with Putin in a Slovenian castle fifteen years earlier, or with Bill Clinton's backslapping sessions with Yeltsin in the 1990s, could not have been greater. Equally notable was the number of world leaders present in Hangzhou who wanted to meet Putin. The isolation of Putin that followed the annexation of Crimea was coming to an end. It would be up to Obama's successor to find a way of putting America – and the West's – relationship with Russia back on track.

24

THREE FACES OF RUSSIA

THE LINGERING AND PAINFUL DEATH OF Alexander Litvinenko was probably the best thing to have happened to Andrei Lugovoi's career. In the decade since he was accused of poisoning the former KGB agent by putting highly radioactive polonium-210 in his tea in a London hotel, Lugovoi has been on a roll. His business interests are flourishing; he sits in the Duma as a member of the Liberal Democratic Party of Russia (LDPR), whose leader, Vladimir Zhirinovsky, has built his career on a particularly strident form of anti-Western populism; and he has established a new career as a presenter of documentaries on Russian television. Appropriately enough, the series Lugovoi fronts is about 'traitors' – men such as Litvinenko, who is seen by many in Russia as having betrayed his country by moving to Britain and teaming up with Boris Berezovsky, the exiled billionaire businessman, and then with MI6.

We have arranged to meet at a restaurant in Moscow owned by Lugovoi. The timing turns out to be fortuitous: a few days earlier, an official inquiry into Litvinenko's death headed by Sir Robert Owen, a senior British judge, has concluded with a report confirming Lugovoi's guilt, and has furthermore ruled that the killing was 'probably' ordered by Putin. The use of the word 'probably' seems odd in a legal document and has been seized on by many in the more nationalist sections of the Russian media as yet another politically motivated assault on their country.

As we approach the entrance to the restaurant through the January snow, Lugovoi emerges from the back of a black chauffeur-driven Mercedes 500. We walk into the restaurant. His wife, Kseniya, a glamorous brunette more than two decades his junior, is seated at a table chatting animatedly with three friends. Otherwise the place is empty. A large number of Moscow's restaurants seem to be empty. It may be because of the economic crisis, which has bitten deeper and deeper. But many establishments seem little more than vanity projects or places where their owners can impress clients. I order tea, resisting the temptation to make a tasteless joke. Lugovoi drinks coffee with honey and a slice of lemon.

In a flurry of interviews with British and Russian media that have accompanied the publication of the report, Lugovoi has condemned Owen's conclusions as a smear on him and on Russia. 'I've seen the nonsense conclusions of your judge who has clearly gone mad,' he told one reporter. 'I saw nothing new there. I am very sorry that ten years on nothing new has been presented, only invention, supposition, rumours. And the fact that such words as "possibly" and "probably" were used in the report means there is no proof, nothing concrete against us.' It was MI6, Lugovoi claims, that was responsible for the trail of polonium, and not him. He speaks with a confidence that comes from the knowledge that there is no way Russia will ever hand him over to the British authorities – however hard Litvinenko's widow, Marina, lobbies.

So did he actually kill Litvinenko? My colleague, Mark Franchetti, the Moscow correspondent of the *Sunday Times*, who set up our meeting and is seated beside me, has interviewed Lugovoi on several occasions since 2006 and spent time on a hunting trip with him for a television documentary. He has put that question countless times and in countless different ways, but has still to receive a straight answer. Instead I ask Lugovoi about the impact of Litvinenko's death on him. 'Every person has a moment in life that allows him to radically change things in his life,' he says. 'This was the case with me.' Although he continues to reap the benefits of his notoriety, he sees Litvinenko's death as a chapter that is now closed; the inquiry, he believes, is an attempt by the British authorities to draw a line under it.

'At some point it was necessary to put an end to this case,' he says.

'The fact that over the past ten years this story has been dragging on and kept on popping up again is because the position of the British government was not clear. Now that the position has officially been made clear by the inquiry, it will not come up again and they will move on.'

We talk instead about him and his life. Despite the extraordinary crime of which he has been accused, Lugovoi is in many ways typical of a generation of Russians who came of age during the last years of the Soviet Union. Brought up in one country with one set of values, he suddenly found himself in another one in which very different rules applied. Born into a military family in 1966, he joined the KGB's ninth directorate, which provided security for top state officials, and went from there to the Federal Protective Service of Russia, where he became deputy head of personal security for Yegor Gaidar, Yeltsin's young reformist prime minister. One of his first trips abroad was when he accompanied the two of them to America in June 1992.

'I only visited Washington DC, but it was enough to see the difference,' he says. 'Everything was so neat there, unlike Moscow where there were people everywhere on the streets selling things. I had a feeling that we had been tricked during the Soviet days. When I came back I told my wife that Gaidar's reforms meant that we would have to suffer a bit, but in a few years we would live just like they live in America.

'It was in the 1990s that the foundations were laid for the suspicion that we have now. There were many foreign advisers and economists around Gaidar. We were quite open towards the West, because we suddenly had the opportunity to travel there. But the exact opposite happened in the West. They had no intention of coming to us. They also kept on criticising us: firstly because of the Chechen war, then because Yeltsin was a heavy drinker and later because of the second Chechen war.

'People from the former Soviet Union have a different mentality from those in the West. In the 1990s we failed to understand each other. And at the moment we see the result of this misunderstanding. The West is scared of how big Russia is. I do not think of the West as an enemy, but I see it as an opponent, which is fighting against us at the moment; not necessarily against the country, but rather to get what they want and fulfil their aims.'

It was the year after Litvinenko's death that Lugovoi received a call from Vladimir Zhirinovsky inviting him to stand for his party in the December 2007 parliamentary elections. His name was put second, after Zhirinovsky's own, on the LDPR's list of candidates. 'After he announced my candidacy, his support rose by four per cent,' says Lugovoi. 'It was very good PR.' Some voters, he believes, backed him because they thought he had killed a traitor; others voted for him because they thought he was the victim of a 'provocation', who had been framed for a killing he had not carried out.

It is this ambiguity that characterises Lugovoi. Traces of polonium-210 were found not just in the Millennium Hotel in Grosvenor Square where Litvinenko drank his lethal tea, but also in other places that Lugovoi visited in London, in the airplanes he took to and from Britain, and even on his own children. But why did the Kremlin choose to kill Litvinenko in such a bizarre way, making use of someone he knew and could identify to British authorities himself, before he died? Had Lugovoi and his alleged accomplice Dmitry Kovtun been told the precise nature of the substance they were to put into Litvinenko's tea and, if so, why were they so cavalier in handling it, at one point even tipping some of it down a hotel toilet?

There are other questions, too, about why, immediately after being accused of the killing, Lugovoi agreed to give an interview to Echo Moskvy, a radio station that is one of the few remnants of Russia's independent media. Was he worried that the Russian security services might try to kill him, too? And did he think that by raising his public profile at home it would provide him with a form of protection? We may never know the answer.

Lugovoi used to enjoy travelling to London but can no longer go to Britain for fear of arrest. Nor, as someone accused of one of the highest-profile crimes of the past decade, can he safely leave Russia without fear of extradition. But he says he has a good life and does not feel like a prisoner in his own country. 'If you have a chance to travel to an exotic place like the Maldives or Bali you want to go there, but when you know it's impossible to do so, then you no longer have the desire,' he says. 'I easily get used to things. I always lived well, but I have a better life now.'

DMITRY KISELYOV CANNOT TRAVEL ABROAD, EITHER, at least not to Europe. One of Russia's most popular and controversial television presenters, he is the only journalist on the sanctions list drawn up by the European Union in response to Russia's annexation of Crimea. He has yet to be informed of his precise offence, although the EU has described him as 'the central figure of the government propaganda supporting the deployment of Russian forces in Ukraine'.

He is angry at his treatment, but is not letting it cramp his plans for the summer: a decade or so ago, while working for Ukrainian television, he bought a holiday home in Crimea and now spends his holidays there. The previous autumn he organised a jazz festival on the peninsula, which, he gleefully notes, featured performers from America and Britain. He invites me to travel with him to Crimea to see how much better life has become on the peninsula since it was taken back by Russia.

The addition of Kiselyov, a bullet-headed, pugnacious character with a sharp, sarcastic wit, to a list of some of Putin's closest cronies is a tribute to the influence of his programme, *Vesti Nedeli* (News of the Week), which is broadcast on the main state television station, Channel One. It is what the Russians call an 'authored programme', which means Kiselyov is free to use the show as a vehicle to express his views. And express them he does. They clearly strike a chord with many Russians: some four million people tune in each week to watch him. Putin is said to be among his fans. His influence extends beyond the programme: since December 2013 he has also been head of Rossiya Segodnya, a media organisation that incorporates the former RIA Novosti news service and the international radio service Voice of Russia.

The week we meet he has turned his attention to the Litvinenko inquiry. Not surprisingly, Kiselyov has little time for claims that Litvinenko was poisoned on the orders of the Kremlin. Russia had not killed Oleg Gordievsky, a Soviet KGB colonel and double agent who was sentenced to death in absentia after he defected to Britain in 1985, so why would it bother with small fry like Litvinenko? 'He was a little person,' said Kiselyov. 'We don't kill such people.' So who does he think did it? He points the finger at the British intelligence services and at Boris Berezovsky, the 'master of intrigue'.

Which brings us to Berezovsky's own untimely death seven years later in March 2013, when he was found hanged in the locked bathroom of his Berkshire mansion. Faced with enormous debts after losing a costly legal battle against Roman Abramovich, his fellow oligarch, Berezovsky was apparently despairing of life in exile, so much so that he even wrote a letter to his old foe, Putin, asking to be allowed to return to Russia – or so the Kremlin claimed. Although the coroner recorded an open verdict, suicide seems the most likely cause of death. But not to Kiselyov, who has made conspiracy theories a leitmotif of his work. 'Maybe he just knew too much for the British intelligence services,' he says.

Britain, I suggest, seems a dangerous place for high-profile Russian exiles, citing the suspicious death of Alexander Perepilichny, a businessman and whistle-blower who collapsed and died while out jogging near his Surrey home four months before the death of Berezovsky. Traces were subsequently found in his stomach of a poisonous fern used by Russian and Chinese contract killers.

Kiselyov responds with a diatribe against British perfidy: it was a British firm, Vickers, that left the Russian imperial army without the shells it needed in 1915, the British government that harboured Lenin and his fellow revolutionaries as they plotted to overthrow the Tsar, and Winston Churchill who in 1947 urged President Harry Truman to carry out a preventive atomic strike on the Kremlin, he says. Not to forget Sir Charles Whitworth, the British ambassador to Russia, who was involved in the plot to assassinate Tsar Paul I, who was stabbed, strangled and trampled to death in his bedroom in 1801. 'England doesn't do fair play,' he says. 'It doesn't play honestly.'

Nor is the West as a whole playing fair with Russia today, according to Kiselyov. Russia, he notes, has saved Europe three times – from the Mongol hordes, from Napoleon and from the Nazis – and is now saving it again, this time from Isis, thanks to its bombing campaign in Syria. But it gets no thanks. Instead the West criticises Russia over its human rights record – although those of other countries such as China and Saudi Arabia are far worse – and tries to impose its own values on it. 'But it turned out that Western patterns did not work here, just like they did not work in Iraq or in Libya,' he says. 'You want to impose your value system here but it won't work.'

Despite the fervour with which he expounds his views, Kiselyov did not always think this way. Like many of Putin's most loyal supporters, he was on the side of the 'democrats' during the 1990s, rejoicing at the fall of communism and dreaming of a 'world of peace, friendship and chewing gum'. He demonstrated his liberal credentials in February 1991 when he refused to broadcast the Kremlin line after Gorbachev sent in tanks to crush Lithuania's bid for independence from the Soviet Union. He went on to present *Window on Europe*, a TV programme produced with the help of an EU grant. The sixth of his seven wives was British and he speaks English, Norwegian and Swedish.

His views changed during Ukraine's Orange Revolution, when he began to doubt Western media's claims of objectivity and came to believe that America was manipulating developments in the country to further its own interests. As a result, when he looks back on the events that followed the collapse of the Soviet Union he sees them very differently from the way he did at the time. His country, he believes, fell victim to a mixture of 'Western propaganda and Russian romanticism', which was all the more effective because of the openness of the Russian soul.

'We were told that once the Soviet Union broke up, we would all be friends and everything would be fine. That it was the system that was to blame', says Kiselyov. 'But no sooner had the system disappeared than NATO started to expand to the east and they began to bomb Yugoslavia.' For that reason, he feels justified in having changed his view of the West. 'I said then what I thought and I say now what I think. That hasn't changed. But my opinion itself has changed. On the basis of my political and social experience I have undergone an evolution along with the whole country.'

Among Kiselyov's most controversial views are those on gays. In a much-quoted broadcast in April 2012 he argued that they 'should be prohibited from donating blood or sperm. And their hearts, in case they die in a car accident, should be buried or burned as unfit for extending anyone's life.' Yet he angrily rejects suggestions that he is homophobic. He is equally indignant at claims that he is a warmonger, following his comment at the height of the Ukraine crisis that Russia is the only country that would be able to reduce America to nuclear ash. 'I only implied that two countries with such capabilities must act responsibly in this world and avoid steps that can spiral into uncontrolled escalation,' he says.

Kiselyov is effusive in his praise for Putin, who, he believes, has restored much-needed order and stability to his country: had it not been for his arrival on the scene, Russia might have fallen apart, with disastrous consequences. 'I am convinced that he was the saviour not just of Russia but of the world.'

ON THE OTHER SIDE OF MOSCOW I visit one of Russia's richest men. His office, reached after passing through several levels of security, is large but simply decorated with expensive pieces of modern art. My host is friendly and unassuming and dressed casually in an open-necked shirt. In his early fifties, he has had an extraordinary career, moving in the 1980s from the town of his birth to Moscow to study and then at the end of the decade taking his first tentative steps into the rapidly evolving world of business. Two decades later, thanks to a series of bold deals, some of them highly controversial, he has amassed a fortune worth several billion pounds. He thrived during the wild capitalism of the 1990s and has continued to thrive under Putin. A key to his success has been his discretion. For that reason, he does not want me to give his name.

So what does he see as the root causes of the current problems between Russia and the West? He considers the rift that has opened up since the end of the Soviet Union to be the result of the fundamental difference between the Protestant and Catholic cultures of America and the West, with their emphasis on individual effort and self-improvement, and the more fatalistic attitude fostered by Russian Orthodoxy. It is no coincidence, he believes, that Christmas is the most important event in the West while Easter is the focus of the Russian religious calendar. The first is the celebration of something joyous but real; the latter something miraculous. The difference seems clear to him as a Jew, able to see the impact of both religious traditions from the outside.

Gaidar and the other young economic reformers who gathered around Yeltsin in the early 1990s failed to understand the depth of this cultural rift, he says. They painstakingly created all the laws and regulations needed to allow the new Russian economy to function along Western lines, but did not see that this would not change the country's underlying 'Asian' mindset. 'They thought all they had to do was pass the laws and open the gates to the West,' he said. While some, like him, seized the chances suddenly presented, many were unwilling or unable to do so, leading to growing disparities in income and wealth. The result was the emergence of 'an anger and hatred' of liberalism and of 'shock therapy', which became synonymous with one another, and a disdain for what became known in retrospect as the 'wild, wild 1990s'. The problem was further compounded by Yeltsin's unwillingness – or inability – to make a complete break with the Soviet past. 'The Communist Party should have been forbidden,' he says. 'We underestimated the impact of ideology. That was why it was necessary to have a purge.'

So how does he view the situation in the 1990s that allowed him and a few others to begin to amass such huge wealth? Was it fair? Aged in his twenties at the time, he sees himself as a member of a lucky generation that was quick and smart enough to seize the opportunity thrown up by the sell-off of state assets. The first, mass phase of privatisation based on vouchers was fair, he believes. If people wanted to sell their voucher for a bottle of vodka rather than invest it in a small piece of industry, then that was their choice, even if the state should have done more to educate them about the choice they were making. What followed was not right, though: the 'loans for shares' scheme set up to help ensure Yeltsin's re-election in 1996 served merely to enrich the president's cronies. 'It was not fair at all,' he says.

Russia under Putin has long since moved on from those days. Although the economy remains a capitalist one, albeit with a far more powerful role for the state, society has in many ways reverted to type. The sink-or-swim individualism of the 1990s that allowed a smart few to enrich themselves and reduced others to selling their possessions by the side of the street has gone. In its place, helped by the surging oil price of the early 2000s, a traditional form of Russian paternalism began to emerge. If people continued in overwhelming numbers to vote for Putin, it was partly because of a belief that he would look after them. 'Putin proposed a deal,' he says. 'You give me power and in return I will care for you.'

For now he is continuing to do well in that system, but he knows that this could change at any moment. The deteriorating economic situation and hostile international climate have changed the nature of Putinism. Nor is it clear what kind of leader will succeed Putin when he finally leaves power. Despite my host's enormous wealth, there is a precariousness about his situation. Everyone in business in Russia is all too aware of the savage treatment meted out to Mikhail Khodorkovsky, once the country's richest man, after he fell foul of Putin. For that reason my host's wife and children live abroad, and he spends much of the year outside Russia. He is always ready to leave the country at the drop of a hat. 'We Jews are used to that,' he says.

EPILOGUE

THE YEAR 2016 WAS A TIME of political surprises. None was as great as the election of Donald Trump as the forty-fifth president of the United States. His victory that November promised to change America's relationship with the Kremlin. Taken together with the rise of populism in Europe, it also looked set to transform Russia's relations with the broader Western world, heralding the start of a new era. Things were suddenly going Vladimir Putin's way.

Trump's warm words about Putin during the campaign suggested that he would be friendlier to Moscow than Obama had been – and certainly friendlier than Hillary Clinton, who had been portrayed in the Russian media as a Russophobe spoiling to start a Third World War. There was talk of finding common ground. Not surprisingly, his success was greeted in Russia with something approaching jubilation. Members of the Duma, in full session at the time, burst into applause at the news. Vladimir Zhirinovsky, head of the nationalist Liberal Democratic Party of Russia, bought 132 bottles of champagne for his fellow parliamentarians and staff, crowing that he expected Trump to help Russia achieve its strategic goals. 'What's Crimea to him? He doesn't even know where it is!' Zhirinovsky declared.

Russian state media carried out an abrupt 180-degree turn. During the campaign, when Clinton looked certain to prevail, it had lambasted the American electoral process as corrupt and unfair. Trump's win was swiftly hailed as a triumph for democracy. Margarita Simonyan, editor-in-chief of RT, linked the result with two equally tumultuous events in Britain: the election of Jeremy Corbyn as Labour leader in September 2015 and the vote to leave the EU the following June. 'Corbyn. Brexit. Trump,' she tweeted. 'The world is sick of the establishment, of its lies, of its lying condescending media. Today I want to ride around Moscow with an American flag in the window.' Simonyan's comments reflected Russia's attempt to depict itself as leading the opposition to the global international liberal order. Now, apparently against all the odds, Clinton, who epitomised that liberal order, had been defeated by a populist revolt. Trump's victory was also Russia's.

Putin was one of the first foreign leaders to congratulate the president elect, sending him a telegram in which he said he hoped that relations between the two world powers would improve 'from their crisis state'. Later that day, after swearing in a group of foreign diplomats in the Kremlin, Putin struck an optimistic note. 'It's not our fault that Russian–American relations are in this poor state,' he said. 'But Russia is ready and wants to restore full-fledged relations with the United States.' The contrast could not have been greater with Obama's election eight years earlier, when President Medvedev 'forgot' to congratulate him. Within the following few weeks, Trump and Putin reportedly spoke by phone at least twice.

The legacy Trump inherited was a difficult one. The reset that Obama attempted after he came to power was aimed at establishing a new partnership with Moscow. But by the end of his second term he was trying to isolate Russia or ignore it, even as Putin ran rings around him, first over Ukraine and then Syria. 'Russia is a regional power that is threatening some of its immediate neighbours, not out of strength but out of weakness,' was Obama's withering response to Putin's annexation of Crimea. 'They don't pose the number one security threat to the United States. I remain much more concerned about the prospect of a nuclear weapon going off in Manhattan.'

Putin was livid – not least because Obama's accusation struck home. Russia may still have been capable of muscling its way into Syria and possessed enough nuclear weapons to destroy America several times over, but its economy was just one sixteenth the size of America's, it had considerably less territory than it had during the Soviet days and its conservative, Orthodox ideology had nothing like the global ideological pull of communism.

Relations reached a low point in October 2016 when Putin suspended an agreement with the United States, concluded in 2000, that bound the two sides to dispose of surplus plutonium originally intended for nuclear weapons. He set stringent conditions for the resumption of cooperation: all sanctions imposed over Crimea should be lifted and compensation paid, the Magnitsky Act repealed and the US military presence reduced in those countries that had joined NATO since September 2000. Putin's announcement came the same day that Washington said it was freezing talks with Russia on trying to end the violence in Syria. Obama's reset had been aimed at 'delinking' intractable issues from those where productive cooperation with Russia might be possible. Now Russia was making clear its determination to use arms control agreements – the basis of post-Cold War cooperation between the two countries – as leverage in other disputes. Putin's move represented a new stage in the degeneration of Russia's relations with the West.

The election offered the potential for a new start. Trump came to the presidency with one clear advantage: he was not Obama. His warm words for Putin during the campaign pointed to a willingness to give the Russian leader the respect he craved. This in turn looked set to raise Russian hopes of a 'grand bargain' with America that might eventually pave the way for the fulfilment of Putin's dream: a return to the days when Washington and Moscow ran the world together – only now perhaps in tandem with China. Inevitably, this fuelled fears in Ukraine, the Baltic states and Russia's other neighbours that any such rapprochement would be at their expense. These concerns were heightened by Trump's lukewarm commitment to NATO and his suggestion that the Alliance should not come to the aid of those countries that did not pay their fair share to defend themselves.

Events in Europe, too, seemed to be moving in Putin's favour, with Britain's Brexit vote providing a foretaste of a surge in anti-establishment feeling similar to the one that brought Trump to power in America. Pro-Russian sentiment was already strong in countries such as Italy and Greece, while Viktor Orban, the Hungarian leader, was an avowed admirer of the Kremlin leader. The weeks after Trump's victory saw the election of two more pro-Russian presidents: in Bulgaria, Rumen Radev, a Socialist former air force general with no political experience, trounced the candidate of the ruling centre-right party, while in the former Soviet republic of Moldova, the contest was won by Igor Dodon, who called for his country, the poorest in Europe, to scrap its association agreement with the EU and instead join Putin's Eurasian Economic Union.

More significant was the choice two weeks later in France of François Fillon as the presidential candidate of the centre-right Républicains in the party's primary, setting the stage for a battle between him and Marine Le Pen of the National Front in the second round of the election in May 2017. While Le Pen's admiration for Putin was well known, Fillon was just as fulsome in his praise of the Kremlin leader, calling for the lifting of sanctions on Russia and for France to work together with Moscow to curb immigration and fight terrorism. The policy appeared straight out of the playbook of Charles de Gaulle, who had tried to steer a path between Moscow and Washington when he ruled France during the 1960s. It was also underpinned by a strong personal relationship between Fillon and Putin that had developed when they were prime ministers in the late 2000s. Both men share a similar conservative approach towards social policy and wariness of multiculturalism and international organisations. Fillon spoke of Putin as 'cher Vladimir'. When his mother died, Putin reportedly sent him a bottle of 1931 wine – the year of her birth.

The result looked almost certain to be a softening of the hardline stance towards the Kremlin that had been followed by Francois Hollande, the Socialist president, even though it would put France at odds with Chancellor Merkel, who remained deeply suspicious of Putin. Yet Merkel was finding herself increasingly isolated: her Social Democrat coalition partners hankered for a return to the days of *Ostpolitik*, when Germany tried to balance West and East, while polls showed ordinary Germans would be reluctant to defend their Eastern neighbours if they became embroiled in a serious conflict with Russia. Britain, Europe's other leading Russia hawk, was increasingly distracted by the challenges of Brexit, while a resounding 'no' vote in Italy in a referendum on constitutional reform in December gave a further challenge to the established order.

In the meantime, Syria was the most pressing international issue facing Trump. In the last years of Obama's second term, the West found itself increasingly torn between the need to crush ISIS and its attempts to use 'moderate' rebels to oust President Assad. By late 2016, that policy was in tatters. Identifying groups that were not in league with the Islamists yet capable of ousting the regime proved an impossible task. At the same time, the West's unwillingness to be drawn into a shooting war with Moscow left it impotent in the face of relentless Russian and Syrian government bombing of Aleppo, which culminated in the fall of the last rebel areas in the East of the city that December. Trump, by contrast, made clear during the campaign that his priority was crushing ISIS. If this meant a de facto recognition of Assad's right to continue in power – albeit only for a limited transitional period – then so be it. Such a policy opened the way to cooperation with Russia, which, given its own large and often troubled Muslim population, has a special interest in the defeat of Islamic fundamentalism.

More intractable was the question of Ukraine, which had led to growing tension and a build-up of military forces on both sides of NATO's border with Russia. The starting point had to be Crimea itself. Given the importance that Putin has attached to reversing the 'historical injustice' of 1954 when Crimea was transferred to Ukraine, it would be politically impossible for him to give up the peninsula. Such a move would also prove unpopular with the local Russian majority. Yet it would be equally difficult for the West to explicitly accept Russian rule over Crimea and its continued involvement in Eastern Ukraine, for fear that it would give the green light to other military adventures. History does provide a possible way out of the impasse, however: the United States, along with Britain and many other countries, refused to recognise Stalin's annexation of Estonia, Latvia and Lithuania in 1940, providing a major morale boost to the Baltic states, but this did not prevent the West from having dealings with the Soviet Union on other issues during the Second World War and in the decades that followed.

This still leaves the problem of Ukraine's war-torn East. Events since 2014 have shown the lost lands will not be recovered through military conquest. The only way to do so is instead by example – by turning the rest of Ukraine into a reformed, Western country that those living in the separatist regions want to join. The government in Kiev still has much to do to achieve that – in particular in tackling chronic corruption. If it were to succeed, it would allow the country eventually to reunite peacefully, as Germany did before it.

Much, though, depends on Ukraine's future military alignment. The situation has changed radically since 2008 when America was pushing for the country to join NATO. All such talk appeared to have gone for good after the Crimea crisis. Yet the Alliance has been reluctant to acknowledge this explicitly. One of the leading voices arguing for a change in policy has been Henry Kissinger. In a series of interviews with *The Atlantic* on the eve of the election, the former secretary of state rejected Obama's policy of isolating Russia and dismissed calls from some Democrats and Neocon Republicans for a military solution to the stalemate over Ukraine. 'Russia is a vast country undergoing a great domestic trauma of defining what it is,' said Kissinger.[1] 'Military transgressions need to be resisted. But Russia needs a sense that it remains significant.'

The status of Ukraine was key to this: attempting to incorporate the country into NATO, which would shift the Alliance's eastern border just 300 miles from Moscow, would be an unnecessary provocation, Kissinger argued. Yet, by the same token, fixing a Russian security border along the western side of Ukraine would be intolerable to Poland, Slovakia and Hungary with their recent memories of Soviet occupation. Kissinger believed Ukraine should instead be turned into a bridge between East and West, much like Finland or Austria during the Cold War, 'free to conduct its own economic and political rela- tionships, including with both Europe and Russia, but not party to any military or security alliance'.

Lest it be interpreted by Moscow as capitulation, such a policy should be combined with a reinforced commitment to the defence of NATO's most recent Eastern members. Like other members of the Alliance, they are covered by Article 5 of the Washington Treaty on collective defence. Yet the decision to take in the former Warsaw Pact countries, starting in 1999, was primarily a political one, which was not matched by the necessary deployment of troops. Sending extra forces to Poland and the Baltic states, as agreed at NATO's Warsaw summit in July 2016, was a step in the right direction, even if there is a danger that the Alliance could still be wrong-footed by a limited Russian intervention in Estonia or Latvia.

This should be coupled with a vigilance towards Russia's other attempts to divide the West and disrupt the established order, both in Europe and in the United States, countering the various attempts at cyber warfare and its propaganda efforts that pollute the information space. There should be attempts to engage with the Russian people, too, even though this has been made more difficult by the Kremlin's clampdown on NGOs, which it characterises as agents of foreign governments. The widespread suspicion of the West and its values now felt by many Russians is an alarming phenomenon that did not exist in communist days, despite the heavy-handed efforts of the Soviet propaganda machine. Efforts should be taken to counter this by encouraging more personal contact, especially within the younger generation.

Given Trump's intention to reach out to Putin, the personal chemistry that develops between the two men will be crucial. Trump's aides predicted he would be happy to flatter Putin's ego by returning to the high-profile summits of past years that had allowed Russia to present itself as America's equal on the world stage. Although they had never met before the election, there was speculation that Putin might come to achieve the same rapport with Trump that he once enjoyed with Berlusconi, another flamboyant showman and businessman turned political leader. When Obama expelled 35 Russian diplomats over cyber hacking in December, Putin did not respond, prompting Trump to describe him as 'very smart'. Mutual flattery can only go so far, however, and it remains to be seen whether such a rapport would survive the inevitable policy differences between Russia and America. Putin's tendency to see foreign policy as a zero sum game and his insistence on dominating any international organisation of which he is a member inevitably complicates relations with the West. For his part, Trump is equally determined to appear a strong leader, which would reduce the scope for him to negotiate any deal that smacks of giving ground.

The extent of Trump's willingness to adopt a new policy towards Russia will also be shaped by those around him. His choices to fill the top jobs in his administration reinforced expectations of a change of course. One of the first to be named, Retired Army Lieutenant General Michael Flynn, Trump's national security advisor, appears to share his boss's enthusiasm for Putin – and was criticised for sitting next to the Russian leader at an event in Moscow. Even more intriguing was Trump's pick for secretary of state. After toying with a number of candidates including Mitt Romney, who had been hawkish on Russia during his failed presidential bid in 2012, Trump finally opted for Rex Tillerson, a veteran Texan oilman who headed ExxonMobil. Tillerson's career had brought him into frequent contact with Putin since their first meeting on the Russian Pacific island of Sakhalin in 1999, when

Exxon had struck a deal with Rosneft. In 2013, Putin awarded him Russia's Order of Friendship medal; photographs that circulated in the media showed the two men drinking champagne. Tillerson was also close to Igor Sechin, the head of Rosneft, one of the most powerful members of Putin's entourage. Not surprisingly, Tillerson was a vocal critic of the sanctions imposed on Russia after the seizure of Ukraine, saying they cost his company hundreds of millions of dollars and prevented its participation in key projects including a deal with Rosneft to explore and pump oil in Siberia. After four decades at Exxon, during which time he had accumulated an estimated $245 million of shares in the company, Tillerson would be open to accusations of conflict of interest in his new job. With even some Republican senators such as Marco Rubio and John McCain critical of him, a tough confirmation hearing seemed assured.

This did not necessarily make Tillerson a soft touch as far as Russia was concerned. His backers pointed to his skills as a tough negotiator, which he could now deploy to advance America's interests rather than Exxon's. Other factors mitigated against a sudden transformation of Russia from foe to friend. Many of America's top generals have made clear that they see Russia, rather than Islamist terrorism, as the principal threat to their country. Vice President Mike Pence, who took charge of Trump's transition team after the election and was expected to play a powerful role in the administration, also appeared suspicious of the Kremlin's intentions. During the vice-presidential debate he referred twice to Putin as 'the small and bullying leader of Russia' and derided his 'crony, corrupt capitalist system' as inferior to the American political system.

Either way, Putin and Trump appear destined to share the world stage for some time to come. The Russian leader is expected to stand for – and win – another term in 2018, ensuring a further six years in office. By that time he will be seventy-one – just a year older than Trump was when he was elected – and may find another way of bending the rules to stand again. He has the means to do so, since the parliamentary majority won by United Russia in the September 2016 election gave it enough votes to change the constitution. A change in American policy could nevertheless answer one of the fundamental questions about US–Russian relations over the past twenty-five years: will a more conciliatory stance by Washington usher in a new era of cooperation between the two erstwhile Cold War rivals or instead be seized upon and exploited by the Kremlin as a sign of weakness?

So, who did lose Russia? The failure of Russia and the West to find a *modus vivendi* has its roots in the inability of both sides to agree on what happened in 1991 and a tendency to conflate the end of the Cold War, the collapse of communism and the break-up of the Soviet Union. The world we have inherited – and, in particular, Russian resentment at being treated as a vanquished foe – stems from this disagreement. Western actions such as the bombing of Yugoslavia, NATO's enlargement to the East and the US-led attacks on Iraq and Afghanistan have also played their part in poisoning relations. So too did memories of the poverty and economic chaos of the 1990s, which were portrayed by critics as the result of the neoliberalism forced on Russia by the West.

A decade on, the war against Saddam has few defenders, while questions can be asked about the manner and intensity of the bombing of Yugoslavia. The expansion of NATO is not so clear cut: if the Soviet Union's former satellites, seeing Russia's weakness in the 1990s, saw a historic opportunity to tie their future to the West rather than to the East, then why should their desire have been subjected to a Kremlin veto? Yet George W. Bush's attempt to extend the alliance to Georgia and Ukraine was a step too far and an unnecessary provocation – and also represented a commitment the Alliance would struggle to honour in the case of a Russian attack. The European Commission's attempt to force Viktor Yanukovych, the Ukrainian leader, to choose between Russia and Europe, proved the final straw.

Yet Putin himself bears much of the responsibility for his country's isolation with his fear of Western plots and desire for respect, which in Russian eyes so often translates into a desire to be feared. The form of exceptionalism he has promoted since returning to power in 2012 is merely the latest manifestation of what Russians have long seen as their special mission, depicting their country variously over the years as the Third Rome, a centre of world communism and now the heart of Eurasia. Putin has used it a way to keep himself in power, bolstering his own reign by transforming the last vestiges of the naïve, euphoric pro-Western sentiment that followed the end of the Cold War into today's popular anti-Americanism. In the process, he has come to appreciate that waging war, first against Chechnya, and then in Ukraine and Syria can do wonders for his ratings.

If anyone is responsible for losing Russia, then it is Putin. It would be wrong, though, to characterise the East–West tensions of the past decade as a 'Putin problem' that will disappear when he eventually leaves the Kremlin. Looking back another quarter of a century from now, it will likely be the pro-Western Russia of the Yeltsin years that is seen as the aberration and the assertive, self-assured Putin era that is the norm.

The final word belongs with George Kennan who, in his 'Long Telegram' from Moscow and an anonymous article for *Foreign Affairs* in 1946, is credited with the devising concept of containment, which underpinned US policy towards the Soviet Union for several decades. In an article in 1951 in *Foreign Affairs*, this time written under his own name, Kennan pondered what might eventually follow the Soviet regime, which, he noted presciently, 'like the capitalist world of its conception, bears within it the seeds of its own decay'. It was foolish, he argued, to expect the emergence of an American-style liberal democratic system in Russia or to believe that 'doctrinaire and impatient well-wishers in the West' would help to produce there 'in short order a replica of the Western democratic dream'.

'Of one thing we may be sure: no great and enduring change in the spirit and practice of government in Russia will ever come about primarily through foreign inspiration or advice,' Kennan added. 'To be genuine, to be enduring and to be worth the hopeful welcome of other peoples such a change would have to flow from the initiatives and efforts of the Russians themselves.'

Acknowledgements

THIS BOOK WAS PROMPTED BY VLADIMIR PUTIN'S annexation of Crimea in 2014, the war in Eastern Ukraine and the geopolitical crisis that followed. As the world wondered what had happened – and why – I decided to attempt an explanation by going back to my experiences in Russia a quarter of a century ago.

I am grateful to Andrew Nurnberg, of Andrew Nurnberg Associates, for working through the initial idea with me and to his colleague, Charlotte Seymour, for taking it on from there. Alex Christofi of Oneworld has been an excellent editor and demonstrated exemplary patience during my multiple attempts to refine and update the text – before finally convincing me it really was time to let go. Jenny Page continued Alex's great work.

I owe special thanks to Mark Franchetti, the veteran Moscow correspondent of *The Sunday Times*, who dipped into his impressive contacts book to set up a number of fascinating meetings in Moscow. I am grateful to all those in Russia and elsewhere who shared their thoughts or memories with me, either on or off the record. Natia Seskuria very efficiently transcribed and translated my interviews.

Last, but certainly not least, I want to commend Julia Dräger on her patience. She has lived with the book over the past year and could be forgiven for wondering in the final weeks whether it was ever going to be finished. It is now.

Notes

PART I: THE TIME OF TROUBLES

CHAPTER 1: THE TIES THAT BIND

1. Yuri Slezkine, 'The USSR as a Communal Apartment, or How a Socialist State Promoted Ethnic Particularism', *Slavic Review*, vol. 53, no. 2 (summer 1994), p. 443.

2. I. Vareikis and I. Zelenskii, *NatsionalPno-gosudarstvennoe razmezhevanie Srednei Azii* (Tashkent: Sredne-Aziatskoe gosudarstvennoe izdatel'stvo, 1924), p. 59.

3. Slezkine, 'The USSR as a Communal Apartment', p. 443.

4. George Bush and Brent Scowcroft, *A World Transformed* (New York: Knopf, 1998), p. 502.

5. Ibid., p. 513.

6. Serhii Plokhy, *The Last Empire: The Final Days of the Soviet Union* (London: Oneworld Publications, 2014), pp. 47–8.

7. Ibid., p. 49.

8. Peters, Gerhard and Woolley, John T. (1991, August 1). *The American Presidency Project*. 'Remarks to the Supreme Soviet of the Republic of the Ukraine in Kiev, Soviet Union', George Bush. [Online]. (URL http://www.presidency.ucsb.edu/ws/?pid=19864). (Accessed 26 September 2016).

9. Memorandum of conversation, 1 August 1991. Bush Presidential Records, George Bush Presidential Library. [Online]. (URL https://bush41library.tamu.edu/files/memcons-telcons/1991-08-01--Kravchuk.pdf). (Accessed 9 October 2016).

10. 'Bush's Slap in Kiev Talk Enrages Rebel Republics', *Chicago Sun-Times*, 14 August 1991.

11. William Safire, 'Essay; After the Fall', *New York Times*, 29 August 1991.

12. Alexander Solzhenitsyn, *Rebuilding Russia* (New York: Farrar, Straus & Giroux, 1991), p. 17.

13. Jack F. Matlock in Dick Combs, *Inside the Soviet Alternate Universe* (Pennsylvania: Pennsylvania State University Press, 2008), p. ix.

14. Ibid.

CHAPTER 2: THE BOYS IN PINK TROUSERS

1. Interview with author, January 2016.

2. *Pravda*, 2 September 1950.

3. Frederick A. Barghoorn, *The Soviet Image of the United States* (New York: Harcourt, Brace & Co., 1950), p. 277.

4. Peter H. Juviler and Henry W. Morton, eds, *Soviet Policy-Making* (New York: Praeger, 1967), p. 17.

5. Sachs, Jeffrey. (2012, March 14). 'What I Did in Russia'. [Online]. (URL http://jeffsachs.org/2012/03/what-i-did-in-russia/). (Accessed 26 September 2016).

CHAPTER 3: IN SEARCH OF A NEW MARSHALL PLAN

1. Craig R. Whitney, 'Russians Sniff at Beef, Miffing British Donors', *New York Times*, 7 January 1992.

2. Sylvia Nasar, 'How to Aid Russians is Debated', *New York Times*, 20 January 1992.

3. Sachs, Jeffrey. (2012, March 14). 'What I Did in Russia'. [Online]. (URL http://jeffsachs.org/2012/03/what-i-did-in-russia/). (Accessed 26 September 2016).

4. William Safire, 'Clinton Wins First Round in Bout with Bush,' *New York Times*, 3 April 1992.

5. Thomas L. Friedman, 'Diplomatic Notebook; The Odd Art of Summitry Without a Cold War', *New York Times*, 14 June 1992.

6. Full text. (1992, August 14). [Online]. (URL www.nytimes.com/1992/08/14/us/the-1992-campaign-excerpts-from-clinton-s-speech-on-foreign-policy-leadership.html?pagewanted=all). (Accessed 17 October 2016).

7. David Remnick, 'A Very Big Delusion', *The New Yorker*, 2 November 1992.

8. Klebnikov, Paul (2002). 'Theft of the Century, Privatization and the Looting of Russia'. [Online]. (URL http://multinationalmonitor.org/mm2002/02jan-feb/jan-feb02interviewklebniko.html). *The Multinational Monitor*, 23 (1 and 2). (Accessed 26 September 2016).

9. Quoted in Rodric Braithwaite, *Across the Moscow River: The World Turned Upside Down* (London: Yale University Press, 2002), p. 315.

CHAPTER 4: STOCKHOLM SYNDROME

1. Bill Clinton, *My Life* (New York: Alfred A. Knopf, 2004), p. 502.

2. Serhii Plokhy, *The Last Empire: The Final Days of the Soviet Union* (London: Oneworld Publications, 2014), p. 112.

3. Clinton, *My Life*, p. 504.

4. Strobe Talbott, *The Russia Hand: A Memoir of Presidential Diplomacy* (New York: Random House, 2002), p. 42.

5. Ibid.

6. Clinton, *My Life*, p. 504.

7. Ibid., p. 505.

8. Talbott, *The Russia Hand*, p. 63.

9. Ibid., p. 64.

10. Ibid.

11. Ibid., pp. 64–5.

12. Clinton, *My Life*, p. 508.

13. Talbott, *The Russia Hand*, p. 79.

14. Ibid., p. 80.

15. Fiona Hill and Pamela Jewett, *Back in the USSR: Russia's Intervention in the Internal Affairs of the Former Soviet Republics and the Implications for United States Policy Toward Russia* (Cambridge, Mass.: Harvard University, John F. Kennedy School of Government, 1994), p. 5.

16. Ibid., p. 1.

17. Ibid., p. 6.

18. Ibid., p. 7.

19. Ibid.

20. Serhii Plokhy, *The Gates of Europe: A History of Ukraine* (London: Allen Lane, 2015) p. 324.

21. Quoted in Hill and Jewett, *Back in the USSR*, p. 87.

22. Talbott, *The Russia Hand*, p. 150.

CHAPTER 5: EASTWARD BOUND

1. SaArchive (1989, 23 September). (National Security Archive). Cold War: Margaret Thatcher conversation with Mikhail Gorbachev (extract from Soviet memcon in Gorbachev Archive) ['Britain & Western Europe are not interested in the unification of Germany']. [Online]. (URL http://www.margaretthatcher.org/archive/displaydocument.asp?docid=112005). (Accessed 26 September 2016).

2. Condoleezza Rice, 'I Preferred to See it as an Acquisition', *Spiegel Online*, 29 September 2010. Retrieved from http://www.spiegel.de/international/world/condoleezza-rice-on-german-reunification-i-preferred-to-see-it-as-an-acquisition-a-719444.html. (Accessed 26 September 2016).

3. *Time* magazine, 30 May 1990.

4. Joanna A. Gorska, *Dealing with a Juggernaut: Analyzing Poland's Policy Toward Russia, 1989–2009* (New York: Lexington Books, 2010), p. 56.

5. Andrzej Drawicz, quoted in Gorska, *Dealing with a Juggernaut*, p. 70.

6. Craig R. Whitney, 'NATO, Victim of Success, Searches for New Strategy', *New York Times*, 26 October 1991.

7. Strobe Talbott, *The Russia Hand: A Memoir of Presidential Diplomacy* (New York: Random House, 2002), p. 98.

8. Madeleine Albright, *Madam Secretary: A Memoir* (London: Miramax Books, 2003), p. 166.

9. Unnamed official quoted in Ted Galen Carpenter, *The Future of NATO (Strategic Studies)*, (Oxford: Routledge, 1995), p. 9.

10. Talbott, *The Russia Hand*, p. 101.

11. Ronald D. Asmus, Richard L. Kugler and Stephen Larrabee, 'Building a New Nato', *Foreign Affairs*, September/October 1993.

12. Pushkov, Alexei (1994). 'Russia and the West: An Endangered Relationship?'. [Online]. (URL http://www.nato.int/docu/review/1994/9401-5.htm). *NATO Review*, 42 (1), pp. 19–23. (Accessed 26 September 2016).

13. Henry Kissinger, 'Not this Partnership', *Washington Post*, 23 November 1993.

14. Albright, *Madam Secretary*, p. 169.

15. Partnership for Peace: Invitation Document. (1994, January 10). [Online]. (URL http://www.nato.int/cps/en/natolive/official_texts_24468.htm). (Accessed 26 September 2016).

CHAPTER 6: BILL AND OL' BORIS

1. Padma Desai, *Conversations on Russia: Reform from Yeltsin to Putin* (New York: Oxford University Press Inc., 2006), p. 81.

2. Michael Specter, 'In Election, Russian Communist Starts to Sound Like a Communist', *New York Times*, 13 December 1995.

3. Craig R. Whitney, 'Soothing Tone by Russian Communist at Business Forum', *New York Times*, 5 February 1996.

4. Interview with author, October 2016.

5. Telephone call between Blair and Clinton, 29 May 1997. [Online]. (URL http://clinton.presidentiallibraries.us/files/original/5aa-4876f138a60330e869d23b372880d.pdf). (Accessed 26 September 2016).

6. Strobe Talbott, *The Russia Hand: A Memoir of Presidential Diplomacy* (New York: Random House, 2002), p. 201.

7. Ibid., p. 204.

8. Boris Yeltsin, *Prezidentskii Marafon* (Moscow: Rosspen, 2008), p. 35.

9. Interview with author, January 2016.

10. Interview with author, January 2016.

11. Bill Browder, *Red Notice* (London: Bantam Press, 2015), p. 87.

12. Treisman, Daniel (2010, March). '"Loans for Shares" Revisited', working paper 15819. [Online]. (URL http://www.nber.org/papers/w15819.pdf). National Bureau of Economic Research. (Accessed 26 September 2016).

13. Desai, *Conversations on Russia*, p. 82.

14. Tatiana Zhurzhenko and Ivan Krastev, 'Gleb Pavlovsky: The Final Act', *Open Democracy*, 15 May 2011.

15. Chrystia Freeland, John Thornhill and Andrew Gowers, 'Moscow's Group of Seven', *Financial Times*, 1 November 1996.

CHAPTER 7: A FATAL ERROR?

1. Katharine Q. Seelye, 'Arms Contractors Spend to Promote an Expanded NATO', *New York Times*, 30 March 1998.

2. Interview with author, March 2016.

3. Quoted in James Goldgeier and Michael McFaul, *Power and Purpose: US Policy toward Russia after the Cold War* (Washington, DC: Brookings Institution Press, 2003), pp. 204–5.

4. Henry Kissinger, 'U.S. Must Embrace the Expansion of NATO', *Los Angeles Times*, 12 January 1997.

5. Susan Eisenhower, 'Russia and the Cold-War Warhorses', *Washington Post*, 20 March 1997.

6. 'Fateful error – A Sage Speaks on Nato Expansion – Americans Should Listen', *The Times*, 7 February 1997.

7. Strobe Talbott, *The Russia Hand: A Memoir of Presidential Diplomacy* (New York: Random House, 2002), p. 232.

8. Anatole Kaletsky and Michael Evans, 'Nato Expansion would be "Biggest Error in 50 Years"', *The Times*, 4 February 1997.

9. Talbott, *The Russia Hand*, p. 232.

10. Ibid., p. 233.

11. Madeleine Albright, *Madam Secretary: A Memoir* (London: Miramax Books, 2003), p. 256.

12. Talbott, *The Russia Hand*, p. 237.

13. Ibid.

14. Bill Clinton, *My Life* (New York: Alfred A. Knopf, 2004), p. 750.

15. Telephone call between Blair and Clinton, 19 April 2000. [Online]. (URL http://clinton.presidentiallibraries.us/files/original/5aa-4876f138a60330e869d23b372880d.pdf). (Accessed 26 September 2016).

16. Talbott, *The Russia Hand*, p. 241.

17. James Rubin, 'Reassuring Eastern Europe', *New York Times*, 11 June 2014.

18. Telephone call between Blair and Clinton, 29 May 1997. [Online]. (URL http://clinton.presidentiallibraries.us/files/original/5aa-4876f138a60330e869d23b372880d.pdf). (Accessed 26 September 2016).

19. Telephone call between Blair and Clinton, 27 August 1998. [Online]. (URL http://clinton.presidentiallibraries.us/files/original/5aa4876f138a6033 oe869d23b372880d.pdf). (Accessed 26 September 2016).

20. Talbott, *The Russia Hand*, p. 286.

21. Ibid., p. 288.

22. Thomas L. Friedman, 'Foreign Affairs; Now a Word From X', *New York Times*, 2 May 1998.

23. Jane Perlez, 'Expanding Alliance: The Overview; Poland, Hungary and the Czechs Join NATO', *New York Times*, 13 March 1999.

24. Tyler Marshall, 'U.S. Gives NATO's 3 Newest Members Official Welcome', *Los Angeles Times*, 13 March 1999.

25. Braithwaite, Roderic (2016, July 7). 'NATO Enlargement: Assurances and Misunderstandings'. [Online]. (URL http://www.ecfr.eu/article/commentary_nato_enlargement_assurances_and_misunderstandings). (Accessed 19 October 2016).

26. Interview with Eduard Shevardnadze: 'We Couldn't Believe that the Warsaw Pact Could Be Dissolved', *Spiegel Online*, 26 November 2009. Retrieved from http://www.spiegel.de/international/europe/interview-with-eduard-shevardnadze -we-couldn-t-believe-that-the-warsaw-pact-could-be-dissolved-a-663595-2.html. (Accessed 26 September 2016).

27. Mikhail Gorbachev, *The New Russia* (Cambridge: Polity Press, 2016), p. 308.

CHAPTER 8: KOSOVO

1. Mike Jackson, *Soldier: The Autobiography* (London: Bantam Press), p. 333.

2. Richard Holbrooke, *To End a War* (New York: Modern Library, 1999), p. 117.

3. Strobe Talbott, *The Russia Hand: A Memoir of Presidential Diplomacy* (New York: Random House, 2002), p. 76.

4. Steven Erlanger, 'Albright Warns Serbs on Kosovo Violence', *New York Times*, 8 March 1998.

5. Madeleine Albright, *Madam Secretary: A Memoir* (London: Miramax Books, 2003), p. 384.

6. Louis Sell, *Slobodan Milošević and the Destruction of Yugoslavia* (Durham, NC: Duke University Press, 2002) p. 299.

7. Boris Yeltsin, *Midnight Diaries* (London: Weidenfeld & Nicolson, 2000), p. 258.

8. Robyn Dixon, 'Gunman Rakes U.S. Embassy in Moscow', *Los Angeles Times*, 29 March 1999.

9. Yeltsin, *Midnight Diaries*, p. 263.

10. Interview with author, January 2016.

11. Charles Gati, 'Weimar Russia', *Washington Post*, 17 March 1995.

12. Lilia Shevtsova, *Lonely Power: Russia's Uneasy Relationship with the West* (Washington, DC: Brookings Institution Press, 2010), p. 14.

13. Rodric Braithwaite, *Across the Moscow River: The World Turned Upside Down* (London: Yale University Press, 2002), p. 315.

14. Garry Kasparov, *Winter is Coming: Why Vladimir Putin and the Enemies of the Free World Must Be Stopped* (London: Atlantic Books, 2015), p. xi.

15. Charles Gati, 'Weimar Russia, 1995–2015', *The American Interest*, 29 June 2015.

16. Walter Laqueur, *Putinism: Russia and Its Future with the West* (New York: Thomas Dunne Books, 2015), p. 201.

PART II: REBIRTH

CHAPTER 9: A NEW START

1. Yeltsin's resignation speech. (1999, December 31). [Online]. (URL http://news.bbc.co.uk/1/hi/world/monitoring/584845.stm). (Accessed 30 September 2016).

2. Eric Schmitt, 'Yeltsin Resigns: In Washington; Power Shift is not Viewed as a Threat to U.S. Ties', *New York Times*, 1 January 2000.

3. Bill Clinton, *My Life* (New York: Alfred A. Knopf, 2004), p. 882.

4. Vladimir Putin and Nataliya Gevorkyan, *First Person: An Astonishingly Frank Self-portrait by Russia's President Vladimir Putin* (New York: PublicAffairs, 2000), p. 70.

5. Bowlby, Chris (2015, 27 March). 'Vladimir Putin's Formative German Years'. [Online]. (URL http://www.bbc.co.uk/news/magazine-32066222). (Accessed 30 September 2016).

6. Ibid.

7. German History in Documents and Images, 'Helmut Kohl's Welcome in Dresden, 19 December 1989' (taken from Helmut Kohl, *Recollections, 1982–1990* (Munich: Droemer Knaur, 2005), pp. 1020–8). [Online]. (URL http://germanhistorydocs.ghi-dc.org/sub_document.cfm?document_id=2889). (Accessed 30 September 2016).

8. Putin and Gevorkyan, *First Person*, p. 80.

9. Padma Desai, *Conversations on Russia: Reform from Yeltsin to Putin* (New York: Oxford University Press Inc., 2006), p. 82.

10. Boris Yeltsin, *Midnight Diaries* (London: Weidenfeld & Nicolson, 2000), p. 213.

11. Desai, *Conversations on Russia*, p. 84.

12. Strobe Talbott, *The Russia Hand: A Memoir of Presidential Diplomacy* (New York: Random House, 2002), p. 355.

13. Interview with author, January 2016.

14. Talbott, *The Russia Hand*, p. 356.

15. Putin and Gevorkyan, *First Person*, pp. 143–4.

16. Sergei Kovalev, 'Putin's War', *New York Review of Books*, 10 February 2000.

17. Steven Lee Myers, *The New Tsar: The Rise and Reign of Vladimir Putin* (London: Simon & Schuster, 2015) p. 163.

18. Interview with author, January 2016.

19. Yeltsin, *Midnight Diaries*, p. 6.

20. Talbott, *The Russia Hand*, p. 367.

21. Yeltsin, *Midnight Diaries*, p. 7.

22. Ibid., p. 8.

23. Talbott, *The Russia Hand*, p. 7.

24. Interview with author, January 2016.

25. Interview with author, January 2016.

26. Interview with author, October 2016.

27. Clinton, *My Life*, p. 869.

28. Jonathan Powell, *The New Machiavelli, How to Wield Power in the Modern World* (London: Bodley Head, 2010, p. 289)

29. Telephone call between Blair and Clinton, 8 February 2000. [Online]. (URL http://clinton.presidentiallibraries.us/files/original/5aa4876f138a6033 0e869d23b372880d.pdf). (Accessed 30 September 2016).

30. Paul Lettow, *Ronald Reagan and His Quest to Abolish Nuclear Weapons* (New York: Random House, 2005), p. 21.

31. Interview with author, January 2016.

32. Talbott, *The Russia Hand*, p. 4.

33. Ibid., p. 5.

34. Ibid., p. 6.

35. Ibid., p. 7.

36. Ibid., p. 8.

37. Telephone call between Blair and Clinton, 23 November 2000. [Online]. (URL http://clinton.presidentiallibraries.us/files/original/5aa4876f138a6033 0e869d23b372880d.pdf). (Accessed 30 September 2016).

38. J. L. Black, *Vladimir Putin and the New World Order: Looking East, Looking West?* (New York: Rowman & Littlefield, 2004), p. 103.

39. Interview with author, January 2016.

CHAPTER 10: A SENSE OF PUTIN'S SOUL

1. Quoted in Tucker Carlson, 'Devil May Care', *Talk Magazine*, September 1999, p. 108.

2. Quoted in Jacob Heilbrunn, 'Condoleezza Rice: George W.'s Realist', *World Policy Journal*, 16, 1999/2000, p. 51.

3. Condoleezza Rice, *No Higher Honor: A Memoir of My Years in Washington* (New York: Random House, 2011) p. 3.

4. Elaine Sciolino, 'The 43rd President: Woman in the News; Compulsion to Achieve – Condoleezza Rice', *New York Times*, 18 December 2000.

5. (2000, 9 August). 'Bush Senior Policy Adviser Condoleezza Rice'. [Online]. (URL http://www.washingtonpost.com/wp-srv/liveonline/oo/politics/freemedia 080900_rice.htm). (Accessed 30 September 2016).

6. Ivo H. Daalder and James M. Lindsay, *America Unbound: The Bush Revolution in Foreign Policy* (Washington, DC: Brookings Institution Press, 2003) pp. 12–13.

7. Gerald F. Seib, 'Note to Allies: There is a Method to Bush Policies', *Wall Street Journal*, 9 May 2001.

8. Interview with author, March 2016.

9. Angela Stent, *The Limits of Partnership: U.S.-Russian Relations in the Twenty-First Century* (Princeton, NJ: Princeton University Press, 2014), p. 59.

10. *Le Figaro*, 10 February 2001.

11. James Risen and Jane Perlez, 'Russian Diplomats Ordered Expelled in a Countermove', *New York Times*, 22 March 2001.

12. (2001, 1 May). Bush's speech to National Defense University, Washington. [Online]. (URL http://fas.org/nuke/control/abmt/news/010501bush.html). (Accessed 30 September 2016).

13. Interview with author, October 2016.

14. Karen Hughes, *Ten Minutes from Normal* (New York: Viking, 2004), p. 218.

15. George W. Bush, *Decision Points* (New York: Random House, 2010), p. 196.

16. Hughes, *Ten Minutes from Normal*, p. 219.

17. Interview with author, March 2016.

18. Robert Draper, *Dead Certain: The Presidency of George W. Bush* (New York: Simon & Schuster, 2007) p. 133.

19. Jane Perlez, 'Cordial Rivals: How Bush and Putin Became Friends', *New York Times*, 18 June 2001.

20. Rice, *No Higher Honor*, p. 63.

CHAPTER 11: FROM 9/11 TO IRAQ

1. Peter Baker and Susan Glasser, *Kremlin Rising: Vladimir Putin's Russia and the End of Revolution* (New York: Simon & Schuster, 2005), p. 122.

2. Condoleezza Rice, *No Higher Honor: A Memoir of My Years in Washington* (New York: Random House, 2011), p. 75.

3. George W. Bush, *Decision Points* (New York: Random House, 2010), p. 196.

4. Baker and Glasser, *Kremlin Rising*, p. 122.

5. Ibid., p. 122, note 5.

6. Bush, *Decision Points*, p. 197.

7. Interview with author, January 2016.

8. Interview with author, January 2016.

9. John Bolton, *Surrender is Not an Option: Defending America at the United Nations* (New York: Simon & Schuster, 2007), p. 74.

10. David E. Singer and Michael Wines, 'Bush and Putin Sign Pact for Steep Nuclear Arms Cuts', *New York Times*, 24 May 2002.

11. Interview with author, January 2016.

12. *Diane Rehm Show*, 27 March 2014.

13. Interview with author, October 2016.

14. Interview with author, (3 Nov 2016)

15. John Tagliabue, 'Rome Journal: A Faux Treaty Room, with Missiles', *New York Times*, 27 May 2002.

16. Anders Fogh Rasmussen, *The Will to Lead: America's Indispensable Role in the Global Fight for Freedom* (New York: HarperCollins Publishers, 2016), p. 175.

17. Lord Robertson (2003, 23 January, updated). 'A New Russian Revolution: Partnership with NATO'. [Online]. (URL http://www.nato.int/docu/speech/2002/s021213a.htm). (Accessed 30 September 2016).

18. Alan Friedman, 'Silvio Berlusconi and Vladimir Putin: The Odd Couple', *Financial Times*, 2 October 2015.

19. Interview with author, October 2016.

20. Interview with author, March 2016.

21. Friedman, 'Silvio Berlusconi and Vladimir Putin: The Odd Couple'.

22. Angela Stent, *The Limits of Partnership: U.S.-Russian Relations in the Twenty-First Century* (Princeton, NJ: Princeton University Press, 2014), p. 77.

23. George W. Bush, 'The Enlargement of NATO is Good for All Who Join Us', *New York Times*, 21 November 2002. Retrieved from http://www.nytimes.com/2002/11/21/world/threats-responses-bush-s-words-enlargement-nato-good-for-all-who-join-us.html. (Accessed 30 September 2016).

24. Elisabeth Bumiller and Patrick E. Tyler, 'Threats and Responses: The President; Putin Questions U.S. Terror Allies', *New York Times*, 23 November 2002.

25. Interview with author, October 2016.

26. Reuters, 18 November 2002.

CHAPTER 12: MISSION ACCOMPLISHED

1. Jean Edward Smith, *Bush* (New York: Simon & Schuster, 2016), p. 234.

2. Richard Clarke, *Against All Enemies: Inside America's War on Terror* (London: Simon & Schuster, 2004), pp. 30–1.

3. Smith, *Bush*, p. 233.

4. George W. Bush, *Decision Points* (New York: Random House, 2010), p. 234.

5. Peter Baker and Susan Glasser, *Kremlin Rising: Vladimir Putin's Russia and the End of Revolution* (New York: Simon & Schuster, 2005), p. 202.

6. (2003, 10 February). 'Joint Declaration on Iraq: Text'. [Online]. (URL http://news.bbc.co.uk/1/hi/world/europe/2746885.stm). (Accessed 30 September 2016).

7. Interview with author, January 2016.

8. Bob Woodward, *Plan of Attack* (London: Simon & Schuster, 2004), p. 404.

9. Bush, *Decision Points*, p. 256.

10. Ibid., p. 257.

11. Interview with author, January 2016.

12. Jonathan Steele, 'Angry Putin Rejects Public Beslan Inquiry', *Guardian*, 7 September 2004.

13. (2004, September). [Online]. (URL http://georgewbush-whitehouse. archives.gov/news/releases/2004/09/images/20040913-2_p42987-08a-515h. html). (Accessed 30 September 2016).

14. Interview with author, March 2016.

CHAPTER 13: THE COLOUR REVOLUTIONS

1. Pavlovsky, interview with author, January 2016.

2. Alexander Solzhenitsyn, *Rebuilding Russia* (New York: Farrar, Straus & Giroux, 1991), p. 17.

3. Condoleezza Rice, *No Higher Honor: A Memoir of My Years in Washington* (New York: Random House, 2011), p. 355.

4. Angus Roxburgh, *The Strongman: Vladimir Putin and the Struggle for Russia* (London: I. B. Tauris, 2012), p. 130.

5. Interview with author, March 2016.

6. Roxburgh, *The Strongman*, p. 130.

7. Interview with author, January 2016.

8. Roxburgh, *The Strongman*, p. 133.

9. William Branigin, 'U.S. Rejects Tally, Warns Ukraine', *New York Times*, 25 November 2004.

10. Tatiana Zhurzhenko and Ivan Krastev, 'Gleb Pavlovsky: The Final Act', *Open Democracy*, 15 May 2011.

CHAPTER 14: MUNICH

1. Interview with author, January 2016.

2. Mike Eckel, 'Putin Calls Soviet Collapse a "Geopolitical Catastrophe",' Associated Press, 26 April 2005.

3. Masha Lipman, 'Putin's "Sovereign Democracy"', *Washington Post*, 15 July 2006.

4. Ibid.

5. Historical Crude Oil Prices. [Online]. (URL http://inflationdata.com/ Inflation /Inflation_Rate/Historical_Oil_Prices_Table.asp). (Accessed 30 September 2016).

6. Peter Baker, 'Russian Relations Under Scrutiny', *Washington Post*, 26 February 2006.

7. Ibid.

8. Angela Stent, *The Limits of Partnership: U.S. – Russian Relations in the Twenty-First Century* (Princeton, NJ: Princeton University Press, 2014), p. 137.

9. Dick Cheney and Liz Cheney, *In My Time: A Personal and Political Memoir* (New York: Simon & Schuster, 2011), p. 428.

10. Steven Lee Myers, 'Cheney Rebukes Russia on Rights', *New York Times*, 5 May 2006.

11. Peter Baker, 'Cheney Switches from Scowls to Smiles', *Washington Post*, 6 May 2006.

12. Philippe Naughton, 'Putin Takes Swipe at Hungry America's "Comrade Wolf"', *The Times*, 10 May 2006.

13. Nick Paton Walsh and Patrick Wintour, 'Putin: Don't Lecture Me about Democracy', *Observer*, 16 July 2006.

CHAPTER 15: THE TRAP

1. (2004, 3 February). [Online]. (URL https://wikileaks.org/plusd/ cables/04YEREVAN282_a.html). (Accessed 9 October 2016).

2. Angus Roxburgh, *The Strongman: Vladimir Putin and the Struggle for Russia* (London: I. B. Tauris, 2012), p. 115.

3. Ibid., p. 116.

4. (2006, 11 January). [Online]. (URL https://wikileaks.org/plusd/cables/06 ALMATY211_a.html). (Accessed 9 October 2016).

5. (2006, 26 January). [Online]. (URL https://wikileaks.org/plusd/cables/ 06MOSCOW789_a.html). (Accessed 9 October 2016).

6. (2006, 24 March). [Online]. (URL https://wikileaks.org/plusd/cables/ 06MOSCOW2974_a.html). (Accessed 9 October 2016).

7. Condoleezza Rice, *No Higher Honor: A Memoir of My Years in Washington* (New York: Random House, 2011), p. 668.

8. Ibid., p. 671.

9. Ibid.

10. Ibid., p. 672.

11. Ibid., p. 675.

12. Anders Fogh Rasmussen, *The Will to Lead: America's Indispensable Role*

in the Global Fight for Freedom (New York: HarperCollins Publishers, 2016), p. 180.

13. Ibid., p. 175.

14. George W. Bush, *Decision Points* (New York: Random House, 2010), p. 431.

15. Ibid.

16. Ibid., p. 433.

17. Ibid.

18. Roxburgh, *The Strongman*, p. 236.

19. Rice, *No Higher Honor*, p. 686.

20. Ibid.

21. Bush, *Decision Points*, p. 434.

22. Rice, *No Higher Honor*, p. 688.

23. Ibid.

24. Ibid., p. 689.

25. Ian Traynor in Brussels, Luke Harding in Tbilisi and Helen Womack in Moscow, 'Moscow Warns it Could Strike Poland over US Missile Shield', *Guardian*, 16 August 2008.

26. Angela Stent, *The Limits of Partnership: U.S.-Russian Relations in the Twenty-First Century* (Princeton, NJ: Princeton University Press, 2014), p. 173.

27. Mikhail Gorbachev, 'A Crisis Russia Did Not Want', *New York Times*, 21 August 2008.

28. Interview with author, January 2016.

29. Interview with author, January 2016.

PART III: THE HOT PEACE

CHAPTER 16: OVERLOAD

1. Mark Landler, *Alter Egos: Hillary Clinton, Barack Obama, and the Twilight Struggle over American Power* (London: W. H. Allen, 2016), p. 278.

2. William J. Broad and David E. Sanger, 'Obama's Youth Shaped his Nuclear-Free Vision', *New York Times*, 4 July 2009.

3. Barack Obama, *The Audacity of Hope: Thoughts on Reclaiming the American Dream* (New York: Random House, 2006) p. 312.

4. Ibid., p. 313.

5. David Remnick, 'Watching the Eclipse', *The New Yorker*, 11–18 August 2014.

6. Elisabeth Bumiller and Michael Falcone, 'Candidates' Reactions to Georgia Conflict Offer Hints at Style on Foreign Affairs', *New York Times*, 9 August 2008.

7. (2008, 26 September). 'The First Presidential Debate'. [Online]. (URL http://edition.cnn.com/TRANSCRIPTS/0809/26/se.01.html). (Accessed 3 October 2016).

8. *Putin, Russia and the West*, BBC2 documentary produced by Norma Percy, Part 4 (2012).

9. Landler, *Alter Egos*, p. 270.

10. Peter Baker, 'Obama Resets Ties to Russia, but Work Remains', *New York Times*, 7 July 2009.

11. Ibid.

12. Anders Fogh Rasmussen, *The Will to Lead: America's Indispensable Role in the Global Fight for Freedom* (New York: HarperCollins Publishers, 2016), p. 173.

13. Ibid., p. 174.

CHAPTER 17: SILICON VALLEY

1. Sergei N. Khrushchev, *Nikita Khrushchev and the Creation of a Superpower* (Pennsylvania: Pennsylvania State University Press, 2000), p. 334.

2. (2016, July). Quoted in 'From Russia with Money, Hillary Clinton, the Russian Reset, and Cronyism', Government Accountability Institute. [Online]. (URL http://www.g-a-i.org/u/2016/08/Report-Skolkvovo-08012016.pdf). (Accessed 3 October 2016).

3. Peter Schweizer, 'The Clinton Foundation, State and Kremlin Connections', *Wall Street Journal*, 31 July 2016.

4. *Putin, Russia and the West*, BBC2 documentary produced by Norma Percy, Part 4 (2012).

5. Tom Parfitt, 'Vladimir Putin Consoles Exposed Russian Spies with "Singalong"', *Guardian*, 25 July 2010.

6. (2011, 21 March). 'Statement by Dmitry Medvedev on the Situation in Libya'. [Online]. (URL http://en.kremlin.ru/events/president/news/10701). (Accessed 3 October 2016).

7. Len Barry, 'In Shift, Russia Agrees to Try to Talk Qaddafi into Leaving', *New York Times*, 27 May 2011.

8. Vladimir Ryzhkov, 'Why Putin Created All-Russia People's Front', *Moscow Times*, 11 May 2011.

9. Mark Franchetti, 'Putin in Face-Off with his Kremlin Protégé', *Sunday Times*, 22 May 2011.

CHAPTER 18: THE RETURN OF THE CHIEF

1. Ellen Barry, 'New U.S. Envoy Steps into Glare of a Russia Eager to Find Fault', *New York Times*, 23 January 2012.

2. Leon Aron, 'Putinology', *The American Interest*, col. 11 (1), 30 July 2015.

3. Anton Barbashin and Hannah Thoburn, 'Putin's Philosopher', *Foreign Affairs*, 20 September 2015.

4. Ivan Nechepurenko, 'The World's a Stage: What the Tannhäuser Scandal Reveals about Russia Today', *The Calvert Journal*, 29 April 2015.

5. Hillary Rodham Clinton, *Hard Choices: A Memoir* (London: Simon & Schuster, 2014), p. 209.

6. Ibid.

7. Helene Cooper, 'Face to Face, Obama Tries to Persuade Putin on Syria', *New York Times*, 18 June 2012.

8. (2012, 6 September). [Online]. (URL http://www.npr.org/2012/09/06/1607 13941/transcript-president-obamas-convention-speech). (Accessed 3 October 2016).

CHAPTER 19: UKRAINE

1. Askold Krushelnycky, 'Neverland Was Never This Vulgar', *Sunday Times*, 23 February 2014.

2. Interview with author, January 2016.

3. Interview with author, Moscow, January 2016.

4. Bojan Pancevski and Matthew Campbell, 'Dithering EU Sowed Seeds of Disaster by Sticking to the Rules', *Sunday Times*, 4 May 2014.

5. Henry Kissinger, 'To Settle the Ukraine Crisis Start at the End', *Washington Post*, 5 March 2014.

CHAPTER 20: A PIECE OF PARADISE

1. Roderic Lyne, 'Reading Russia, Rewiring the West', *Open Democracy*, 12 October 2008.

2. Daniel Treisman, 'Why Putin Took Crimea', *Foreign Affairs*, May/June 2016.

3. Interview with author, January 2016.

4. Bojan Pancevski, 'Putin's Anti-Gay Tirade Ends pas de deux with Merkel', *Sunday Times*, 30 November 2014.

5. Neil MacFarquhar, 'For Many, a Nation that Seems Less Free From Moscow's Dominance than Ever', *New York Times*, 22 September 2014.

6. Andrew E. Kramer, 'A Bleak Future in Eastern Ukraine's Frozen Zone', *New York Times*, 10 November 2015.

7. International Partnership for Human Rights, 'Where Did the Shells Come From?' June 2016.

CHAPTER 21: 'YOU DO IT TOO'

1. Benjamin Bidder, 'Paid as a Pro-Kremlin Troll: "The Hatred Spills over into the Real World"', *Spiegel Online*, 1 June 2015. Retrieved from http://www.spiegel.de/international/world/interview-with-ex-russian-internet-troll-lyudmila -savchuk-a-1036539.html. (Accessed 17 October 2016).

2. Interview with author, January 2016.

3. Roman Skaskiw, 'Nine Lessons of Russian Propaganda', *Small Wars Journal*, 27 March 2016.

4. Peter Pomerantsev, 'Why We're Post-Fact', *Granta*, 20 July, 2016. Retrieved from https://granta.com/why-were-post-fact/. (Accessed 19 October 2016).

5. Angus Roxburgh, *The Strongman: Vladimir Putin and the Struggle for Russia* (London: I. B. Tauris, 2012), p. 190.

6. Andrew Gilligan, 'Stop the War Linked to Putin Puppets', *The Times*, 16 October 2016.

7. Anne Applebaum, 'Authoritarianism's Fellow Travelers', *Slate*, 16 October 2015.

8. Valery Gerasimov, 'The Value of Science is in the Foresight: New Challenges Demand Rethinking the Forms and Methods of Carrying out Combat Operations', *Military-Industrial Courier*, 27 February 2013.

9. Orysia Lutsevych, 'Agents of the Russian World Proxy Groups in the Contested Neighbourhood', Chatham House, April 2016.

10. Melanie Amann and Pavel Lokshin, 'Moscow's Fifth Column: German Populists Forge Ties with Russia', *Spiegel Online*, 27 April 2016. Retrieved from http://www.spiegel.de/international/germany/german-populists-forge-deeper-ties-with-russia-a-1089562.html. (Accessed 17 October 2016).

11. Anne Applebaum and Edward Lucas, 'The Danger of Russian Disinformation', *Washington Post*, 6 May 2016.

12. Michael McFaul, 'How to Counter the Putin Playbook', *New York Times*, 30 July 2016.

CHAPTER 22: TOWARDS EURASIA

1. Maria Tsvetkova, 'Russia, Despite Draw Down, Shipping More to Syria than Removing', Reuters, 30 March 2016.

2. Andrew E. Kramer, 'Ukraine Struggles to Shake Off Legacy of Corruption', *New York Times*, 6 June 2016.

3. Interview with author, June 2016.

4. Shaun Walker, 'What Russia Thinks of Brexit – and How it Could Gain from a Fractured Europe', *Guardian*, 11 July 2016.

CHAPTER 23: THE SIBERIAN CANDIDATE

1. Aleksandr Minkin, 'Twenty-Five Years of Imprisonment', *Moskovsky Komsomolets*, 18 August 2016.

2. Mark Bennetts, 'Putin U-Turn on Celebration of KGB's Defeat', *The Times*, 19 August 2016.

3. Kara-Murza, Vladimir (2016). 'Russia's 2016 Election: Despair, Apathy – and Hope?' [Online]. (URL http://www.worldaffairsjournal.org/blog/vladimir-kara-murza/russia%E2%80%99s-2016-election-despair-apathy%E2%80%94and-hope). *World Affairs Journal*. (Accessed 26 September 2016).

4. Jeffrey Goldberg, 'Hillary Clinton: "Failure" to Help Syrian Rebels Led to the Rise of ISIS', *The Atlantic*, 10 August 2014.

5. Mary Jordan, 'Anxious about Trump? Try Being a Foreign Ambassador', *Washington Post*, 17 March 2016.

6. Michael Isikoff, 'U.S. Intel Officials Probe Ties Between Trump Adviser and Kremlin', *Yahoo News*, 23 September 2016. Retrieved from https://uk.news.yahoo.
com/u-s-intel-officials-probe-ties-between-trump-adviser-and-kremlin-175046002.html. (Accessed 17 October 2016).

7. Ross Douthat, 'Our Russia Problem', *New York Times*, 10 September 2016.

EPILOGUE

1. Jeffrey Goldberg, 'World Chaos and World Order: Conversations with Henry Kissinger', *The Atlantic*, 10 Nov, 2016.

Index

Abashidze, Aslan 188, 196
Abkhazia 13, 165, 187, 188, 189–90, 192, 193
   and independence 200
   and Russia 195
Abraham Lincoln, USS 155–6
Abramovich, Roman 25, 126, 329
Abromavičius, Aivaras 301
Adenauer, Konrad 102
adoption laws 241
advertising 28, 98
Afghanistan 24, 140, 141, 193, 203, 245
Ahtisaari, Martti 191
aid 31–5, 100–1, 167
Aksyonov, Sergey 263
Albania 89, 190
Albright, Madeleine 61, 65, 94, 95, 97
   and NATO 80, 82, 88, 123
Aliyev, Ilham 182
All-Russia People's Front 228
Alliance, *see* NATO
Alternative für Deutschland (AfD) 288–9, 305
Alyokhina, Maria 233
Ames, Aldrich 134
Andropov, Yuri 122
Anti-Ballistic Missile Treaty 122, 134, 142–3
Anti-Globalisation Movement of Russia (AGMR) 286
anti-Semitism 68
Apollo-Soyuz mission 23
Applebaum, Anne 286–7, 291
Aptekar, Pavel 309
Arab Spring 225–6, 234
Araud, Gérard 306
armed forces 50–1
Armenia 7, 9
Armitage, Richard 130
arms manufacturers 76–7
Aron, Leon 234–5
arts, the 237
Ashton, Catherine 253
Åslund, Anders 180, 181
Asmus, Ronald D. 62–3
Aspin, Les 61
al-Assad, Bashar xi, 238–9, 243–4, 245, 296–7, 298, 300
   and Clinton 315

   and Trump 337
Assange, Julian 292
Australia 153
Austria 16, 56, 289, 338
Avakov, Arsen 258, 263
Azerbaijan 7, 50, 182

Babich, Dmitry 310
Baker, James 33, 89, 90, 165
Balkans, the 61, 121
Baltic states, *see* Estonia; Latvia; Lithuania
Bandera, Stepan 250, 259
Barghoorn, Frederick 23
Barroso, José Manuel 252, 253
Basayev, Shamil 113, 114, 159
Belarus 3, 4, 6, 48, 184, 275
   and gas 158
   and independence 52
Belavezha 3–4, 14, 16, 18, 51, 251
Ben Ali, Zine El Abidine 226
Berezovsky, Boris 25, 72, 75, 324, 328–9
   and Putin 112, 126
Berger, Sandy 82, 123
Berkut riot police 247, 253, 254
Berlin Wall 19, 40, 57
Berlusconi, Silvio 146–7, 148, 202, 339
Beseda, Sergei 258
Beslan massacre 159, 160
Beyrle, John 216
Biden, Joe 208, 218, 226, 292–3
Bin Laden, Osama 152, 161
Black Sea Fleet 51, 162, 193, 250, 262, 266
Blair, Tony 81, 82–3, 85, 96, 145, 202
   and Iraq 153
   and Putin 120–1, 127
Blinken, Tony 257
Boehner, John 246
Bolsheviks 5, 74, 236, 280
Bolton, John 142
Bonner, Elena 54
Bortnikov, Alexander 266
Bosnia 42, 92, 93
Bouazizi, Mohamed 225
Braithwaite, Rodric 69, 90, 101, 321–2
Brennan, John 319
Brezhnev, Leonid 47

Brin, Sergey 221
Britain, *see* Great Britain
Browder, Bill 71–2, 239–40
Brzezinski, Zbigniew xiii, 52–3, 78, 162
Bulgaria 89, 150, 335–6
Burns, William 189, 214, 231
Bush, George H. W. 9, 10–12, 14, 18–19, 40, 130
   and aid 32, 33–5
   and Cold War 36–7
Bush, George W. xii, 128–9, 130, 132, 141, 213
   and democracy 173–4, 182–3
   and Georgia 189, 197–8
   and Iraq 152–3, 154–7
   and NATO 150, 151, 192, 341
   and 9/11 138–9, 140
   and nuclear weapons 142–3
   and Putin 134–7, 193–5
   and Russia 160–1

Cameron, David 244, 257
capitalism xii, xiii, 20–3, 98, 332
Cardin, Ben 240
Carter, Ashton 297
Castro, Fidel 10
Castro, Raúl 295
Catherine the Great 261, 269
Caucasus 8, 15
Ceaușescu, Nicolae 57, 258
censorship 24, 163, 280
Central Asia 6, 7, 14, 15
Chapman, Anna 224–5
Chechnya 53–4, 67, 99, 107, 151
   and Iraq 154
   and Islamists 159–60
   and Putin 113–15, 141, 142
chemical weapons 209, 243, 244, 245
Cheney, Dick 139, 180–2
Chernenko, Konstantin 75
Chernomyrdin, Viktor 41, 79, 84, 85, 86–7, 96, 131–2
Chilcot, Sir John 153
China 96, 122, 127, 134, 180, 295
Chirac, Jacques 77, 82, 96–7, 127
   and Iraq 153, 154, 156
Chornovil, Viacheslav 163
Christopher, Warren 45, 52, 70
Chubais, Anatoly 37, 71, 72, 73–4, 79
Churchill, Winston 65
Churov, Vladimir 231
CIA 258, 280, 296, 319, 321
Clapper, James 244, 292
Clark, Wesley 92–3
Clarke, Richard 152
Clinton, Bill 34, 36, 37, 40, 55, 63
   and independent states 48–9
   and Kosovo 93, 96
   and NATO 60–1, 77–8, 79, 80–1, 82–3, 87
   and Putin 121, 122–5, 127, 202
   and Russia 43, 52–3, 54, 85–6, 131
   and Yeltsin 44–6, 69–70, 75, 101, 107–8
Clinton, Hillary 207, 222, 223, 226, 251, 292
   and Putin 230, 238, 241–2, 317
   and Russia 313–15, 318–19, 333, 334

Cold War xii, xiii, 18–19, 30, 45, 100
   and Bush 36–7
Colour Revolutions 177, 212, 231, 253, 259, 321
Comey, James 318
commerce 27–8, 98
Committee to Expand NATO 76–7
Commonwealth of Independent States 16, 50, 51, 251
communism xii–xiii, 36, 37, 47, 86
   and Eastern Europe 55–7
   and GDR 108–10
   and Ukraine 162–3
   and Zyuganov 68, 70, 74
Conference on Security and Cooperation in Europe (CSCE) 41, 42–3, 58
Congress of People's Deputies 8, 34, 40–1, 46–7
conspiracy theories 281, 284, 329
Conventional Forces in Europe (CFE) Treaty 77–8
Cook, Robin 94
cooperative movement 24–5
Corbyn, Jeremy 334
corruption 69, 102, 157, 163, 249, 301–2
Cossacks 288
Crimea xiii–xiv, 162, 193, 261–8, 274–5, 276–7
   and Kiselyov 328
   and the media 284–5, 286
   and sanctions 335
   and Trump 316–17
   and Ukraine 337
Croatia 150, 190
Cuba 10, 23, 142
cyberwarfare 287, 290, 291–3, 318, 319, 338
Czech Republic 55, 56, 59, 65, 289
   and NATO 82, 83, 88–9

Dannath, Siegried 110
Däubler-Gmelin, Herta 153
De Hoop Scheffer, Jan 177
defections 22
democracy xiii, 7, 8, 19, 42, 173
   and Russia 177, 178–9, 180
Democratic National Committee (DNC) 291–2, 318, 319
Denikin, Anton 236
Dialogue of Civilizations Research Institute 286
Doctor Zhivago (Pasternak) 24, 41
Dodon, Igor 336
Donbass 250, 270, 272, 274
Donetsk 268, 269, 272, 273, 274
Douthat, Ross 319–20
Drach, Ivan 12
Dubček, Alexander 56
Dudayev, Dzhokhar 53
Dugin, Aleksandr 235
Dvorkovich, Arkady 229
Dyachenko, Tatyana 71, 106, 117

Eagleburger, Lawrence 32, 42
East Germany, *see* German Democratic Republic
Eastern Europe 55–66, 90, 217–18
EastStratCom Task Force 291

Egypt 226, 239, 298
Eisenhower, Susan 78
espionage 133–4, 142, 222, 224–5
Estonia 8, 9, 153, 290, 337
    and independence 14, 17, 18
    and NATO 80, 83, 89, 150, 302–4
ethnic cleansing 94, 198
ethnic minorities 5–8, 15, 53, 64
Eurasian Customs Union 251–2, 321
Euroasianism 235
Euromaidan 247, 252–4, 258–9
Europe 42, 335–6
European Union (EU) 120, 148, 149, 267–8, 279
    and Brexit 304–5, 334
    and Georgia 187, 189
    and sanctions 271, 273
    and Ukraine 172, 250–2, 253, 255, 259–60
ExxonMobil 339

Fallon, Michael 304
FBI 133, 224–5
Federal Security Service (FSB) 108, 114, 222, 258
Fillon, Francois 336
Finland 303, 305, 338
Flynn, Gen Michael 318, 339
food 31, 98, 111, 271, 275
For Fair Elections 230–2
foreign travel 98
France 94, 192, 226, 288, 305, 336
Franchetti, Mark 325
Fridman, Mikhail 25
Fyodorov, Boris 72

G7: 30
G8: 80, 81, 127, 238
    2006 summit 178, 180, 183
G20: 213, 214–15, 238–9, 245, 319, 322–3
Gaddafi, Muammar 226, 227
Gaidar, Yegor 25, 26, 27, 30, 32, 39, 41
    and elections 63
    and Lugovoi 326
    and Yeltsin 68, 69
Gamsakhurdia, Zviad 165
gas 38, 179, 250, 255, 266, 275
Gates, Robert 176, 177
Gati, Charles 99, 102
Gazprom 38–9, 118, 285
Genscher, Hans-Dietrich 90
Georgia 7, 9, 15, 50, 165–6, 172
    and NATO 190–3
    and Russia 195–7
    and South Ossetia 186–7, 189–90
    and USA 187–8, 189, 196–7, 201–2, 212, 215,
        218
    and war 197–9, 200–1, 321
Gerashchenko, Viktor 27
Gerasimov, Gennadi 56
Gerasimov, Gen Valery 287
Geremek, Bronisław 88
Gergiev, Valery 298, 299
German Democratic Republic (GDR) 108–11
Germany 9, 16–17, 30, 56, 153, 290–1
    and AfD 288–9, 305

and reunification 57–8, 60, 90, 91
    and Russia 271–2, 336
    and Weimar Republic 99, 102
    see also German Democratic Republic; West
        Germany
glasnost ('openness') 24, 35, 109
Goldman, Marshall 32
Göncz, Árpád 55
Gongadze, Heorhii 163
Gorbachev, Mikhail xiii, 3–4, 7, 8–11, 18–19, 24
    and Bush 36–7
    and coup 12, 13, 14, 106
    and Eastern Europe 56–7
    and economics 30–1
    and Germany 57–8
    and Lithuania 330
    and NATO 60, 89, 90–1, 307
    and Putin 109–10
    and Thatcher 120
    and the West 201
Gore, Al 54, 79, 95, 128, 131–2
Gozman, Leonid 275
Grachev, Gen Pavel 53
Graham, Thomas 132, 137, 149, 167
Great Britain 60, 153, 226, 324–6, 328, 329
    and Brexit 304–5, 334, 336
    see also Blair, Tony
Greece 335
Grinin, Vladimir 290–1
Gromov, Gen Boris 54
GRU 292
Guantánamo Bay 241
Gudkov, Dmitry 312
Gudkov, Lev 309–10
Gusinsky, Vladimir 25, 72, 118, 126

Haass, Richard 144
Hadley, Stephen 130, 199, 200
Halonen, Tarja 174
Hamas 179
Hanssen, Robert 133
Harrison, Miles 241
Havel, Václav 55, 60–1, 217
Herbst, John 167, 249
Hitler, Adolf 24, 55, 153
Holbrooke, Richard 93, 95
Hollande, François 244, 336
Holtzman, Marc 72
homosexuality 236, 237, 243, 272, 286, 330
Honecker, Erich 56, 109
Hughes, Karen 135, 136
human rights 121, 181, 182, 243, 329
    and Magnitsky 239, 240–1
Hungary 9, 56, 59, 65, 289, 335
    and NATO 82, 83, 88–9
    and Ukraine 338

Ilyin, Ivan 235–6
industry 37–8, 101–2
Institute of Democracy and Cooperation 286
Institute of Globalisation and Social Movements
    (IGSO) 286
intelligence services 140, 149, 292

International Monetary Fund (IMF) 31–2, 83, 84, 131, 180
Internet Research Agency 278–80
Iran 121, 134, 179, 193, 203, 244
    and nuclear weapons 143–4, 181, 214, 238, 295–6
Iraq 122, 152–7, 183, 203, 245, 341
    and Georgia 189
    and Isis 300
    and Obama 210, 212
Isis 296–7, 298, 300, 329, 336, 337
Islamic terrorism 138–40, 142, 159–60, 203, 337
Israel 179
Italy 94, 146–7, 335, 336
Ivanov, Igor 94, 97, 119, 145, 177, 203
    and Georgia 188, 189
Ivanov, Sergei 138, 184
Ivashov, Gen Leonid 89

Jackson, Bruce P. 76
Jackson, Gen Sir Mike 92–3
Japan 30, 34, 127, 153
Jaruzelski, Wojciech 56
Jiang Zemin 96
Jobs, Steve 220
Johnson, Boris 299

Kallas, Siim 153
Kara-Murza, Vladimir 312–13
Karaganov, Sergei 18, 100
Karimov, Islam 179
Kasatanov, Adm Igor 51
Kasparov, Garry 101
Kasyanov, Mikhail 118, 179, 311
Katyn massacre 24
Kavan, Jan 88
Kazakhstan 4, 7, 13–14, 48, 52, 182
Kennan, George 78–9, 88, 342
KGB 108, 109, 110–11, 281
Kharitonov, Nikolay 158
Khatami, Mohammad 134
Khodorkovsky, Mikhail 157, 227, 332
Khrushchev, Nikita 22, 23, 47, 220, 261
Kievan Rus' 164
Kinkel, Klaus 43
Kirill of Moscow and all Rus', Patriarch 235
Kiriyenko, Sergei 84, 85
Kiselyov, Dmitry 328–31
Kissinger, Henry 65, 78, 260, 338
Klitschko, Vitali 254–5, 257
Kohl, Helmut 57–8, 77, 89, 110
Kolbin, Gennady 7
Kolomoisky, Ihor 269
Komar, Dmitry 308
Konayev, Dinmukhamed 7
Korzhakov, Aleksandr 71, 73–4
Kosovo 92–7, 99, 191
Kovalev, Sergei 114
Kovtun, Dmitry 327
Kozyrev, Andrei 41–3, 49–50, 61, 93
Kravchuk, Leonid 4, 12, 48, 162
Krichevsky, Ilya 308
Kuchma, Leonid 162–3, 167, 168, 169, 170, 171

Kudrin, Alexei 229
Kugler, Richard L. 62–3
Kursk (submarine) 126
Kuwait 9, 19
Kwaśniewski, Aleksander 171, 181, 217
Kyrgyzstan 172–3

Laar, Mart 217
Lake, Anthony 45, 210–11
Laqueur, Walter 102
Larrabee, F. Stephen 63
Latvia 8, 9, 14, 17, 337
    and NATO 80, 83, 89, 150, 302–4
Lavrov, Sergey 198, 207, 290–1
Le Pen, Marine 288, 336
Lebed, Aleksandr 73
Lebedev, Platon 157
Lenin, Vladimir 5, 7
Leontyev, Mikhail 231–2
Lewinsky, Monica 85, 86, 87
Liberal Democratic Party of Russia (LDPR) 324, 327
Libya 226–7, 239, 245
Lipman, Masha 179
literature 24
Lithuania 8, 9, 14, 17, 330, 337
    and NATO 62, 80, 83, 89, 150, 302–4
Litvinenko, Alexander 324, 325–6, 327, 328
living standards 28, 63, 98
'loans for shares' scheme 72–3, 75, 332
Lockheed Martin 76, 77
Lucas, Edward 291
Lugar, Richard 64–5, 171, 209
Lugovoi, Andrei 324–7
Luhansk 268, 269, 272, 273
Lukashenko, Aleksandr 158
Lukin, Vladimir 49, 256–7, 259
Luzhkov, Yury 113
Lyne, Roderic 265–6

McCaffrey, Lt Gen Barry 61
McCain, John 177, 180, 212, 254, 268, 276, 340
McCurry, Mike 54
McDonald's 20–1
McDonough, Denis 244
Macedonia 89, 190
McFaul, Michael 137, 211, 214, 215, 217, 231–2
    and cyberwarfare 293
    and Putin 239
Maduro, Nicolás 295
Magnitsky, Sergei 239, 240–1
Major, John 90
Malaysian Airlines Flight MH17: 269–71
Mamedov, Yuri 79
Manafort, Paul 249, 317–18
Mariinsky Theatre concert 298–9
Martonyi, János 88, 89
Marxism 22–3
Maskhadov, Aslan 113
Massoud, Ahmad Shah 140
Matlock, Jack 19
media, the 24, 98, 126, 234, 280–5, 328

and propaganda 289–91
see also social media
Medvedev, Dmitry 158, 184–5, 195–6, 197–8, 200, 204
and economy 311
and Libya 226
and NATO 218
and nuclear weapons 219
and Obama 223–4, 237–8, 334
and Putin 215–17, 227–8, 229
and social media 280
and technology 220–2
and Ukraine 250, 252
and USA 213–15
Menendez, Robert 246
Merkel, Angela 176, 191, 200, 290–1, 305
and Crimea 268
and Putin 271–2, 336
and Syria 244
and Ukraine 255, 256
Metrojet Airbus 320 crash 298
MI6: 324, 325
Middle East 10, 203
Miles, Richard 189
Milošević, Slobodan 15, 92, 93, 94, 95, 96–7
and war crimes 171
Minkin, Alexander 309
Mitterand, François 57
Moldova 8, 9, 15, 50, 336
Molotov-Ribbentrop Pact 8, 24, 81
Morell, Michael 319
Mori, Yoshiro 127
Mubarak, Hosni 226
Mugabe, Robert 295
Munich Security Conferences 176–7, 208
Mutual Assured Destruction (MAD) 122

Nagorno-Karabakh 7
Narochnitskaya, Natalia 286
Nashi youth group 177, 231
national anthem 126
National Front 288, 305, 336
nationalism 7–8, 68
NATO 42, 55, 58, 291, 306–7, 335
and Baltic States 302–4
and Crimea 266–7, 268
and Eastern Europe 59–66
and expansion 76–83, 87–91, 135, 149–51, 341
and Georgia 189, 190–3, 201
and Kosovo 92–3, 94–6, 97
and Putin 119–20, 123, 218–19
and Russia 144–9, 199–200, 321
and Ukraine 172, 250, 265–6, 338
Navalny, Alexei 230, 231, 232, 233
Nayyem, Mustafa 252
Nazarbayev, Nursultan 13–14, 182, 294
Negroponte, John 181
Nemtsov, Boris 89, 96, 111–12, 278
Netherlands, the 305
Nicaragua 167
Nicholas II, Tsar 47, 280
Night Wolves 288

Niinistö, Sauli 303
9/11 attacks 138–42, 151, 202–3
Nixon, Richard 32–3, 44
NKVD 24
Nogovitsyn, Col Gen Anatoly 200
Non-Proliferation of Nuclear Weapons (NPT) 51
North Caucasus, see Chechnya
North Korea 122, 127, 238
novie russkie 28–9
Novorossiya 269
Nowak, Jan 65
nuclear weapons 9, 12, 14, 48, 142–4, 208
and arms control 23, 36
and Bush (G.W.) 134
and Iran 295–6
and Medvedev 213
and Obama 209–10, 214
and plutonium 335
and Russia 50
and START 10, 121–3, 215, 219
and Ukraine 51–2
Nuland, Victoria 253–5, 259, 292

Obama, Barack xiv, 204, 207–11, 212–15, 314, 319
and Crimea 264, 267
and Libya 226
and Medvedev 216–17, 223–4, 237–8
and nuclear weapons 219
and Putin 322
and Russia 240–1, 242–3, 334
and Syria 238–9, 243–4, 245, 296
and Ukraine 275–6, 277
oil 26, 38, 179–80, 195, 221
and Crimea 266, 275
and Iraq 153–4
oligarchs 25, 71–3, 75, 112, 118, 126
and Ukraine 162, 269
Olympic Games 24, 194, 243, 255
Operation Provide Hope 31
Orange Revolution 170–2, 173, 203, 249, 330
Orban, Viktor 335
Organisation for Security and Co-operation in Europe (OSCE) 119
organised crime 28, 53
Ortega, Daniel 167
Oslon, Aleksandr 22, 25, 71, 97
and Putin 113, 115, 116, 127
Other Russia, The 178
Owen, Sir Robert 324, 325

Page, Carter 318
Palazhchenko, Pavel 217
Pamfilova, Ella 310, 312
paramilitary groups 288
Partnership for Peace (PFP) 62, 64–5, 76
Patrushev, Nikolai 114, 266
Pavlovsky, Gleb 167–8, 170, 174, 229
Pavluk, Stepan 12
Pelosi, Nancy 246
Pence, Mike 340
pensions 115–16, 311
Pereplilchny, Alexander 329
perestroika ('restructuring') 35

Perheentupa, Olli 175
Perle, Richard 130
Perot, Ross 44
Peskov, Dmitry 266–7
Philotheus of Pskov 235
Phoenix Initiative 211–12
Podesta, John 292, 318
poisonings 169, 324, 325, 327, 329
Poland 9, 29, 37, 65, 77, 338
    and NATO 59, 82, 83, 88–9, 191, 192,
        200
    and Soviet Union 55–6
Poltorak, Stepan 274
Pomerantsev, Peter 284
Ponomaryov, Lev 308
populism 333, 334
Poroshenko, Petro 169, 269, 272, 273, 279, 301
Potanin, Vladimir 72, 75
Potemkin, Prince Grigory 261, 269
Powell, Colin 144, 171
Powell, Jonathan 120, 145
Power, Samantha 299
Pozner, Vladimir 281–2
Pretzell, Marcus 288
price controls 20, 21, 26, 27
Primakov, Yevgeny 80, 87, 95, 113, 154
private enterprise 24–5, 37–9, 68–9, 98, 332
propaganda 17, 236, 280–91, 338
    and Ukraine 262, 264, 265, 268
protests 178, 230–4, 241
    and Ukraine 247–9, 252–4, 255–9, 268
Pushkov, Alexei 64
Pussy Riot 232–3, 236–7
Putin, Vladimir 22, 70, 202, 236–7, 313, 340–2
    and authoritarianism 157, 158–9
    and Berlusconi 146
    and Brexit 304–5
    and Bush 134–7, 174–5, 193–5
    and Chechnya 114–15, 159–60
    and Crimea 262–3, 264, 266–7, 268
    and Eurasian Customs Union 251, 321
    and first presidency 106–8, 116–19
    and France 336
    and GDR 108–11
    and Georgia 187–8
    and human rights 241
    and Iraq 153, 154, 155, 156–7
    and Kiselyov 330–1
    and Medvedev 215–17, 227–8
    and Merkel 271–2
    and Munich speech 176–7
    and NATO 144–5, 147–8, 149, 150–1, 218–19
    and 9/11 attacks 138, 139–41
    and nuclear weapons 142–3
    and Obama 240
    and Poland 181
    and premiership 183–5
    and propaganda 280, 283, 284, 285, 288
    and reforms 125–6
    and second presidency 229–32, 233
    and Second World War anniversary 294,
        295
    and Soviet Union 177–8

and Syria xi, xii, 238–9, 296–7, 298–9, 300
and treason 225, 234
and Trump 316, 317, 318–19, 339–40
and 2016 election 310–11
and Ukraine 165, 169–70, 173, 256, 274, 277
and USA 245–6, 334–5
and the West 119–21, 122–4, 127, 322–3
and Yeltsin 112–13
Pyatt, Geoffrey 254–5, 259

Al Qaeda 140, 141, 152, 161, 208

Radev, Rumen 335–6
Rasmussen, Anders Fogh 148, 192, 193, 218–19
Reagan, Ronald 122, 167
refugee crisis 297
Reid, Harry 318
Reines, Philippe 208
religion 235, 331
Reynolds, Albert 67–8
Rice, Condoleezza 57, 129–31, 133, 137, 165, 181
    and Georgia 195, 196–7, 198–9, 201–2
    and Iraq 154
    and NATO 190, 191–2
    and 9/11 attacks 139–40
Rice, Susan 211
Robertson, George, Lord 119–20, 135, 145, 147,
    148, 151
Roldugin, Sergei 298–9
Romania 57, 82, 89, 150
Romney, Mitt 238, 240, 339
Roosevelt, Franklin D. 65
Rose Revolution 166, 167, 187, 203
Rosneft 339
Rossiya Segodnya 284, 328
Roxburgh, Angus 285
Rubin, Eric 216
Rubin, James 82
Rubio, Marco 340
Rühe, Volker 60
Rumsfeld, Donald 134
Russia 4–5, 16–17, 98–102, 234–7, 340–2
    and Baltic States 302–4
    and constitution 46–8, 183–4, 340
    and Crimea 263–6, 274–5, 276–7
    and cyberwarfare 291–3
    and defence 201
    and economy 25–9, 30–5, 41, 83–6, 87, 159,
        179–80, 310–11
    and elections 310–13
    and Georgia 189, 195–8
    and governance 160, 177, 178–9, 184–5,
        215–16
    and independent states 49–50
    and Iraq 153–4
    and Kosovo 92–3, 94, 95–7
    and NATO 63–4, 77–83, 89, 190–1
    and privatisation 37–9
    and propaganda 280–91
    and Putin 125–6, 127
    and South Ossetia 187
    and Syria 296–300
    and technology 221–3

and Trump 318–19, 320, 333–4
and Ukraine 162, 164–5, 167–70, 171, 172–3, 259
and USA 35–6, 131–4, 174, 182–3, 193–4, 202–4, 207–8
and the West 320–2, 338–9
see also Putin, Vladimir; Soviet Union; Yeltsin, Boris
Russia Today (RT) 283–5
Russian army 263–4, 271, 272
Russian language 250, 268
Russian Military Doctrine 50, 52–3
Russian Orthodox Church 234, 235, 236, 287, 331
Rutskoi, Aleksandr 13, 27, 46
Rybachuk, Oleh 168–9

Saakashvili, Mikheil 166, 174–5, 187–90, 195–8, 199, 201–2
and Ukraine 301–2
Sachs, Jeffrey 26, 27, 29, 31–2
Saddam Hussein 9, 152, 153, 154
Sakharov, Andrei 54
Samutsevich, Yekaterina 233
sanctions 42, 240, 275, 305, 267–8
and Ukraine 271, 273
Sanders, Bernie 292
Sarkozy, Nicolas 198, 199, 213
Savchuk, Lyudmila 279–80
Sawers, John 120
Schröder, Gerhard 127, 153, 154, 156, 285
Schulze, Peter 286
Schwarzenegger, Arnold 221
Schweizer, Peter 223
Scowcroft, Brent 129
Sechin, Igor 227, 318, 340
Second World War 6, 294–5
Serbia 15, 93–5, 96, 97
Sergeyev, Igor 119
Shalikashvili, John 61–2, 65
Shea, Jamie 77, 161
Shevardnadze, Eduard 90, 165–6
Shirreff, Gen Sir Richard 304
Shoygu, Sergey xi, 279
Siberia 340
Sikorski, Radek 192, 257
Silicon Valley 220–1
Simonyan, Margarita 283, 333–4
Skaskiw, Roman 283
Skolkovo Innovation Center 221–3
Slavs 16
Slezkine, Yuri 7
Slovakia 82, 89, 150, 289, 338
Slovenia 82, 89, 150
Snowden, Edward 242, 243
Sobchak, Anatoly 13, 70, 112, 309
Sobyanin, Sergei 304 5
social media 220, 230, 278–80
soft power 286, 287–8
Solidarność 55, 88
Solzhenitsyn, Alexander 16, 165
Soros, George 166, 259
Soskovets, Oleg 71
South Ossetia 165, 186–7, 188, 189–90, 192, 193

and independence 200
and Obama 212
and war 197, 198
Soviet Union 5–7, 8–9, 12–18
and collapse xii–xiii, 3–5, 18–19, 308–10
and Crimea 261–2, 267
and Eastern Europe 55–6
and GDR 109–11
and the media 280–2
and Putin 126, 177–8
see also Gorbachev, Mikhail
space 23
Spogli, Ronald 146
Stalin, Joseph 6, 7, 8, 24, 274
and Baltic States 337
and Poland 65
Stasi 109, 110
Steinmeier, Frank-Walter 192, 305
Stepashin, Sergei 87, 112
Stop the War 286
Strategic Arms Reduction Treaty (START) 10, 121–3, 215, 219
Strategic Offensive Reductions Treaty (SORT) 143
Straw, Jack 145
Suchocka, Hanna 59
Summers, Lawrence H. 31–2
Surkov, Vladislav 178–9
Syria xi–xii, xiii, 238–9, 243–5, 296–300, 336–7
and Clinton 315
and USA 335

Tajikistan 141
Tak, Brig Gen Nico 272
Talbott, Strobe 43, 45, 48, 49, 52, 97–8
and Chechnya 54
and NATO 61, 62, 79, 80, 81
and PFP 64, 65
and Putin 113, 116, 117, 124
and Yeltsin 86
Taliban 140, 141, 203, 208
Talvitie, Heike 187
Tatars 263
technology 220–3
Tenet, George 154
terrorism 113–14, 138–42, 151; *see also* Islamic terrorism
Thatcher, Margaret 57, 120
think-tanks 285–7
Tillerson, Rex 339, 340
Tolokonnikova, Nadezhda 233
Trade Act (1974) 240
treason 225, 234
Treisman, Daniel 166
Trenin, Dmitry 183
Trump, Donald xiv, 292, 313–14, 333–4, 337
and Russia 315–20, 335, 339–40
Tsars 5
Tsypko, Maria 289–90
Tunisia 225–6
Turchynov, Oleksandr 268
Turkestan 6
Tyahnybok, Oleh 255, 257

Tymoshenko, Yulia 164, 169, 172, 190, 248, 249–50
  and imprisonment 251, 252, 257

Ukraine xii, xiii, 6, 8, 162–5, 337–8, 340
  and corruption 300–2
  and Crimea 261–6, 306
  and elections 166–72
  and gas 179
  and independence 4, 13–14, 15
  and the media 279, 284, 286, 289–90
  and missile strike 269–71
  and NATO 190–2, 193, 201
  and nuclear weapons 48, 49, 51–2
  and protests 253–4, 255–9
  and Russia 16, 17–18
  and separatists 268–9, 272–4, 276–7
  and Trump 316–18
  and USA 11–12, 172, 173, 218, 254–5, 275–6
  and Yanukovych 247–53, 259–60
United Nations (UN) 94, 176, 226
United Russia party 158, 177, 178, 229, 230
  and 2016 election 310–13, 340
United States of America (USA) 10–12, 18–19,
    22–3, 30, 176, 232
  and aid 31, 32–5
  and arms 76–7
  and cyberwarfare 291–3
  and foreign policy 315–16
  and Georgia 187–8, 198–9
  and Germany 57, 58
  and Kosovo 96
  and NATO 148–9
  and Russia 21, 35–6, 99–101, 131–4, 180–3,
    193–4, 202–4, 207–8, 319–20, 321, 334–5
  and Syria 296–7, 299–300
  and technology 220–1, 222
  and Ukraine 164, 167, 171, 172, 173, 249,
    253–5, 259, 275–6
  see also Bush, George H. W.; Bush, George
    W.; Clinton, Bill; Obama, Barack; Trump,
    Donald
Unity Party 116–17
US Agency for International Development
    (USAID) 167, 234
Usoltsev, Vladimir 109
Usov, Vladimir 308
USSR, see Soviet Union
Uzbekistan 141, 179

Valdai Discussion Club 285
Vareikis, I. 6–7
Vershbow, Alexander 133
Vietnam 142
Vietor, Tommy 230
Voloshin, Aleksandr 106, 118, 119, 123, 143–4, 158
  and Iraq 154–5
  and 9/11 attacks 141, 142
voucher scheme 37–9, 332

Wahl, Liz 284–5
Wałęsa, Lech 55, 60–1, 62, 65, 217
Warsaw Pact 56, 58–9, 90, 91, 306

weapons of mass destruction (WMDs) 152, 154
West Germany 102
West, the 20–1, 22–4, 25, 98, 100–1, 102
  and denigration 278–80, 281–3
  and Putin 119–21
  and Russia 320–2, 329–32, 338–9
  see also European Union; United States of
    America
Western Alliance, see NATO
Westerwelle, Guido 253
WikiLeaks 292
Wolfowitz, Paul 130, 134
World Bank 84
World Trade Organization (WTO) 80, 81, 223,
    237
  and Jackson-Vanik amendment 240, 335
Wörner, Manfred 60
Wurst, Conchita 237

Xi Jinping 294, 295

Yakovlev, Dmitri 241
Yakunin, Vladimir 184, 286
Yanayev, Gennady 12
Yanukovych, Viktor 163–4, 167, 168, 169–70, 171,
    341
  and leadership 249–53, 255, 256–7, 258
  and removal 247–9, 259, 260, 266
Yatsenyuk, Arseniy 255, 257
Yazov, Dmitri 90
Yeltsin, Boris 3–4, 12–13, 14, 15, 22, 30
  and Chernomyrdin 84, 85, 86–7
  and Clinton 44–6, 69–70, 101
  and ethnic minorities 64
  and independent states 49
  and Kosovo 94, 96–7
  and NATO 62, 80–1
  and Nemtsov 111–12
  and 1996 election 67–8, 71–2, 73–5
  and parliament 40–1, 46–8
  and Putin 112–13, 116, 117, 124–5, 322
  and resignation 105–6, 107
  and USA 35–6
Young Guard 231
Yugoslavia 15, 42, 92, 93, 226, 341
Yukos 157
Yumashev, Valentin 106
Yushchenko, Viktor 164, 167, 168–9, 170, 190, 249
  and USA 172, 173

Zakharova, Maria 307
Zaldostanov, Alexander 288
Zapadniki ('Westernisers') 21
Zavarzin, Viktor 92
Zhirinovsky, Vladimir 63, 102, 185, 324, 327, 333
Zlenko, Anatoliy 43
Zubkov, Viktor 184
Zurabov, Mikhail 257
Zygar, Mikhail 265
Zyuganov, Gennady 67, 68–9, 70, 71–2, 73, 74
  and Putin 118
  and 2008 election 185